Indigenous-Industry Agreements, Natural Resources and the Law

This edited collection is an interdisciplinary and international collaborative book that critically investigates the growing phenomenon of Indigenous-industry agreements—agreements that are formed between Indigenous peoples and companies involved in the extractive natural resource industry. These agreements are growing in number and relevance, but there has yet to be a systematic study of their formation and implementation. This groundbreaking collection is situated within frameworks that critically analyze and navigate relationships between Indigenous peoples and the extraction of natural resources. These relationships generate important questions in the context of Indigenous-industry agreements in diverse resource-rich countries including Australia and Canada, and regions such as Africa and Latin America. Beyond domestic legal and political contexts, the collection also interprets, navigates, and deploys international instruments such as the United Nations Declaration on the Rights of Indigenous Peoples in order to fully comprehend the diverse expressions of Indigenous-industry agreements.

Indigenous-Industry Agreements, Natural Resources and the Law presents chapters that comprehensively review agreements between Indigenous peoples and extractive companies. It situates these agreements within the broader framework of domestic and international law and politics, which define and are defined by the relationships between Indigenous peoples, extractive companies, governments, and other actors. The book presents the latest state of knowledge and insights on the subject and will be of value to researchers, academics, practitioners, Indigenous communities, policymakers, and students interested in extractive industries, public international law, Indigenous rights, contracts, natural resources law, and environmental law.

Ibironke T. Odumosu-Ayanu is Associate Professor at the College of Law, University of Saskatchewan, Canada.

Dwight Newman is Professor of Law & Canada Research Chair in Indigenous Rights in Constitutional and International Law at the University of Saskatchewan, Canada.

Routledge Research in International Law

The Far-Right in International and European Law
Natalie Alkiviadou

International Law and Revolution
Owen Taylor

The Responsibility to Protect in International Law
Philosophical Investigations
Natalie Oman

The Responsibility to Protect in Libya and Syria
Mass Atrocities, Human Protection, and International Law
Yasmine Nahlawi

Public Private Partnership Contracts
The Middle East and North Africa
Mohamed Ismail

WTO Jurisprudence
Governments, Private Rights, and International Trade
Wenwei Guan

State Territory and International Law
Josephat Ezenwajiaku

Territorial Disputes and State Sovereignty
International Law and Politics
Jorge E. Núñez

Indigenous-Industry Agreements, Natural Resources and the Law
Edited by Ibironke T. Odumosu-Ayanu and Dwight Newman

For more information about this series, please visit www.routledge.com/Routledge-Research-in-International-Law/book-series/INTNLLAW

Indigenous-Industry Agreements, Natural Resources and the Law

Edited by Ibironke T. Odumosu-Ayanu and Dwight Newman

Routledge
Taylor & Francis Group
NEW YORK AND LONDON

First published 2021
by Routledge
52 Vanderbilt Avenue, New York, NY 10017

and by Routledge
2 Park Square, Milton Park, Abingdon, Oxon, OX14 4RN

Routledge is an imprint of the Taylor & Francis Group, an informa business

Library of Congress Cataloging-in-Publication Data
A catalog record for this title has been requested

ISBN: 978-1-138-58491-4 (hbk)
ISBN: 978-0-429-50563-8 (ebk)

Typeset in Galiard
by KnowledgeWorks Global Ltd.

Contents

Contributors

Angela Cameron is an Associate Professor, University of Ottawa Faculty of Law, Canada.

Ken Coates is Canada Research Chair in Regional Innovation, Johnson-Shoyama Graduate School of Regional Innovation, University of Saskatchewan, Canada.

Kaitlin Y. Cordes is Head: Land and Agriculture and Lead: Human Rights and Investment at the Columbia Center on Sustainable Investment, New York, USA.

Karen Drake is an Associate Professor and Associate Dean (Students) at Osgoode Hall Law School at York University, Toronto, Canada.

George K. Foster is a Professor of Law at Lewis & Clark Law School in Portland, Oregon, USA.

Franklin Gaffney is Principal of PBC Legal & Consultancy Services in Western Australia, Australia.

Sari Graben is Associate Professor and Associate Dean, Ryerson Faculty of Law, Canada.

Levi Graham is a JD candidate at the University of Saskatchewan College of Law, Canada.

Arend J.A. Hoekstra is an Associate at Cassels, Brock & Blackwell LLP, Vancouver, Canada.

Thomas Isaac is a Partner at Cassels, Brock & Blackwell LLP, Vancouver, Canada.

Charis Kamphuis is an Associate Professor in the Faculty of Law at Thompson Rivers University, Canada, and a co-founder of the Justice & Corporate Accountability Project (JCAP).

Jason MacLean is an Assistant Professor in the Faculty of Law at the University of New Brunswick, and an Adjunct Professor in the School of Environment and Sustainability at the University of Saskatchewan, Canada.

Tehtena Mebratu-Tsegaye is a Senior Legal Researcher at the Columbia Center on Sustainable Investment in New York, USA.

Matthew I. Mitchell is an Assistant Professor in the Department of Political Studies at the University of Saskatchewan, Canada.

Sarah Morales is Associate Professor, University of Victoria Faculty of Law, Canada.

Dwight Newman is Professor of Law & Canada Research Chair in Indigenous Rights in Constitutional and International Law at the University of Saskatchewan, Canada.

Bram Noble is a Professor in the Department of Geography and Planning at the University of Saskatchewan, Canada.

Ciaran O'Faircheallaigh is Professor of Politics and Public Policy at Griffith University, Brisbane, Australia.

Ibironke T. Odumosu-Ayanu is Associate Professor at the College of Law, University of Saskatchewan, Canada.

Damilola S. Olawuyi is an Associate Professor of petroleum, energy, and environmental law at Hamad Bin Khalifa University, College of Law, Qatar, and chancellor's fellow at the Institute for Oil, Gas, Energy, Environment and Sustainable Development (OGEES Institute), Afe Babalola University, Nigeria.

Sam Szoke-Burke is a Senior Legal Researcher at the Columbia Center on Sustainable Investment in New York, USA.

Preface

The increasing recognition of the rights of Indigenous peoples is an important development of recent decades, one achieved in large part through ongoing activism and legal efforts of Indigenous peoples. Apart from rights realized against states, ongoing exploration and development related to extractive industries increasingly takes place with an awareness that Indigenous rights have significant implications for such activities. It is unsurprising, then, that the world has seen a growing wave of Indigenous-industry agreements (under a variety of different names) that purport to be consensual arrangements between Indigenous rights-holders and industry stakeholders.

While domestic legal developments have given a particular push to such agreements in some jurisdictions like Australia and Canada—and those jurisdictions now have numerous Indigenous-industry agreements in place—other developments, including the increasing recognition of norms related to "free, prior, and informed consent" (FPIC), have contributed to the spread of such agreements at a more global level, including in resource-rich regions in Africa and Latin America.

Even while these developments have occurred on the ground, scholarship has not kept pace, and the phenomenon of Indigenous-industry agreements has not yet been subject to the sort of scholarly interrogation it warrants. This collection seeks to examine Indigenous-industry agreements from a variety of different perspectives, ultimately contributing to an interdisciplinary and international conversation on this important legal phenomenon drawing on the best researchers we could draw in who had worked on the scholarship and practice of Indigenous-industry agreements in different forms. Those participating include legal scholars and scholars of politics and policy, practitioners, environmental assessment experts, and legal advocates for Indigenous peoples and for industry. The authors include Indigenous scholars as well as experts on regions where Indigenous-industry agreements are a newly expanding phenomenon. Overall, the collection hopes not to finish conversations but to commence them.

While the authors present a variety of different perspectives, as explained at more length in the introduction, they all link their chapters in some manner to the FPIC concept that has become a norm guiding many conversations in the international arena and consequently in many domestic arenas. Some authors see a more straightforward link between FPIC and Indigenous-industry agreements (at least in some particular forms), and others see these links as more complex and contestable. In any event, the collection addresses important developments on Indigenous rights that concern not simply the nexus with states but relationships between Indigenous peoples and natural resource industries, moving beyond state-centric paradigms towards the broader array of ways in which Indigenous rights matter.

Acknowledgements

In completing a project of this nature, one typically enlists assistance from several quarters. This has been our experience over the years that we worked on this edited collection. From the time we first started to explore our mutual interests in Indigenous peoples' agreement-making in natural resource development, we have been the beneficiaries of colleagues' intellectual contributions, research grants, institutional support, research assistance, and the incredible generosity of family.

We appreciate the work of all the contributors to this collection; they prepared excellent chapters with the utmost professionalism. Most of the contributors participated in a workshop hosted at the College of Law, University of Saskatchewan in October 2017—*Law and Politics of Indigenous-Industry Agreements in Extractive Industries.* Many travelled to Saskatoon and offered rich contributions to the subject of this collection. We would also like to thank other workshop participants, including commentators, who participated in insightful discussions at the workshop. We are appreciative of Ciaran O'Faircheallaigh (Griffiths University) who delivered a public keynote lecture at the workshop and Larry Chartrand (University of Ottawa) who presented the response to the lecture, as well as to Ginger Gibson and Jerome Slavik who also participated in the workshop and offered valuable comments. Staff at the University of Saskatchewan, especially Ms Katie Richard, ensured that the workshop functioned seamlessly, and we extend our thanks to Ms Richard and all University of Saskatchewan staff who facilitated delivery of a successful workshop. We are also grateful for the invaluable institutional support that the College of Law, University of Saskatchewan provided for the workshop and our research.

The project that resulted in this collection received generous funding from several sources. We received a Social Sciences and Humanities Research Council (SSHRC) Connections Grant titled *Law and Politics of Indigenous-Industry Agreements in Extractive Industries* in June 2017 to fund the October 2017 workshop which is the intellectual foundation for this collection. The Canada Research Chair (CRC) in Indigenous Rights in Constitutional and International Law also generously made funds available for the workshop. Ibironke's (Ronke's) interest in the subject of this collection was largely spurred by research that was funded through SSHRC grants—a one-year SSHRC Standard Research Grant in 2011/2012 and a SSHRC Insight Development Grant which was awarded in 2014. Research funded by a Law Foundation of Saskatchewan Fellowship also fostered this interest and helped develop the research questions that culminated in this project. We appreciate financial contributions of SSHRC, the CRC, and the Law Foundation of Saskatchewan to the workshop and research that serve as foundation for this collection.

Student research assistants—Courtenay Catlin, Rachael Ostroff, and Olivia Salkeld—and Research Associate, Shannon Hale, completed excellent work ensuring that the chapters complied with Routledge's format. We are grateful for their excellent work. We also extend thanks to students—Nnaemeka Ezeani and Katherine Starks—who helped summarize proceedings during the workshop and helped with some other tasks after the workshop, and to Gideon Odionu who was also a research assistant. This collection benefited immensely from the expert review of anonymous reviewers. We submitted the chapters to anonymous reviewers who provided excellent comments that helped ensure that the individual chapters and the collection are compelling pieces of academic work.

As always, our families and friends supported our work as we completed this project and we are grateful to them. Ronke appreciates and thanks Olabisi, Demilade, and Tamilore who make home the best place in the world. Their love, support, and precious smiles are priceless. Ronke is grateful to and thanks her mother, Gladys Odumosu who is an educator, and her late father, Olaitan Odumosu who loved knowledge and learning. They fostered a quest for research, inquiry, and community that inspire her community-focussed questions. Ronke's incredibly helpful siblings as well as friends provided exceptional support and she thanks them for their kindness and generosity. Dwight thanks all of the students with whom he has discussed matters related to this collection, his colleague Michael Plaxton for various discussions, and various friends and family for their support.

Part I

Theoretical and Conceptual Frameworks

1 Indigenous-Industry Agreements, Natural Resources, and the Law: An Introduction

Ibironke T. Odumosu-Ayanu and Dwight Newman

Agreements between Indigenous peoples and industry actors (typically in the natural resource sector)—what we will call Indigenous-industry agreements—raise important scholarly questions warranting attention. Scholarly attention to Indigenous-industry agreements has been limited thus far. This collection sets out to try to change that by bringing together a series of different scholarly perspectives on Indigenous-industry agreements and some of the key issues they raise.

Our discussion takes place against a backdrop of natural resource development generating significant attention and debate in the last half century. The practice and discourse of natural resource development have mostly been dominated by a limited range of actors encompassing states, natural resource proponents and developers (industry) and, in the case of many developing countries, international financial institutions such as the World Bank. The last few decades witnessed small, albeit important, shifts in the discourse and practice, yet the communities that host and are impacted by resource development have not yet received much formal attention.

In many cases, these host and impacted communities are Indigenous peoples. A significant proportion of the world's remaining natural resources are located on Indigenous lands and traditional territories.[1] Due, in part, to Indigenous peoples' advocacy and activism in domestic and international fora, recognition in some jurisdictions of sovereignty that Indigenous peoples have asserted for centuries, the ascendance of free, prior, and informed consent (FPIC) and contentions over its scope,[2] governments' interpretation of the duty to consult Indigenous peoples prior to resource development,[3] and industry's turn to the "social license to operate," agreements between Indigenous peoples and industry have proliferated in recent decades.[4] Agreements between Indigenous peoples and other actors are not new. They have existed since colonial times.[5] What is relatively new is Indigenous peoples' participation as parties in agreements that are related to resource development.

Indigenous peoples in Canada and Australia have been at the forefront of agreement-making with industry with different areas of focus such as environmental management[6] and benefits negotiations.[7] The most substantial prior study of Indigenous-industry agreements, a leading book by Ciaran O'Faircheallaigh, undertook a comparative study of the development of Indigenous-industry agreements in these two jurisdictions, examined factors that led to stronger or weaker Indigenous-industry agreements in particular contexts, and generally set out some matters that we do and do not know about Indigenous-industry agreements.[8] However, the inherent limits on the scope of that book's largely empirical study also made clear that there are numerous normative and analytical angles from which Indigenous-industry agreements ought to still be studied, in addition to the possibility of reaching beyond the Australian and Canadian contexts.

This collection considers issues related to Indigenous-industry agreements between Indigenous peoples and industry proponents on continents as diverse as Africa, Australia, North America, and South America.[9] These agreements, which are known by different terminologies including Impact Benefit Agreements (IBAs) in Canada, Community Development Agreements (CDAs) in Ghana, Global Memoranda of Understanding in Nigeria's oil and gas industry, and Participation Agreements in Australia, are growing in number and relevance and have been referred to as "an emerging global phenomenon."[10] The collection studies Indigenous-industry agreements, though with some contributors discussing agreement-making with peoples or communities with contested or debated Indigenous status or not having Indigenous status on present legal definitions.

While the incidence of Indigenous-industry agreements is becoming increasingly widespread, there remains limited analysis of their negotiation, contents, implementation, and impacts. Contributors to this collection were invited to reflect on these issues by developing theoretical and conceptual frameworks for assessing Indigenous-industry agreements, investigating jurisdictional case studies that demonstrate some of the challenges and any emerging best practices regarding the agreements, analysing specific areas such as gender and the environment, and assessing the implications of Indigenous-industry agreements for FPIC and vice versa. Indeed, the developing norm of FPIC is the connecting thread among all the pieces in the collection. Each author engages with FPIC in some way, very appropriately so in the context of the central place of this norm in contemporary Indigenous rights discourse and its potential significance to resource development activity.[11]

This book is situated within the framework of the relationship between Indigenous peoples and natural resource development. It is an interdisciplinary collection of international scope that critically analyses legal, political, normative, conceptual, and practical questions regarding the growing phenomenon of Indigenous-industry agreements. In light of the overarching objective of opening a conversation on various key questions on Indigenous-industry agreements, this collection seeks to achieve four purposes.

First, the collection presents analyses aimed at developing theoretical and conceptual frameworks for analysing Indigenous-industry agreements (Odumosu-Ayanu; Foster; Newman & Graham; Graben, Cameron & Morales; O'Faircheallaigh). There have yet to be established conceptual frameworks, in part, because this is a relatively novel subject. Second, contributors provide targeted analyses of specific relevant areas including gender (Graben, Cameron, and Morales), the environment (Noble; Maclean), and politics (Mitchell). Third, in order to situate the analyses, contributors present case studies from countries such as Australia, Canada, Peru, and several others and regions such as Africa, the Middle East, and Latin America (Kamphuis; Gaffney; Cordes, Mebratu-Tsegaye & Szoke-Burke; Olawuyi; Isaac & Hoekstra; and Coates), with complexities on Indigenous status in some of these regions leading to a broader discussion of agreements with host communities. Fourth, FPIC is an overarching theme in all the chapters. In discussing the emerging internationally recognized norm of FPIC, the contributors present novel analyses on what could be the next frontier in Indigenous peoples' engagement with other stakeholders in extractive industries. They critically explore the law and politics of Indigenous-industry agreements, using FPIC as the basis for this essential simultaneous legal and political reading.

In responding to the four purposes outlined in the preceding paragraph, the contributors also engage with specific normative questions. At this stage in the development of Indigenous-industry agreements, Indigenous peoples, industry, states, and other actors are still confronted with questions such as what these agreements should seek to achieve and whether they should be centrally regulated by the state. Relying on specific agreements in their analysis, among other relevant normative questions, the contributors, to varying degrees, assess the impacts of colonialism on the negotiation and implementation of Indigenous-industry agreements, ask whether these agreements mitigate risk and uncertainty or whether they contribute to uncertainty, assess legitimacy and perceptions of the legitimacy of these agreements, and critically examine the objectives that they (should) achieve.

Central to the collection's conceptual legal questions is the recognition that law is contested. Contributors recognize that legal perspectives from diverse legal traditions including Indigenous law, domestic state law, and international law are germane to the full development of robust Indigenous-industry agreements. Some contributors (including Odumosu-Ayanu; Graben, Cameron, and Morales) are critical of insufficient engagement with Indigenous laws in Indigenous-industry agreements while others (including Newman & Graham; Isaac & Hoekstra; Gaffney) descriptively emphasize domestic state law, which is the law that mostly regulates these agreements especially from industry's perspective.

In addition to engendering analysis based on multiple legal sources, Indigenous-industry agreements are sites for navigating and negotiating diverse and sometimes competing interests and views between Indigenous peoples and industry. However, presenting Indigenous peoples' and industry's competing interests is incomplete without accounting for the interests of the state and the public that it represents. For, even when the state is not a party to Indigenous-industry agreements, the agreements are negotiated, formed, and implemented in the context of complex natural resource relationships of which the state is a major part. Closely related to these interests is the identity of the actors, which is by no means monolithic, but which has a significant impact on how they view the agreements. As contributors to this collection demonstrate, the identity of the Indigenous rights-holder as well as the sometimes-competing interests and political structures within Indigenous communities are crucial to analyses of Indigenous-industry agreements. The identity and interests of industry actors are also germane to understanding the complex interactions that these agreements generate. The goals that industry seeks to achieve through these agreements (addressing uncertainty, mitigating risk, seeking a social licence to operate, etc.), the differences in the sectors (including mining, oil and gas, forestry, and agriculture), and the scope of industry's duty under the law and internal policies on voluntary obligations, remain relevant factors that impact how they view the agreements. Hence, Indigenous-industry agreements emerge as a complex site of negotiation that contributors explore in this collection.

As the unfolding chapters make clear from the first section of the book, Indigenous-industry agreements raise an array of conceptual legal questions including their interaction with areas of domestic law such as contract, constitutional, and administrative law as well as the extent to which these agreements are regulated or not regulated by domestic state law. As Odumosu-Ayanu argues in her chapter, these interactions raise questions about the nature of the agreements and cast these agreements as instruments that extend beyond mainstream conceptions of common law contracts as private regimes.[12] She analyses the nature of Indigenous-industry agreements noting that content, context, and sometimes consent, impact the nature of specific agreements. Based on her analysis, these agreements, which are impacted by the complex legal and political environment in which they are situated, could be legal, political, and/or public–private instruments. Odumosu-Ayanu observes that the laws that currently inform Indigenous-industry agreements mostly flow from legal traditions that states and industry favour and argues for consideration of a legal pluralist framework that adequately accounts for Indigenous legal traditions which may be more reflective of the potential that these agreements have but are yet to achieve.

Apart from the legal questions, legitimacy issues arise. In presenting his conceptual analysis of Indigenous-industry agreements, Foster develops preconditions for legitimacy that navigate both procedural and substantive legitimacy. These preconditions—community leverage, host state policy, compatibility of project impacts with community values, and the bargaining process for the agreements—form a framework for determining the feasibility of Indigenous-industry agreements and which agreements are able to garner broad community support.

Newman and Graham engage with some of the tensions on various areas of law in their chapter where they argue that although Indigenous-industry agreements serve risk allocation and uncertainty-mitigating functions, uncertainty remains especially with regard to the intervention of institutions such as courts in the interpretation of agreements and potential developments around FPIC. Overall, their chapter argues that Indigenous-industry agreements actually have a variety of complex relationships to the concepts of risk and uncertainty. The chapter ultimately nuances statements made about them in this regard and shows some of the need to interrogate and navigate issues related to Indigenous-industry agreements with great care.

Contributors to this collection deploy multiple analytical and critical perspectives for understanding Indigenous-industry agreements including perspectives situated in Indigenous legal traditions, consent, feminist analysis, and conflict theories. O'Faircheallaigh traces the mine life cycle in relation to Indigenous-industry agreements and considers the intersection with FPIC, arguing that present approaches to Indigenous-industry agreements in Australia and Canada seldom achieve genuine Indigenous consent. On his argument, this is because Indigenous-industry agreements too often tend to provide simply for a form of consent around the time of regulatory approval and do not provide for consent at the time of each major decision or project activity during the project life cycle. In their chapter, Graben, Cameron, and Morales problematize consent from the critical standpoint of Indigenous feminisms and intersectional feminist analysis. Understanding colonialism and its gendered aspects is crucial to understanding Indigenous-industry agreements from a gendered perspective. Graben, Cameron, and Morales offer critical insight into the negotiation of Indigenous-industry agreements and the participation of Indigenous women in IBAs via participation in Indigenous governance and IBA negotiation and the "potentially disruptive effect" of these on perceptions of community. Drake's chapter directly engages community. A major issue that Indigenous-industry agreements encounter is the identification of the Indigenous party to the agreement. Using FPIC as a framework for analysis, Drake explores issues related to the peoples involved in Indigenous-industry agreements by relying on the particularly apt experience of the Metis. She analyses bases for identifying the Metis rights-holder for the purposes of consultation and consent. The contentious historical relationship between Indigenous peoples and the state and the continued violence in some jurisdictions make conflict theories relevant to Indigenous-industry agreements. Mitchell applies a "sons of the soil" conflict perspective in his analysis of IBAs in Canada as an analytical tool and a conceptual approach for understanding the conflicts that surround IBAs.

Targeted analyses of specific issues related to Indigenous-industry agreements forms the second area of focus of this book. In addition to the chapter by Graben, Cameron, and Morales on gender, the chapter by Noble on environmental assessment (EA) and that by MacLean on sustainability and confidentiality are examples of analyses of specific and often contentious issues. The environment has been one of the main areas of debate in the discourse and practice of Indigenous-industry agreements. Levels of attention to the environment range from none to significant depending on the jurisdiction and, perhaps, the organizational and other capacity of the Indigenous parties to the agreements.[13] Some of the questions addressed through the targeted analyses include whether Indigenous-industry agreements with environmental protection clauses lead to greater levels of environmental protection and the extent of the relationship between EA and Indigenous-industry agreements. In his analysis of IBAs, confidentiality, and sustainability, MacLean regards IBAs as "sustainability experiments." He argues that IBAs have the capacity to, and in fact, sometimes include provisions that exceed regulatory environmental requirements. However, given their mostly confidential nature, MacLean takes the view that they may be unable to fulfil their potential as "living laboratories of sustainability supportive of Indigenous rights."

In his intervention, Noble questions the relationship between Indigenous-industry agreements and EA. He situates these agreements at various phases of the EA review process including the period prior to commencement of EA, during the EA process, and after the process. In certain cases, agreement negotiation may extend across these phases. For Noble, the preferred time for negotiating and forming Indigenous-industry agreements is during the EA process when the potential impacts of a project have become known but before the EA approval is granted. He regards the relationship as a "complex" one. For Noble, the impacts of Indigenous-industry agreement formation vary, sometimes strengthening the engagement of Indigenous peoples in the EA process and at other times undermining the process. This relationship is especially pertinent in establishing the place of these agreements as fundamental documents that have the potential to significantly impact public processes.

A significant portion of this collection is dedicated to jurisdictional case studies. One of the key elements of this part of the collection is to present diverse types of agreements that exist in different countries and how the political relationship between Indigenous peoples and states, the laws in different countries, local content requirements, the extent to which industry behaves responsibly in a jurisdiction, and other factors, impact the contents and effects of Indigenous-industry agreements in different jurisdictions. Kamphuis' chapter analyses Indigenous-industry agreements in Latin America with a focus on Peru. She challenges the notion that these agreements are based on the peoples' consent, given the glaring power differentials, and questions their legitimacy. Kamphuis' chapter demonstrates that Indigenous-industry agreements and the extent of Indigenous participation and expressed agency may vary significantly across regions. Cordes, Mebratu-Tsegaye, and Szoke-Burke offer a perspective from African countries. They rely on an empirical analysis of 42 agreements related to agricultural and forestry projects from seven African countries as well as agreements from Indonesia. Given the limited literature on these types of agreements, the paper's analysis of the agreements' provisions as well as recommendations for developing better agreements is insightful. Olawuyi turns attention to the Middle East as well as Australia, Canada, Nigeria, and the United Kingdom in his multijurisdictional analysis of negotiated agreements and local content requirements. Whether all of the communities involved qualify specifically as Indigenous under domestic and/or international law becomes complex. Olawuyi thus situates Indigenous-industry agreements issues in a broader context by examining negotiated agreements with communities, state-investor contracts, and legislation, interpreting some provisions of these instruments as local content requirements, and analysing how local content requirements can foster agreements. In this frame, these agreements essentially take the form of governance instruments.

The balance of the jurisdictional case studies turn attention to Australia and Canada, which are the two countries with the most established record of Indigenous-industry agreements. Gaffney's chapter involves empirical analysis of a practical question, that of whether Indigenous-industry agreements between the Pilbara-based Aboriginal people in Western Australia and industry have served as "a vehicle for economic prosperity" over a period of 20 years. Assessment of Indigenous-industry agreements' contribution to economic development is crucial given that this is one of the main purposes of these instruments. Isaac and Hoekstra focus on IBAs in Canada. Their chapter provides an overview of IBAs, situate these agreements in existing Canadian law and politics, and draw examples from several IBAs. Isaac and Hoekstra ultimately urge caution on government regulation of IBAs. Coates' chapter completes the collection with the argument that it must not be taken for granted that Indigenous-industry agreements will continue in the form that they presently take. Drawing examples for his analysis from Canada, Coates argues that there is a trend towards "comprehensive engagement" throughout the life cycle of projects, thus partly speaking back to O'Faircheallaigh's chapter with a possibly optimistic note about the future of Indigenous-industry agreements and the ways they will evolve so as to realize deeper conceptions of FPIC even while operating in grounded, practical ways that provide tangible benefits for communities.

In fulfilling the collection's fourth objective, all the contributors examine the potential for Indigenous-Industry agreements to move the conversation beyond consultation of Indigenous peoples to FPIC. In their assessment of the legal and political implications of FPIC, contributors recognize that the very definition of FPIC is contested. FPIC is central to the notion of consent in Indigenous-Industry agreements, it could serve as a mechanism for asserting Indigenous authority, and it is a concept that has implications for interpretations of the duty to consult. Yet, one can challenge the utility of FPIC especially given its political implications and the resistance to more robust interpretations of FPIC. As some contributors emphasize, some Indigenous-industry agreements may not support FPIC as they are sometimes formed because of a sense of compulsion and enduring inequities within the system, many are not formed prior to decisions to proceed with projects, and many do not provide sufficient information for people to make informed choices. They note that some of these agreements, are at best, means for industry to acquire a social licence to operate. Some of these challenges inform O'Faircheallaigh's chapter and Noble's chapter in their discussion of timing of agreement negotiation. FPIC serves as an opportunity to assess Indigenous peoples' views regarding Indigenous-industry agreements and it is a theme that each contributor assesses in their chapters.

In order to bring a scholarly lens to Indigenous-industry agreements, contributors develop and apply conceptual and analytical approaches for understanding Indigenous-industry agreements, explore targeted subjects such as the agreements' relationship with the environment, and present jurisdictional case studies to ground the arguments, while also addressing the foundational role and implication of the agreements for FPIC and vice versa.

Notes

1. James Anaya, Report of the Special Rapporteur on the Rights of Indigenous Peoples: Extractive Industries and Indigenous Peoples, UN Doc A/HRC/24/41, (1 July 2012) para. 1.
2. Dwight Newman, "Interpreting FPIC in UNDRIP" (2020) 27 Int'l J Min & Group Rights 233; Cathal Doyle, *Indigenous Peoples, Title to Territory, Rights and Resources* (Routledge 2015).
3. See Dwight Newman, *Revisiting the Duty to Consult Aboriginal Peoples* (Purich Publishing 2014).
4. James Thuo Gathii and Ibironke T. Odumosu-Ayanu. "The Turn to Contractual Responsibility in the Global Extractive Industry" (2015) 1 Bus & Hum Rts J 69.
5. Saliha Belmessous (ed) *Empire by Treaty: Negotiating European Expansion, 1600–1900* (OUP 2015); Antony Anghie, *Imperialism, Sovereignty and the Making of International Law* (CUP 2005).
6. Natasha A. Affolder, "Rethinking Environmental Contracting" (2010) 21 J Env'l L & Practice 155; Courtney Fidler and Michael Hitch, "Impact Benefit Agreements: A Contentious Issue for Environmental and Aboriginal Justice" (2007) 35(2) Environments Journal 49.
7. See the chapters in this volume.
8. Ciaran O'Faircheallaigh, *Negotiations in the Indigenous World: Aboriginal Peoples and the Extractive Industry in Australia and Canada* (Routledge 2015). O'Faircheallaigh delivered a keynote address mainly based on this book at a workshop where we gathered a number of the participants in this collection, but he has written an original chapter for this collection.
9. Chilenye Nwapi, "Legal and Institutional Frameworks for Community Development Agreements in the Mining Sector in Africa" (2017) 4 Extractive Industries & Society 202; Jennifer Loutit, Jacqueline Mandelbaum and Sam Szoke-Burke, "Emerging Practices in Community Development Agreements" (2016) 7 J Sustain Dev Law & Policy 64.
10. Ciaran O'Faircheallaigh, "Community Development Agreements in the Mining Industry: An Emerging Global Phenomenon" (2013) 44 Community Dev 222.
11. Newman (n 2); Doyle (n 2); Mauro Barelli, "Free, Prior, and Informed Consent in the UNDRIP: Articles 10, 19, 29(2), and 32(2)," in Jessie Hohmann & Marc Weller (eds) *The UN Declaration on the Rights of Indigenous Peoples: A Commentary* (OUP 2018) 247; *Free, Prior and Informed Consent: A Human Rights-Based Approach*, Study of the Expert Mechanism on the Rights of Indigenous Peoples, UN Doc A/HRC/39/62 (10 August 2018).
12. Note that Isaac and Hoekstra regard IBAs as private agreements.
13. O'Faircheallaigh (n 8).

2 The (Legal) Nature of Indigenous Peoples' Agreements with Extractive Companies

*Ibironke T. Odumosu-Ayanu**

I. Introduction

Parentheses inspire curiosity. They clarify and they augment. Yet the absence of their content may not compromise completeness. By placing the word "legal" in parentheses in the title, this chapter's aim is to emphasize the legal nature of agreements between Indigenous peoples and extractive resource companies/developers (industry) while acknowledging that Indigenous-industry agreements (IIAs) are multifaceted instruments with political and other ramifications that are not always present in the myriad types of agreement that actors may form. It prevents an assumption, without analysis and evidence, that the agreements are legal instruments and it allows an assessment of *whose* and *which* law drives IIAs.

Indigenous peoples have formed agreements with non-Indigenous actors for generations.[1] While agreement-making is not a new method of engagement between Indigenous peoples and other actors, their implications have not always been without significant consequence including positive and very negative implications.[2] The former Special Rapporteur on the Rights of Indigenous Peoples emphasized the relevance of agreement-making between Indigenous peoples and industry when he noted that "direct negotiations between companies and indigenous peoples may be the most efficient and desirable way of arriving at agreed-upon arrangements for extraction of natural resources within indigenous territories."[3]

Extractive industry agreements vary greatly.[4] Natural resource agreements traditionally involve state actors and industry, or are formed between two or more industry actors. In recent decades, there has been greater participation of Indigenous communities in natural resource (-related) agreements. Sometimes, these agreements such as Natural Gas Pipeline Benefits Agreements and Economic and Community Development Agreements are formed between Indigenous communities and federal or provincial governments.[5] Others are tripartite agreements among Indigenous peoples, federal and/or provincial governments, and industry.[6]

Of the several forms of IIAs, this chapter focusses on agreements formed in Australia and Canada between Indigenous communities and industry that, *inter alia*, transfer some benefits to communities. It also draws examples from

Ghana and Nigeria. There is debate regarding the Indigenous status of people in the African context.[7] Hence, references to agreements with communities in Ghana and Nigeria may not always involve (recognized) Indigenous peoples. However, Ghana and Nigeria are included in this chapter as they provide useful cross-jurisdictional comparison with the agreements concluded in Australia and Canada. The chapter draws examples from agreements known in Canada mostly as Impact Benefit Agreements (IBAs), as Participation Agreements (PAs) in Australia, as Community Development Agreements (CDAs) in Ghana and in Nigeria's mining industry, and as Global Memorandum of Understanding (GMOU) in Nigeria's oil and gas industry. Growing interest in these agreements has earned them the distinction of being regarded as "an emerging global phenomenon."[8]

In spite of their increasing status as a "global phenomenon," the agreements vary from country to country and from project to project. IBAs in Canada are often adopted in mining and other projects. They operate within a complex legal system that attempts to negotiate relationships between Indigenous peoples, the governments of the provinces, and Canada. IBAs, which are typically negotiated on a case-by-case basis, usually include provisions on training, employment, business opportunities, and sometimes include related provisions on finances and environmental protection.[9] Similar agreements in other parts of the world including PAs in Australia, CDAs in Ghana and Nigeria, and GMOUs in Nigeria, include similar provisions but they reflect different levels of attention to vital issues such as consent, content, and the overall purpose that they seek to achieve. They also reflect varying degrees of challenges including power differentials, colonial underpinnings, and implications on communities' access to legal options that are available to citizens who have not formed agreements with industry.

This chapter's assessment of IIAs is a critical and sometimes normative analysis of their nature as public–private instruments, as political arrangements, and as legal instruments impacted by states' contracts laws. It also subjects the agreements to the scrutiny of consent through the lens of the principle of free, prior and informed consent (FPIC) and assesses the contributions of consent to the legal and/or political nature of IIAs. This chapter's critique of IIAs should not be interpreted as a rejection of negotiated agreements as a mechanism for navigating the relationship between Indigenous and non-Indigenous actors. In fact, it adopts the view that agreements, including IIAs, are valuable tools for Indigenous peoples' engagement with other actors but emphasizes that the conditions must be right for these agreements to achieve the highest level of potential that they possess for the parties. This chapter analyzes two of those conditions, that is, making and interpreting agreements using laws that reflect the parties' perspectives and ensuring that Indigenous parties express FPIC to projects. The chapter's assessment commences with an analysis of questions regarding incommensurability and the location of IIAs within potentially irreconcilable Indigenous legal traditions and the neo-liberal legal tradition that the laws of the states draw on. The incommensurability question is not only significant because it facilitates discussion regarding the reconciliation of views, perspectives and legal traditions, but because it directs attention to the nature of IIAs by addressing the question: Whose law/legal tradition?

II. Incommensurability, Indigenous Law, and Indigenous-Industry Agreements

The view of contract law that dominates law schools, law firms, and extractive companies is based on a capitalist neo-liberal framework that some Indigenous peoples contest.[10] Indigenous legal traditions and the capitalist neo-liberal legal tradition are foundationally different.[11] In view of this, one must ask whether meaningful analyses of the nature of IIAs can view these agreements not only from the lens of the neo-liberal perspective but from a deliberate plural perspective that engages the law and perspectives of the Indigenous communities involved in the agreements. The agreements are, after all, situated within broader socio-political relationships between Indigenous peoples and the state, which sometimes engenders questions of competing sovereignties. This section analyzes two issues. First, it assesses incommensurability as a challenge that, perhaps, irremediably impacts IIAs.[12] Second, it explores the nature of IIAs as potential Indigenous *and* industry agreements rather than industry agreements to which Indigenous peoples are signatory. This second issue involves at least two levels of engagement. The first level reflects the current practice of some detailed and well-crafted IIAs with regard to Indigenous law which involves referring to Indigenous legal traditions in parts of the IIAs. However, at this level, Indigenous law does not define the IIAs. The second level, which does not reflect current practice, would involve structuring IIAs according to both state and Indigenous laws and adopting this plural system as the basic framework that drives the parties' understanding of the foundational concepts and ways of knowing that shape their relationship.

International institutions, adjudicatory bodies, and commentators recognize the need to engage on the basis of Indigenous peoples' perspectives. The preamble to the *United Nations Declaration on the Rights of Indigenous Peoples* (UNDRIP) recognizes that "respect for indigenous knowledge, cultures and traditional practices contributes to sustainable and equitable development and proper management of the environment."[13] Similarly, the nature and the capacity for significant impact of IIAs is closely linked to recognition of the "considerable potential for cross-cultural understanding (and indeed, learning) and for cross-cultural community."[14] As the Inter-American Court of Human Rights noted in the *Case of the Saramaka People v. Suriname* ("*Saramaka Case*"), where "large scale development or investment projects … would have a major impact" there is a duty to consult and also to obtain the peoples' "free, prior, and informed consent, *according to their customs and traditions.*"[15] The *Nunavut Land Claims Agreement* (NLCA) expresses a similar view when it notes at article 26.3.3(a) that benefits under Inuit Impact Benefits Agreements ("IIBAs") "shall be consistent with and promote Inuit cultural goals."[16]

A holistic analysis of the nature of IIAs is susceptible to the argument that Indigenous laws and the business laws that extractive companies rely on are competing, incommensurable, and, perhaps, irreconcilable. Specifically, the potential incommensurability of the neo-liberal project and self-determination appears to be a foremost challenge. In addition, fundamental views about natural resources and the personhood of other living organisms and inorganic components of the earth, which are germane to natural resource development, are sometimes different.[17] IIAs are based on a neo-liberal perspective that state law, politics, and economics rely on. They mostly require Indigenous parties to have "a substantial mastery of the vernacular of the dominant," which in this case is the state's business law that industry adopts.[18]

Notwithstanding significant differences, challenges of incommensurability to a meaningful relationship between Indigenous peoples and industry actors expressed through agreements are not insurmountable. As James Gathii and I have expressed in other work, in fact, negotiated agreements could reflect self-determination in a manner that is not readily apparent.[19] But adopting the position that meaningful engagement between Indigenous peoples and industry could occur through IIAs does not suggest that the contestations, pluralisms, and complexities related to the engagement are taken for granted. Dianne Otto insightfully adopts the view that it is possible to identify "transformative possibilities for addressing questions of *difference*, without assimilation" and suggests that "the … assumption that multiplicity and order are themselves incommensurable must be unlearned."[20]

Some Indigenous peoples in Canada have expressed a willingness to permit natural resource development and, in some cases, to participate in such development. They express a willingness, sometimes, to engage neoliberalism towards self-determination.[21] The *NLCA*, for example, situates IIBAs within the realm of the "common law of contract."[22] In recent developments in Canada, the Trans Mountain pipeline expansion project (Trans Mountain Project) demonstrates that there is no single narrative of Indigenous peoples' position regarding natural resource development.[23] It serves as an example of the complexities of Indigenous peoples' engagement with natural resource development.

Where Indigenous peoples engage with resource development, the question remains "whether it is possible to give voice, without assimilation, to the difference" between the perspectives and interests of Indigenous peoples and industry in the formation and implementation of IIAs.[24] While not writing in the specific context of IIAs but in outlining the plural nature of Canada's legal system and advocating multi-juridicalism, Borrows expresses optimism about the co-existence of Indigenous legal traditions with other legal traditions.[25] He notes that "Indigenous legal traditions do not cease being Indigenous if they are called upon to deal with matters such as computer technology, stem-cell research, or insider trading in securities law. The authenticity of Indigenous law and governance is not measured by how closely they mirror the perceived past, but by how consistent they are with the current idea of their communities."[26] In fact, he states categorically that "Indigenous and non-Indigenous worldviews are not necessarily incommensurable."[27] In Canada, Indigenous law sometimes coexists with federal and provincial law. The *Nisga'a Final Agreement* referenced Nisga'a law and Nisga'a laws are operational in conjunction with federal and provincial law.[28] As well, Inuit legal traditions are implemented through the Nunavut Territorial Government by virtue of, *inter alia*, the land claims agreement.[29]

Borrows also cautions against making "broad, almost irreconcilable distinctions between Indigenous legal traditions and western legal sources"[30] and suggests that Indigenous legal traditions "could interact with other legal traditions in autonomous and interdependent ways."[31] Irreconcilability may not, in fact, be the main challenge for IIAs. Rather the terms of engagement, including the processes and applicable law, between Indigenous peoples and industry appear to be more pertinent. By engaging both Indigenous laws and non-Indigenous laws, difference is written into IIAs thereby creating meaningful interaction between "the dominant elite position of knowing" and what Otto calls "the multifarious and disruptive positions of subaltern knowledges."[32] When such interaction occurs, we can describe the nature of the agreements as *Indigenous* and *industry*; as *Indigenous-industry agreements.*

Beyond negotiating relationships between Indigenous communities and industry actors, IIAs have the potential to engender a narrative that navigates difference without assimilation. They have the potential to serve as instruments of self-determination and as legal instruments that re-define the relationship between Indigenous peoples and resource companies. Law often serves as an instrument of domination, but it remains "a site where the limits of the readability of narrative of difference, community and democracy are constantly contested. It provides one forum for re-presenting the incommensurability of difference ..."[33]

At the first level of IIAs' engagement with Indigenous laws, that is, including references to Indigenous law in parts of agreements without Indigenous law defining the agreements, the IIAs remain largely neo-liberal instruments.[34] These references typically appear in IIA provisions that address decision-making capacity of the representatives and some environmental provisions. The *Argyle Diamond Mine Participation Agreement* (*Argyle PA*), which is an IIA that adopted the first level of engagement with Indigenous law, illustrates this approach.[35] It demonstrates that Indigenous law and industry's business law can co-exist in IIAs. The *Argyle PA* embraces its common law of contract roots. It includes general common law contract clauses such as the consideration that the parties provide for the agreement, dispute resolution, and transfer of rights under the agreement. The parties added references to Indigenous legal traditions to this common law contract focus. These include references in clause 2.1 to respect for the traditional rights of the traditional owners (TOs).

In clause 11, the *Argyle PA* clearly situates itself in state law but retains some engagement with Indigenous law. It defines "law" as "the laws applicable in the State of Western Australia from time to time, both statutory and common law" but goes further to indicate that "traditional rights" are "rights and interests ... held by the TOs under Aboriginal laws and customs in relation to the Agreement Area, including rights and interests which, although not recognised by the Law, are, subject to this agreement, exercisable in relation to the entire Agreement Area." It also acknowledges senior TOs as TOs "with the authority and right to speak for land and waters in the Work Program Area under Aboriginal law and custom." They are "authorised under traditional Aboriginal law and custom to make decisions on behalf of TOs in relation to the land and waters ..."[36] A counterpart *ILUA* to the *Argyle PA* affirms at article 2.1 that the TOs own "the Agreement Area in accordance with traditional Aboriginal laws and customs."[37]

The *Argyle PA's* conception of environmental law in its Management Plan 5 adopted Western Australia's laws relating to the environment. Clause 4 of Management Plan 5, however, "acknowledges that the TOs have responsibilities under their traditional laws and customs in relation to land matters in the Agreement Area" but the company is not bound to adopt a proposal that TOs submit regarding suggestions on "land management measures." Similar provisions are included in clause 5 of the Land Management Plan regarding water management and the roles of TOs. Essentially, the *Argyle PA* engages Indigenous law at the first level. Indigenous law does not drive the basic framework for the agreement in conjunction with state law. Rather, Indigenous law is acknowledged as law that guides the actions of the TOs who are core actors under the agreement. Admittedly, by the TOs being guided by Indigenous law in their interactions under the agreement, there is potential for Indigenous law to influence the parties' relationship, if not the formation, framework, and structure of the agreement.

The second level of engagement with Indigenous law in IIAs, which this discussion has not explored in detail, would involve organizing IIAs according to state and Indigenous laws. It raises a number of challenges including the accessibility of Indigenous law and the differences in Indigenous legal traditions across Indigenous Nations. These challenges are not new. Legal scholars have addressed accessibility and other challenges to mainstreaming Indigenous law and provided suggestions for responding to the concerns.[38] Several Indigenous Nations are also codifying their laws and presenting them in forms that are accessible to non-Indigenous audiences.[39] Hence, accessibility and other challenges are being mitigated, making these kinds of challenges to plural IIAs surmountable. The most significant challenge to plural IIAs that is likely to remain is a systemic resistance to Indigenous law and the unlikelihood that industry will be willing to engage on the basis of Indigenous law. Students of natural resource contracts recognize that industry actors prefer the laws of some jurisdictions such that industry often contracts out of the law of some states, especially in the Third World. Hence a practical challenge that does not hinge on limitations regarding Indigenous law but on industry's acceptance of laws other than those to which they are accustomed, exists. Responses to this challenge must be developed before the second level of engagement with Indigenous laws in IIAs can become a subject of practice that exists beyond academic commentary such as the present one. Currently, IIAs that engage Indigenous law do so at the first level of engagement. These IIAs demonstrate that irreconcilability between Indigenous and neo-liberal legal traditions in IIAs is not inevitable. Yet the state of the practice is that many IIAs do not (yet) take sufficient (if any) cognizance of Indigenous law, making them mostly industry law-centric agreements.

While IIAs may not suffer from insurmountable incommensurability and irreconcilability questions, the very idea of agreement-making raises questions for some commentators. As Aaron Mills notes in an indictment of contract in relation to Indigenous peoples, "[w]e need not contract into community; we just need to learn how to live well together, across our difference, in a relationship that is always changing but which has always been."[40] While we may not need to "contract into community" as we are "always-already in relationship" as a political community, suitably crafted and designed IIAs that are appropriately situated within the legal traditions of the parties could, perhaps, serve as mechanisms for living well together.[41] In this frame, they would serve as mechanisms for building and sustaining relationship between partners rather than only as mechanisms, for distributing benefits, that may create winners and losers. This view is open to the charge that the instruments would become political instruments if cast in this frame. Indeed, as this chapter demonstrates, IIAs are not apolitical and they are not formed outside the politics of Indigenous peoples' engagement with the state.

III. Indigenous-Industry Agreements and the Common Law

The reference to "common law" in this section's title and subsequently in this chapter, is a fitting adoption of terminology to distinguish the law discussed in this section from Indigenous law. The common law is a convenient term as all the jurisdictions discussed in this chapter, at a time in their history, adopted the English common law through the transplant of this system of law as a result of colonialism. The common law here, then, denotes a system of state law including statute in these countries, as opposed to Indigenous law discussed in the previous section.[42]

The first reaction of students and practitioners of the common law is to regard IIAs as contracts located within the private law of contracts under the common law. The reality does not, however, reflect this view. Rather, IIAs implicate several areas of law. It is trite that in Canada, Indigenous rights are being negotiated under section 35 of the Canadian Constitution.[43] IBAs engender questions regarding the duty to consult, making IBAs part of the narrative of Indigenous peoples' engagement with the Canadian state.[44] As this chapter demonstrates, many IBAs are common law contracts but they also raise constitutional law questions. In Australia, PAs exist within the broader framework of Indigenous Land Use Agreements (ILUAs) and the *Native Title Act*.[45] IIAs also often involve Indigenous governments. While government involvement in an agreement does not necessarily transform the agreement into a public instrument, the implications of IIAs for Indigenous communities, other citizens, natural resource development, and the relevance of constitutional law in some countries, situate these agreements within both public and private law.

In some jurisdictions, agreements are required under statutes and other instruments; while the agreements are often formed without mandatory requirements for their formation under the laws of other jurisdictions. Ghana's CDAs are not mandated by law and neither are the GMOUs in Nigeria's oil and gas industry; and in many parts of Canada, IBAs are formed without legal requirements for their formation. The fact that some IIAs are required by statute lends credence to the view that the agreements are legal instruments rather than unenforceable political instruments. Statutory backing alone is, however, insufficient to determine the nature of an agreement.

Statutory provisions requiring IIAs mostly provide a limited scope for the agreements as they focus on employment, training, and similar issues.[46] These provisions often do not require formation of IIAs prior to the issuance of operating licences.[47] Some Land Claims Agreements, including the *NLCA*, also require the formation of IBAs.[48] The *Labrador Inuit Land Claims Agreement* (*LILCA*), in article 6.7.6, takes the view that if an IIBA has not been formed at the time that a permit or authorization is issued, such "permit or authorization may be issued subject to the condition that it is of no force or effect, and that no Construction of the Major Development may commence, until the conclusion of an Inuit Impacts and Benefits Agreement."[49] The practice regarding timing of IIA formation is not consistent. With some agreements such as Nigeria's GMOUs, operating licences would have been granted and resources committed to projects before agreements are formed, thereby potentially limiting the contributions that the agreements could make and leaving communities in a situation where they remain without much choice but to garner whatever benefit that they can from a project that would almost inevitably proceed or has commenced. In other cases, such as the Trans Mountain Project in Canada, IIAs were formed prior to project approval.[50]

The *NLCA* includes extensive provisions on the requirements for an IIBA. By virtue of article 26.2.1, major development projects cannot "commence until an IIBA is finalized." IIBAs are contracts.[51] While the *NLCA* includes a list of matters that may be included in an IIBA, the overarching philosophy is that the agreements "may include any matter connected with the Major Development Project that could have a detrimental impact on Inuit or that could reasonably confer a benefit on Inuit, on a Nunavut Settlement Area-wide, regional or local basis."[52]

The *Nigerian Minerals and Mining Act's* CDA provisions are also specific.[53] They focus on projects' social and economic contributions. By virtue of section 116(1) of the Act, CDAs are to be formed prior to commencement of development activity but after the mining lease has been granted. The Act's model is "a classic CSR approach with a focus on service provision."[54] While the *Nigerian Minerals and Mining Act* includes requirements for CDAs, the oil and gas industry's GMOU in Nigeria is a voluntary initiative of oil and gas companies such as Chevron and Shell.[55] By virtue of the GMOUs, which are limited in scope, Chevron and Shell provide services and other "development funding" to communities in exchange for "guarantees of uninterrupted operations."[56] GMOUs are corporate social responsibility (CSR) "agreements where the corporations provide development funding to host communities."[57]

The Newmont-Ahafo CDAs are not required by statute and they closely mirror similar agreements. They are related to a mining project developed by Newmont in the Ahafo community in Ghana.[58] Over a period of three years, the Ahafo communities formed three agreements with Newmont. The Ahafo Social Responsibility Forum was also created. Commitments exchanged in the *Ahafo Social Responsibility Agreement*, which was formed between ten community towns that are part of the Ahafo mine community, include sustainable economic and social development on the part of Newmont while the communities committed to discussions and consultations with Newmont.[59] The *Newmont Ahafo Development Foundation Agreement* focussed on the utilization of funds and outlining sources of funds for the Newmont Ahafo Development Foundation.[60] One of these sources is Newmont's commitment to contribute one US dollar for every ounce of gold that it sells in its operations under the Ahafo Mining Lease to the Foundation. For its part, the *Local Employment Agreement* focusses on employment policies.[61]

Detailed agreements such as some IBAs are contracts under the common law. The *NLCA*, in articles 26.4.2 and 26.5.2, notes that IIBAs "shall be written in the form of a contract." Article 26.9.1 of the *NLCA* is insightful. It states that IIBAs are contracts enforceable under the common law of contract and refers to terms such as liquidated damages, penalty, and specific performance, which are well-known to students and practitioners of the common law of contracts. However, beyond the application of the common law, it calls for the protection of "Inuit lifestyle and culture" making a simultaneous reading of the common law of contracts and Inuit legal traditions necessary. The *LILCA* is more emphatic in stating in articles 6.7.6 and 7.7.8 that: an IIBA "shall be a contract."

Regarding IIAs as contracts to which the common law of contracts applies has significant implications. Elements of contract formation and enforcement including the doctrine of consideration as well as remedies for breach of contract become applicable. At common law, consideration involves exchange and raises questions regarding what Indigenous communities exchange as parties to IIAs. The common law also recognizes that consideration could involve a minute exchange as long as it has value. As such, Indigenous peoples may not need to make significant concessions where they are hesitant to do so, but the feasibility of applying nominal consideration in the practice of IIAs remains an open question. Debates regarding nominal consideration may be unnecessary as Indigenous peoples make a significant contribution by granting access to their traditional territory with resultant impacts on their way of life.

Consideration under some IBAs involves releasing the non-Indigenous party/parties from liability for interfering with Aboriginal rights.[62] The *Lower Churchill Project Impacts and Benefits Agreement*, part of the *New Dawn Agreements*, provides benefits such as "five per cent of net project revenue," five million dollars per year, employment and training, and establishment of a committee for environmental management.[63] However, by section 3(a) "the payments … represent the full and final settlement to Innu Nation, its successor and assigns for all past, present and future claims, activities and compensation relating to the Project." From the perspective of the party making the payment, this is a beneficial clause, but it suggests that it is possible to envisage all possible implications of the project and bargain for them in the agreement. In some cases, Indigenous communities exchange consent to or support for a project as consideration.[64]

Enforceability is also germane to understanding the nature of IIAs. Some IIAs specifically include provisions that affirm that they are enforceable agreements. However, the fact that an agreement does not include provisions on enforcement does not suggest that it is not recognized under the laws of the Indigenous parties or the common law. The *Argyle PA* specifically notes that the "Management Plans form part of this agreement and are binding upon and enforceable by the parties according to their terms."[65] Enforcement and dispute resolution provisions of IBAs in Canada vary.[66] Substantively, article 7.1(e)(vi) of the *Pinehouse Agreement* refers to remedies such as damages or other remedies "in law or equity," squarely placing the remedial options within the common law of contracts. PAs in Australia also include dispute settlement provisions. The *Argyle PA,* in clause 8, outlines the rules that govern disputes between the parties. In Ghana, while the *Newmont Ahafo Development Foundation Agreement* permits arbitration under Ghana's *Arbitration Act*, the parties to the *Ahafo Local Employment Agreement* "renounce their rights" to litigation or arbitration and may only settle disputes by mediation or conciliation.[67] The illegality provision in article 4.0 of the *Local Employment Agreement* however appears to suggest, perhaps inadvertently, that the parts of the agreement that are not impacted by illegality would be enforceable. The *Ahafo Social Responsibility Agreement* for its part is unambiguous in noting at article 4.2 that the "document does not create any legally enforceable rights to the benefit of either of" the parties.

Agreements discussed in this section are situated within states' legal frameworks. Most of them are contracts under the common law and enforceable as such. Viewing these agreements as common law contracts brings the transactional character of contracts into focus. Foremost in this regard is the application of the doctrine of consideration and the sometimes-problematic exchanges that the agreements require. Locating the agreements within the legal framework of the state does not, however, dispense with pertinent questions regarding consent and the politics of the instruments.

IV. Indigenous-Industry Agreements and Free, Prior and Informed Consent

The growing incidence of IIAs does not suggest that Indigenous contestation regarding natural resource extraction has diminished. In spite of, or perhaps because of, the frequency of their formation, these agreements generate questions regarding consent. With IIAs the pertinent consent question is not usually whether the parties have reached an agreement regarding the contents of their agreement; rather, the question is whether IIAs demonstrate that the Indigenous parties fully consent to the project. The Trans Mountain Project, for example, demonstrates that the existence of an IIA is not synonymous with consent to the project, and the absence of an IIA does not imply opposition to the project.[68] Hence, it is necessary to explore the location of these agreements within the norm of FPIC, which is regarded as a specific right by some organs of the United Nations.[69] This section focusses on an analysis of IIAs from the lens of FPIC, which is one of the principal norms that drive Indigenous peoples' engagement with regard to natural resource development as evidenced, *inter alia*, by UNDRIP's significant reliance on FPIC in articulating its provisions.[70] FPIC is essential to assessing and understanding the nature of IIAs. Given the variations in IIAs, there is also significant variation in their compliance with FPIC.

According to the UN Office of the High Commissioner for Human Rights (OHCHR), FPIC has "normative foundations" in treaty-protected rights such as the right to self-determination and the right to develop and maintain cultures.[71] Consent is *free* where "there is no coercion, intimidation or manipulation"; it is *prior* when "sought sufficiently in advance of any authorization or commencement of activities and respect is shown to the time requirements of Indigenous consultation/consensus processes"; and it is *informed* when "information is provided that covers a range of aspects ..."[72] As the OHCHR notes, the "process may include the option of withholding consent."[73] But interpreting FPIC as including a veto exercisable by Indigenous peoples has led to debate and objections by some states.[74]

The meaning of consent has been a subject of debate for centuries and with natural resource extraction, it continues to remain an important issue.[75] As Webber notes, the "ability to give consent ... is severely bounded by the circumstances in which we find ourselves. How can one transcend the consequences of the past so that one can give free assent, undistorted by past inequities or simply by the sedimented positions and expectations of past relations?"[76] Webber's observations, which are related to consent in the formation of political community, are particularly apt with regard to FPIC and IIAs.

As I have argued in other work, several factors impact an agreement's FPIC standing including: the scope, significance, and extent of the issues that the agreement covers; the process through which Indigenous peoples' consent is acquired and how such consent is recorded; and Indigenous peoples' understanding and interpretations of the agreement.[77] O'Faircheallaigh's work details "seven issues that are of crucial importance to Aboriginal peoples in Australia and Canada"[78] including: environmental management, cultural heritage protection, rights and interests in land, financial payments, employment and training, business development, and implementation measures.[79] The breadth of an IIA's coverage and the extent to which it addresses these pertinent issues could determine the extent to which it reflects FPIC regarding the project as opposed to only consent to receiving benefits under an IIA. It simultaneously demonstrates the extent to which an agreement is a political instrument for seeking a social licence to operate or a legal instrument that also provides a social licence but extends beyond the social licence to serve as a legal mechanism of governance and reflection of consent.

Consent triggers thoughts regarding the concept of agreement and the elements of a valid contract in the common law of contract. However, besides the common law, Indigenous understandings of consent, the process of reaching consent and the necessity of continuous consent are essential. As the *Saramaka Case* notes, there is a duty to obtain the peoples' "free, prior, and informed consent, according to their customs and traditions."[80] Timing of agreement formation is also significant for consent. It is insufficient to state that consent has been granted for all time on the basis of one agreement, as extractive projects hardly admit of a single point at which Indigenous peoples may offer consent that is valid for the life of a project.[81] Consent is significantly more complicated and if it indeed mirrors relationship, it, perhaps, needs to be continuous. The nature of extractive projects also dictates the continuous consent, or consent as relationship, approach as it is difficult to comply with all FPIC principles at any single time in a project.

Where an IIA is formed early—before impact assessments are conducted or project approvals are granted—it might represent prior consent but if it is completed too early, there might be insufficient information at the time of negotiation.[82] Such consent may not be informed. If an IIA is formed after regulatory approvals have been granted, the agreement may no longer be part of prior consent, but an almost inevitable arrangement. The OHCHR suggests that consent "sought sufficiently in advance of any authorization *or* commencement of activities" is prior.[83] However, once authorizations are granted, the dynamics change (as the state signals its support through authorizations) even if project activities have not commenced. Szablowski's view regarding Indigenous peoples' consent being "sought but not required"[84] in some cases also reflects the state of many IIAs. He notes concerning the Ekati diamond mine project that the formation of the IBA was affected by "a lack of information and very short timelines" as well as the fact that Indigenous peoples "understood that they would not be allowed to reject the Ekati project by withdrawing from IBA negotiations."[85] IBAs generated through such process do not reflect FPIC. Also, Ghana's Newmont CDAs, Nigeria's mining CDAs and Nigeria's oil and gas GMOUs are not reflections of communities' FPIC to the projects. The agreements' coverage is limited, consent is not prior, and it is not seriously sought. In fact, some commentators perceive GMOUs as impositions on communities.[86] They are essentially used to mitigate unrest in Nigeria's Niger Delta.

Some IIAs provide evidence that communities exchange their support (or consent) for a project for the benefits that they receive under the agreement. Section 4(d) of the *New Dawn Agreement*'s IBA explicitly states that "the parties agree that ratification and execution of the IBA by Innu Nation and the First Nations constitutes full and final consent of the Innu of Labrador to the Project proceeding." Article 5 of the *Pinehouse Agreement* also states that Pinehouse provides "explicit support" for the companies' operations and captures support for existing and proposed projects. The *Argyle ILUA* at article 3.2 also expresses the communities' consent to operations including future activities, subject to Argyle's compliance with the law and the agreement.

In addition to timing, the concern that some agreements do not admit of situations where communities withdraw consent is pertinent.[87] The process of obtaining consent could involve multiple expressions of consent during the life of a project. Viewing an agreement as a final expression of consent may be insufficient as many Indigenous peoples view consent as an ongoing, relational process that may not be adequately reflected in a single agreement that does not permit renegotiation.[88] For some Indigenous communities, consent may need to be continuous and situated in relationship between the actors to the agreement.[89] As Mills notes, "[f]or the majority of Anishinaabe communities, most of the time, the central issue for consideration isn't about a yes or no response to development, but rather about process and relationships."[90] Industry also has a legitimate interest in consent; in this case, with a focus on certainty and some degree of finality. For industry, it helps for consent to signal certainty and finality. Yet, a view of contract as an arbiter of finality and certainty does not accommodate the consent as relationship approach.[91] Hence, consent is a complex issue that does not admit of many ready answers although current practice regarding IIAs' approach to consent suggests that, if they are legal instruments, IIAs are mostly located within the common law's traditions of exchange and certainty.

V. The Politics of Indigenous-Industry Agreements

This chapter has mostly adopted the term 'agreement' to avoid pre-empting the nature of IIAs as contracts to which the common law of contracts applies in terms of validity and enforcement. It has sought to establish, first, that it cannot be assumed that every IIA is an enforceable legal instrument. Second, if an IIA is a legal instrument, the question of whose and which law remains and both state law and Indigenous law have valid claims to applicability.

Given that IIAs are not consistent across projects and jurisdictions, the nature of the agreements also varies. As noted in section three, IIAs are public–private instruments; they are not entirely private or wholly public instruments. They transcend the public–private distinction and sometimes serve as a governance mechanism between the parties. Beyond the private life of contracts, IIAs' public nature is evidenced by the significant public interest involved in resource extraction, the impact on the lives and livelihoods of Indigenous peoples who are directly affected, involvement of Indigenous governments in these agreements, and constitutional ramifications of the duty to consult Indigenous peoples.[92] They are instruments situated within a complex environment and underlying political relationships. While liberal models prefer to privatize engagements and locate them away from the complex world of politics, IIAs do not admit of such depoliticization. Hence, regarding an IIA as a legal instrument does not divorce it from the politics that permeate Indigenous peoples' relationship with the state and other actors involved in resource development.

Some IIAs are simultaneously political and legal instruments. Here, there is no presumption of superiority of political instruments over legal instruments or *vice-versa*. Regarding an agreement as a political instrument does not diminish its usefulness even though it may be unenforceable. To borrow from the distinction in international law between treaties as legal instruments and UN General Assembly Declarations as political instruments, the latter class of instruments often generate impressive results notwithstanding their categorization, UNDRIP being an apposite example. IIAs make political statements regarding the value of engagement between core actors. Nigeria's GMOUs are more reflective of instruments that focus on acquiring a social licence to operate after the required legal licences have been granted. GMOUs are non-binding memoranda of understanding and do not meet the FPIC standard. They are better viewed as political instruments for acquiring a social licence to *continue to* operate and respond to the unrest in the Niger Delta. In the words of Chevron, GMOUs are instruments designed "to bring peace and stability to areas where Chevron operates."[93]

Unlike Nigeria's GMOUs, many IIAs in Canada and Australia are legal instruments. They rely on the status of Indigenous peoples, which Indigenous Nations have sought to affirm in their legal and political struggles with states, to form agreements that recognize the rights of Indigenous peoples. Many of them remain limited arrangements but there is much potential for greater coordination and more significant agreements between Indigenous peoples and industry that extend beyond benefits to impacting the legal licence to operate. In spite of the legal nature of some IIAs, majority of the agreements do not have an impact on the legal licence to operate, which is the principal licence, but seek to serve as mechanisms for acquiring a social licence to operate, which is a secondary but pertinent licence. Third in this continuum is a social licence to *continue to* operate given that some agreements do not interact with FPIC in any meaningful manner but appear to provide Indigenous peoples' support for the continued operation of a project.

Essentially, IIAs are public–private instruments; they are subject to the scrutiny of FPIC and many fail to meet the FPIC standard; some are contracts that are governed by common law contract principles such as consideration and contract enforcement; and all are impacted by political considerations. The extent to which the agreements involve a marriage of legal traditions is also significantly impacted by the political relationships between Indigenous peoples, the state, state law, and industry.

VI. Conclusion

The Cree Nation of Wemindji signed the *Opinagow Collaboration Agreement* in February 2011 as part of the development of the Eleonore mine project operated by Goldcorp.[94] This agreement is one of the measures that the Cree Nation is taking with regard to natural resource engagement. The measures include the articulation of a Cree Nation Mining Policy that *inter alia* "recognizes the importance of agreements" and views them as a "most appropriate instrument."[95] The Cree are only one example of Indigenous nations that have demonstrated a willingness to engage the state and industry on their own terms. The Anishinabek Nation also articulated "positivist" natural resources law[96] while the Tahltan Central Government presented an Industry Review as recently as 2019.[97] For the Tahltan Nation, agreements must be "consistent with Tahltan decision-making processes."[98] The Cree, Anishinabek, Tahltan, and many other Indigenous Nations around the world are giving us reasons to pause and pay attention to the changing dynamics of natural resource extraction. Indigenous peoples engage. The terms of engagement vary from Indigenous nation to nation. Engagement takes various forms including agreement-making and the terms of those agreements vary. Regardless of the terms of engagement, given the current purchase of agreements as a mode of engagement and the rate at which IIAs are being concluded, it is necessary to continue to study the dynamics, impacts and contributions of these instruments.

Indigenous peoples, as Napoleon and Friedland note, are "incredibly diverse" and we must be careful to refrain from "sweeping pan-Indigenous generalities."[99] What this chapter has sought to do is to draw insights from several examples of Indigenous peoples' engagements with industry. It does not suggest that the examples it has relied on are monolithic. Rather, these diverse examples allow us to extrapolate from these engagements in order to determine the nature of IIAs.

Many challenges, which this chapter has not canvassed, remain. From differences in bargaining power to equity and distribution, the challenges are significant.[100] Two specific challenges bear mentioning. First, colonialism and its impacts cannot be separated from agreements with Indigenous peoples regarding natural resources. In fact, it is at the core of engagement with Indigenous peoples and measures being taken today are intended, at least in part, to remedy colonialism. But if those measures are not carefully crafted and the agreements carefully negotiated and drafted to actively account for Indigenous perspectives, they would entrench colonialism. Second, the IIAs that this chapter discussed, which are the most prevalent form of agreements between Indigenous peoples and industry, are mostly limited agreements that are focussed on benefits. They do not address many of the core issues regarding natural resource extraction, which are often already decided before many IIAs are formed. Defining the nature of IIAs and determining their contributions and challenges are essential to law and policy makers taking them seriously and, more importantly, to the parties fully negotiating these instruments with the view that they could be potentially definitive.

Notes

* Corresponding author: Parts of this chapter were presented at conferences and workshops including the 7th JELP Environmental Law Conference, the University of Helsinki Workshop on Extractive Industries and Indigenous Livelihoods, the University of Saskatchewan workshop on Law and Politics of Indigenous-Industry Agreements in Extractive Industries, and conferences/workshops organized by the Centre for International Governance Innovation and by the Canadian Law and Society Association. I thank the conference and workshop participants for their comments. I appreciate the research assistance of Janelle Souter. I also appreciate

Dwight Newman's comments and the comments of two anonymous reviewers. I received a Law Foundation of Saskatchewan Fellowship which provided research funds at the early stages of this work and I am grateful to the Law Foundation for its support.

1. John Borrows, *Indigenous Legal Traditions in Canada: Report for the Law Commission of Canada* (Law Commission of Canada January 2006) 109 [Borrows, *Indigenous Legal Traditions*].
2. David A. Wishart, "Contract, Oppression and Agreements with Indigenous Peoples" (2005) 28(3) UNSWLJ 780.
3. James Anaya (Special Rapporteur on the Rights of Indigenous Peoples), "Extractive Industries and Indigenous Peoples" UN Doc A/HRC/24/41 (1 July 2013) [61].
4. See James Gathii and Ibironke Odumosu-Ayanu, "The Turn to Contractual Responsibility in the Extractive Industry" [2016] 1 Bus & Hum Rts J 69 [Gathii & Odumosu-Ayanu].
5. See Government of British Columbia, "First Nations Negotiations" <http://www2.gov.bc.ca/gov/content/environment/natural-resource-stewardship/consulting-with-first-nations/first-nations-negotiations>.
6. *Environmental Agreement between Her Majesty the Queen in Right of Canada and the Government of the Northwest Territories and Diavik Diamond Mines Inc. and Dogrib Treaty 11 Council and Lutsel K'E Dene Band and Yellowknives Dene First Nation and North Slave Metis Alliance and Kitikmeot Inuit Association* (8 March 2000) <https://www.emab.ca/sites/default/files/diavik_enviro_agree.pdf>.
7. See African Commission on Human and Peoples' Rights & International Work Group for Indigenous Affairs, *Report of the African Commission's Working Group of Experts on Indigenous Populations/Communities* (Eks/Skolens Trykkeri, 2005) <http://pro169.org/res/materials/en/identification/ACHPR%20Report%20on%20indigenous%20populations-communities.pdf>.
8. Ciaran O'Faircheallaigh, "Community Development Agreements in the Mining Industry: An Emerging Global Phenomenon" [2013] 44 Comm Dev 222, 228 [O'Faircheallaigh, "CDAS"].
9. Ken J. Caine and Naomi Krogman, "Powerful or Just Plain Power-Full? A Power Analysis of Impact and Benefit Agreements in Canada's North" [2010] 23 Org & Envt 76.
10. Aaron Mills, "The Lifeworlds of Law: On Revitalizing Indigenous Legal Orders Today" [2016] 61 McGill LJ 847.
11. An analysis of legal traditions, including Indigenous legal traditions, is beyond the scope of this chapter. On Indigenous laws in Canada, see John Borrows, *Canada's Indigenous Constitution* (University of Toronto Press 2010); Michael Coyle, 'Indigenous Legal Orders in Canada—A Literature Review' [2017] Law Publications 92 <http://ir.lib.uwo.ca/lawpub/92>.
12. See Aaron Mills, "Aki, Anishinaabek, kaye tahsh Crown" [2010] 9 Indigenous LJ 107 [Mills, "Anishinaabe Law"] 112 (noting that Anishinaabe and Canadian law "have historically been and at present time remain irreconcilable"). However, Mills notes that this "irreconcilability of Canadian and Anishinaabe law is contingent" and "it need not be there": ibid 148.
13. *United Nations Declaration on the Rights of Indigenous Peoples*, GA Res 61/295, UN Doc A/RES/61/295 (13 September 2007) [UNDRIP].
14. Jeremy Webber, "The Meanings of Consent" in Jeremy Webber & Colin M. Macleod (eds), *Between Consenting Peoples: Political Community and the Meaning of Consent* (UBC Press 2010) 3, 34 [Webber].
15. *Case of the Saramaka People v Suriname* (Preliminary Objections, Merits, Reparations and Costs) Judgment, Inter-Am Ct HR (ser. C) No. 172, [134] (28 November 2007) [*Saramaka Case*] Emphasis added.

16. *Agreement between the Inuit of the Nunavut Settlement Area and Her Majesty the Queen in Right of Canada* (25 May 1993) <http://publications.gc.ca/collections/Collection/R32-134-1993E.pdf> [*NLCA*].
17. See Mills, "Anishinaabe Law" (n 12) 117.
18. Naeem Inayatullah & David L. Blaney, *International Relations and the Problem of Difference* (Routledge 2004) 220.
19. Gathii & Odumosu-Ayanu (n 4) 93.
20. Dianne Otto, "Subalternity and International Law: The Problems of Global Community and the Incommensurability of Difference" [1996] 5 Soc & Leg Stud 337, 339 [Otto].
21. Gabrielle Slowey, *Navigating Neoliberalism: Self-Determination and the Mikisew Cree First Nation* (UBC Press 2008).
22. *NLCA* (n 16) art 26.9.1.
23. Tristin Hopper, "What do First Nations Really Think about Trans Mountain? Some Love It, Some Hate It, and Some Want a Better Deal" (*National Post*, 19 April 2018) <https://nationalpost.com/news/canada/what-do-first-nations-really-think-about-trans-mountain> [Hopper].
24. Otto (n 20) 355.
25. Borrows, *Indigenous Legal Traditions* (n 1).
26. Ibid 14.
27. John Borrows, "Heroes, Tricksters, Monsters and Caretakers: Indigenous Law and Legal Education" [2016] 61 McGill LJ 795, 813.
28. *Nisga'a Final Agreement* (27 April 1999) <http://www.nnkn.ca/files/u28/nis-eng.pdf>[Nisga'a Final Agreement]; Borrows, *Indigenous Legal Traditions* (n 1) 69–73.
29. Borrows, *Indigenous Legal Traditions* (n 1) 74–77.
30. Ibid 78.
31. Ibid 91. He notes at 122 that: "Changing cultural circumstances might lead some Indigenous groups to embed common law or civil law principles in their traditions. If this is the self-determining response of the group, it could appropriately recognize the reality of their normative values in modern terms."
32. Otto (n 20) 358.
33. Ibid 360.
34. See Emily Cameron & Tyler Levitan, "Impact and Benefit Agreements and the Neoliberalization of Resource Governance and indigenous-State Relations in Northern Canada" [2014] 93 Stud in Pol Econ 25.
35. *Argyle Diamond Mine Participation Agreement: Management Plan Agreement between Argyle Diamonds Limited and Argyle Diamond Mines Pty Limited and Traditional Owners* <http://opencommunitycontracts.org/contract/native-title-holders-argyle-2004-management-plan-agreement/> ["*Argyle PA*"]. An ILUA was executed in addition to this Management Agreement: *Argyle Diamond Mine Participation Agreement—Indigenous Land Use Agreement between Argyle Diamonds Limited and Argyle Diamond Mines Pty Limited and Traditional Owners and Kimberley Land Council Aboriginal Corporation* (8 April 2005) <http://opencommunitycontracts.org/contract/native-title-holders-argyle-2005-land-use-agreement/> ["*Argyle ILUA*"].
36. *Argyle PA* (n 35) 37.
37. *Argyle ILUA* (n 35). See also the warranties in art 15.1.
38. See, for example, Borrows, *Indigenous Legal Traditions* (n 1) 118–124.
39. See, *infra*, the examples in Section VI.
40. Aaron Mills, "What Is a Treaty?: On Contract and Mutual Aid" in John Borrows & Michael Coyle (eds), *The Right Relationship: Reimagining the Implementation of Historical Treaties* (University of Toronto Press 2017) 208, 210–211.
41. Ibid 210–211, 212.

42. This does not suggest that English common law applies in every part of these countries. For example, Quebec in Canada adopts the civil law tradition.
43. *The Constitution Act*, 1982 being Schedule B to the *Canada Act* 1982 (UK), 1982, c 11.
44. See Michael Coyle, "From Consultation to Consent: Squaring the Circle?" [2016] 67 UNBLJ 235.
45. *Native Title Act 1993* as amended (Australia), No. 110 1993 <https://www.legislation.gov.au/Details/C2012C00273>.
46. For statutory provisions that require CDAs, see Kristi Disney Bruckner, 'Community Development Agreements in Mining Projects' [2016] 44 Denv J Int'l L & Pol'y 413, 422–423.
47. But see David Szablowski, "Operationalizing Free, Prior, and Informed Consent in the Extractive Industry Sector? Examining the Challenges of a Negotiated Model of Justice" [2010] 30 Can J Dev Stud 111, 117 [Szablowski] (reporting that by virtue of a ministerial directive, an IBA was required to be formed before the water licences for the Ekati mine in Canada were granted).
48. *NLCA* (n 16) art 26. See also pts 6.7 and 7.7 of the *Land Claims Agreement between the Inuit of Labrador and Her Majesty the Queen in Right of Newfoundland and Labrador and Her Majesty the Queen in Right of Canada* (2005) <https://www.nunatsiavut.com/wp-content/uploads/2014/07/Labrador-Inuit-Land-Claims-Agreement.pdf> [*LILCA*] and ss 10 and 16 (11)–(12) of the *Inuvialuit Final Agreement* (April 2005) <https://www.irc.inuvialuit.com/system/files/Inuvialuit%20Final%20Agreement%202005.pdf>.
49. *LILCA* (n 48).
50. "43 Indigenous Groups Have Signed Agreements in Support of the Trans Mountain Expansion Project" (*Trans Mountain*, 19 April 2018) <https://www.transmountain.com/news/2018/43-aboriginal-groups-have-signed-agreements-in-support-of-the-trans-mountain-expansion-project>. For a more nuanced framing of Indigenous peoples' position regarding the pipeline, see: Brenda Owen, "We've Good New Trans Mountain Data and We're Sharing It" (*APTN National News*, 3 July 2018) <https://aptnnews.ca/2018/07/03/weve-got-new-trans-mountain-data-and-were-sharing-it/> [Owen].
51. *NLCA* (n 16) art 26.4.2.
52. Ibid art 26.2.1.
53. *Nigerian Minerals and Mining Act*, 2007.
54. Ibironke T. Odumosu-Ayanu, "Foreign Direct Investment Catalysts in West Africa Interaction with Local Content Laws and industry-Community Agreements" [2012] 35 NCCLR 401 [Odumosu-Ayanu, "FDI Catalysts"] 420.
55. See Ibironke T. Odumosu-Ayanu, "Governments, Investors and Local Communities: Analysis of a Multi-Actor Investment Contract Framework" [2014] 15 Melb JIL 473 [Odumosu-Ayanu, "Multi-Actor Contracts"].
56. Stephen A. Faleti, "Challenges of Chevron's GMOU Implementation in Itsekiri Communities of Western Niger Delta" (Paper, Peace & Conflict Studies Programme, University of Ibadan, 28 December 2010) 25 [Faleti].
57. Odumosu-Ayanu, "Multi-Actor Contracts" (n 55) 487.
58. See Odumosu-Ayanu, "FDI Catalysts" (n 54) 420–424.
59. Ibid 421.
60. Ibid 422.
61. Ibid.
62. Other, more fundamental, agreements also include release clauses. See, for example, *Nisga'a Final Agreement* (n 28) cl 26, 27.
63. NewfoundlandandLabradorExecutiveCouncil,"ANewDawnfortheLabradorInnu" (*Government of Newfoundland and Labrador*, 18 November 2011) <http://www.releases.gov.nl.ca/releases/2011/exec/1118n11.htm> [*New Dawn Agreement's*

IBA]; *The Tshash Petapen Agreement between Her Majesty the Queen in the Right of Newfoundland and Labrador and Energy Corporation of Newfoundland and Labrador and Innu Nation* <https://www.releases.gov.nl.ca/releases/2008/exec/0926n07agreement.pdf>.

64. See *Collaboration Agreement between the Northern Village of Pinehouse and Kineepik Metis Local Inc. and Cameco Corporation and Areva Resources Canada Inc.* (12 December 2012) <http://opencommunitycontracts.org/contract/northern-village-of-pinehouse-kineepik-metis-local-inc-cameco-corporation-areva-resources-canada-inc-2012-collaboration-agreement/> art 5.1 [*Pinehouse Agreement*]. See *New Dawn Agreement's* IBA (n 63) s 3(f).
65. *Argyle PA* (n 35) art 3.1.
66. See *Pinehouse Agreement* (n 64) art 7.
67. *Agreement between Newmont Ghana Gold Ltd. and the Ahafo Mine Local Community on Local Employment* (29 May 2008) <http://opencommunitycontracts.org/contract/the-ahafo-mine-local-community-newmont-ghana-gold-limited-2008-local-employment-agreement/> s 1.2.
68. Hopper (n 23); Owen (n 50).
69. See Food and Agriculture Organization (FAO) of the United Nations, "Free, Prior and Informed Consent: An Indigenous Peoples' Right and a Good Practice for Local Communities—Manual for Project Practitioners" (2016) [The FAO FPIC Manual].
70. See, for example, UNDRIP (n 13) art 32(2).
71. United Nations Office of the High Commissioner for Human Rights, "Free, Prior and Informed Consent of Indigenous Peoples" (September 2013) [OHCHR].
72. Ibid.
73. Ibid.
74. See Cathal M. Doyle, *Indigenous Peoples, Title to Territory, Rights and Resources: The Transformative Role of Free Prior and Informed Consent* (Routledge 2015) 161–168.
75. Webber (n 14) 5.
76. Ibid.
77. See Ibironke T. Odumosu-Ayanu, "Indigenous Peoples, International Law and Extractive Industry Contracts" [2016] 109 AJIL Unbound 220.
78. Ciaran O'Faircheallaigh, *Negotiations in the Indigenous World: Aboriginal People and the Extractive Industry in Australia and Canada* (Routledge 2016) 4.
79. Ibid Ch 4.
80. *Saramaka Case* (n 15).
81. On consent and the life cycle of projects, see Ciaran O'Faircheallaigh, "Negotiated Agreements, Indigenous FPIC and the Mine Life Cycle" in Ibironke T. Odumosu-Ayanu and Dwight Newman (eds.), *Indigenous-Industry Agreements, Natural Resources and the Law* (Routledge 2021).
82. On timing of IIA formation and environmental assessment, see Bram Noble, "The Relationship between Indigenous-Industry Agreements and Environmental Assessment: Enhanced Credibility and Collaboration, or Undermining the Project Review Process?" in Ibironke T. Odumosu-Ayanu and Dwight Newman (eds.), *Indigenous-Industry Agreements, Natural Resources and the Law* (Routledge 2021).
83. OHCHR (n 71) Emphasis added.
84. Szablowski (n 47) 117.
85. Ibid.
86. Faleti (n 56) 21–24.
87. The FAO FPIC Manual (n 69) 13 notes: "Once they have given their consent, they can withdraw it at any stage."
88. Mills, "Anishinaabe Law" (n 12) 143, 145 discusses the relational dimensions of Indigenous peoples' engagement with industry and other actors.

89. By art 26.10.1 of the *NLCA* (n 16), "an IIBA shall provide for its renegotiation."
90. Mills, "Anishinaabe Law" (n 12) 162.
91. See ibid 146 (discussing consent under Anishinaabe law).
92. See Dwight G. Newman, *Revisiting the Duty to Consult Aboriginal Peoples* (Purich Publishing 2014).
93. 'Nigeria: In the Community' (*Chevron*, May 2014) <http://www.chevron.com/countries/nigeria/inthecommunity/>.
94. Newmont Goldcorp, "2015 Sustainability Report" <http://csr.goldcorp.com/2015/_pdf2print/pdfs/0_0_goldcorp_csr_2015_full.pdf?v=2> 84.
95. "Cree Nation Mining Policy: Policy 2010-07" (*Cree Nation Government*, 2017) <https://www.cngov.ca/wp-content/uploads/2018/03/cree_nation_mining_policy-1.pdf>. The Cree Nation of Eeyou Istchee have a written constitution and they have formed several agreements with Canada's federal and provincial governments. See "List of agreements of the Cree Nation of Eeyou Istchee" (Cree Nation Government) <https://www.cngov.ca/resources/agreements/>.
96. Mills, "Anishinaabe Law" (n 12) 142.
97. Tahltan Central Government "Industry Review 2019" (*Tahltan Central Government*, 2019) <https://tahltan.org/2019-industry-review/>.
98. Ibid 3.
99. Val Napoleon & Hadley Friedland, "Indigenous Legal Traditions: Roots to Renaissance" in Markus D. Dubber & Tatjana Hornle (eds), *The Oxford Handbook of Criminal Law* (Oxford University Press 2014) 225, 226.
100. O'Faircheallaigh, "CDAS" (n 8) 231–235.

3 Essential Preconditions for an Indigenous-Industry Agreement with Community Legitimacy

George K. Foster

I. Introduction

Indigenous-industry agreements (IIAs)[1] are increasingly common in many countries. These agreements are widely credited with giving community parties a greater voice in development projects, an active role in mitigating project impacts, and an opportunity to share in economic benefits.[2] At the same time, some projects with impacts on Indigenous communities are still carried out without any agreement in place between the community and the developer, often over the community's vigorous objection. And even when an IIA is signed, the agreement does not necessarily reflect the informed will of the community. While many IIAs enjoy broad support, others are tainted by rumours of corruption or are otherwise controversial.[3]

This chapter offers a framework to explain why IIAs are signed in some instances and not in others, as well as to account for disparate outcomes in the perceived legitimacy of agreements. I use the term "legitimacy" broadly, to encompass two distinct concepts: procedural legitimacy (meaning that the agreement was concluded in conformity with the Indigenous group's own institutions and procedures)[4] and sociological legitimacy (meaning that the agreement is broadly perceived within the community as fair and reasonable).[5] I posit that four preconditions must exist in order for an IIA to be negotiated, and for those negotiations to be conducive to an agreement possessing both types of legitimacy. These include: the existence of substantial leverage on the part of the community vis-à-vis the developer; host state policy that does not unduly impede or pre-empt an IIA; compatibility of project impacts with community values; and a bargaining process that effectively channels the will of the community.

While many of the factors relevant to the viability or legitimacy of IIAs have been examined elsewhere in the literature, this chapter contributes to the discourse by demonstrating how a distinct constellation of circumstances must coalesce before an agreement with broad-based community support will be feasible. This chapter also explores the role that communities can play in creating conditions conducive to such an agreement. While some preconditions are fortuitous in that there is little or nothing that communities can do to influence them, others can be established—at least in part—through careful planning, targeted application of resources, and appropriate community policies. Accordingly, the framework set forth herein is designed to assist in predicting when IIA negotiations are likely to be worthwhile, as well as to supply a broad roadmap for how an Indigenous community can approach negotiations to maximize prospects for a successful outcome.

II. The Community Must Have Substantial Leverage over the Developer

The first precondition for a legitimate IIA is that the Indigenous community must have enough leverage that the developer perceives itself as better off accommodating the community, if it can feasibly do so. In negotiation theory, leverage can be either positive or negative. Positive leverage constitutes a party's ability to satisfy the counterparty's interests.[6] In the context of developer-community relations, positive leverage would be the ability to provide something that will contribute to the project's success. Negative leverage, by contrast, is a party's ability to impose costs on the counterparty.[7] In this context, negative leverage would be the ability to hinder the project or damage the developer's reputation.

1. Positive Leverage

One source of positive leverage arises if the Indigenous group has a recognized ownership interest in the lands or resources that the developer seeks to exploit, to which the group can provide access.[8] In most countries, any such ownership interest is limited to the land itself or surface resources.[9] Yet some Indigenous groups have recognized rights to subsurface resources as well. In Canada, for example, certain Aboriginal groups have negotiated Land Claims Agreements (LCAs) with the federal government that give them ownership over subsurface minerals and require their permission to explore for or exploit the same.[10] Similarly, Native American tribes in the United States have beneficial ownership over natural resources located on tribal lands (including subsurface resources), which are held in trust by the federal government.[11] Tribes have the power to contract with private companies to exploit these resources, subject to federal oversight.[12]

In addition, some Indigenous groups have acquired technical expertise or capital that they can contribute to a development project, particularly if they have played active roles in similar projects in the past. For example, some Alaska Native Corporations have acquired expertise in resource development and associated business activities through decades of partnering with industry. Some have also built up large reserves of capital through those endeavours, as well as through their receipt, over time, of a share of state resource revenues.[13] Similarly, the Southern Ute Tribe of Colorado is highly experienced in energy resource development and has amassed a growth fund estimated to be worth $4 billion.[14]

Indigenous communities may also possess positive leverage if local law provides special incentives for projects carried out in partnership with Indigenous-owned entities. In the United States, for example, a joint venture between a tribally owned business and a non-Native corporation may secure federal contracting opportunities under the Small Business Administration's 8(a) Business Development Program, which the non-Native corporation could not access on its own.[15] In addition, non-Native companies can benefit from substantial tax credits if they invest in projects in partnership with qualifying tribal entities pursuant to a federal program known as the New Market Tax Credit Program.[16]

An Indigenous community may also be able to provide a supply of labour, which may be particularly valued by the developer if the project will take place in a remote location.[17]

2. *Negative Leverage*

While Indigenous groups can have various types of positive leverage, negative leverage is often critical in bringing the developer to the table. Negative leverage may be derived from a variety of sources, including legal rights and powers possessed by the Indigenous community under domestic or international law, financial institution policies that condition project funding on Indigenous stakeholders' consent, and protest movements.

a. Legal Rights and Powers

The most common form of negative leverage possessed by an Indigenous group over a developer is the ability to invoke legal rights or powers to the developer's detriment. In recent decades, Indigenous groups have gained significant new sources of influence under both domestic and international law, and it is no coincidence that IIAs have developed and proliferated during the same timeframe. In fact, IIAs often require the community signatories to agree not to invoke certain rights or powers against the project, or to acknowledge that particular rights have been satisfied.[18] When an IIA so provides, it is a clear indication that the rights or powers in question were a factor in the developer's decision to conclude the agreement.

Regulatory powers devolved by state authorities to Indigenous governing bodies are one potential source of leverage along these lines. For example, LCAs in Canada give Aboriginal bodies authority over land and water use, requiring developers to seek permits from these bodies.[19] Native tribes in the United States likewise have substantial regulatory powers on tribal lands,[20] which may include even the power to enforce federal environmental laws.[21]

Indigenous groups may also derive leverage from legal rules adopted in many countries that require the host state to consult with Indigenous groups that may be affected by a development project before approving the project.[22] Such consultation typically takes place as part of the environmental impact assessment (EIA) process required in most countries for any activity that may have a significant environmental impact.[23] While the duty to consult is generally owed by state authorities rather than developers, project proponents may feel compelled to negotiate agreements with Indigenous groups to ensure that they do not challenge the sufficiency of consultations.[24]

In fact, some international authorities assert that states must do more than consult with Indigenous groups under some circumstances: they must refrain from approving the development activity unless consultations result in the group's free, prior and informed consent (FPIC). For example, the United Nations Declaration on the Rights of Indigenous Peoples (a non binding statement of the rights of Indigenous peoples adopted by the U.N. General Assembly in 2007),[25] provides that states must secure FPIC prior to authorizing any project that would require an Indigenous people's relocation,[26] or expose the community to hazardous materials.[27]

The existence of an obligation under international law to secure FPIC remains contested, and applies at most in cases with relatively extreme impacts on Indigenous communities.[28] Nevertheless, even states that do not recognize a duty to secure FPIC may cancel or require modifications to a development proposal in response to concerns expressed by Indigenous stakeholders during consultations.[29] This can provide a strong incentive to developers to reach an understanding with Indigenous stakeholders.

Finally, some countries have established a legal requirement that companies seeking to undertake mining projects enter into an agreement with affected communities providing for some form of benefit sharing.[30] Although these laws do not give an affected community the right to veto the project,[31] they place pressure on the developer to reach an accommodation because the government may be less likely to approve the project if no agreement is reached.[32]

b. Financial Institution Standards

Indigenous groups may also derive leverage over developers from policies adopted by some financial institutions. In particular, the International Finance Corporation (IFC) and some private institutions adhering to the Equator Principles, require private-sector borrowers to consult with and secure FPIC from affected Indigenous communities under some circumstances. Namely, FPIC is required if the project will have adverse effects on the community's lands or natural resources, will require its relocation, or will have significant project impacts on critical cultural heritage.[33] Hence FPIC may be needed for certain projects by virtue of financial institution standards even if not required by host state law.

c. Extra-Legal Forms of Pressure

Communities may also place pressure on a developer by carrying out protests against the project or otherwise generating adverse publicity.[34] Such efforts can hinder operations or cause reputational damage and are often credited with motivating developers to reach accommodations with local communities.[35]

Nevertheless, even sustained protests and adverse publicity do not always provide compelling leverage over a developer, as exhibited by events surrounding the Dakota Access Pipeline (DAPL) in the United States. The DAPL transports oil produced from the Bakken Formation in Montana to a pre-existing pipeline in Illinois.[36] The project developer, Energy Transfer Partners, routed the pipeline so that it would pass just outside the Standing Rock Sioux Reservation in South Dakota and under a lake that provides the reservation's main source of water.[37] The Standing Rock and other local Native American tribes objected to the DAPL, fearing that the pipeline could rupture and release harmful chemicals into their water supplies, and that the construction would destroy sacred sites and burials.[38] The tribes and other concerned citizens mounted massive protests against the DAPL for many months, attracting worldwide attention.[39] These efforts convinced the Obama Administration to delay the issuance of necessary permits several times, but ultimately failed to block the project.[40] After taking office, President Trump directed the Army Corps of Engineers to issue the necessary permits and the developer soon completed the pipeline.[41]

By mentioning this example I do not intend to suggest that the Standing Rock and other local tribes were open to negotiating an IIA and would have done so if they had only possessed more leverage over the developer. While some have suggested that an IIA might have been possible if the developer had offered economic benefits to the tribes and other concessions,[42] it is by no means certain that the developer could have addressed risks to water quality and sacred sites to the tribes' satisfaction. The DAPL saga does illustrate, however, that leverage from extra-legal forms of pressure is sometimes limited. The tribes would have been in a much stronger position if the pipeline had crossed lands over which they had a recognized ownership interest, such that their permission would have been required. In that event, the tribes could have secured concessions sufficient to address their concerns or simply withheld consent.

The DAPL saga also illustrates the limits to leverage provided by the duty to consult. Although the United States government recognized an obligation to consult with local tribes and purported to do so,[43] the tribes' objections did not prevent the government from authorizing the project. By contrast, in certain other cases the United States government has given serious weight to tribal objections, even cancelling projects after concluding that it would have a significant adverse effect on the tribe or its treaty rights to hunt or fish.[44] A key factor in such cases is the magnitude of the perceived impact on the Indigenous group or its recognized rights—the higher the impact, the more likely the government will defer to the group's views.[45]

III. Host State Policy Must Not Unduly Impede or Pre-empt the Negotiation of an IIA

Another precondition for the negotiation of a legitimate IIA is that governmental policy in the host state must not unduly impede or pre-empt such an agreement. As explained in Part I, some countries' legal frameworks provide

Indigenous communities with leverage that may interest the developer in negotiating an IIA. Yet law or policy in the host state may also create barriers to the negotiation of an IIA or promote alternative mechanisms—apart from a developer-community contract—for channelling benefits to local communities. Indeed, even if the host state purports to encourage IIAs, an active role by the state in negotiating such agreements may sometimes inhibit the bargaining process or undermine the legitimacy of any resulting agreement.

One way that host state policy may impede IIAs is if the government requires such agreements to be submitted to the government for approval, and makes the review process time consuming or onerous. In the United States, for example, the federal government generally must review and approve agreements between a Native American tribe and a project developer in connection with lands or resources held in trust for the tribe.[46] The review process has been described as slow and burdensome, potentially deterring some projects that could bring economic development to Native communities.[47] Some speculate, in fact, that Energy Transfer Partners may have avoided seeking to negotiate an IIA with the Standing Rock over the DAPL in part because the developer would have encountered these burdensome federal policies even if the tribe had been amenable to a deal.[48]

Alternatively, host state policy may effectively pre-empt an IIA by establishing other, state-centric means for delivering benefits to affected communities or securing impact mitigations. For example, if the state or a state-owned entity enters into a contract with the developer (such as a mineral development agreement or a production sharing agreement), the state party may itself negotiate terms for the benefit of local communities, rather than leaving those details to be worked out between the developer and communities.[49]

In addition, legislation in certain countries—such as Peru, Burkina Faso, and Laos—requires mining companies to pay specified amounts into funds established by the state for the benefit of local communities.[50] In other countries—such as the Central African Republic, the Democratic Republic of the Congo, and South Africa—the state requires developers to prepare a "community development plan," and to present that plan to the state for approval.[51] Legislation in South Africa, for example, requires mining proponents to submit a Social and Labour Plan (SLP) to the Department of Mineral Resources (DMR) outlining benefits to be provided to affected communities.[52] SLPs must be approved by the DMR, but not by the communities themselves.[53] Communities reportedly have little or no input into the content of SLPs and lack standing to enforce their terms.[54]

When the host state interposes itself between developers and communities in any of these ways it does not necessarily operate to communities' disadvantage. The state may consider itself better positioned to extract concessions from developers or contend that it has greater capacity to evaluate substantive terms. The latter is notably the justification offered by the United States government for its ongoing role in reviewing industry-tribal agreements: the notion that some tribes may lack the capacity to protect their own interests when negotiating with a developer.[55]

Moreover, if the host state mandates or negotiates particular terms on behalf of local communities it does not necessarily preclude separate developer-community bargaining. There may still be room for an IIA, or the developer and the community may collaborate in managing the amounts contributed to a state-mandated fund.[56] It stands to reason, however, that when the state makes important decisions on behalf of local communities it necessarily limits—and may even pre-empt—negotiation or collaboration between developers and communities.

Furthermore, state interventionism may sometimes be misguided or self-serving. Authorities may underestimate communities' capacity to protect their own interests, and may lack sufficient motivation to represent community interests when negotiating or enforcing developer obligations.[57] In the worst of cases, authorities may seek to control benefit sharing in order to promote their *own* interests rather than those of affected communities. For example, authorities may divert or misappropriate amounts collected on behalf of local communities.[58] Officials may also insist that the state serve as an intermediary for benefit sharing so that they can use funds derived from development projects to build patronage networks that enhance their own power.[59]

In fact, even if host states favour IIAs as a vehicle for community engagement and benefit sharing, the state may unwittingly impede an agreement or undermine its legitimacy. Namely, if local communities have distrust for state authorities as a result of past conflicts, a state role in the IIA may discourage community engagement.[60] The state may also place undue pressure on the community or its representatives to sign an IIA.[61]

IV. The Project's Environmental and Social Impacts Must Be Compatible with Community Values

Assuming that the Indigenous community has enough leverage to bring the developer to the bargaining table, and that host state policy does not impede or pre-empt the negotiation of an agreement, then an IIA is potentially viable. However, a third precondition must be satisfied before an IIA will be worth negotiating from the perspective of the Indigenous community: the project's environmental and social risks must be compatible with community values.

1. The Impact of Impacts on Community Receptivity to a Deal

All large-scale development projects have some environmental and social costs, but these can be particularly severe for Indigenous communities. Some Indigenous communities depend on traditional means of subsistence, which can give them greater exposure to pollution from a development project, or make them more vulnerable to any harm to local fish, plants, or wildlife.[62] Moreover, Indigenous groups have close connections to particular lands, resources, and spiritual sites. When these are damaged or the group's access to them is disrupted, it can threaten the group's culture, way of life, and social order.[63] Consequently, when an Indigenous group opposes a development project it is often because of concerns about the project's environmental or social impacts. Nevertheless, in some cases the risks are sufficiently limited that the community will agree to accept them.

The experience of the Haisla First Nation in British Columbia illustrates how the same Indigenous community may oppose one project, and welcome others based on the nature of anticipated impacts. The Haisla are based in Kitamaat Village on British Columbia's north coast. Kitamaat Village is on the Douglas Channel—a lengthy, narrow fjord rich in Chinook salmon, orcas, and other fish and wildlife central to Haisla traditions and spiritual beliefs.[64] The Haisla were among the most vocal opponents of the Northern Gateway Pipeline, a project intended to bring crude oil from the Oil Sands of Alberta to a marine terminal on the Douglas Channel, where it would have been loaded onto super tankers bound for Asia.[65] Many Haisla feared that a catastrophic spill of crude oil could occur as super tankers wove their way along the narrow Channel, and felt that no amount of economic benefit would be worth the risk.[66]

Yet the Haisla are certainly not anti-development. The Haisla have been perfectly willing to work with project developers when it appears that the environmental and social risks can be managed in a way that they consider acceptable. Notably, the Haisla negotiated equity stakes in projects to construct liquefied natural gas (LNG) terminals near Kitamaat Village, after investigating and concluding that LNG has a better safety record than crude oil.[67] The Haisla have entered into joint ventures with developers in other sectors as well, including reforestation, waste management, construction, and marine services, among others.[68]

2. *Informed Decision Making Requires Effective Impact Assessment*

For an Indigenous community to evaluate project impacts and make an informed decision about any potential IIA, the quality of the EIA process is vital. Significantly, however, conventional EIA processes may not identify the full range of impacts suffered by Indigenous peoples, which may be different from those experienced in other contexts.[69] Consequently, several international instruments, domestic EIA regimes, and non-binding guidelines emphasize the need to identify the particular types of environmental, social, and cultural impacts that may arise for an indigenous community and provide guidance on how to identify and evaluate such impacts.[70]

Notably, an effective EIA requires broad-based community participation in each stage of the process.[71] The community should be notified early on about the potential project, and procedures should be put in place for exchanging information with community members and recording their views and concerns.[72] Community participation has the potential to identify impacts and mitigations that would otherwise be overlooked, by drawing on the community's traditional knowledge and familiarity with the local geography, environment, and sacred sites.[73] It can also improve the community's understanding of potential impacts, as well as the legitimacy of the EIA process itself.[74]

3. Complicating Factors

While an Indigenous group's decision whether or not to conclude an IIA will often be driven in part by its perception of the project's environmental and social risks, several factors can complicate the group's decision-making process in this regard.

One such factor is that divisions often manifest within a community, with some members willing to tolerate anticipated impacts and others refusing to do so.[75] A potential dividing line is between individuals who have the skills and inclination to work for the developer as wage labourers or contractors, and community members who seek to maintain traditional practices of living off the land.[76] The former are more likely to see themselves as benefitting from the economic opportunities that the project will provide, and the latter more likely to balk at impacts on plants, fish, or wildlife.

Another potential complication is that state authorities may be prepared to approve the project whether or not the community agrees to support it. In such circumstances, the community may feel compelled to sign an IIA as the only way to secure benefits from the project, notwithstanding serious concerns about project impacts.[77] Yet an IIA signed under such circumstances is unlikely to enjoy legitimacy within the community over the long term, and may only sow the seeds of future conflict—poised to sprout once adverse effects manifest.

V. The Bargaining Process for the IIA Must Effectively Channel the Will of the Community

While IIAs are often hailed as vehicles for Indigenous empowerment and emblems of corporate social responsibility, concerns are sometimes raised about the integrity of an agreement's formation. In particular, critics sometimes contend that the community representatives who negotiated an agreement were not fully informed, were adversely influenced by threats or corruption, or otherwise did not represent the community effectively. This leads us to a fourth essential precondition for a legitimate IIA: a bargaining process must be employed that effectively channels the will of the community.

1. Community Negotiators Must Have the Capacity and Freedom to Protect the Community's Interests

In order for negotiators to express the community's will effectively, they must have the means to articulate—and protect in an agreement—the community's values and goals, and must also be free from threats or corruption.

Leadership may already have some familiarity with the matters that need to be negotiated if the community has concluded similar deals in the past. Otherwise community negotiators generally must rely on advice from legal, financial, and technical experts, access to which can vary considerably from community to community.[78]

In addition, negotiations must not be undermined by corruption or intimidation. There have been dozens of reports, from all over the world, of developers or state authorities attempting to influence Indigenous leaders improperly during consultations over a development project.[79] Sometimes the developer or state authorities are said to have threatened community representatives with harm if they refused to sign the deal,[80] but more often some form of corruption is alleged. The alleged corruption may consist of outright bribes, clouding negotiators' judgment with alcohol or lavish entertainment, or promising the negotiators lucrative jobs or contracts in connection with the project.[81]

To be sure, not all economic transactions between project developers and Indigenous leaders are improper. After all, one of the central purposes of an IIA is generally to secure economic benefits for community members, including the community's leaders. Nevertheless, some offers or payments may affect the integrity of the agreement and may even violate anti-corruption laws.[82] Corrupt intent is more likely to be found if any benefits flowing to a representative are disproportionate to those received by community members generally, and do not satisfy an arm's length standard.[83]

As a safeguard against corruption risks, it may be prudent for the group's governing authority to adopt a conflict of interest policy that limits opportunities for developers to influence leaders. Such a policy could not only prohibit representatives from accepting gifts and other items of value, but also require that any negotiations be held locally, foreclosing the need for representatives to travel to a distant location where they could be subjected to improper tactics by the developer. The policy could also require that any contracts, employment opportunities, or other transactions between leaders and the developer be approved in advance by independent and disinterested community representatives, or by the community as a whole, and meet certain substantive standards. For example, the policy could require that any contracts between a community representative—or to a company that he or she controls—reflect the fair market value of the services rendered and be the product of competitive bidding.

2. *Community Negotiators Must Be Validly Selected and Provide Adequate Opportunities for Input from the Broader Community*

To produce an IIA that has legitimacy in the community, it is not enough for community negotiators to exercise their own will during the bargaining process. The process must also channel the collective will of the community, and be perceived as doing so.

One potential problem is that the developer may choose to negotiate with individuals who are not an Indigenous group's established leadership. In some cases this may occur inadvertently, but developers are sometimes accused of singling out individuals or bodies considered more likely to favour the project.[84] If an IIA is negotiated in this manner—by representatives whose legitimacy is not established within the community—then the legitimacy of the agreement itself is likely to be questioned.[85]

Indeed, problems can manifest even if the community's representatives *are* selected according to the community's established procedures. Some Indigenous groups have adopted procedures or criteria for leadership elections that favour certain types of individuals, often those having more education and fluency in the dominant language of the country.[86] Such individuals may be more likely to favour development projects that offer employment opportunities or other economic benefits than community members who follow a traditional lifestyle.[87] Yet an IIA approved by negotiators who reflect only a subset of viewpoints is more likely to generate conflict. Accordingly, it may be advisable to establish a special committee of community members drawn from each material element within the population to carry out the negotiations.[88] Having negotiations conducted by a diverse committee may decrease the likelihood that an IIA will be signed, but should increase the likelihood that any deal negotiated will enjoy broad support.

Another concern that is sometimes raised about an IIA is that it was negotiated behind closed doors between the group's representatives and the developer, with little or no input from the broader community.[89] To avoid these concerns, there should be effective community participation not only in the EIA process, but also in connection with any IIA—or at least any long-term or definitive agreement. Hence the community should be notified of the IIA negotiations, and procedures should be established to solicit input and record community members' views and concerns about any agreement or potential agreement before its essential terms become a fait accompli. Efforts should also be made, as appropriate, to build the community's capacity to provide that input.

It may even be advisable for the IIA to be subject to approval in a community referendum. Ratification by the community may not always be necessary or appropriate,[90] but can potentially diffuse conflict and enhance the agreement's legitimacy.[91] In fact, announcing at the outset that any agreement will be subject to community ratification may give the developer—and the community's own leadership—more incentive to address stakeholder concerns when drafting the agreement.

VI. Conclusion

IIAs have the potential to give Indigenous communities a vital voice in the development process, critical protections against adverse project impacts, and economic benefits and opportunities that can transform their lifestyles and future prospects in positive ways. Yet development projects and IIAs can also present serious risks for Indigenous communities, and some may never have an opportunity to negotiate a deal with the developer, let alone decide whether the project should take place at all.

This chapter has shown that for an IIA to be negotiated—and to have legitimacy within the community—certain preconditions must exist. Oftentimes whether or not particular factors are present is beyond the community's control, but not always. An Indigenous group cannot control law and policy in the country where it resides, the nature of resources on its lands, or the vulnerability of local fish or wildlife. Communities may have little or no control over how much money is at their disposal to invest in a project, fund EIAs, or hire experts. Yet communities open to the possibility of an agreement can maximize their prospects for securing a favourable one by leveraging whatever rights and resources the community does possess, adopting policies that require effective community participation in EIAs and contract negotiations, and establishing safeguards against corruption.

Communities and their advocates can also strive to influence law and policy over time. Indeed, the diverse sources of community leverage that exist at present—as well as the IIA itself as a contractual device—are all products of political pressure and innovation by communities and their advocates in years past.[92] The more such efforts are sustained in the future, the more Indigenous groups will bring developers to the bargaining table when they desire to do so, and the more legitimate any agreements are likely to be in the eyes of the communities in whose names they are signed.

Notes

1. The term "IIA" is used herein to refer to a community development agreement (CDA) concluded between an Indigenous community and a commercial project developer.
2. See, for example, World Bank, *Mining Community Development Agreements Source Book* (World Bank 2012), 5, 8, 20–21; M. Cecilia G. Dalupan, "Community Agreements and Mining: A New Frontier for Social Impact Investments" (One Earth Future Foundation and RTC Impact Fund 2015) <https://oefresearch.org/sites/default/files/documents/publications/communityagreementsminingdigital.pdf> accessed 15 July 2019 [Dalupan] (describing CDAs as "hallmarks of sustainable development" that "can demonstrate mutual recognition and respect, incorporate human rights protections, and facilitate socioeconomic benefits").
3. Ibid CDA Source Book 9 (highlighting a risk of "perceptions that a community or group has been misled or coerced into signing a deal, or that a 'backroom deal' has been brokered with one or more parties to the detriment of others.").
4. Kevin A. Kordana and David H. Tabachnick, 'Rawls and Contract Law' [2005] 73 Geo Wash L Rev 598, 628.
5. *See* Jaya Ramji-Nogales, "Designing Bespoke Transitional Justice: A Pluralist Process Approach" [2010] 32 Mich J Int'l L 1, 15.
6. Paul F. Kirgis, "Bargaining with Consequences: Leverage and Coercion in Negotiation" [2014] 19 Har Negotiation L Rev 69, 74.
7. Ibid.
8. Dalupan (n 2) 9.
9. *See* ibid 3.
10. Carly A. Dokis, *Where the Rivers Meet: Pipelines, Participatory Resource Management and Aboriginal-State Relations in the Northwest Territories* (University of British Columbia Press 2015) 98.
11. Felix S. Cohen, *Handbook of Federal Indian Law* (Nell Jessup Newton edn, USGPO 2012) § 17.03.
12. Colette Routel and Jeffrey Holth, "Toward Genuine Tribal Consultation in the Twenty-first Century" [2013] 46 U Mich J L Reform 417, 434.

13. *See* "Alaska Native Corporations" (*Resource Development Council*) <www.akrdc.org/alaska-native-corporations> accessed 15 July 2019 (listing Alaska Native Corporations and providing examples of their partnerships with non-Native developers).
14. Shawn Regan, "Unlocking the Wealth of Indian Nations: Overcoming Obstacles to Tribal Energy Development" (*Property and Environment Research Center*, February 2014) <www.perc.org/2014/02/18/unlocking-the-wealth-of-indian-nations-overcoming-obstacles-to-tribal-energy-development/> accessed 15 July 2019.
15. *See* Emily M. Maass, "Navigating Unchartered Waters: Alaska Native Corporations in a New Era of 8(a) Contracting" [2012] 29 Alaska L Rev 51, 56 (describing the 8(a) program and noting that "[w]hen necessary or desirable, an 8(a) firm can even enter into a joint venture agreement with one or more non-8(a) firms to work together for a limited duration on a specific contract.").
16. For a summary of the NMTC Program and examples of projects involving tribal organizations, see Ecotrust, "New Market Tax Credit Program" (*United States Department of Agriculture*) <www.rd.usda.gov/files/EricFoley-ECOTRUST.pdf> accessed 15 July 2019.
17. Dwight G. Newman, *Revisiting the Duty to Consult Aboriginal People* (Purich Publishing Limited 2014) 82–83.
18. Newman (n 17) 83.
19. Dokis (n 10) 151.
20. Joseph P. Kalt, "Energy and Mineral Development in Indian Country: The Legal Landscape" [2014] 2014-5 RMMLF PROC 4.
21. Cohen (n 11) § 10.03.
22. For a detailed treatment of the duty to consult as it has developed in Canada, see Newman (n 17). Newman also provides an overview of consultation obligations in several other countries, including Australia, the United States, Peru, and Bolivia, among others. Ibid 153–162.
23. George K. Foster, "Community Participation in Development" [2018] 51 Vand J Transnat'l L 1.
24. See, for example, Newman (n 17) 112; Ciaran O'Faircheallaigh, "Effectiveness in Social Impact Assessment: Aboriginal Peoples and Resource Development in Australia" (2009) 27(2) Impact Assessment and Project Appraisal 95, 101 [O'Faircheallaigh].
25. United Nations Declaration on the Rights of Indigenous Peoples, GA Res 61/295, UN Doc A/RES/61/295 (13 September 2007); 46 ILM 1013 art 25 [hereinafter UNDRIP].
26. Ibid art 10 ("Indigenous peoples shall not be forcibly removed from their lands or territories. No relocation shall take place without the free, prior and informed consent of the Indigenous peoples concerned and after agreement on just and fair compensation and, where possible, with the option of return.").
27. Ibid art 29(2) ("States shall take effective measures to ensure that no storage or disposal of hazardous materials shall take place in the lands or territories of Indigenous peoples without their free, prior and informed consent.").
28. See Newman (n 17) 163–164; Carla F. Fredericks, *Operationalizing Free, Prior, and Informed Consent* [2017] 80 Alb L Rev 429, 465 [Fredericks].
29. See, for example, Newman (n 17) 105–106 (providing an example of a major mining project in British Columbia that was cancelled because the developer's proposals were "found to be likely to lead to significant impacts on a lake that was of spiritual significance to a local Aboriginal community").
30. Kendra E. Dupuy, "Community Development Requirements in Mining Laws" [2014] 1 Extractive Industries & Soc'y 200, 200–202 [Dupuy] (describing CDA mandates in Sierra Leone, Nigeria, Guinea, Mali, South Sudan, Afghanistan, and Yemen); Ibironke T. Odumosu-Ayanu, "Foreign Direct Investment Catalysts in West Africa: Interactions with Local Content Laws and Industry-Community

Agreements" [2012] 35 NC Central Law Rev 65, 83–84 (summarizing CDA legislation in Nigeria); Lucas Moalusi, "Community Development Agreements" [2015] 2015-3 RMMLF PROC 11C [Moalusi] ("In countries such as [Papua New Guinea], Nigeria, Mozambique and Mongolia there is a legal requirement on mining companies to negotiate and conclude lease agreements with landowners.").

31. James M. Otto, "Community Development Agreement Model Regulations and Example Guidelines" (*World Bank Group*, 2010) 22 <http://documents1.worldbank.org/curated/en/278161468009022969/pdf/614820WP0P11781nal0Report0June02010.pdf> accessed 23 October 2020.
32. See, for example, Moalusi (n 30).
33. "Performance Standard 7" (International Finance Corporation, 2012), [32] <www.ifc.org/wps/wcm/connect/topics_ext_content/ifc_external_corporate_site/sustainability-at-ifc/policies-standards/performance-standards/ps7> accessed 15 July 2019; "The Equator Principles" (Equator Principles, 2013), principle 5 <https://equator-principles.com/wp-content/uploads/2017/03/equator_principles_III.pdf> accessed 15 July 2019.
34. See, for example, Ginger Gibson and Ciaran O'Faircheallaigh, *IBA Community Toolkit: Negotiation and Implementation of Impact and Benefit Agreements* (Gordon Found 2015) 35.
35. See, for example, William M. Laurin and Joann P. Jamieson, "Aligning Energy Development with the Interests of Aboriginal Peoples in Canada" [2015] 53 Alberta L Rev 453, 462; Dr. Roy Maconachie, Radhika Srinivasan, and Nicholas Menzies, "Responding to the Challenge of Fragility and Security in West Africa: Natural Resources, Extractive Industry Investment, and Social Conflict" (World Bank Fragility, Conflict, and Violence Group, 2015) 22 <http://documents.worldbank.org/curated/en/169321468189569256/pdf/98902-WP-AFR-P148420-Box-393185B-PUBLIC-Extractives-FINAL.pdf> accessed 15 July 2019 [Maconachie, Srinivasan, and Menzies].
36. Fredericks (n 28) 473.
37. Catherine Thorbecke, "Why a Previously Proposed Route for the Dakota Access Pipeline Was Rejected" (*ABC News*, 3 November 2016) <http://abcnews.go.com/US/previously-proposed-route-dakota-access-pipeline-rejected/story?id=43274356>.
38. Ibid 474–475; Aaron Sidder, "Understanding the Controversy Behind the Dakota Access Pipeline: What to Know as Protesters and the Oil Company Continue to Clash" (*Smithsonian*, 14 September 2016) <www.smithsonianmag.com/smart-news/understanding-controversy-behind-dakota-access-pipeline-180960450/?no-ist> accessed 15 July 2019 [Sidder].
39. Fredericks (n 28) 475; Sidder (n 38).
40. Ibid Fredericks475–476.
41. Robinson Meyer, "Oil Is Flowing Through the Dakota Access Pipeline" (*Atlantic*, 9 June 2017) <www.theatlantic.com/science/archive/2017/06/oil-is-flowing-through-the-dakota-access-pipeline/529707/> accessed 15 July 2019.
42. See, for example, Alicia Adamczyk, "The Dakota Pipeline Could Devastate Some of the Poorest People in America" (*TIME*, 1 November 2016) <http://time.com/money/4551726/dakota-access-pipeline-standing-rock-sioux-tribe-devastate-poorest-people/> accessed 15 July 2019 ("[P]erhaps the state and Energy Transfer Partners could have worked with the tribe to build the pipeline through the reservation, rather than under the water supply, so that the Sioux could reap some of the tax benefits from the project").
43. *See Standing Rock Sioux Tribe* v *United States Army Corps of Engineers*, 205 F Supp 3d 4 (DDC 2016) (discussing the legal standard for the required consultations, summarizing discussions that took place, and denying an injunction sought by tribes who challenged the sufficiency of consultations).

44. Kirk Johnson, "Tribe's Fishing Rights Halt Proposed Coal Terminal" (*New York Times*, 10 May 2016) A11 (asserting that the Army Corps of Engineer denied a permit for a coal terminal near Seattle because it would impede the Lummi Nation's water access and undermine the tribe's fishing rights).
45. The Supreme Court of Canada has explained that the duty to consult requires a spectrum analysis, such that the degree of consultation required varies depending on the strength of the asserted rights and the magnitude of the potential interference with those rights. Newman (n 17) 17; *See also* Fredericks (n 28) 464.
46. Routel and Holth (n 12) 434 ("[F]ederal law provides that these leases are void until approved by the federal government in its role as trustee over tribal resources."). There are certain exemptions to the requirement for federal review, but they rarely apply in practice.
47. *See* Elizabeth Ann Kronk Warner, "Tribal Renewable Energy Development Under the Hearth Act: An Independently Rational, but Collectively Deficient, Option" [2013] 55 Ariz L Rev 1031, 1046.
48. See, for example, Terry L. Anderson and Shawn Regan, "No Wonder the Standing Rock Sioux Opposed the Pipeline" (*National Review*, 12 December 2016) <www.nationalreview.com/2016/12/standing-rock-dakota-access-victory-tribes-deserve-more-control-federal-regulations/> accessed 15 July 2019.
49. See, for example, Dupuy (n 30) 201 (providing examples of projects in Liberia and Ghana in which the state renegotiated mining agreements to require the mining company to implement community development projects); Moalusi (n 30) (discussing requirements for community protections and benefits in state contracts in Mozambique).
50. World Bank, *Mining Foundations, Trusts and Funds: A Source Book* (World Bank 2010) 73–76 (describing social funds established by the Peruvian state to which mining developers must make contributions for the benefit of local communities) [World Bank]; Keith Slack, "Unpacking Burkina Faso's '1% Campaign'" (Oxfam, 23 July 2015) <https://politicsofpoverty.oxfamamerica.org/2015/07/unpacking-burkina-fasos-1-campaign/> accessed 15 July 2019 (describing legislation adopted in Burkina Faso that requires mining companies to pay one percent of their gross revenues into community development funds, while highlighting uncertainty over how the funds will be managed and utilized); Earth Systems, "Briefing Note 1: Community Development in the Lao Mining Sector" (World Bank 2011) 8 <http://documents.worldbank.org/curated/en/857791468036884909/pdf/702270ESW0P1220nt0Lao0Mining0Sector.pdf> accessed 15 July 2019 [Earth Systems] (describing mining legislation in Laos that requires mining companies to contribute to community development funds).
51. *See* "Requirements for Community Development in Mining Laws" (Columbia Center on Sustainable Development, February 2017) <http://ccsi.columbia.edu/files/2014/09/Mining-Community-Development-Requirements-Summary-Table-CCSI-2017_February.pdf> accessed 23 October 2020 (identifying various countries that require the developer to submit a community development plan for state approval, and contrasting these plans with developer-community agreements).
52. Moalusi (n 30).
53. Ibid.
54. *See* Centre for Applied Legal Studies, "Social and Labour Plan Mining Community Toolkit" (University of the Witwatersrand, Johannesburg) <www.wits.ac.za/media/wits-university/faculties-and-schools/commerce-law-and-management/research-entities/cals/documents/programmes/environment/resources/SLP%20Community%20Toolkit%202%20March%202017.pdf> accessed 15 July 2019 ("SLPs are often designed without consulting the people who should benefit from them, and so they may not effectively respond to the challenges experienced by people in the communities. … [N]ot everything that is promised in an SLP is delivered, and the

[DMR] does not always follow up to check that these promises are kept.").

55. Routel and Holth (n 12) 434.
56. World Bank (n 50) 77 (describing a social fund in Peru administered by a body that includes "representation from the directly impacted stakeholders and the mining company."); Earth Systems (n 50) 9 (discussing a community development fund in Laos administered by a committee that is co-chaired by the mining company and the government, but includes village representatives).
57. See, for example, Centre for Applied Legal Studies (n 54) 13 ("[In South Africa,] if the mine does not comply with the SLP, then the DMR can suspend or even cancel their mining right. However, in practice this is very unlikely. Part of the problem is that the DMR does not currently have enough inspectors to monitor how all mines comply with their SLPs, and another part is that there is not much motivation to undertake this monitoring.").
58. *See* "Burkina Faso: as good as gold" (*Mining Africa Online*, 19 October 2016) <https://miningafricaonline.co.za/index.php/mining-features/mining-in-africa/2685-burkina-faso-as-good-as-gold> accessed 15 July 2019 ("There are instances where very little of these revenues are distributed to the local communities, adversely affecting the reputations of mining companies.").
59. Maconachie, Srinivasan & Menzies (n 35) 13, 16.
60. *See* Dalupan (n 2) 28 ("If community trust of government is low, involving the state in the process will inhibit cooperative and effective agreement making").
61. Ibid 17 ("When the FPIC process is facilitated by the government, communities often believe that the project is a done deal and that they are left with no other option but to enter into [an IIA] for the project.").
62. O'Faircheallaigh (n 24) 101; Roy E. Kwiatkowski, "Indigenous Community Based Participatory Research and Health Impact Assessment" [2011] 31 Environmental Impact Assessment Rev 445, 446 [Kwiatkowski].
63. Kwiatkowski ibid 446 ("Social community health may also then be impacted as individuals face a loss of cultural identity and impacts on their quality of life associated with traditional lifestyles. Furthermore, socio-cultural wellbeing can be affected by increasing stress, anxiety, and feelings of alienation as their link to mother earth is broken.").
64. Chelsea Gutzman, "Northern Getaway: What Ecotourism Advocates Say about the Plan to Divide BC with a Pipeline" [2012] 38 Alternatives Journal 28 (describing the proposed route for oil transport and the ecological significance of the Douglas Channel); Jacquie Green, Ray Green, and Mary Green, "Haisla Nuuyum: Cultural Conservation and Regulation Methods within Traditional Fishing and Hunting" [2013] 2 Decolonization: Indigeneity Educ. & Soc'y 57 (describing traditional hunting and fishing practices along the Douglas Channel and the significance of these activities for Haisla culture).
65. Grace Nosek, "Re-imagining Indigenous Peoples' Role in Natural Resource Development Decision Making: Implementing Free, Prior and Informed Consent in Canada through Indigenous Legal Traditions" [2017] 50 UBC L Rev 95, 129–130.
66. Derrick Penner, "Coastal First Nations Promise to Keep up Fight" *Calgary Herald* (Calgary, 18 June 2014) D4 (discussing Haisla opposition to the Northern Gateway project).
67. "Bridging the Last Divide" *Alberta Oil Magazine* (March 2012) <http://haisla.ca/bridging-the-last-divide-2/>accessed 15 July 2019.
68. "Haisla First Nation" (Indigenous Business and Investment Council) <www.bcabic.ca/success-stories/haisla-first-nation/> accessed 15 July 2019.
69. Dokis (n 10) 77–80.
70. *See* Foster, "Community Participation in Development" (n 23) 67–77 (summarizing requirements for impact assessment in ILO Convention No. 169, UNDRIP, US and Canadian law, the Convention on Biological Diversity, and the Akwé: Kon Guidelines).

71. *See* Secretariat of the Convention on Biological Diversity, "Akwé: Kon Voluntary Guidelines for the Conduct of Cultural, Environmental and Social Impact Assessment regarding Developments Proposed to Take Place on, or which are Likely to Impact on, Sacred Sites and on Lands and Waters Traditionally Occupied or Used by Indigenous and Local Communities" (Convention on Biological Diversity, 2004) 8–9 [Akwé: Kon Guidelines].
72. Ibid 8–9, 21, 24.
73. *See* O'Faircheallaigh (n 24); Philippe Hanna and others, "Improving the Effectiveness of Impact Assessment Pertaining to Indigenous Peoples in the Brazilian Environmental Licensing Procedure" [2014] 46 Envt'l Impact Assessment Rev 58, 60.
74. Kwiatkowski (n 62) 448–449.
75. Ciaran O'Faircheallaigh and Tony Corbett, "Indigenous Participation in Environmental Management of Mining Projects: The Role of Negotiated Agreements, Environmental Politics" [2005] 14 Envt'l Pol 629, 636.
76. Dokis (n 10) 120–121, 153.
77. Ciaran O'Faircheallaigh, "Extractive Industries and Indigenous Peoples: A Changing Dynamic?" [2013] 30 J Rural Stud 20, 26–27; Dokis (n 10) 120.
78. Dalupan (n 2) 12.
79. See George K. Foster, "Combating Bribery of Indigenous Leaders in International Business" [2015] 54 Colum J Transnat'l L 59, 68–76 [Foster] (summarizing reports of improper tactics by developers during negotiations with Indigenous representatives in Latin America, the Asia-Pacific Region, and Africa).
80. See, for example, Lindsay Fendt, "Indigenous and Afro-Caribbeans claim they were forced to negotiate over Nicaragua Canal" (*Tico Times*, 14 January 2016) <https://ticotimes.net/2016/01/14/indigenous-afro-caribbeans-claim-forced-negotiate-nicaragua-canal> accessed 15 July 2019.
81. See, for example, Foster (n 79) 69 (discussing allegations involving an oil project in Belize); Dokis (n 10) 117–118 (discussing concerns about negotiating practices in Canada).
82. Ibid Foster 76–107 (outlining circumstances under which offers or payments to Indigenous leaders would violate the Foreign Corrupt Practices Act and other anti-corruption legislation in the United States).
83. Ibid 102.
84. Gibson and O'Faircheallaigh (n 34) 168; "On Improving Tribal-Corporate Relations in the Mining Sector: A White Paper on Strategies for Both Sides of the Table" (The Harvard Project on American Indian Economic Development, 2014) 51.
85. Ciaran O'Faircheallaigh, "Community Development Agreements in the Mining Industry: An Emerging Global Phenomenon" [2013] 44 Community Dev 222, 232.
86. Dokis (n 10) 118.
87. Ibid.
88. Gibson and O'Faircheallaigh (n 34) 65.
89. Dokis (n 10) 117; (n 54) 10.
90. Gibson and O'Faircheallaigh (n 34) 179.
91. Trevor Jang, "Breaking Tradition: Why Consent From the Entire Community Is Crucial When It Comes to Getting First Nations' Approval for Resource Projects" (*Disclosure Media*, 28 July 2017) <www.impactresolutions.ca/single-post/2017/07/24/Breaking-tradition-Why-consent-from-the-entire-community-is-crucial-when-it-comes-to-getting-First-Nations-approval-for-resource-projects> accessed 15 July 2019 (discussing conflict within an Aboriginal community in Canada over an IIA that negotiators did not originally intend to submit to community ratification).
92. *See* Foster (n 23) 87–90, 95–96.

4 Indigenous-Industry Agreements, Legal Uncertainty, and Risk Allocations

Dwight Newman and Levi Graham

I. Introduction

Indigenous-Industry Agreements have a complex set of relationships to legal uncertainty, some of which we will seek to examine in this chapter. Overall, we will argue that legal uncertainty may both facilitate and flummox the practice of Indigenous-Industry Agreements. The conclusion is that while Indigenous-Industry Agreements may seem like a response to certain types of legal uncertainty about Indigenous rights, they may also serve that role on only an interim basis. In the result, at a broader policy level, there may be ongoing questions about whether the resolution of legal uncertainty on Indigenous rights more broadly would be more constructive than relying upon this privatised response.[1]

In making the argument, we discuss two particular relationships between legal uncertainty and the practice of Indigenous-Industry Agreements. Notably, we extrapolate principally from the Canadian context, where the duty to consult doctrine has played a massive, albeit non-exclusive role in incentivising Indigenous-Industry Agreements,[2] but which we also think has lessons for elsewhere. Thus, we also attempt to make some deliberate connections to other domestic contexts and the international arena where these starting points offer some illumination.

In terms of the two particular relationships we will examine, first, legal uncertainty provides a context in which Indigenous-Industry Agreements can flourish, as industry seeks to enter into agreements that remove uncertainty. Indigenous-Industry Agreements can appear to have the potential to transform uncertainty into a set of managed risks and even incentivise the reduction of some of these risks, and the paper will begin by offering a conceptualisation of typical forms of Indigenous-Industry Agreements as relating not simply to benefit-sharing but as importantly to removal of uncertainty and allocation of risk.

Second, Indigenous-Industry Agreements may themselves be subjected to more legal uncertainty than has been realized thus far. Some of this latter uncertainty, we suggest, arises from potential future developments related to Free, Prior, and Informed Consent (FPIC). The real possibility exists of later legal challenges to Indigenous-Industry Agreements far more so than has often been realized.[3] This possibility raises issues about the role that Indigenous-Industry

Agreements have or have not played during a certain period of increasingly privatised relationships with Indigenous communities in relation to their land and resource claims.

This discussion is grounded in a set of background concepts concerning legal uncertainty and risk. Uncertainty refers to unpredictable, uncontrollable outcomes; by contrast, risk generically refers to different potential outcomes being subject to a range of probabilities, with the possibility existing of a more or less successful outcome on certain criteria, or refers specifically to a particular factor that affects those probabilities.[4] For industry engaged in a resource development project, a certain range of risks are unavoidable and are part of doing business, and legal risk specifically has become a larger part of the business landscape across various sectors.[5] However, the fact that there can be attempts to measure or control risks makes them a manageable part of doing business, albeit with certain costs attached. Uncertainty, in the strict sense, may turn doing business into little more than gambling and, on traditional accounts, will have strong implications against investment unless it can be transformed into manageable risk.[6]

Indigenous-Industry Agreements may serve certain purposes in terms of distributing known benefits and costs from certain developments. However, large parts of their function relate to transformation of uncertainty into managed risks and to the actual management of these risks. Notably, where there is legal uncertainty for a potential project due to Indigenous rights norms—the possibility that the project will be unable to proceed due to a potential clash with established or potential future legal norms related to Indigenous rights—one way of dealing with that uncertainty is by transforming it into a set of managed risks and allocating these risks as part of a larger agreement related to the project.

In discussing Indigenous-Industry agreements fundamentally in relation to issues of risk and uncertainty, we obviously focus on one particular dimension of these agreements. However, it is an important one that affects various aspects of how we understand the phenomenon of Indigenous-Industry Agreements. Correlatively, it also has implications for any policy-maker engagement with Indigenous-Industry Agreements, as we discuss further in the conclusion.

II. Legal Uncertainty and Risk Management as Backdrop to Indigenous-Industry Agreements

One key relationship between uncertainty and Indigenous-Industry Agreements is the phenomenon of such agreements being negotiated, at least from the industry proponent's perspective, so as to attempt to remove uncertainty. Legal uncertainty about the scope of Indigenous rights has been prevalent in the Canadian jurisprudence.[7] While the duty to consult doctrine was developed in part to manage situations of uncertainty,[8] it also generates both uncertainties and risks of its own, partly stemming from its reliance on the underlying rights norms that are subject to ongoing development and partly from the dependence of projects on interactions between governments and Indigenous rights-holders.

In Canada, then, there may be legal uncertainty for a resource development project specifically because of the duty to consult doctrine, which mandates that there must be consultation with Indigenous communities when the Crown has actual or constructive knowledge of a potential adverse effect on asserted Aboriginal or treaty rights arising from a contemplated government decision.[9] Meaningful consultation has a range of requirements in it, including accommodation that attempts to avoid negative impacts on Aboriginal and treaty rights and which in principle includes the possibility of not proceeding with the decision.[10]

Where there is a government failure to meet the requirements of the duty to consult, something which is to some degree inherently outside the control of a project proponent, that failure will be subjected to a remedy that generally requires going back and meeting the requirements of consultation, resulting in delay at minimum and the ongoing possibility of a reversal of a project approval.[11] For example, in the context of the multi-billion dollar Enbridge Northern Gateway pipeline project, an initial regulatory and governmental approval of that project was quashed at the Federal Court of Appeal over imperfections in the last stage of consultation, ultimately resulting in an unexpected cancellation of the project when a new federal government chose not to proceed with further consultations as would have been required to consider reissuing the approval.[12] A similar problem arose with the Trans Mountain pipeline, with its certificate of approval also being quashed at the Federal Court of Appeal, although later decisions by various actors would seem to be permitting that project to move forward.[13]

The legal uncertainties attached to Canada's duty to consult doctrine have greatly incentivised the use of Indigenous-Industry Agreements, known in Canada specifically as Impact Benefit Agreements (IBAs).[14] While the focus of much discussion of these agreements is on the resulting distribution of benefits and impacts from the project, it has also been widely realized that a key function of these agreements from an industry perspective is to transform uncertainty into managed risks. In particular, a relatively standard clause in Canadian IBAs is the so-called "support clause" under which the community agrees to support the project in the context of consultation and other legal processes as part of what it offers in exchange for the range of benefits it receives under the agreement.[15] By such a clause, not only have uncertainties concerning the duty to consult been transformed into managed risks, but also there is actually a management of these risks in a way that incentivises their reduction in so far as the party that could most elevate the uncertainty has now contractually agreed not to do so and derives ongoing contractual benefits from not doing so.

The form of a support clause in a Canadian IBA can vary to some degree. Some clauses may continue to permit Indigenous communities to raise some issues in government consultation processes, whereas others may entail support for the project across a range of different forums so as to remove various potential uncertainties for the project.[16] Some clauses have run into significant controversy, such as those that would attempt to require the Indigenous community in the IBA to discourage its members from commenting negatively about the project—so-called "gag order" provisions.[17] Different IBAs may end up involving different forms of support clauses, depending in part on how extensive various uncertainties appear to be on a particular project, some of which may not relate precisely to legal risks but to broader risks related to social acceptance of the project. Different forms of support clause share a common aim of reducing the pertinent uncertainties for the proponent.

Canadian IBAs respond to a meaningful degree to an environment of legal uncertainty. Some might initially perceive this characteristic as singularly Canadian. However, realizing that the legal uncertainty addressed coexists with other uncertainties helps to make clear the broader application of this characteristic of Indigenous-industry agreements. In Australia, Indigenous-industry agreements between mining companies and Indigenous communities also operate to reduce uncertainties that would otherwise exist. Agreements under the "right to negotiate" provisions in Australia's *Native Title Act* operate in a space in which the specific rights of Indigenous communities in relation to minerals are not clearly defined, so companies that negotiate such agreements achieve specificity on the Indigenous entitlements in particular circumstances while also lessening broader risks of unrest in relation to a project.[18]

However, apart from the support clause, one can read more clauses of a typical IBA as related to risk allocation than may first be apparent. An agreement will also provide, for instance, for ongoing consultative processes between the industry proponent and the Indigenous community related to future environmental issues or unexpected impacts. On one reading, such a clause transforms uncertainty and manages risk related to future issues that could arise by submitting them to an agreed process rather than making them something that raises questions about the agreement itself.

Apart from Impact Benefit Agreements (IBAs) which traditionally exchanged a range of benefits and allocated a range of risks, an emergent phenomenon in terms of Indigenous-Industry Agreements in Canada has been the increasing development of equity partnerships between industry proponents and Indigenous communities. While not necessarily "partnerships" in the technical legal sense, these arrangements effectively mean that Indigenous communities take a partial ownership stake in a project. For example, in the context of the Northern Gateway pipeline, dozens of Indigenous communities along the route had become future owners of the project, with up to one third of the ownership of the project destined for these Indigenous communities. In the context of this sort of Indigenous-Industry Agreement, communities are inherently incentivised to support the project because their economic interests are actually directly aligned with those of the industry proponent. The legal uncertainty that might have arisen out of potential community opposition instead becomes a naturally managed risk.

In many respects, Indigenous-Industry Agreements are functioning here much like any other contract, and they must be understood as part of the broader contractual context for resource development projects. Contracts are important for business projects for a variety of reasons. Simply put, they allow a business to organize and order an array of business collaborations, they provide certainty for planners and underwriters, and they allow for efficient allocation of risk. However, beyond discrete transactions, they also provide a basis for guiding commercial relationships. Contracts allow "immediate parties to a transaction to align incentives and to craft governance structures that are better attuned to their exchange needs."[19] To illustrate, consider what is required to establish a mineral mining project. Once an economically viable resource deposit has been proven, the company must gain approval for the project, design the extraction facility, and arrange for supporting infrastructure. This may include power, water, port facilities, processing plants, communication facilities, transportation, refining, and product marketing.[20] In many cases, logistics and transportation may rival the cost of extraction.[21] Contracts allow an owner to gather and align specialized firms to provide services without being vertically integrated and other necessary parties for a project to move forward.

In general terms, contracting also allows planners and underwriters to determine whether a project or business is economically viable. For the owner, negotiation may help "smoke out" critical facts that might be important for planning and costing an enterprise.[22] To finance a project, a bank or investor must also have certainty to underwrite an investment. For example, in the mining context, where commodities are traded in US Dollars, exchange-rate and commodity risks are critical.[23] Proponents often sell future contracts—contractual obligations to sell a certain quantity of goods at a certain price.[24] These contracts hedge against future commodities and currency rates, either through public exchanges or through over-the-counter derivatives.[25] Therefore, to manage market exposure companies may "lock in" revenue streams through contracts. This in turn reduces venture risk and aids in underwriting.

Apart from the Indigenous-Industry Agreement context, contracts are key risk allocation tools. Warranties and *force majeure* clauses allocate known and unknown risks. When contractors, sub-contractors, and suppliers are involved in a project, risk is allocated by the contractual terms and prices are adjusted accordingly.[26] It is a widely accepted principle that risks should be allocated to the party best able to manage or mitigate those risks.[27] For example, transport companies have industry expertise and are better situated to manage logistic risks.[28] Therefore, contract law reduces transaction costs, enables better risk allocation, and furthers greater prosperity for all parties than would otherwise be achieved. Indigenous-Industry Agreements must function as part of this complex contractual environment for any given project.

Apart from their role as excellent planning and risk mitigation tools, it is important to realise that many contracts must also structure relationships that are long-term, dynamic, and complex, as opposed to being merely transactional.[29] Commercial disputes are often resolved by reference to norms which are distinct from the legal process.[30] This relational aspect of contracts highlights that legal certainty is not an end unto itself. Flexibility and ambiguity may be necessary and desirable. Negotiation is costly, and perfect precision of terms may not be feasible;[31] flexibility may be desired to accommodate unconsidered risks.[32]

Indeed, litigious and distrustful business relationships can be marked by higher transaction costs.[33] An IBA is an excellent example of a relational contract. IBAs may provide detailed responsibilities for each party while leaving many terms open for future growth.[34] They provide numerous mechanisms, such as arbitration and mediation clauses, that govern ongoing relationships.

Impact Benefit Agreements (IBAs) have gained popularity among Canadian project proponents, in large part, to ensure legal certainty regarding the duty to consult, but with that purpose also needing to be understood within the larger contractual matrix involved in a project, what Indigenous communities bring to the project, and the broader relationships involved.[35] This said, these Indigenous-Industry Agreements may leave open or even create a number of potential uncertainties in their own right, as we next address.

III. Future Uncertainties with Indigenous-Industry Agreements

While the role of Indigenous-Industry Agreements in shaping relationships may itself imply departure from some narrower conceptions of certainty, the legal environment in which Indigenous-Industry Agreements are located may also pose larger future uncertainties concerning the legal standing of such agreements in the first place. Here, we explore some of these potential uncertainties, identifying sources in contract law principles and in aspects of the evolving landscape of Indigenous rights jurisprudence more generally.

To be clear, though, attention to the relationship-building aspects of Indigenous-Industry Agreements directs us towards a broader conception of certainty than that with which some might first begin. In a fascinating piece on certainty in the common law, John Linarelli draws a distinction between two types of legal certainty that are arguably preferred, respectively, in the United Kingdom and the United States. These are legal certainty in a conceptual sense and legal certainty in an instrumental sense, with the American conception having focussed in particular on economic efficiency.[36] The law can be predictable on either version of certainty, with conceptual certainty allowing those predictions based on concepts within the law itself and instrumental certainty allowing those predictions based on the instrumental values the law advances and an analysis, in the American context, of what future legal rules will best achieve economic efficiency. While the latter approach may leave more possibilities open, it does not render prediction impossible.

The certainty achieved by an Indigenous-Industry Agreement will not always be a conceptual certainty that locks in precise legal commitments on every dimension within the agreement. It may nonetheless offer a form of instrumental certainty, not in this context directed solely at economic efficiency but directed towards the value of maintaining the relationship between a resource company and a community. Terms of the Indigenous-Industry Agreement may achieve certainty through more complex mechanisms than would fit with the narrower conception of certainty some would employ.

That said, different terms of the agreement that are meant to offer conceptual and/or relational certainty may still be subjected to broader uncertainties from the legal environment in which Indigenous-Industry Agreements are located. In particular, without a different choice of law clause, Indigenous-Industry Agreements will be subjected to the proper law of the contract. That will normally be the national/provincial/territorial law. The legal uncertainties embedded within the respective contract law jurisprudence of these jurisdictions become embedded into the agreement itself.[37]

Canadian contract law could conceivably identify a number of circumstances in which an Indigenous-Industry Agreement could be subjected to a later legal challenge, although these may not arise so much from contract law on its own as from the interfaces between contract law and Indigenous rights law. For example, there would be contract law issues if a particular agreement were be procured through coercion or bad faith. A vivid example of "illegitimate" agreements can be found in parts of Latin America where many similar agreements are extracted by coercion, duress, or gross power imbalance.[38] However, IBAs in Canada more typically arise from negotiations between sophisticated parties. This is aided by funding schemes that provide communities with means to employ professional counsel during the process. The high standards to void an agreement for duress will not arise often, even in the context of arguments about the precarious economic position of many Indigenous communities.

Some might wonder whether broader uncertainties in contract law will make their way into the IBA context. For example, in *Bhasin v. Hrynew*, the Supreme Court of Canada recently enunciated a new organizing principle of good faith which in turn gives rise to a more specific duty of honest performance.[39] The general duty of good faith operates irrespective of the intentions of the parties and therefore cannot be excluded by terms on any agreement—including an IBA.[40] However, again, there are high thresholds for these principles to permit an effective challenge to an Indigenous-Industry Agreement. The test for the duty of honest performance could be conceptualized as a two-step process. The first step is to establish that a party lied or knowingly misled another—not merely a failure to disclose.[41] The second element is to establish that the dishonest act was directly and intimately connected to the dishonest party's contractual performance.[42] However, this principle would not be likely to apply in respect of systemic features of the IBA process, and all of these considerations are in any case within the control of the negotiating proponent and thus do not represent an uncertainty for it.

More challenging for proponents, though, may be situations where broader doctrines of Canadian Aboriginal law or Indigenous rights law have the potential to raise contract law issues in the context of an Indigenous-Industry Agreement. Such situations might arise, for instance, where there are problems in the way in which a community has signed on to an agreement, there are arguments about which representative(s) were able to negotiate the agreement, or there are arguments that representatives of a community have agreed to something going beyond what the community is legally permitted to do.

First, to the extent that Canadian Aboriginal law prescribes aspects of contract formation with Indigenous communities, notably with First Nations operating under the *Indian Act*,[43] it may contain elements that could raise issues. While lower courts have read an implied power to contract with bands, this contractual power is subject to s 2(3)(b) of the *Indian Act* which states that "a power conferred on the council of a band shall be deemed not to be exercised unless it is exercised pursuant to the consent of a majority of the councillors of the band present at a meeting of the council duly convened."[44] Judicial consideration of this provision has highlighted that it can have complicating effects where, for example, band councillors sign off on a decision but have not done so through a duly constituted meeting.[45] The effects for a band that were to deal with a particular issue through traditional protocol remain untested.

Second, there will in some instances be disputes about whether a band council government is the appropriate representation for purposes of a First Nations community's entry into an Indigenous-Industry Agreement.[46] One might highlight here situations like those involving disputes between elected *Indian Act* governments and hereditary or other traditional governments.[47] To the extent that the law has not resolved which government has legal authority on behalf of a community, there is potential legal uncertainty for proponents who enter into negotiations with communities that have such internal disputes.[48]

Third, there could be further uncertainties given the way that Indigenous rights law has developed thus far, notably in so far as the Canadian courts have suggested that there may be limits on the scope of the authority of present representatives of a community to agree to certain uses of land where these uses would reduce the value of the land for future generations of the community.[49] The judicially imposed inherent limits on the use of Aboriginal title land have become relatively uncertain, meaning that it is not clear whether communities can enter into agreements for certain types of resource development at all.[50]

This last situation may appear to be an artefact of a particular phase of development of Canada's approach to Indigenous rights law,[51] and indeed it may turn out to be the case that Canadian courts in future find constructive approaches that avoid uncertain restrictions on Indigenous communities' permitted uses of their own lands. But one challenge that will not change is that an Indigenous-Industry Agreement is usually meant to endure over a significant period of time. It thus needs to take account not just of present law but of future law as well. Something like the scope of application and content of the Free, Prior, and Informed Consent (FPIC) norm in international law has been subjected to significant flux over recent decades. Today, there continue to be different possible reads on what the meaning of the FPIC norm is.[52] An Indigenous-Industry Agreement reached today needs to take account of different ways such a norm might evolve, including ways that the concept of FPIC as developed by some future point might be used to challenge a particular Indigenous-Industry Agreement. The making of Indigenous-Industry Agreements must actually operate in a context of some very challenging uncertainties indeed.

IV. Conclusions

Indigenous-Industry Agreements have a set of complex relationships to uncertainty, only some of which we have been able to address here. While some from an industry perspective will take a view that the achievement of clear terms in an Indigenous-Agreement is precisely for the sake of attaining certainty against a backdrop of various legal uncertainties, the way in which an Indigenous-Industry Agreement promotes certainty can be more complex than first thought. We have discussed not only conceptual certainty but also relational certainty, and both matter. The presence of certain legal uncertainties no doubt promoted the practice of Indigenous-Industry Agreements, especially in Canada, but these agreements also grapple with uncertainty in a more complex set of forms.

At the same time, emerging uncertainties in the ways in which Aboriginal law and Indigenous rights law perpetuate and expand different sorts of uncertainties can create new challenges for the practice of Indigenous-Industry Agreements. Realising just some of the complexities of the interface of Indigenous-Industry Agreements and uncertainty highlights just what an important field of study Indigenous-Industry Agreements present. They warrant ongoing attention from a rich variety of perspectives, and we are glad to write as part of a collection engaging with some of these.

Notes

1. We do not, though, adopt a completely definitive view on that point. In some of his past work, Newman has suggested there are circumstances where legal uncertainty in the consultation context has had negative consequences. In some of his work in progress, Graham identifies arguments based on the economics of information that may identify particular circumstances where legal uncertainty can actually promote efficient agreement-making. There are thus more complex considerations at issue, and our chapter is focussed simply on identifying some relationships between Indigenous-Industry Agreements and uncertainty.
2. See Dwight Newman, ***Revisiting the Duty to Consult Aboriginal Peoples*** (Purich 2014) 82–83; Dwight Newman, ***The Rule and Role of Law: The Duty to Consult, Aboriginal Communities, and the Canadian Resource Sector*** (Macdonald-Laurier Institute 2014) 12–13. For some of the fundamental uncertainties in Canadian Indigenous rights jurisprudence, see also Malcolm Lavoie, "Aboriginal Rights and the Rule of Law" (2019) 92 Supreme Ct L Rev (2d) 155. For the widespread nature of Impact Benefit Agreements (IBAs) in Canada, with consultation-based, statute-required, and business-based underpinnings, see also Darwin Hanna, ***Legal Issues on Indigenous Economic Development*** (LexisNexis Canada 2017) 123–124, 126. Hanna considers arguments that the proliferation of IBAs represents shifting norms on corporate social responsibility and/or that they represent principally a desire to reduce uncertainty but does not seek to decide between these explanations, though he does say they are at least partially in response to risks on duty to consult.
3. Cf. also Charis Kamphuis, "Contesting Indigenous-Industry Agreements in Latin America", in Ibironke T. Odumosu-Ayanu and Dwight Newman (eds.), ***Indigenous-Industry Agreements, Natural Resources, and the Law*** (Routledge 2021).
4. The classic distinction between uncertainty and risk derives from FH Knight, ***Risk, Uncertainty, and Profit*** (Houghton Mifflin 1921), although the reality of which is the applicable concept can become murky in the context of the issues at stake.

5. For discussion on increased challenges of legal risk worldwide, see generally Peter Kurer, *Legal and Compliance Risk: A Strategic Response to a Rising Threat for Global Business* (OUP 2015).
6. See generally Knight (n 4). For a recent, rich set of discussions on legal uncertainty, some of which may call for some adaptations to this traditional picture (as discussed further below), see generally Mark Fenwick, Mathias Siems & Stefan Wrbka (eds) *The Shifting Meaning of Legal Certainty in Comparative and Transnational Law* (Bloomsbury 2017).
7. Lavoie (n 2).
8. Newman, *Revisiting the Duty to Consult* (n 2) 29–30.
9. *Id* 26, 37–57; *Haida Nation v British Columbia (Minister of Forests)* [2004] 3 SCR 511, [11].
10. Newman *Revisiting the Duty to Consult* (n 2) 86–88.
11. *Cf id* 78–79.
12. *Gitxaala Nation v Canada*, 2016 FCA 187, [2016] 4 FCR 418. For some discussion of whether this decision was consistent with how the Supreme Court of Canada would have approached matters had there been an appeal, see Dwight Newman, "Changing Duty to Consult Expectations for Energy Regulators: Broader Implications from the Supreme Court of Canada's Decisions in *Chippewas of the Thames and Clyde River*" (2017) 5:4 Energy Regulation Q 21.
13. For the quashing, see *Tsleil-Waututh Nation v. Canada (Attorney General)*, 2018 FCA 153. For the approval of the subsequently recompleted consultation process, see *Coldwater Indian Band v. Canada (Attorney General)*, 2020 FCA 34.
14. Some proponents may follow a two-track system of trying to advance through regulatory and consultation processes while simultaneously seeking to negotiate with communities, making a later determination on which path offers better business outcomes: Keith Bergner, "Navigating a Changing Landscape: Challenges and Practical Approaches for Project Proponents and Indigenous Communities in the Context of the Review and Assessment of Major Projects" in Dwight Newman (ed), *Business Implications of Aboriginal Law* (LexisNexis Canada 2018) 193.
15. See discussion in Dwight Newman, *Natural Resource Jurisdiction in Canada* (LexisNexis Toronto 2013) 98–100; Dwight Newman, *Mining Law of Canada* (LexisNexis Toronto 2018) 40–42; Thomas Isaac and Arend J.A. Hoekstra, "Canadian Law and Realpolitik Regarding Indigenous-Industry Agreements", in Odumosu-Ayanu and Newman (eds.) (n 3).
16. Cf. Brad Gilmour & Bruce Mellett "The Role of Impact and Benefits Agreements in the Resolution of Project Issues with First Nations" (2013) 51 Alberta L Rev 385, 391.
17. *Id.* For a recent example, see August 2019 media discussion of the leaked agreement between the Nak'azdli Whut'en Nation and TC Energy on the Coastal GasLink Pipeline, which contained a provision requiring the Nation to dissuade its members from taking part "in any media or social media campaign" against the pipeline.
18. Cf. Ciaran O'Faircheallaigh, *Negotiations in the Indigenous World: Aboriginal Peoples and the Extractive Industry in Australia and Canada* (Routledge New York 2016) 53–54.
19. Oliver Williamson, "The Theory of the Firm as Governance Structure: From Choice to Contract" (2002) 16 J Economic Perspectives 172. See also Ronald Coase, "The Nature of the Firm" (1937) 4 Economica 386; Chester Barnard, *The Functions of the Executive* (HUP 1938).
20. Victor Rudenno, *The Mining Valuation Handbook*, 3rd ed. (Wrightbooks 2009) 59–60 [*Rudenno*].
21. Ibid 137.
22. Charles Fox, *Working with Contracts* (Practicing Law Institute, 2008) 10.
23. *Rudenno* (n 20) 193.
24. *Id* 194.

25. *Id* 194, 196, 201.
26. Hon Justice L Ricchetti and Timothy Murphy, *Construction Law in Canada* (LexisNexis Canada 2010) 177–179; Phillip Scheibel, "Understanding Construction Warranties in Canada" [2015] J Cdn College Construction Lawyers 137, 140.
27. John Haythorne and Mollie Deyong, "Fairness and Transparency in Large Project Public Procuremen" [2018] J Cdn College Construction Lawyers 59, 77–78; Haythorne argues that this principle is ideal, but that risk is often allocated based on leverage or industry norms in reality.
28. Another excellent, albeit abstract, example can be found in the financial hedging example above.
29. Ian Macneil, "Contracts: Adjustment of Long-Term Economic Relations under Classical, Neoclassical, and Relational Contract Law" (1978) 72 NW U L Rev 854 [*Macneil*].
30. See Stewart Macaulay, "Non-Contractual Relations in Business, A Preliminary Study" in MP Furmston, *The Law of Contracts*, 16th ed. (OUP 2012) 30n34.
31. See Richard A Posner, "The Law and Economics of Contract Interpretation" (2005) 83 Texas L Rev 1581.
32. Macneil (n 29) 867; see also Richard A. Posner, *Economic Analysis of Law* 1st ed. (Little Brown & Co 1973) 44.
33. Ramy Zaghloul & Francis Hartman, "Construction Contracts: The Cost of Mistrust" (2003) 21 Intl J Project Management 419.
34. Irene Sosa & Karyn Keenan, "Impact Benefit Agreements Between Aboriginal Communities and Mining Companies: Their Use in Canada," online: (2001) Environmental Mining Council of British Columbia, the Canadian Environmental Law Association and Cooper Accion: Accion Solidaria para el Desarrollo <http://www.cela.ca/sites/cela.ca/files/uploads/IBAeng.pdf> at 18.
35. See Isaac and Hoekstra (n 15).
36. John Linarelli, "Legal Certainty: A Common Law View and a Critique," in Fenwick, Siems & Wrbka (n 6) 159.
37. It would of course be possible for the parties to agree to have the agreement governed by Indigenous law, and there will no doubt be future pressures in this direction: Ibironke T. Odumosu-Ayanu, "The (Legal) Nature of Indigenous-Industry Agreements with Extractive Companies", in Odumosu-Ayanu and Newman (eds.) (n 3). However, as with contracting with any government, subjecting the law of the contract to something changeable by one of the parties has certain risks. In broader contexts, investors entering agreements with states seek to get those agreements outside the scope of the domestic law of those states, whether through choice of law clauses or international investor-state agreements. In the United States, there is much discussion of getting waivers of tribal sovereign immunity in the context of business deals with American Indian tribal governments, essentially motivated by similar considerations.
38. Kamphuis (n 3).
39. *Bhasin v. Hrynew*, 2014 SCC 71, [2014] 3 S.C.R. 494.
40. *Id* [74].
41. *Id* [86].
42. *Id* [73].
43. RSC 1985, c I-5 (Canada).
44. *Id* s 2(3)(b).
45. See *W. Downer Holdings Ltd v Red Pheasant First Nation*, 2012 SKQB 468.
46. The question of who represents a Métis community may be yet more complex, and we will thus not deal with it at length here. See generally *R v Powley*, [2003] 2 S.C.R. 207, 2003 SCC 43, [23] and [27]. Given these issues, a proponent could end up contracting with the wrong party. These uncertainties reduce the effectiveness of IBA in mitigating future problems and may drive some proponents to forego

IBA negotiation with Métis groups altogether. Not only is a loss for Métis communities but also demonstrates how legal uncertainty can interfere with the spirit of reconciliation by reinforcing the stereotypical notion that Métis rights are of "lesser value." For a further perspective on these issues, see Karen Drake, "Who are the Métis? The Role of Free, Prior, and Informed Consent in Identifying a Métis Rights-Holder", in Odumosu-Ayanu and Newman (eds.) (n 3).

47. For a judicial decision that was forced to engage with some such disputes, see *Coastal GasLink Pipeline Ltd. v Huson*, 2019 BCSC 2264.
48. Notably, the sometimes-floated claims that the Supreme Court of Canada's *Delgamuukw* decision indicated that traditional hereditary leaders always have priority in the context of underlying rights of Aboriginal title are not consistent with the decision which appeared to recognise the hereditary leaders for purposes of standing on behalf of the community but also sent the case back on procedural defects on the very basis that they were erroneously claiming Aboriginal title interests as individual claimants and saying that there needed to be a claim by the community. See generally *Delgamuukw v British Columbia (Attorney General)*, [1997] 3 SCR 1010.
49. See *Tsilhqot'in Nation v British Columbia*, 2014 SCC 14, [116], [140].
50. Cf Dwight Newman, *The Top Ten Uncertainties of Aboriginal Title after Tsilhqot'in* (Fraser Institute 2017); Dwight Newman, "The Economic Characteristics of Indigenous Property Rights: A Canadian Case Study" (2016) 95 Nebraska L Rev 432; Isaac and Hoekstra (n 15).
51. Cf Dwight Newman, "Judicial Power, Living Tree-ism, and Alterations of Private Rights by Unconstrained Public Law Reasoning" (2017) 36 U Queensland LJ 247.
52. See generally Dwight Newman, "Interpreting FPIC in UNDRIP" (2020) 27 Int'l J Min & Group Rights 233.

Part II

Analytical and Critical Perspectives

5 Negotiated Agreements, Indigenous FPIC, and the Mine Life Cycle

Ciaran O'Faircheallaigh

I. Introduction

Negotiated agreements between Indigenous peoples and industry, especially extractive industry, have been widely used in Australia and Canada for over 20 years, and are increasingly a feature of relations between industry, Indigenous peoples, and customary landowners in the Global South. While they vary greatly in style and content, negotiated agreements share a common core. They seek to mitigate negative effects of a project and ensure that affected Indigenous peoples share in its benefits. They include some form of consent or support for the project concerned by the Indigenous parties. They are generally contractual in nature and so make consent explicit and, at least in principle, offer some certainty that the benefits and impact mitigation promised in return for Indigenous consent will actually materialize.[1]

Because of these characteristics, negotiated agreements have the potential to offer an important platform for the implementation of the right of Indigenous Free Prior and Informed Consent (IFPIC). However if this potential is to be achieved, a number of conditions must be met. These include the condition that Indigenous people enter agreements fully informed about the likely impacts, negative and positive, of the extractive activities they contemplate, and that they do so without duress. In addition, and this is a particular focus of this chapter, agreements must provide for Indigenous consent for critical decisions and key activities throughout the mine life cycle, as each component of that cycle has the potential to have major impacts on Indigenous peoples and their interests.

This chapter seeks to identify whether, and in what circumstances, negotiated agreements in the extractive industries of Australia and Canada meet the conditions required to achieve IFPIC. It concludes that certain agreements in Australia and Canada can be regarded as effective expressions of IFPIC. However, structural barriers arising from legislative frameworks, state and corporate policies, and unequal access to resources mean that agreement making has serious shortcomings in this regard. One particular problem is that agreements frequently fail to address decisions at points in the mine life cycle other than when a mining project receives regulatory approval to proceed. The chapter concludes by identifying structural changes that must occur if the potential of negotiated agreements as a vehicle for expressing IFPIC is to be realized.

II. IFPIC and the Mine Life Cycle

The international norm of IFPIC requires that Indigenous people should have the right, free from duress and in possession of full information regarding proposed developments on their ancestral lands, to provide or withhold their consent to those developments prior to any authorization of development activity by state authorities or developers. According to the United Nations Economic and Social Council, "free" means the absence of coercion, intimidation or manipulation. "Prior" implies that consent has been sought sufficiently in advance of any authorization or commencement of activity and that respect is shown for the time requirements of Indigenous consultation and decision-making processes. "Informed" implies that information is provided to Indigenous peoples in relation to any proposed activity on their ancestral estates, in a form accessible and understandable to them and in a time frame sufficient to allow them to fully consider it. Information should cover at least the nature, size, pace, location, duration, reversibility, and scope of any proposed activity; the reasons for it; the activity's likely economic, social, cultural and environmental impacts, including potential risks and proposals for benefit sharing; the personnel likely to be involved; and procedures the activity is likely to entail. Consent involves "meaningful participation" by Indigenous peoples in all aspects of decision-making in relation to a proposed activity through their freely chosen representatives, and the ability to permit or to prohibit, proposed development activities on their ancestral lands.[2]

IFPIC raises important issues regarding the mineral development process, and the legislative regimes that regulate it. Mineral development involves a series of discrete stages (the "mine life cycle").[3] These may be characterized as exploration designed to locate and test an orebody's physical properties and economic viability; approval and construction of a project; project modification and/or expansion; and mine closure and rehabilitation. Each of these stages typically involves "authorizations" by state authorities or developers, including investment decisions and the grant of exploration and mining licences, and of environmental and planning approvals. Every stage involves decisions that can have serious consequences for affected Indigenous peoples. The grant of an exploration licence constitutes a decision that, in principle, land or water may at some time in the future be subject to mining. Large-scale exploration activity can have substantial impacts, and indeed in some respects its effects may be even more significant than those of a mine because they occur over much larger areas.[4] For instance, construction of roads and tracks by exploration teams can allow much freer access by outsiders to Indigenous lands, leading to hunting of game on which Indigenous people rely, and damage to sites of cultural and spiritual significance.[5] Project approval involves a final decision by a developer to invest substantial capital in mine construction and operations, and by state regulators to permit this investment to proceed, with obvious consequences for Indigenous landowners and communities. Few large mining projects do not undergo substantial changes during the course of their operating lives. Some of these, for example a decision to switch from underground to open cut mining to extract additional ore, can have major economic and environmental consequences.

Critical decisions do not end because a mine reaches the end of its economic life. Issues arise, for instance, in terms of who will pay for safe closure of a mine and rehabilitation of affected areas; by whom and for how long monitoring will be continued to ensure that toxic substances escaping from closed mines are not adversely affecting the environment; how and when a mine operator will be relieved of further responsibility for a mine site; and what final land form and land use should follow mine closure. These decisions have particular significance for Indigenous peoples whose homelands continue to be affected by any adverse effects after miners, investors and regulators have departed.

As noted above, a key issue involves the extent to which agreement making provides a vehicle for expression of IFPIC by incorporating the consent of Indigenous peoples for decisions and actions that affect them at each stage of the mine life cycle. To focus on this issue, I consider the relationship between negotiated agreements and FPIC at the exploration, project approval, and post-approval stages of the cycle, drawing on experience in Australia and Canada.

1. *Mineral Exploration*

Historically in both Australia and Canada "free entry" systems have been used to grant prospecting or exploration licences. In such systems a mining company can apply to the relevant government authority for an exploration permit and, as long as the area is not already under licence and the applicant meets statutory conditions related, for instance, to technical and financial competence, the licence is granted automatically. There is no reference to the Indigenous owners of the area concerned.[6] Free entry systems still apply in much of Canada, with some exceptions, including on Indian Reserves;[7] the proportion of comprehensive land claim settlement areas where Aboriginal peoples own sub-surface rights or where their consent is required before licence applicants can gain access for exploration;[8] and in cases where land claim agreements require government to consult with the Aboriginal parties prior to the opening up of land to exploration.[9] The last of these does not of course ensure that Aboriginal opposition to exploration will result in a government decision not to grant licences, because governments may consult and then decide not to be bound by the views expressed by the people consulted. The same point applies to the Yukon Court of Appeal's ruling in 2012 that the government of Yukon had a duty to consult the Ross River Dena Council before registering a mining claim within an area in which the Council claimed Aboriginal title.[10] In 2014, the Supreme Court of Canada expressed the view in the *Tsilhqot'in* decision that governments should seek the consent of Aboriginal title holders when proposing to use their land.[11] However, the Court also made it clear that where resource development was in the public interest, government could override Aboriginal opposition and allow it to proceed.[12]

While these decisions are evidence of a change in judicial thinking in relation to free entry and Aboriginal rights, in the absence of a statutory requirement to seek Aboriginal consent, agreements are often not negotiated at the exploration stage. While a project approval agreement might subsequently record Aboriginal consent to the (earlier) grant of exploration licences, the "prior" component of FPIC is clearly breached in these circumstances. There can also be wider consequences for FPIC other than the failure to seek consent for the specific activities involved in exploration. Once any mineral tenure is granted, there is a tendency for government actors, and in some cases the general public, to assume that mining constitutes the most valuable use for the land concerned. If a project proceeds to the mining stage, this can create pressure on Aboriginal landowners to approve a project, weakening their bargaining position and undermining the "free" component of FPIC.

In Australia, free entry systems are enshrined in many of the country's mining laws, but their operation is moderated by the effect of legislation recognizing Indigenous rights in land. For example, when the country's first land rights legislation, the *Aboriginal Land Rights (Northern Territory) Act 1976*, was enacted, it provided that Aboriginal consent was required for exploration on Aboriginal freehold land, which covers about half of the Territory. However, the mining industry argued that this created a disincentive to investment as a mining company might commit substantial funds to exploration only to have subsequent development of an orebody prohibited by Aboriginal landowners.[13] The Australian Government responded in 1987 by amending the *Act* so that if Traditional Owners approve an exploration licence they must at the same time provide approval for mining. It could be argued that in cases where Traditional Owners decide to prohibit any mineral development activity, the principle of FPIC is complied with. On the other hand if they approve exploration they must also approve a mining project whose characteristics are largely unknown when consent is provided, breaching the "informed" component of FPIC.[14]

Australia's *Native Title Act 1993* (*NTA*), which applies to the grant of mineral tenures across about half of Australia's land area, is applied separately to the exploration and mining stages. However, it has a fundamental weakness from the Indigenous perspective in that it does not require Indigenous consent before exploration or mining can proceed, but only provides an opportunity for Indigenous landowners to negotiate the conditions under which it can do so.[15] (This situation is discussed in detail in the next section.) In addition, while there is a separate "Right to Negotiate" on applications for exploration licences, these applications are subject to what is termed an "expedited procedure." This means that if the state governments believe that exploration activity will have minimal impact on native title rights, the Right to Negotiate does not apply, and governments are only required to notify native title holders of the impending explorations. Aboriginal landowners can object to the grant of an "expedited procedure" through a government tribunal, the National Native Title

Tribunal (NNTT), which after hearing submissions from both sides determines whether the expedited procedure should apply.[16] In reality Aboriginal organizations, especially those in areas of high mineral activity, lack the resources to even examine in detail the hundreds of exploration permit applications that can be lodged in a year, let alone fund an objection process in the NNTT.[17] They must focus on a small number of applications that affect areas of high cultural or environmental value and/or are believed to have particularly high impacts. Even in relation to this small number of cases their objections may not be successful.[18] The end result is that FPIC is entirely absent in relation to a very high proportion of exploration activity.

Given the statutory context in Australia and Canada, agreements providing for Aboriginal consent to exploration usually occur only where Aboriginal peoples have the political capacity to insist on agreements, or where corporate policies require agreements to be in place. These two factors are closely related. Companies are much more inclined to seek agreement in the absence of a statutory requirement to do so, where they assess that Aboriginal peoples and organizations have the capacity to disrupt their operations or cause them reputational damage.[19] In Australia, some of the more powerful regional Aboriginal land organizations have been able to insist that mining companies sign agreements before they commence exploration. The Kimberley Land Council, a regional land council in the North-West of Western Australia, for example, uses a template agreement that provides consent from Aboriginal landowners in the area of the proposed exploration activity. In return the explorer makes binding undertakings in relation to protection of the environment and of Aboriginal cultural heritage, to provision of Aboriginal employment and business development opportunities, and to provision of financial benefits (calculated as a percentage of on-ground exploration expenditure).

The use of template agreements can substantially reduce the time and cost involved in negotiations, as attention can focus only on those elements that do not align with a specific operational context or the requirements of an individual explorer. Transaction costs are further reduced in cases, as in South Australia, where Aboriginal consent is negotiated through claim-wide agreements with industry peak bodies and state regulators. A case in point is the Indigenous Land Use Agreement between a native title claim group, Antakirinja Land Management Aboriginal Corporation (ALMAC), the South Australian Government, and South Australia's peak mining industry body, the South Australian Chamber of Mines and Energy. Under this Agreement, ALMAC provides its consent to grant of exploration licences and the conduct of activities allowed under them provided the grantee commits to contract conditions that are set out in the Agreement. These include payments to ALMAC, preservation of native title rights, protection of Aboriginal cultural heritage, environmental rehabilitation, and measures to promote Aboriginal employment.[20] The willingness of the peak industry body to sign this agreement indicates that, in fact, having separate Indigenous agreements for exploration and mining is not seen as a disincentive to investment. Other elements of the regulatory framework, for example environmental impact assessments and grant of tenures and environmental approvals, treat exploration and mining separately, and there is no guarantee that government consent for exploration will result in government consent for mining. There is no reason why Indigenous consent should be treated any differently.

It must be acknowledged that template agreements may, while reducing transaction costs, create a risk that the requirements of IFPIC are not achieved because separate decision-making processes are not conducted in relation to each grant of an exploration licence. However any such risk can be substantially minimized if two conditions are met. First, Indigenous landowners must be closely involved in negotiating, and must approve any template agreements, and the processes involved to secure their consent must occur prior to finalization of agreements must be based on provision of information that is comprehensive and accessible, and be inclusive of all landowner interests that may be affected by operation of an agreement. Second, landowners or their representative organization must have the capacity to monitor exploration plans, activities, and impacts to ensure that they align with the requirements of template agreements and that no unanticipated activities or impacts occur that would render them non-compliant with those agreements.

In the absence of consent agreements, mineral exploration activity is conducted in clear breach of the principle of IFPIC. This breach has enormous implications given the potential impact of exploration on peoples and lands, and the very large areas under exploration licences in both Australia and Canada.

2. *Project Approval*

In Australia and Canada the overwhelming component of agreement making relates to the project approval point in the Mine Life Cycle. The context for negotiation of agreements at this point varies enormously. In both countries, some agreement making occurs in a context where there is no legal requirement for agreements to be negotiated, and they result from corporate social responsibility (CSR) policies, political pressure by Indigenous peoples, or a combination of the two. In Canada, Indigenous-industry agreements result from requirements of comprehensive land claim settlements; Territorial legislation; or legislative rights exercised on Indian Reserves. In Australia, many agreements result from operation of the *Native Title Act 1993* (*NTA*), the Australian government's legislative response to the High Court's 1992 *Mabo* decision which established the existence of inherent Indigenous rights to land in Australia. The *NTA* is especially important because native title claims that have been the subject of positive determinations or are still before the courts cover more than half of Australia's land mass. Agreements are also negotiated pursuant to state and territory land rights legislation. It is not possible to consider agreement making in each of these numerous contexts separately. Rather the approach is to identify issues in relation to FPIC that arise in the majority of negotiations across all of them.

Critical questions arise in nearly every case in relation to the "informed" component of IFPIC. What information is available in relation to the planned project and its impacts? In both Australia and Canada information usually emerges from the statutory environmental impact assessments (EIAs) that are required for most large projects, though not for many smaller ones. EIAs are conducted by project proponents and consultants they employ on the basis of terms of reference established by regulatory authorities. However, the ability of EIAs to provide information required for the exercise of Indigenous informed consent through agreements is limited. EIAs may not have been completed by the time that an Indigenous-company agreement is negotiated.[21] They tend to be voluminous, written in highly technical English, and so not easily accessible to affected Indigenous peoples.[22] Their scope is often limited, focussing on biophysical impacts and paying much less attention to social and especially to cultural impacts. They may define a project's "zone of impact" narrowly, reflecting a more general and well-documented tendency of project-controlled impact assessment to underestimate the scale and severity of negative impacts.[23] Indirect impacts resulting from in-migration of outsiders attracted by the prospect of employment, for example, or cumulative effects generated in combination with other planned or existing projects, are often ignored.

The time frames EIAs use in assessing impacts can also be a problem. These typically are related to the economic life of a project, whereas from an Indigenous perspective, impacts may be understood in much longer, inter-generational time frames. At a broader level, EIAs tend to ignore Indigenous world views and systems of knowledge, which can result in whole categories of impacts being ignored, for instance those on human—animals relations, or on inter-connected clusters of cultural sites that extend well beyond a conventional "project footprint."

In a small but growing number of cases, Indigenous peoples in Australia and Canada are now conducting their own impact assessment studies as a precursor, depending on their outcomes, either to negotiation of an agreement, or to a decision to oppose the project concerned.[24] A comparison of Indigenous and "conventional" impact assessments for similar projects[25] illustrates the obvious superiority of the former in providing a basis for informed decision-making. However, the cost of undertaking comprehensive impact assessments of major and complex projects is high, and they demand considerable administrative and technical capacity on the part of the Indigenous organizations involved. In the absence of cooperation from corporate and regulatory authorities, it can also be difficult to obtain the project information required to conduct accurate impact assessment. These factors help explain why use of Indigenous impact assessment is still limited. In the absence of major reforms to statutory EIA processes, Indigenous impact assessment must be extended very considerably if there is any possibility that agreement making for project approval can provide a firm basis for exercise of FPIC.

Another key issue involves definition of the Indigenous entity that is to give its consent, related in turn to the nature of interests in land and water and the definition of project impact. In some cases there may be a statutory basis for identifying what is deemed to be the relevant decision-making group, for instance the registered members a First Nation when a project is located on Reserve land in Canada, or the native title holders where it is located within a native title determination in Australia. However, it is often the case that there is not a neat "fit" between an Indigenous group defined by statute and an Aboriginal people whose ancestral territory is host to a proposed project.[26] In addition, location of a project on a defined area of land does not mean that its impact is restricted to that area. If toxic substances escape from a project into a waterway, for example, their impact may be felt across a much wider area. Another problem is that the definition of interests in land that underpin relevant legislation may not incorporate all affected Indigenous interests. Those interests can be "layered" and multifaceted, including a right to occupy and permanently use an area, to exploit its resources on a seasonal basis, knowledge of and interests in cultural features of a landscape, and particular rights arising, for instance, from adoption, being born on land, or having kin buried there.

Unless there are mechanisms in place to fully identify Indigenous interests in land and water, people with legitimate interests will not be involved in decision-making and cannot give or withhold their consent. For this reason Aboriginal impact assessments conducted in Australia are typically accompanied by anthropological and land use studies designed to identify the full range of interests that can be expected to be affected by a project. In some cases these studies have resulted in a considerable expansion of the initial population whose consent was deemed to be required.[27]

Also important is the manner of community members' involvement in the agreement making process. At one extreme is a situation which has occurred in both Australia and Canada, where Indigenous community members may have little access to information during negotiations and little opportunity to shape negotiation positions. Negotiations may be conducted between their representatives and company or state officials, with community members only involved in approving or rejecting a summary of a draft final agreement.[28] Such approaches fall short of the requirement for informed consent. On the other hand some agreements in both Australia and Canada have resulted from extensive community engagement processes before negotiations begin, continued engagement during negotiations, and sustained efforts to disseminate information about the project concerned and about negotiation issues and options prior to community decisions about whether or not to approve proposed agreements.[29]

Turning to the "free" dimension of IFPIC, Indigenous "consent" provided through agreements can only be thought of as given freely if Indigenous peoples have a right to withhold that consent. Thus any legislative regime that allows government to override decisions of Indigenous peoples creates a structural impediment to the exercise of FPIC, even if that regime results in agreements involving Indigenous participation. For example, under the *NTA,* native title holders can refuse their consent to an application for a mining lease. However the company concerned can apply to the NNTT to have the lease granted, and in virtually every case where this occurs, company applications are successful.[30] If the NNTT determines that a lease may be granted, it is not permitted to make a royalty-type payment by the proponent a condition of the lease, whereas royalties can be negotiated as part of an Indigenous—company consent agreement. This places enormous pressure on the Indigenous parties to reach agreement, while there is no comparable pressure on the proponent. While in a formal, legal sense the Indigenous group may "consent" to a project, it is very difficult to argue that this consent has been "freely" given.

The threat of compulsory acquisition of Indigenous lands by the State constitutes a further denial of IFPIC. For instance after a change of government in Western Australia in 2008, the State Premier threatened to compulsorily acquire land under native title claim for a proposed Liquefied Natural Gas (LNG) project unless the native title claimants entered into an agreement for the project to proceed. A large majority agreed to do so, primarily because they felt that their obligation to look after their ancestral lands required them to negotiate a role in managing the LNG project. The subsequent agreement records their consent to the project, but that consent was certainly not given freely.[31]

In Canada, there are some specific cases where there is an unequivocal legal requirement to obtain Aboriginal consent before project approval can be granted. As with exploration, these include Indian Reserves, and those portions of land claim settlements (usually a small percentage of the total settlement area) that include sub-surface rights. Land claim settlements typically involve larger areas where Aboriginal ownership of surface rights is recognized and Aboriginal agreement is required for commercial interests to access these lands.[32] The practical requirement might be Aboriginal consent if there are no economically viable alternative access points. More broadly, where there is legal recognition of Aboriginal rights in land, the Crown's "duty to consult" may provide an opportunity for Aboriginal landowners to negotiate the terms on which they will consent to a project proceeding. However, the duty to consult may fall well short of granting Aboriginal peoples the ability to prevent developments to which they are opposed,[33] and as such does not guarantee compliance with the principle of IFPIC.

Yet another potential threat to the "free" component of IFPIC involves company funding of community consultations and negotiations. In most cases in Australia and Canada, Indigenous communities do not themselves have the considerable resources required to consult with community members, carry out impact assessment, gain access to relevant technical information, and maintain a negotiation effort that typically lasts for many months, if not years. They must rely on company funding, and there is always a risk that company negotiators will, at critical points in the negotiation, withdraw or threaten to withdraw funding, placing undue pressure on Indigenous negotiators. This risk can be reduced by reaching a formal funding agreement before negotiations start, but if negotiation last longer or costs more than expected, the need to extend or amend a funding agreement can become a "pressure point."

It is not the case that Aboriginal people in Australia and Canada have been unable to insist that the consent they provide in agreements is free and informed.

The Innu and Inuit, for instance, used direct action, litigation, and capacity to push back project time frames to force Inco, the developer of the Voisey's Bay project, and the governments of Canada and Newfoundland and Labrador, to abandon their attempts to proceed with the project without Aboriginal consent.[34] Similar cases have occurred in Australia. However, such outcomes inevitably reflect the application of significant political and organizational resources, and many Aboriginal groups in both countries lack such resources. This reality also means that the net benefits obtained by Aboriginal signatories to agreements vary greatly from case to case-an outcome that is resulting in significant inequalities between Aboriginal groups affected by mining.[35]

In summary, legislative and policy contexts place Aboriginal peoples in Australia and Canada at a serious disadvantage when they negotiate agreements for project approval, and this in turn creates major problems in ensuring that agreements form a basis for realization of IFPIC. This does not mean that negotiation of agreements is contrary to Aboriginal interests. Given the political realities, the negotiation of agreements may be the only opportunity for Aboriginal peoples to play a role in managing the impacts of mining on their land and culture, and the only way in which they can share in the benefits of resource development. However, large-scale structural reform is required before it can be assumed that agreements providing project approval reflect the principle of IFPIC. I return to this point in the Conclusion.

3. *Project Modification and Mine Closure*

It is unusual to be able to predict the course of a project over its life when it is initially approved. Often a mine will be expanded once it has proved a commercial success, or its life may be extended well beyond what was initially planned. For example, BHP applied for approval to expand its Ekati diamond mine in Canada's Northwest Territories just three years after production commenced, a possibility not envisaged in its original EIA or in the agreements BHP negotiated with a number of Aboriginal groups.[36] Expanding a mine or extending its life can change project configuration substantially, which in turn may result in major changes to its environmental impacts. For instance, extension of the planned life of the McArthur River lead/zinc mine in Australia's Northern Territory required diversion of a large river, an outcome not even remotely envisaged when the agreement approving the project was signed by Indigenous landowners.[37]

Unless agreements provide for their renegotiation when significant changes to a project are proposed, there is no opportunity for Indigenous consent and the principle of IFPIC is therefore breached. This is because, in effect, a new or amended agreement is needed, requiring Indigenous consent. In the absence of consent, the proposed change cannot happen. A small number of agreements do contain such a provision, with one example being in an Australian petroleum production agreement concluded in 2012. However, many agreements only provide for their periodic review and require the agreement of all parties before any changes can be made, in effect denying Indigenous parties the right to insist on changes to agreements when the scale, nature or impact of a project changes from that envisaged at the time an agreement was signed.

The final stage of the mine life cycle, closure, raises numerous issues for affected Indigenous peoples. It has long been recognized that unless mine remediation and environmental rehabilitation are effective, abandoned mines can create lasting and serious health and environmental impacts on Indigenous peoples. Numerous such cases have been documented in Canada, including the effects of uranium mines developed in the 1950s and 1960s and the Giant gold mine, within the city limits of Yellowknife, capital of the Northwest Territories. During its life the Giant mine, now closed, deposited 237,000 tonnes of arsenic trioxide, a proven non-threshold carcinogen which dissolves easily in water, underground. The chambers in which it is stored are leaking arsenic into the mine water, which is currently treated before it eventually reaches Yellowknife Bay. As the mine reached the end of its life the operating company went into receivership and minutes later its entire board of directors resigned, leaving the problem of how to deal with the long-term impacts of the stored arsenic trioxide in the hands of government and the affected Aboriginal communities.[38] Such outcomes appear likely to increase as a result of a growing practice by multinational firms to dispose of mines close to the end of their lives to "junior" companies, at nominal cost. The latter may extend mine life for some years, but junior companies lack the financial capacity to pay for the costs of closure and rehabilitation, which then inevitably fall on the public purse and on affected communities.[39] More broadly, there are issues regarding the standards to which mined land should be rehabilitated; what land uses are feasible and desirable on closed mine sites; and how Indigenous people can deal with the irreversible impacts of mining on landscapes and cultural sites.

Environmental legacies are especially significant for Indigenous peoples because of the long time frames over which environmental impacts can persist. For example, under the proposed approach to closure of Glencore, the operator of the McArthur River lead/zinc mine, it will take 300 years to rehabilitate toxic waste dumps created by mining.[40] There is virtually no prospect that Glencore will continue to exist as a corporate entity over this period of time, raising obvious questions about who will bear responsibility for ensuring that rehabilitation is completed. The issue of long-term responsibility for managing post-closure impacts assumes proportions that are difficult to grasp in the case of waste from uranium mines. Radioactive waste left on the lands of Athabasca First Peoples in Northern Saskatchewan or Mirrar Traditional Owners in Australia's Northern Territory, for instance, has a half-life of about 10,000 years.

In recent years there has been a growing recognition that the issues around closure extend beyond the environmental impact.[41] Particularly in remote areas where few other economic activities occur, closure can severely disrupt the livelihoods of Indigenous communities previously dependent on mining. Such disruption can in turn have major cultural and social effects, often because of the departure of younger community members in search of work, loss of self-esteem associated with subsequent unemployment, and removal of wage income used to support land-based activities. Moreover, in Indigenous communities in the far north of Canada, wages from mine work have been used to buy and maintain hunting equipment such as snowmobiles, while in the Pilbara region in Australia's north west wages and business income from a booming iron ore industry have supported the revival of large-scale, regional ceremonial activity. Closure can also create economic opportunities, for instance from use of mine infrastructure in tourist ventures and from the income that can be generated by long-term environmental monitoring and rehabilitation programs.

The critical issue in relation to IFPIC is that closure involves highly significant choices in relation to the scope, focus, duration, and financing of environmental monitoring and remediation; post-closure mine use; disposal of project assets, particularly of multi-use infrastructure; and management of social and cultural impacts arising from closure. Regulatory regimes governing closure in Australia and Canada generally provide no avenues for seeking Indigenous consent in relation to proposed responses to closure issues. For example, Parts 10.6 (Closure) and 10.7 (Reclamation) of British Columbia's key instrument for regulating mine rehabilitation and closure make no provision for any form of Indigenous input.[42]

To date, most Indigenous—industry agreements have similarly failed to provide for Indigenous inputs into key decisions regarding mine closure. With few exceptions, agreements which do address the question of Indigenous input provide only an advisory role for Aboriginal signatories, with ultimate decision-making retained by project operators and regulators. There is no legal or technical reason why this should be the case. It is entirely feasible, for example, for agreements to provide that the mine rehabilitation and closure plans required by most jurisdictions in Australia and Canada cannot be submitted to regulators until they receive the consent of the Indigenous owners of land on which mines are located. One Australian agreement does achieve this outcome by requiring that a closure plan cannot be submitted unless it has the unanimous approval of an implementation comprised of company and Indigenous landowner representatives. The agreement between the Tahltan Nation and Nova Gold for development of the Galore Creek copper/gold project provides for the Tahltan to carry out an independent evaluation to ensure obligations of the closure plan have been reached before NovaGold can reclaim the security deposit it is obliged to lodge with the Provincial Government.[43] There is of course no guarantee that government regulators will accept closure plans endorsed by project operators and Indigenous landowners. However, even if regulators require some modifications to them, such plans are much more likely to reflect Indigenous interests than a situation in which Indigenous peoples have no role, or only an advisory role, in the mine closure process.

III. Conclusion

I wish to stress that nothing in this chapter should be taken as an argument against the negotiation of Indigenous—industry agreements in the extractive sector. Agreements often constitute the only mechanism available to Indigenous peoples to fulfil their obligations to minimize the effects of mining on their ancestral lands and their cultural and spiritual sites, by allowing them to negotiate mitigation measures more effective than those provided by government regulation, and to participate in project management. Agreements are usually also the only means by which Indigenous peoples can share in the economic opportunities created by mining on their lands, opportunities highly valued in communities than frequently face serious economic and social disadvantage.

At the same time, the significant shortcomings of many agreements as expressions of Indigenous FPIC must be recognized and addressed. A fundamental problem is that agreements often fail to address key components of the mine life cycle, in particular grant of exploration licences, expansions or reconfigurations of operating projects, and mine closure. Indigenous FPIC should be required before exploration is allowed on Indigenous land. Especially where effective use is made of template agreements, including by taking care that they comply with the requirements of FPIC, compliance can be achieved with little additional cost to industry and without deterring investment. Project approval agreements should include provisions for their re-negotiation where subsequent expansions or mine life extensions involve significant changes to the project configurations on which Indigenous consent was originally provided. In relation to mine closure, more radical change is required. Legislative and regulatory regimes must acknowledge the depth and longevity of Indigenous interest in mine closure and reclamation, by allowing for Indigenous participation in setting the financial security required of companies to cover the cost of closure; in setting standards for environmental rehabilitation and in designing post-closure monitoring regimes; and in decisions about post-mining land use. Appropriate provisions could then be negotiated in agreements to allow for Indigenous—company cooperation in developing closure plans for submission to regulators.

Whatever its scope, agreement making can only offer full expression to IFPIC if the legal frameworks within which it occurs allow Indigenous people to withhold their consent to mining. Across much of Australia and Canada, this is not currently the case. Indeed in most situations Aboriginal peoples in both countries have only been able to insist that their consent be sought by mobilizing political resources. If this situation is to change, governments must heed the Supreme Court of Canada's advice that they should seek the consent of Aboriginal title holders when it proposes to use their land. Government support is also needed to ensure that Indigenous peoples have access to the substantial resources they require to conduct their own impact assessment studies and participate in the complex technical processes typically involved in approval and regulation of large resource projects. The alternative is that Indigenous peoples will not be "informed" and will experience duress at the hands of corporate negotiators. Finally, the internal decision-making processes of Indigenous communities must themselves reflect the principle of IFPIC, allowing for meaningful citizen participation throughout the agreement making processes.

These changes will not be easy to achieve. The fact that a minority of existing agreements in Australia and Canada are based on application of FPIC indicates that the challenges involved, while formidable, can be overcome. They must be overcome if the potential of negotiated agreements to assist in achieving Indigenous FPIC in the extractive industries is to be realized.

Notes

1. For a detailed discussion see Ciaran O'Faircheallaigh, *Negotiation in the Indigenous World: Aboriginal Peoples and the Extractive Industries in Australia and Canada* (Routledge 2015).
2. United Nations Economic and Social Council (UNESC), *Standard Setting: Preliminary working paper on the principle of free, prior informed consent,* E/CN.4/Sub.2/AC.4/2004/4, 6–8; UNESC, *Report of the International Workshop on Methodologies regarding Free, Prior and Informed Consent and Indigenous Peoples,* E/C.19/2005/3, 11–13; For a discussion of the principle of IFPIC and its application to natural resources industries see: Fergus MacKay, *Indigenous Peoples' Right to Free, Prior and Informed Consent and the World Bank's Extractive Industries Review* (Forest Peoples Programme 2004); Cathal M. Doyle and Kill Cariño, "Making Free Prior & Informed Consent a Reality Indigenous Peoples and the Extractive Sector" [2013] PIPLinks Links https://www.ecojesuit.com/wp-content/uploads/2014/09/Making-FPIC-a-Reality-Report.pdf.
3. For a detailed discussion of these stages see Ginger Gibson and Ciaran O'Faircheallaigh, *IBA Community Toolkit: Negotiation and Implementation of Impact and Benefit Agreements* (Walter & Duncan Gordon Foundation 2010) 17–21.
4. Emma LeClerc and Arn Keeling, "From Cutlines to Traplines: Post-Industrial Land Use at the Pine Point Mine" (2015) 2(1) The Extractive Industries and Society 7, 11–12.
5. Leah S. Horowitz and others, "Indigenous peoples' relationships to large-scale mining in post/colonial contexts: Toward multidisciplinary comparative perspectives" (2018) 5(3) The Extractive Industries and Society 404, 406 <https://www.sciencedirect.com/science/article/pii/S2214790X1830039X>.
6. See for example Sam Adkins and Thomas Isaac, "Ross River Dene Council v Government of Yukon" (*McCarthy Tetrault*, 2013) <http://www.mondaq.com/canada/x/217520/Mining/Ross+River+Dena+Council+v+Government+Of+Yukon>.
7. *Indian Mining Regulations*, CRC, c 956, s 6.1 (2009).
8. See, for example, *Labrador Inuit Land Claims Agreement*, SNL 2004, c L-3.1, s 4.11.13.
9. See, for example *Tlicho Land Claims and Self-Government Agreement*, 25 August 2003, s 23.3.1.
10. Adkins & Isaac (n 6).
11. Ken Coates and Dwight Newman, *The End Is Not Nigh: Reason Over Alarmism in Analysing the Tsilhqot'in Decision* (Macdonald-Laurier Institute, September 2014).
12. Ibid.
13. Ciaran O'Faircheallaigh, "Land Rights and Mineral Exploration: The Northern Territory Experience" (1988) 60(1) The Australian Quarterly 70.
14. Siobhan McKenna, "Negotiating Mining Agreements under the Native Title Act 1993" (1995) 2(3) Agenda: A Journal of Policy Analysis and Reform 301, 301–303.
15. Ibid.
16. National Native Title Tribunal, "Expedited Procedure Objections" (*National Native Title Tribunal*) <http://www.nntt.gov.au/futureacts/Pages/Expedited-procedure-objections.aspx>.

17. The serious resource constraints faced by Aboriginal land councils that deal with exploration permit applications have been documented in detail by these organizations and acknowledged by the mining industry and state and local governments. See, for example, Parliament of the Commonwealth of Australia, Parliamentary Joint Committee on Native Title and the Aboriginal and Torres Strait Islander Land Account, *Report on the operation of Native Title Representative Bodies* (2006) <https://apo.org.au/sites/default/fil es/resource-files/2006/03/apo-nid1552-1132311.pdf>.
18. National Native Title Tribunal (n 16).
19. O'Faircheallaigh, (n 1) 213–214.
20. The documents that constitute this Agreement can be found at Government of South Australia, "Antakirinja Land Management Corporation (ALMAC) ILUA" (*Department for Energy and Mining*, 2018) <http://minerals.statedevelopment.sa.gov.au/land_access/native_title_and_aboriginal_land/Antakirinja_Land_Management_Corporation_ALMAC_ILUA>; For a Canadian example of an exploration template, see BC First Nations Mining and Energy Council, "Mining Exploration Agreement Template" (2015) <https://docs.google.com/viewerng/viewer?url=http://fnemc.ca/wp-content/uploads/2015/07/Mining-Agreement-Templates-2011.doc>.
21. Courtney Riley Fidler, "Aboriginal Participation in Mineral Development: Environmental Assessment and Impact and Benefit Agreements" (Master of Applied Science Thesis, University of British Columbia 2008).
22. See, for example, Helen Davidson's account of the efforts of Aboriginal Traditional Owners to make sense of the EIA for the proposed expansion of the McArthur river lead/zinc mine, which she describes as "a scientific document that, printed and stacked, stands the height of a small child": Helen Davidson, "'They'll get rich and go': Glencore's McArthur River Mine Could Take 300 Years to Clean up" (*The Guardian*, 15 May 2017) <https://www.theguardian.com/australia-news/2017/may/15/theyll-get-rich-and-go-glencores-mcarthur-river-mine-could-take-300-years-to-clean-up>.
23. Ciaran O'Faircheallaigh, "Shaping Projects, Shaping Impacts" (2017) 38(5) Third World Quarterly 1181.
24. See, for example, Kimberley Land Council, "Indigenous Impacts Report: Kimberley LNG Precinct Strategic Assessment Six Volumes" (2010) <http://www.jtsi.wa.gov.au/what-we-do/offer-project-support/lng-precincts/browse-kimberley/browse-lng—environment/appendices-to-strategic-assessment-report/strategic-assessment-report-appendix>; Matsqui First Nation, "An Assessment of Impacts from the Trans Mountain Expansion Project on Matsqui First Nation" (2015) <https://docs2.neb-one.gc.ca/ll-eng/llisapi.dll/fetch/2000/90464/90552/548311/956726/2392873/2449925/2451197/2785415/C227-7-5_-_Matsqui_First_Nation_Impact_Assessment_%28part1of2%29_-_A4L8J2.pdf?nodeid=2784643&vernum=-2>; Athabasca Chipewyan First Nation, "Integrated Knowledge and Land Use Report and Assessment for Shell Canada's Proposed Jackpine Mine Expansion and Pierre River Mine" (2011) <https://ceaa-acee.gc.ca/050/documents_staticpost/59540/82080/Appendix_D_-_Part_01.pdf>.
25. See O'Faircheallaigh (n 23) for a comparison of conventional and Indigenous social impact assessments for very similar Liquefied Natural Gas (LNG) projects in Australia's North West.
26. For a discussion of this point in the Canadian context see Adkins & Isaac (n 6).
27. O'Faircheallaigh, (n 1) 102.

28. Fidler documents such a process in relation to negotiation of the Tahltan—Nova-Gold participation agreement. In this case community members only gained access to the full text of the agreement three years after they ratified it, Fidler (n 21) 56–57. O'Neill documents a similar situation in relation to native title claim group ratification of agreements for development Liquefied Natural Gas projects in central Queensland (L O'Neill, "A Tale of Two Agreements: Negotiating Aboriginal Land Access Agreements in Australia's Natural Gas Industry" (PhD Thesis, University of Melbourne 2016), 179–180.
29. Ciaran O'Faircheallaigh, "Negotiating Major Project Agreements: The 'Cape York Model'" [2000] Australian Institute for Aboriginal and Torres Strait Islander Studies; Innu Nation Task Force on Mining Activities, "Ntesinan Nteshiniminan Nteniunan: Between a Rock and a Hard Place" [2006] Innu Nation; Kimberley Land Council, "Indigenous Impacts Report" [2010] Kimberley Land Council and Griffith University.
30. For example, as of January 2016 the National Native Title Tribunal had refused to allow just three "future act" applications, while allowing 90 to proceed. (L. O'Neill (n 28) 82).
31. Ciaran O'Faircheallaigh, "ESD and community participation: the Strategic Assessment of the proposed Kimberley LNG Precinct, 2007–2013" (2015) 22(46) Australasian Journal of Environmental Management <https://www.tandfonline.com/doi/abs/10.1080/14486563.2014.999726>.
32. For example: *Tlicho Agreement* (n 9) s 19.1.1.
33. M Olszynski, "The Duty to Consult and Accommodate: An Overview and Discussion" (Canadian Chamber of Commerce 2016); Coates and Newman (n 11).
34. O'Faircheallaigh, (n 1) Ch 6, 9.
35. Ibid.
36. See, ibid 148–73, for a history of the Ekati project. The Aboriginal agreements for the project are confidential but are available to the author.
37. Anthony Young, "McArthur River Mine: the Making of an Environmental Catastrophe" (2015) 2(1) Australian Environmental Law Digest 15.
38. Kevin O'Reilly, "Liability, Legacy, and Perpetual Care: Government Ownership and Management of the Giant Mine, 1999–2015" in Arn Keeling and John Sandlos (eds), *Mining and Communities in Northern Canada: History, Politics, and Memory* (UBC Press 2015).
39. Jess Lodge, "Queensland Mining Companies Avoid Clean-Up Costs with Government Consent, Lawyers Say" (*ABC News Online*, 14 April 2016) <http://www.abc.net.au/news/2016-04-15/mining-companies-avoiding-cleanup-costs-say-lawyers/7329716> accessed 9 March 2017.
40. Helen Davidson, "'They'll get rich and go': Glencore's McArthur River mine could take 300 years to clean up" (*The Guardian* Australia, 14 May 2017).
41. See, in particular, A Keeling and J Sandlos (n 38).
42. Ministry of Energy and Mines, British Columbia, "Health, Safety and Reclamation Code for Mines in British Columbia" (*Ministry of Energy and Mines,* 2017); for a similar example from Australia, see Queensland Government, "Mined Land Rehabilitation Policy" (Queensland Government 2018).
43. Fidler (n 21) 58–59.

6 Gender Impact Analysis of Impact Benefit Agreements: Representation Clauses and UNDRIP

Sari Graben, Angela Cameron and Sarah Morales

As a general rule, Indigenous feminist scholarship is inimical to large-scale resource extraction taking precedence over environmental stewardship, human rights protection, the integrity of Indigenous laws, and Indigenous understandings of gender equality.[1] We argue here that the use of Impact Benefit Agreements (IBA) to facilitate large-scale resource extraction renders contracts which facilitate extraction subject to similar scrutiny.[2] While cognizant that legal devices that facilitate unsustainable or harmful resource extraction may be irreconcilable with many Indigenous feminist worldviews, the authors use intersectional feminist theories to interrogate the capacity of bilateral private negotiations in the extractive sector to speak to the impacts of resource development on Indigenous women.[3] This project addresses the reality that the use of IBAs as a tool of resource governance has continued at an accelerating rate but no feminist analysis or gendered analysis of IBA terms or their capacity to generate good measurable outcomes for women has been undertaken.[4] An emergent scholarship has identified the underrepresentation of Indigenous women in the negotiation,[5] approval,[6] and implementation of IBAs.[7] However, no research has evaluated what impact IBAs' terms have on the propagation of gender inequities or the capacity of IBA terms to rectify them. In light of this gap in the literature, and the growing reliance on IBAs to evidence community consent in accordance with UNDRIP's Free, Prior, and Informed Consent,[8] a feminist analysis of IBA terms is critical and timely for communities, scholars, and practitioners.

In this chapter, the authors interrogate the prospect posed by law reformists that IBAs are mechanisms where concerns about inequality and inequity could be mitigated. As devices used to literally represent community consent and implement substantive terms that predict measurable positive outcomes, this type of study is key to identifying the circumstances under which IBAs could deliver more equitable outcomes and, for those who resist their adoption, those circumstances where they cannot reconcile fundamental values.

To this end, we raise questions needed to begin the analysis of gender equity and IBAs and, by way of example, provide a preliminary gender impact analysis of Representations clauses in IBAs (i.e., those clauses that provide assurances as to the capacity of the parties to agree to the terms of the IBA). A full gender assessment of an IBA would evaluate each individual term on its merit as well as the effect of the term as a part of the whole. A robust intersectional feminist analysis, which includes Indigenous feminist perspectives, would require taking up a particular IBA, on particular Indigenous territories, and empirical research with Indigenous women (particularly Elders) from that community, related to the relevant Indigenous law(s). That is work we plan to undertake together in the coming years and months.[9] Given space constraints here, a preliminary focus on one clause allows us to explore the kinds of questions we need to ask in such an analysis, and identify the numerous places where there are serious research gaps.

Through this inquiry we are able to draw a few conclusions of note. First, how gender-neutral terms fail to reflect upon existing inequities related to the participation of women in public government. Second, there is scant research on the number of Indigenous women who negotiate IBAs but there is also a need for knowledge about the mechanisms needed to acquire authority to negotiate and what barriers prevent women acquiring and maintaining that authority. Third, in contexts where Indigenous laws and legal orders play a role in furthering women's participation, either in primary form of governance, in hereditary structures, or in traditional institutions and sites that reflect gendered responsibilities, the methods by which participation is affected may be different from those that mark liberal democratic structures. As such, the central inquiry for the purposes of representation clauses is whether these Indigenous sites in which women participate are identified as political institutions in which certain women's perspectives are aggregated, and whether the views expressed by its participants are incorporated into IBA negotiations.

I. Indigenous Feminism and Problematizing Consent

1. Contract as Consent

The response of many Indigenous community members, scholars, and legal practitioners to the rising use of IBAs has been positive for several reasons outlined in the literature in, and in other chapters in, this book.[10] Despite these positive reviews, a significant body of critical scholarship has identified the problematic use of IBAs as a technology of resource governance rather than community building.[11] Scholars and community members have questioned the private context of negotiations,[12] the effect of power inequities in bargaining and implementation,[13] and the use of IBAs by government institutions to distance themselves from the responsibilities inherent to resource development and the legal duty to consult.[14] These critiques are not universal but they seem to explain much of what is problematic when IBAs fail to provide promised improvements or distribute those improvements unevenly.

Legally, IBAs have been situated in the realm of private contract. Because contract discourse is characterized by freedom to consent, IBAs have been understood as the penultimate manifestation of a liberal Indigenous society in which Indigenous nations have the freedom to exercise their private financial interests. Within this context, representation clauses in IBAs, those that warrant the authority of the signatories to bind those they represent to the agreed terms, are theorized, as a product of private choice. While the collective character of

Indigenous authority is at the core of the Indigenous signatories' power to contract, the method by which the parties choose to internally organize themselves is relevant only to the extent that the contract can be enforced against the Indigenous government as a singular signatory.

Nonetheless, despite its association with private choice, IBAs have triggered a host of assumptions about the political preconditions by which they are formed. The decidedly public purpose of IBAs to ensure social, economic, and cultural well-being of the signatory nations, as well as the embedding of consent in the ownership and political representation of Indigenous governments, makes it difficult to avoid their public character. The signatories' arrangements are generally triggered by the duty to consult and public interest requirements.[15] Several Indigenous land laws reflect a similar characterization of resource development as public in nature, and therefore subject to public discourse.[16] Moreover, IBAs are maintained, governed, or terminated through the operation of state law, including Indigenous legislative enactments. The reading of representation clauses, in this more complex legal context, allows its users to situate them as part of the political and public character of IBAs for Indigenous communities. A political framing of IBAs contextualizes the entitlement to negotiate private power in something more than ownership. Moreover, it opens the document to a much richer analysis than would arise from seeing the agreements as a simple transaction—an exchange of money for access to land and resources. Instead of transaction, the degree to which the negotiated terms achieve their broader social objectives of consent, choice, and the self-determination of Indigenous nations and collectivities can be assessed in the specific and on the whole.

a. Insights from Indigenous Feminisms

Existing feminist scholarship that locates the perspectives and experiences of Indigenous women at the centre of resource contracting bring the preconditions of contract (agency) into question as well as the impact of its terms in public (work and civic) and private (home) spaces.[17] This scholarship provides important insights into the unquestioning adoption of IBAs as beneficial tools of resource governance and the role of Indigenous women in efforts to resist their use. Most importantly, feminist critiques situate IBA outcomes within the duty to consult and implicate contracts in addressing gender inequalities in women's participation in natural resource governance and their representation in IBAs.

Seeing what is common in everyday orderings as contested and contingent has been one of the key contributions of feminist scholarship. Western feminism made clear that the assignment of duties, responsibilities, and the concomitant assumption of identity could be reconstructed differently in both the public and private lives of diverse women.[18] Moreover, the traditional focus on equality, as expressed in the first and second waves of western feminism, has by all accounts, informed the idea of workplace equality in all industries, including the extractive industry.[19] However, in reality, the lived experience of Indigenous women would be better reflected in a more consciously intersectional analysis that takes into account race, class, sex, ethnicity, and colonialism.[20]

An intersectional methodology identifies that Indigenous women's experiences of colonialism may be different in important ways from that of their male counterparts. While gender inequality is ubiquitous in Canadian society, gendered social inequality can take particular forms within Indigenous communities and collectivities, and for Indigenous women living in urban centres. In particular, with the introduction of extractive economies, Indigenous women are more at risk of violent victimization.[21] Indigenous women are more likely than non-Indigenous women to live in overcrowded and under-maintained housing.[22] Indigenous women have the lowest median total income when compared to Indigenous men, non-Indigenous men, and non-Indigenous women,[23] and are more likely than any other comparator group to be the lone head of a household.[24] Despite having higher rates of secondary and post-secondary education than their Indigenous male counterparts, Indigenous women have lower employment levels[25] and are more likely to live off reserve, in urban areas.[26]

Taken together, these comparisons illustrate the way Indigenous feminist perspectives can identify that women and men do not begin their relationships with IBAs from positions of equal social and economic power. Nor can it be presumed that Indigenous women have equal access to the resources that support them in speaking to their interests in IBA negotiations. To analyze the benefits from IBAs to Indigenous communities as a homogenous whole obscures a more complex and complete understanding of relative benefit and privilege.[27] There can therefore be no presumption that any benefits flowing from IBAs attach to all community members in an equal way, providing equal benefit and advantage to all who participate.

Beyond identifying the problematic distribution of benefits, Indigenous feminism can also explain why solutions to inequalities are not easy to implement. For example, better representation of women in the workforce appears to be something that can be addressed by an IBA. However, women will express deeper concerns about community integrity and health related to inherently fixed problems with resource extraction (i.e., boom and bust development cycles, distant work sites, social stress, and environmental degradation). Thus, the incompatibilities of public/work and private/home manifest differently and may seem even more intractable for Indigenous women. In this way, Indigenous feminism has identified that apart from increased income that is often unevenly distributed across a community, there is little evidence that the exploitation of resources leads to greater social, economic, or physical well-being for Indigenous women or the community as a whole. This means that even one traditional focus of feminism, equality in the workforce, is not easily addressed in IBAs.

Lastly, Indigenous feminism raises questions about the ways that a gendered approach to Indigenous law might be implicated in a more complete analysis of IBAs. The revitalization of Indigenous laws is key to the project of reconciliation[28] and IBAs are an important site to imagine Indigenous laws doing this work. In some cases, Indigenous laws are already recognized in IBAs and are already interpreted and implemented in some communities. As will be discussed below, terms that represent and warrant that community consent has been obtained using traditional processes explicitly import Indigenous legal traditions into the IBAs themselves. This is equally true of IBA implementation committees that address treatment of sacred sites or community protests that premise their claims on breaches of Indigenous laws, accommodation allowances for work sites so men can undertake seasonal hunting, or leave requirements for community mourning. While the text of IBAs rarely reference Indigenous laws, these examples illustrate that they certainly create or recognize processes where Indigenous laws are at work.

All this being said, consideration of Indigenous laws in an IBA introduces complicating factors for gender assessment.[29] For instance, Indigenous laws are not often written and accessible to western legal actors.[30] Much like any engagement with law, the interpretation and translation of law therefore remains, partial, contingent, and contested.

Moreover, this translation is not straightforward. Indigenous women, and their relationship to Indigenous and common or civil laws, are not homogenous. Some Indigenous communities, including women, have arguably embraced and deployed the neo-liberal ideologies reflected in IBAs as a means of economic development and reconciliation.[31] To these groups, the conscious adoption of Indigenous laws can challenge the seemingly agnostic character of contracts but still maintain them. Others might simply reject IBAs as a path to reconciliation, thereby undermining its relevance as a tool of resource governance.[32] IBAs can be, in these places, a continuation of this legacy of using common and civil law to reach into Indigenous territories, lives, and laws and colonize them. Given the range in views, it must be acknowledged that Indigenous laws themselves are not homogenous, nor are the roles of women within them harmonized.

We therefore respond here to calls from legal scholars Hadley Friedland and Val Napoleon to engage with Indigenous laws "... not just articulation and recognition, but also mindful, intentional acts of recovery and revitalization."[33] While some of the legal practices discussed in this chapter are in the process of conscious revitalization, their use and consideration illustrate how revitalization of Indigenous laws can be used as tools for dealing with contemporary, gendered issues.[34] In taking on this task, we raise the challenge for IBA negotiators to be responsive to not only the place-based reconciliation and the revitalization context surrounding the negotiations, but more importantly, to take into account the roles of women with respect to Indigenous laws and their impacts on contract terms. Any gendered examination of negotiation and deployment has to ask hard questions about whether and how Indigenous law and jurisdiction are being taken seriously, and, if not, what stands in their stead.

II. A Gendered Analysis of Representation and Warranty Clauses

In order to better identify key research issues and priorities we examined a selection of IBA terms that have been made public, technical reports and regulatory reviews of IBA performance more generally, as well as the existing literature that has taken on the impact of resource development on Indigenous women.[35] In this chapter, we focus on the use of representations and warranties in IBAs as a way to examine what considerations could be taken up in a gender-based analysis. Guiding our thinking are questions about how women are empowered or disempowered by gender neutral language and what type of language or broad interpretations of terms would ensure IBAs provide women the opportunity to make their own choices, self-govern, and return to Indigenous traditions that in some communities are tied to the land.

1. The Role of Representations and Warranties in IBAs

Representation clauses are essential clauses in IBAs that typically outline the power and authority of each signatory as well as confirm that authorizing resolutions will be implemented by the government and company. As a general rule, a representations clause will often involve a statement that the signatories have the requisite authority to bind the government of the relevant Indigenous nation and set out the procedures that were followed to establish the requisite participation of community members, and can include a Band Council Resolution, a community vote, or a traditional procedure.[36]

An example of representations made by an Indigenous nation to a resource company include the following types of terms:

- The Council of the Indigenous nation is the duly constituted council on behalf of the Indigenous nation under the *Indian Act* and under the Indigenous nation's constitution;
- That the signatory has good and sufficient power, authority and right to enter into and perform its obligations under this agreement;
- That the agreement is, upon execution, a valid and legally binding obligation of the Indigenous nation, and
- A Band Council Resolution approving the execution of this agreement will be delivered concurrently with the agreement.[37]

The representations clause can also consider if some Indigenous legal provisions should apply. Language to this effect is as follows:

- The Indigenous nation will warrant that it has taken all steps required by the Indigenous nation's traditional law and procedures to authorize the agreement.

While the formal legal purpose of the terms is to confirm the binding effect of the agreement on the organizations that the signatories represent, the multiple ways that effect might be achieved indicates that this section is used primarily to validate the knowledge and participation of the community. As such, this is a key place in IBAs where questions about the participation of women in these validating processes as well as in negotiations themselves could be raised and addressed.

2. *Women and Participation in IBAs*

If IBAs represent and warrant capacity to bind a community, it seems relatively clear that the starting point of analysis is to identify the ways that Indigenous women are represented in relation to those processes that bind them to negotiated terms. Pragmatically, this involves identifying what roles women occupy in determining the terms of IBAs, adopting them, implementing them, as well as contesting them. However, given the wide variety of ways that women can engage with IBAs, and resource management more generally, there is a tendency to point to one or two examples of engagement without examining systemic barriers and thereby overlooking systemic means of addressing them.

This chapter contributes to an understanding of the choices facing Indigenous communities and industry in determining capacity by focussing on a central question; that of participation. Participation arises as a key variable in making representations and warranties about the capacity to sign an IBA in three distinct ways: (a) participation in the governmental bodies; (b) participation in IBA negotiation; and (c) consultations with Indigenous women, prior to and during implementation.

a. Participation in Government

A key way that women's participation arises in discussions that impact capacity is the politically representative nature of Band Councils or other types of Indigenous governance. In this section, we explore the kinds of questions an intersectional feminist analysis might ask about Indigenous women's participation in Indigenous government and legal structures, keeping in mind that unlike liberal democracies in Canada who function under common or civil law, Indigenous governance takes multiple forms across multiple Indigenous jurisdictions, sometimes with extreme variation. In particular, besides variation in Indigenous laws across territories, many Indigenous governments may take the shape of an *Indian Act* band, a hereditary Indigenous legal structure, or some combination of these models.

Indigenous governments are the ultimate decision-maker as to whether an IBA is signed and ratified by a community. Therefore, in so far as private negotiation can incorporate community perspectives, a number of scholars in diverse fields of study would likely agree with the characterization of IBAs as participatory in theory. As Jane Holder explains, private negotiation marks a vital shift in favour of law that allows for negotiation and deliberation between government, industry, and the public, and makes room for innovation and creativity in decision-making.[38]

While theorizing negotiated initiatives as participatory is on the rise, criticisms about political representation reflect a concern that the interests of certain community members or sub-groups can be sidelined in negotiation.[39] Reliance on representative government presumes there to be unitary internal processes by which a representative obtains authority to negotiate. To be sure, negotiations necessitate formal legal authority, which, from a legal perspective, is best situated in the Indigenous government. However, it also presumes that the representative possesses a high degree of normative authority. While liberal democratic theory can collapse these two requirements, effective representation of community interests does not necessarily follow from a position in local government. Rather, the regular struggle over leadership among community members and the continuing importance of hereditary chiefs and Elders as sources of guidance means that elected officials do not necessarily represent the normative positions of community members or sub-communities. The following sections explore the implications of this for IBA terms in more detail.

i. INDIAN ACT BANDS

There are important questions that must be raised and addressed about the downstream effects of systemic gender discrimination on participation in *Indian Act* Band Councils and ultimately IBA terms. Scholars have long identified the effects of some male-dominated *Indian Act* Band Councils on marginalizing the role of women and their issues within communities.[40] Kim Anderson, a Metis-Cree scholar, notes that in some cases "… the hierarchical nature of the (*Indian Act*) system places men at the top of the pecking order."[41]

Processes that include women in community decision-making depend partially on the representative character of Band Council operating pursuant to the *Indian Act*.[42] Indigenous women have fought, and still fight, long legal battles in Canadian common law courts to rectify the sex discrimination written into the *Indian Act*.[43] Explicit exclusion of women has now been eliminated from the Indian Act. However, the effects of hundreds of years of legislated sex discrimination are multi-faceted, but include a disproportionate number of disenfranchised Indigenous women living in urban areas away from their traditional territories, making participation in local government more difficult. Resistance, including litigation[44], on the part of some *Indian Act* bands to the re-integration of Indigenous women who regain Band status[45] has also created barriers for women's full access to the limited resources allocated to Indigenous communities.[46]

This original normative structure and its lasting effects are particularly important when considering whether the voices of women are lost when companies negotiate with Band Councils rather than engaging with broader community structures.[47] As a result, key issues to be determined are: in what ways IBA methodologies that rely on Band Council approval are representative of women's insights; and whether participation arises in alternative fora, including referenda, consultation, and internal community dialogue, which may or may not be captured by terms used in IBAs. Also in need of study are simple questions about what ways membership, status, and residency impact the type and scope of women's participation.

Lastly, questions about who leads a community on different issues prompts questions about who is forwarding arguments that IBA representations and warranties align with Indigenous laws and traditions on the substantive matter of resource extraction but also on the rules regarding political representation. More specifically, debunking assumptions about the participation of women in Band Councils opens up questions about how women participate in determining the normative value of resource extraction and its effects on certain Indigenous worldviews about responsibility to territory. The following section discusses how hereditary Indigenous governance structures address these questions.

ii. HEREDITARY INDIGENOUS GOVERNANCE

Clauses in IBAs that reference traditional processes integrate traditional structures into representations and warranties. As will be outlined below, effective leaders will draw on multiple sources of authority to obtain support.[48] However, this is not always the case and may be difficult to obtain in relation to IBAs, where the terms are constantly in flux and negotiated in relation to each other and where alternative language may not be available to communities to discuss.[49] These variations raise questions about women's roles in the conflict between groups, whose voices get submerged, and the kinds of compromises women may have to make to be heard.

In contexts where Indigenous laws and legal orders play a role of some kind, either as a primary form of governance, or working alongside *Indian Act* bands, or common and civil law, the questions we ask about participation may be different from those we ask of liberal democratic governance structures. Indigenous women, writing about their own laws and gender, point the way in this inquiry. Lina Sunseri describes Oneida women as having both power and responsibility, and says that these two characteristics of leadership go hand in hand to avoid domination and power imbalances within the Oneida nation.[50] Sylvia Maracle (Skonaganleh:ra) and Marlyn Kane (Osennontion) note that Mohawk women take up positions of political leadership in ways that may be considered oblique by Western standards.[51] According to Maracle and Kane, while Mohawk men hold visible public positions of leadership, they are selected and groomed by women,[52] who have a responsibility to keep Mohawk laws alive and to correct those who are not following the laws.[53] Men are given "great and serious responsibilities ... (but) ... are not considered to be at the top of a hierarchy with authority that is subject to abuse."[54] Similarly, Kim Anderson describes Anishnabeeg women as leaders within their communities[55] who simultaneously have responsibilities of caring for the young and the old[56] and holding positions as decision-makers within their nations.[57] Both Anishnaabeg law[58] and Mohawk law[59] hold up older women as important legal decision-makers, medicine people, and teachers.[60] What this demonstrates is that although the types of responsibilities, decision-making authority, and power of Indigenous women varies from nation to nation and between legal traditions, what is constant is that Indigenous women play a significant role in community governance structures.

Despite this recognition, a gender analysis would be meaningless if it romanticized women's participation in traditional governance structures. As in non-Indigenous communities, Indigenous women faced challenges and power struggles within their own traditional systems, even before colonialism.[61] An intersectional feminist inquiry into women's participation in governance structures must begin with the experiences of women within these Indigenous communities themselves. How would a variety of Mohawk women measure participatory success within Mohawk governance structures? Have those goals been met? What aspects or interpretations of Mohawk law might they challenge or question in order to attain satisfactory forms of participation?[62] How do these gendered forms of Mohawk participatory governance fit into an IBA negotiation? How are Mohawk leadership and legitimacy laws translated into private contract negotiations with a party who does not follow Mohawk law?

An intersectional approach will incorporate these considerations but should also allow those reconciling women's participation with Indigenous law to move beyond the identification of Indigenous law and into critical assessment of its implications for Indigenous women.[63] This form of critical Indigenous feminism rejects essentialist practices that take Indigenous law as dogma. Instead, critical approaches use other legal traditions and other Indigenous laws to question how laws manifest in and in relation to contemporary institutions in which gendered roles are established and forward interpretations that reflect the complex identities of Indigenous women and the layered legal traditions in which they live. In this analysis, it is not taken for granted that traditional forms of participation are effective for Indigenous women in contemporary settings but even where not, they too can be reimagined and refashioned based on a community's laws.

For example, several Indigenous women have held the role of chief negotiator in Canadian Indigenous communities. Women's participation in the Voisey Bay Agreement was significant both due to the scale of economic benefits negotiated, and because of the innovative and extensive provisions regarding Indigenous participation prior to signing the IBA and in the environmental management provisions of the IBA.[64] The agreement contains several commitments by the company to promote equality of Innu and Inuit men and women; to work with the LIA and the Innu Nation to identify and remove any barriers to the employment and advancement of Innu and Inuit women; to provide gender sensitivity training for the project workforce; and to report on a quarterly basis on the number of Innu/Inuit women hired.[65]

Reflections on the different ways that political representation manifests within Indigenous communities opens our minds to the way that pro forma representation and warranties clauses paper over the messy processes by which women do or do not participate in IBAs through public government. While we know that women have very low political representation in Band Councils and this has an effect on what issues come before a council and how they are decided, we do not know if other processes fill the void or how to create accountability that ensures they do. More to the point, the discussion here illustrates the risk that effective representation and capacity poses to decision-making related to IBAs, as women may reject it. While the cynic might see this reality as affirming the separation of IBAs from too much public engagement, inattention to this issue means that those negotiating IBAs become complicit in reinforcing sexist norms.

b. Participation in Negotiation

A second branch of investigation related to representations focusses on the participation of women in negotiating mining agreements in various jurisdictions. The overwhelming impression gained from reviewing existing published work is that women are largely excluded from negotiating agreements. Several global reviews of corporate engagement have concluded that women are inadequately represented or excluded entirely.[66] These studies have identified the fact that few women are tasked with representation in negotiations and have postulated that their absence negatively effects the type of outcomes achieved through IBAs, such as whether women are beneficiaries of employment and contracting prioritizations, or whether they receive royalties or compensation.[67]

While there is significant agreement that the increased role of Indigenous women in negotiations is a fertile area for further growth, the research demonstrates that the issue is not simply quantitative.[68] Several studies have identified circumstances where women played a direct and central role as negotiators yet these studies have come to varying conclusions about the impact of participation on outcomes, raising questions about the conditions that made their participation possible and the impact of their participation on negotiation processes and outcomes.

These emergent studies indicate that there is a gap in the research on the gender diversity of IBA negotiations. Certainly, there is scant research on the number of IBAs signed by Indigenous women members. However, there also a need for knowledge about the mechanisms needed to acquire authority to sign and what barriers prevent women acquiring and maintaining that authority. Understanding gender composition will allow for a richer analysis of gender power dynamics, women's agency as expressed by their signing authority, and the methods used to organize stakeholders during negotiations individually and collectively in relation to terms regarding the Indigenous government's capacity to sign.

These accounts highlight the need to study how women organize as stakeholders during negotiations, garner support, and represent themselves in relation to the terms of IBAs.[69] While few Indigenous women act as official negotiators, many play key leadership roles in relation to resource extraction, negotiation, protest, and policy. A feminist examination of IBAs should also take into account complementary ways Indigenous women leaders are speaking to, and influencing resource development issues. For example, the group First Nations Women Advocating Responsible Mining has developed policy advocacy expertise promoting resource extraction that minimizes environmental and social harm.[70] Similarly, Chief Sheila North Wilson is the Grand Chief of the Manitoba Keewatinowi Okimakanak, a non-profit political advocacy organization that provides a collective voice on issues of inherent Treaty, Aboriginal and human rights for First Nations who are signatory to treaties 4, 5, 6 and 10. Grand Chief North Wilson has demonstrated a deep knowledge of the complexities of resource benefit negotiations and strong advocacy on behalf of missing and murdered Indigenous women.[71] Her role illustrates that Indigenous women have experience, knowledge, and leadership skills that support their communities in ways that are difficult to capture in IBAs.

c. Participation in Reform and Resistance?

Lastly, matters related to representation manifest in questions of how the input of women in the community is achieved through internal community consultation and political organization.[72] Consultation and decision-making processes within communities that explicitly take women's needs and interests into account are much more likely to result in an IBA that has legitimacy for diverse community members.

Political scholars describe approaches that simplify community representation as unreliable descriptors of how communities effect resource conservation.[73] Instead, empirical studies and common sense reveal a much more complex conceptualization of community at work. As in all places, Indigenous communities are comprised of sub-groups, and individuals, with varying preferences for resource use and distribution, and varying institutional sites in which those preferences are communicated. Recognition of heterogeneity indicates that decentralization is better described as the devolution of authority to a set of institutions and actors that mediate, structure, mold, accentuate, and facilitate particular outcomes and actions.[74] In short, one cannot characterize a community without characterizing the institutions that make the decisions.

Women are identified in this narrative of participation as individuals who are engaged as any other community member might be engaged or as sub-groups with distinct interests that are represented by leaders in negotiations. One effect of framing women in this way is to raise questions about the manner in which women organize in communities, and whether governments and proponents actually recognize these institutions as representative.[75] For example, in a report by Weitzer the experience of Lutsel K'e Dene First Nation indicates that greater time allotted for negotiation allowed for a greater involvement of women, and that Lutsel K'e Dene women felt they were well represented in the IBAs being studied. Brenda Gunn argues that the inclusion of Indigenous women and their laws in self-determination practices increases the legitimacy of such processes.[76] Missing from this research is what best practices for engaging Indigenous women in communities might be, and how often these best practices are met.

Moreover, where Indigenous nations' laws are gendered,[77] men and women[78] can have distinct, but potentially equally respected, roles and responsibilities within legal orders.[79] This gendering of roles raises questions about whether the law can account for gender in ways that ensure women's participation. Kim Anderson notes that these equality-balancing mechanisms in Anishnaabeg law have evolved and changed over time to deal with contemporary issues while remaining rooted in pre-contact law.[80] According to Aimee Craft, Anishnaabeg laws, unlike common and civil law, understand human legal relationships to land and water primarily as responsibilities, rather than rights over resources.[81] Reconfiguring participation as responsibility might provide some answer to this question. These two foundational cornerstones of many Indigenous legal theories—that the law can be gendered and that there may be legal responsibilities beyond those owed to humans—could fundamentally alter the landscape for IBAs, potentially adding legal interests that will require representation in negotiation or a specialized council to represent gendered roles and responsibilities in the negotiation and execution of IBA agreements.[82]

Lastly, there are questions about how to recognize the role of Indigenous women in resistance as valid participation in IBA making. Indigenous women have been engaged in resistance to development that they perceive to be contrary to environmental stewardship, human rights protection, the integrity of Indigenous laws, or Indigenous understandings of gender equality. This resistance has manifested in political movements that campaign against mining companies and operations in the local communities. However, women have also led principled opposition to resource development through their own laws.[83] For example, Sylvia McAdams (Saysewahum) has led her family and community in fighting against logging on Cree territory as part of her wider leadership on legal revitalization.[84] As one of the founders of the Idle No More[85] movement, Saysewahum has taught, marched, protested, and blockaded in support of many Indigenous peoples' resistance to unwanted resource development in their territory, rooting her critique of such development in Cree legal principles of responsibility to the earth.[86]

Taken together, this discussion identifies the potentially disruptive effect that women's participation can have on external and internal perceptions of who is the community and how unified they are in relation to IBAs.

III. Conclusions

In this chapter, the authors have canvassed three principal arenas in which the participation of Indigenous women might arise or could be engaged but, to date, have not: government, negotiation, and community organization. First, we identified how gender-neutral terms fail to reflect upon existing inequities related to the participation of women in public government. The failure to reflect upon who frames the priorities of IBAs is a caution to IBA negotiators to pay attention to the systemic discrimination underpinning the structure of Band Councils or other Indigenous governments, and to ensure the discriminatory structures which maintain gender imbalances in government are not brought forward in the framing of IBA terms and outcomes. The legacy of embedded sexism is reconstructed in legal documents and governance regimes that fail to reflect on it and leaves one to consider the silencing of women's voices when companies negotiate with Band Councils rather than broader community structures.

Second, we identified that there is scant research on the number of Indigenous women who negotiate IBAs, the mechanisms they need to acquire authority to negotiate, and what barriers prevent women acquiring and maintaining that authority. Understanding gender composition will allow for a richer analysis of gender power dynamics, as well as women's agency as expressed by their signing authority.

Third, we identified contexts where Indigenous laws and legal orders play a role in furthering women's participation in formal governments, in hereditary structures, or in traditional institutions that reflect gendered responsibilities. The methods by which participation is affected may be different from those that mark liberal democratic structures. As such, the central inquiry for the purposes of representation clauses is whether these alternative modes and sites in which women participate are identified as political institutions in which certain women's perspectives are aggregated, and whether the views expressed by its participants are incorporated into IBA negotiations.

Through this analysis, the authors have turned an intersectional and critical lens on IBA terms that relate to representations and warranties, devices meant to provide legal surety that those who sign it have the legal capacity to bind its members. While these terms appear, at first blush, to be relatively innocuous, the above discussion has illustrated that they are not. Instead, the authors have illustrated that representation and warranty clauses can be characterized as unimportant only if deficiencies in Indigenous women's participation is ignored. Rather than standing as formal recognition of community participation, the limited participation of Indigenous women as governmental representatives, as hereditary chiefs, as negotiators, or as community organizers limits the ability to rely on the term for that purpose.

Notes

1. See, for example, Joyce Green (ed), *Making Space for Indigenous Feminism* (2nd ed, Fernwood Publishing 2017); Brenda L Gunn, "Self-Determination and Indigenous Women: Increasing Legitimacy through Inclusion" (2014) 26(2) CJWL 241 (Gunn, "Self-determination and Indigenous Women"); Isabel Altamirano-Jimenez, *Living on the Land: Indigenous Women Understandings of Place* (AU Press 2016); Minnie Grey, "From the Tundra to the Boardroom to Everywhere in Between: Politics and the Changing roles of Inuit Women in the Arctic" in Cheryl Suzack and others (eds), *Indigenous Women and Feminism: Politics, Activism, Culture* (UBC Press 2010) 25; Joyce Green, "From Colonialism to Reconciliation Through Indigenous Rights" in Joyce Green (ed) *Indivisible: Indigenous Human Rights* (Fernwood Press 2014) 33; See, for example, Leanne Betasamosake Simpson, *As We have Always Done: Indigenous Freedom Through Radical Resistance* (University of Minnesota Press 2017) 72–73; Sylvia McAdams (Saysewahum), *Nationhood Interrupted: Revitalising nehiyaw Legal Systems* (Purich 2015) 54–55 (McAdams (Saysewahum); Lynn Gehl (Gii-Zhigate-Mniddo-Kwe), *Mkadengwe: Sharing Canada's Colonial Process through Black Face Methodology* (Algonquin Anishnabe-Kwe Publishing 2014) 9.
2. Deborah Stienstra and others, "Gendered and Intersectional Implications of Energy Resource Extraction in Resource Based Communities in Canada's North" (Feminist Northern Network, 13 May 2016) http://fnn.criaw-icref.ca/images/userfiles/files/SSHRC%20KS%20Report.pdf; Deborah Stienstra, "Northern Crises: Women's Relationships and Resistances to Resource Extractions" (2015) 17(4)

Intel Feminist J of Politics 630; Ginger Gibson and Deanna Kemp, "Corporate Engagement with Indigenous Women in the Minerals Industry: Making Space for Theory" in O'Faircheallaigh and Saleem Ali (eds) *Earth Matters: Indigenous Peoples, the Extractive Industries and Corporate Social Responsibility* (Greenleaf Publishing 2008) 104 (Gibson and Kemp); Linda Archibald and Mary Crnkovich, "If Gender Mattered: A Case Study of Inuit Women, Land Claims and the Voisey Bay's Nickel Project" (Government of Canada, November 1999) http://publications.gc.ca/collections/Collection/SW21-39-1999E.pdf (Archibald and Crnkovich "If Gender Mattered"); "Where We Stand: Serious Questions Deserve Some Serious Answers" *Canadian Mining Journal* (13 January 2016) 22.

3. For intersectional approaches to law, see Val Napoelon, "Aboriginal Discourse: Gender, Identity, and Community," in Benjamin J. Richardson, Shin Imai and Kent McNeil (eds) *Indigenous Peoples and the Law: Comparative and Critical Perspectives* (Hart 2009) 233; Emily Snyder, *Gender, Power and Representations of Cree Law* (UBC Press 2018); Emily Snyder, "Gender and Indigenous Law, A Report Prepared for the University of Victoria Indigenous Law Unit, the Indigenous Bar Association and the Truth and Reconciliation Commission" (Indigenous Bar, 31 March 2013) <http://indigenousbar.ca/indigenouslaw/wp-content/uploads/2013/04/Gender-and-Indigenous-Law-report-March-31-2013-ESnyder1.pdf> (Snyder); Emma LaRocque, "The Colonization of a Native Woman Scholar" in Christine Miller and Patricia Chuchryk (eds) *Women of the First Nations: Power, Wisdom, and Strength* (University of Manitoba Press 1996) 11.
4. See, for example, Ciaran O'Faircheallaigh "Social Equity and Large Mining Projects: Voluntary Industry Initiatives, Public Regulation and Community Development Agreements" (2015) 132(91) J Bus Ethics 91.
5. Ciaran O'Faircheallaigh, "Indigenous Women and Mining Agreement Negotiations: Australia and Canada" in Kuntala Lahiri-Dutt (ed) *Gendering the Field: Towards Sustainable Livelihoods for Mining Communities* (Australian National University Press 2011) 87 [O'Faircheallaigh, "Indigenous Women and Mining Agreement Negotiations"]; Gibson and Kemp (n 2) 104.
6. Gunn, "Self-determination and Indigenous Women" (n 1).
7. Ben Bradshaw and Adam Wright, "Review of IBA Literature and Analysis of Gaps in Knowledge" (*Yukon Research Centre: Resource and Sustainable Development in the Arctic*, 2013) <http://yukonresearch.yukoncollege.yk.ca/resda/wp-content/uploads/sites/2/2013/09/9-Bradshaw-and-Wright-draft-paper1.pdf>. Janelle Kuntz, "Tłı̨chǫ Women and Environmental Assessment of the NICO Project proposed by Fortune Minerals Limited" (MA Thesis, University of Victoria Department of Anthropology 2012).
8. United Nations Declaration on the Rights of Indigenous Peoples, GA Res 61/295, UN Doc A/RES/61/295 (13 September 2007).
9. See, for example, Val Napoleon and Emily Snyder, "Housing on Reserve: Developing a Critical Indigenous Feminist Property Theory" in Angela Cameron, Sari Graben & Val Napoleon (eds) *Creating Indigenous Property: Power, Rights and Relationships* (UTP 2020) (Napoleon and Snyder).
10. Drew Meerveld, "Assessing Value: A Comprehensive Study of Impact Benefit Agreements on Indigenous Communities of Canada" (MA Thesis, University of Ottawa Graduate School of Public and International Affairs 2016).
11. Martin Papillon and T. Rodon, "Indigenous Consent and Natural Resource Extraction: Foundations for a Made-in-Canada Approach" [2017] 16 Institute for Research on Public Policy.
12. Sari Graben, "Assessing Stakeholder Participation in Sub-Arctic Co-Management: Administrative Rulemaking and Private Agreements" (2011) 29(1) Windsor Yearbook of Access to Justice 195 (Graben, "Assessing Stakeholder Participation"); Ken J. Caine and Naomi Krogman, "Powerful or Just Plain Power-Full? A Power

Analysis of Impact and Benefit Agreements in Canada's North" [2010] 23(1) Organization & Environment 76 (Caine and Krogman); Michael Hitch and Courtney Fidler, "Impact and Benefit Agreements: A Contentious Issue for Environmental Justice" (2007) 35(2) Environments Journal 45.

13. Jason Prno, "Assessing the Effectiveness of Impact and Benefit Agreements from the Perspective of their Aboriginal Signatories" (MA Thesis, University of Guelph 2007).
14. Lindsay Galbraith, Ben Bradshaw, and Murray Rutherford, "Towards a New Supraregulatory Approach to Environmental Assessment in Northern Canada" (2007) 25(1) Impact Assessment and Project Appraisal 27 (Galbraith, Bradshaw and Rutherford).
15. For illustration, see Graben, "Assessing Stakeholder Participation" (n 12)
16. See, for example, Sarah Morales and Brian Thom, "The Principle of Sharing and the Shadow of Canadian Property Law" in Angela Cameron, Sari Graben and Val Napoleon (eds) *Creating Indigenous Property: Power, Rights and Relationships* (University of Toronto Press, 2020); Sarah Morales, "Sh-tiiwun: Respect, Responsibility & Reconciliation in a Period of Increased Extractive Development in the Coast Salish World" in Brenda Gunn and Karen Drake (eds) *Renewing Relationships: Indigenous Peoples and Canada* (University of Saskatchewan Native Law Centre 2019); Richard Overstall, "Encountering the Spirit in the Land: 'Property' in a Kin-Ship Based Legal Order" in Bruce Ziff and others (ed) *A Property Reader: Cases, Questions and Commentary* (4th ed, Carswell 2016).
17. David Cox and Suzanne Mills, "Gendering Environmental Assessment: Women's Participation and Employment Outcomes at Voisey's Bay" (2015) 68(2) Arctic 246 (Cox and Mills, "Gendering Environmental Assessment"); Stephanie Labelle, "Aboriginal Women, Mining Negortiations, and Project Development: Analyzing the Motivations and priorities Shaping Leadership and Participation" (MA Thesis, University of Manitoba Department of Native Studies 2015); Drew Meervald, "Assessing Value: A Comprehensive Study of Impact Benefit Agreements on Indigenous Communities in Canada" (Major Research Paper, University of Ottawa Graduate School of Public and International Affairs 2016)
18. See, for example, Susan B Boyd (ed), *Challenging the Public/Private Divide* (University of Toronto Press 1997).
19. Joyce Green, "Taking Account of Indigenous Feminism" in Joyce Green (ed) *Making Space for Indigenous Feminism* (2nd ed, Fernwood 2017) 49 (Green, "Taking Account").
20. Napoleon and Snyder (n 9); ibid Green, "Taking Account"; Archibald and Crnkovich "If Gender Mattered" (n 2); William Hipwell and others, "Aboriginal Peoples and Mining in Canada: Consultation, Participation and Prospects for Change: Working Discussion Paper" (The North-South Institute January 2002) (Hipwell); Ann Varley, "Gender and Property Formalisation: Conventional and Alternative Approaches" [2007] 35 World Development 1739.
21. Jillian Boyce, "Victimization of Aboriginal people in Canada, 2014" (Statistics Canada 28 June 2016) 9.
22. Paula Arriagada, "Women in Canada: A Gender-based Statistical Report: First Nations, Métis and Inuit Women" (*Statistics Canada*, 23 February 2016) 15, 51.
23. "Aboriginal Women in Canada: A Statistical Profile from the 2006 Census" (Aboriginal Affairs and Northern Development Canada 2012) 30, 51.
24. Ibid 59.
25. Ibid 19.
26. Ibid.
27. Green, "Taking Account" (n 19) 58.
28. Brenda Gunn, "Protecting Indigenous Peoples' Lands: Making Room for the Application of Indigenous Peoples' laws within the Canadian Legal System" [2007] 6 Indigenous LJ 31; Hadley Friedland, "Wanasika: Re Imagining the Future with Indigenous Legal Traditions" [2016] 33 Windsor YB Access Just 85.

29. Val Napoleon and Hadley Friedland, "Gathering the Threads: Developing a Methodology for Research and Rebuilding Indigenous Legal Traditions" (2016) 1(1) Lakehead LJ 17, 44.
30. See, for example, Kim Anderson, *Life Stages and Native Women* (University of Manitoba Press 2011) (Anderson, *Life Stages and Native Women*); Kim Anderson, *A Recognition of Being: Reconstructing Native Womanhood* (2nd ed, Women's Press 2016) (Anderson, *A Recognition of Being*); Nancy Sandy, "Stsqey'ulecw re st'exelcemc (St'Exelemc Laws from the Land)" [2016] 33 Windsor YB Access Just 187, 216; Maria Campbell, *Halfbreed* (Saturday Review Press 1973).
31. See, for example, Gabrielle Slowley, *Navigating Neoliberalism: Self-Determination and the Mikisew Cree First Nation* (UBC Press 2008). It is worth noting, however, that Slowley's analysis does not take up gendered differences, therefore we used the term "arguably."
32. See, for example, Osennontion and Skonaganleh:ra, "Our World" (1989) 10(2) CJWS 7 (Osennontion and Skonaganleh:ra); Aimee Craft, "Giving and Receiving Life from Water" in Jocelyn Thorpe, Stephanie Rutherford and L. Anders Sandberg (eds) *Methodological Challenges in Nature-Culture and Environmental History Research* (Routledge 2017) 9 (Craft).
33. Napoleon and Friedland (n 29) 17.
34. Val Napolean and Hadley Friedland, "Working with Indigenous Law" (*University of Victoria Law*, 2019) <https://www.uvic.ca/law/about/indigenous/workwithindigenouslaw/index.php>.
35. Jane Stinson and Leah Levac, "Requiring Gender Based Analysis Plus (GBA+) in Environmental Assessments" (*Canadian Research Institute for the Advancement of Women*, 12 May 2016) <http://fnn.criaw-icref.ca/images/userfiles/files/EA%20Review(FNN%20Submission)(final).pdf>.
36. See, for example, Paul C Wilson and Charlene D Hiller, "Negotiation and Structuring Business Transactions with First Nations: Drafting Impact Benefit Agreements" [2011] CLE BC 2.1.1 (Wilson and Hiller).
37. Ibid.
38. Jane Holder, *Environmental Assessment: The Regulation of Decision-Making*, (Oxford University Press 2004); Caine and Krogman (n 12); Galbraith, Bradshaw and Rutherford (n 14)
39. Graben, "Assessing Stakeholder Participation" (n 12).
40. Sharon McIvor, "Aboriginal Women's Rights as 'Existing Rights'" (1995) 15(2–3) Can Woman Studies 34; Mary Ellen Turpel, "Patriarchy and Paternalism: The Legacy of the Canadian State for Women" (1993) 6(1) CJWL 174; Emma LaRocque, "Re-examining Culturally Appropriate Models in Criminal Justice Applications" in Michael Asch (ed) *Aboriginal and Treaty Rights in Canada: Essays on Law, Equality, and Respect for Difference* (UBC Press 1997) 75.
41. Kim Anderson, "Affirmations of an Indigenous Feminist" in Cheryl Suzack et al (eds) *Indigenous Women and Feminism: Politics, Activism, Culture* (UBC Press 2010) 84–85.
42. Wilson and Hiller (n 36); See David C Natcher, "Gender and Resource Co-Management in Northern Canada" (2013) 66(2) Arctic, 218–221 (see for application to representation by women on co-management boards).
43. See Gwen Brodsky, "Indian Act Sex Discrimination: Enough Inquiry Already, Just Fix It" (2016) 28 CJWL 314 (For the latest on the still unresolved sex discrimination in the *Indian Act*).
44. See, for example, *Sawridge Band* v *Canada*, [1995] 4 CNLR 121 (FCTD).
45. See Pam Palmater, *Beyond Blood: Rethinking Indigenous Identity* (Purich Publishing 2011) 110–111.
46. Ibid120.
47. See, for example, ibid 110–111.

48. See, for example, John Goddard, *Last Stand of the Lubicon Cree* (Douglas and Mcintyre 1991).
49. Graben, "Assessing Stakeholder Participation" (n 12).
50. Lina Sunseri, *Being Again of One Mind: Oneida Women and the Struggle for Decolonization* (UBC Press 2011) 127.
51. Osennontion and Skonaganleh:ra (n 32)
52. Ibid 14.
53. Ibid 13.
54. Ibid 14.
55. Anderson, *Life Stages and Native Women* (n 30) 82.
56. Ibid 97.
57. Ibid 130.
58. Ibid 148.
59. Osennontion and Skonaganleh:ra (n 32) 18.
60. Anderson, *Life Stages and Native Women* (n 30) 148.
61. See Valerie Napoleon, Emily Snyder and John Borrows, "Gender and Violence: Drawing on Indigenous Legal Resources" (2015) 48(2) UBC Law Rev 593.
62. Snyder (n 3); Napoleon and Snyder (n 9).
63. Ibid.
64. O'Faircheallaigh, "Indigenous Women and Mining Agreement Negotiations" (n 5) 91.
65. Ibid 96.
66. Cox and Mills, "Gendering Environmental Assessment" (n 17); Gibson and Kemp (n 2) 107 (citing cases in Australia, Papua New Guinea, Indonesia, and India); B Campbell, "Indigenous Views on the Terms of Participation in the Development of Biodiversity Conservation in Nepal" in A Bicker, P Sillitoe and J Pottier (eds) *Investigating Local Knowledge: New Directions, New Approaches* (Ashgate 2004); Hipwell (n 20); M Simatauw, "The Polarization of the People and the State on the Interests of the Political Economy and Women's Struggle to Defend their Existence: A Critique of Mining Policy in Indonesia" in I Macdonald and C Rowlands (eds) *Tunnel Vision: Women, Mining and Communities* (Oxfam Community Aid Abroad 2002) 35, 38–39.
67. Ingrid Macdonald, "Tunnel Vision: Women's Rights Undermined?" (Women in Mining Conference, Madang, 3 August 2003) 6.
68. Gibson and Kemp (n 2) 109.
69. Drew Meervald, "Assessing Value: A Comprehensive Study of Impact Benefit Agreements on Indigenous Communities in Canada" (Major Research Paper, University of Ottawa Graduate School of Public and International Affairs 2016).
70. First Nations Women Advocating Responsible Mining <http://fnwarm.com/>.
71. Canada, House of Commons, Standing Committee on Indigenous and Northern Affairs, *Evidence*, 42nd Parl, 1st Sess (27 September 27).
72. See, for example, Osennontion and Skonaganleh:ra (n 32) 12; Lina Sunseri, *Being Again of One Mind: Oneida Women and the Struggle for Decolonisation* (UBC Press 2011) 99.
73. Arun Agrawal and Clark Gibson, "Enchantment and Disenchantment: The Role of Community in Natural Resource Conservation" (1999) 27(4) World Development 629, 633; Graben, "Assessing Stakeholder Participation" (n 12).
74. Ibid.
75. Ginger Gibson and Ciaran O'Faircheallaigh, "*IBA Community Toolkit: Negotiation and Implementation of Impact Benefit Agreement*," (Summer 2015 ed, The Gordon Foundation 2011) <http://gordonfoundation.ca/app/uploads/2017/03/IBA_toolkit_web_Sept_2015_low_res_0.pdf>; Graben, "Assessing Stakeholder Participation" (n 12).

76. Gunn, "Self-determination and Indigenous Women" (n 1).
77. Napoleon and Snyder (n 9).
78. See, for example, Andrea Smith, "Queer Theory and Native Studies: The Heteronormativity of Settler Colonialism" (2010) 16(1) GLQ: A Journal of Gay & Lesbian Studies 41 (While men and women are often understood as the primary organizing legal categories, some Indigenous laws and legal orders contain mechanisms to allow for gender non-conformity); Val Napoleon, "The Raven's Garden: A Discussion about Aboriginal Sexual Orientation and Transgender Issues" [2002] 17 CJLS 149.
79. See, for example, Craft (n 32) 108; Anderson, *A Recognition of Being* (n 30) at xxiv.
80. Ibid 34.
81. Craft (n 32)108.
82. See, for example, Anderson, *Life Stages and Native Women* (n 30) 128; Osennontion & Skonaganleh:ra (n 32) 18.
83. See, for example, Shiri Pasternak, *Grounded Authority* (University of Minnesota Press 2017) 95, 101.
84. McAdams (Saysewahum) (n 1) 43–45.
85. Idle No More <http://www.idlenomore.ca/>.
86. McAdams (Saysewahum) (n 1) 25–26.

7 Who Are the Métis? The Role of Free, Prior and Informed Consent in Identifying a Métis Rights-Holder

Karen Drake[1]

I. Introduction

The rise of the duty to consult and accommodate has generated an increase in Indigenous-industry agreements.[2] For proponents tasked with carrying out the procedural aspects of the duty, Indigenous-industry agreements offer relative certainty compared to the ambiguity involved in determining whether the duty has been legally satisfied.[3] For Indigenous peoples, although the drawbacks of Indigenous-industry agreements are well documented,[4] these agreements can potentially instantiate the principle of free, prior and informed consent. Compared to First Nation and Inuit peoples, though, Métis rights-holders are entering into comparatively fewer Indigenous-industry agreements.[5] One cause of this phenomenon is the supposed uncertainty surrounding the question of who are the Métis, which can be divided into three sub-questions: (1) Who qualifies as a Métis rights-holder to whom the duty to consult and accommodate is owed? (2) How do we determine the geographic scope of the Métis rights-holder? (3) Who is entitled to represent the Métis rights-holder for the purposes of engaging in consultation about the right?

Recently, governments have sought to avoid the duty to consult and accommodate by attempting to insert these three sub-questions into the test for triggering the duty to consult and by arguing that Métis rights-holders cannot satisfactorily answer the three sub-questions. If the duty is not triggered, proponents have little or no incentive to negotiate an Indigenous-industry agreement. The lower court decisions adopting the three sub-questions should be rejected because they contradict Supreme Court of Canada jurisprudence affirming a low threshold for triggering the duty to consult.[6] In the meantime, to get to the negotiation table, Métis rights-holders need a strategy for answering these three sub-questions.

In this chapter, I examine the jurisprudence on the three sub-questions with a focus on the latter two, given the exhaustive literature already devoted to the first.[7] I argue that the Métis Nation of Ontario's approach to consultation—which has been lauded by independent experts[8]—not only provides clear answers to the three sub-questions, but also ensures consent given by the Métis Nation of Ontario to Indigenous-industry agreements is fully informed. The Métis

Nation of Ontario's approach can guide other Aboriginal peoples seeking to enter into Indigenous-industry agreements.

Readers who are unfamiliar with the Métis nation may desire, at the outset, a definition of Métis people. This is precisely the issue raised by the three sub-questions discussed throughout this chapter, and especially by the first sub-question. In the context of this analysis, any pithy, introductory definition of the Métis would be unhelpful.[9]

II. The Duty to Consult and Accommodate and the Principle of Free, Prior and Informed Consent

Proponents may be reluctant to enter into Indigenous-industry agreements with the Métis for two reasons. First, proponents might assume that consent is required from the Métis nation less often than it is required from First Nation or Inuit peoples. Second, governments have argued that the duty is not triggered if the rights-bearing Métis people cannot be sufficiently identified.[10] This section dispels the first concern; subsequent sections address the second concern.

The duty to consult and accommodate arises in at least three distinct situations, only two of which are discussed here: asserted rights and established rights.[11] First, the duty arises when Aboriginal rights protected by section 35(1) of the *Constitution Act, 1982*[12] are asserted but not yet proven in court or admitted by the Crown.[13] In the context of asserted rights, the Crown is not required to obtain the consent of the affected Aboriginal people; that is, the Supreme Court of Canada has held that Aboriginal peoples do not have a veto prior to Crown or court recognition of their rights.[14] The duty is not a duty to agree.[15]

Second, the duty to consult and accommodate continues to apply even after Aboriginal rights have been established in court. At this stage, though, the duty to consult and accommodate is only one of several requirements that governments must satisfy in order to justify an infringement of an Aboriginal right.[16] Unlike the context of asserted rights, in some cases of established rights—such as established Aboriginal title—the Crown must obtain the full consent of the Aboriginal people before courts will allow the Crown to infringe the right.[17]

To summarize, consent is not required in the context of asserted rights but can be required in some cases of established rights. Given the dearth of appellate level decisions about the Aboriginal rights of the Métis compared to the Aboriginal rights of First Nations,[18] proponents might assume that Métis rights are primarily asserted and not established. When consent is not required because the right is merely asserted, proponents might assume they have less incentive to negotiate an Indigenous-industry agreement.

The legal reality, though, is more nuanced than this simple binary between asserted and established rights might suggest. Rights which are asserted either are, or should be, in the process of being established or admitted, given the Crown's obligation to negotiate a resolution of asserted Aboriginal rights, which is a legal duty on the Crown and not merely a moral or political exhortation.[19] What happens if the Crown approves a project while the right is merely asserted, without obtaining the consent of the Aboriginal people, and then the right is subsequently established? The Supreme Court of Canada in *Tsilhqot'in Nation* explains that in this scenario, the Crown might be required to cancel the project.[20] This is true even if the Crown fully satisfied the duty to consult and accommodate as it existed at the time when the right was still merely asserted. As the Court states, "the level of consultation required may change as the process goes on and new information comes to light."[21] Proponents might be tempted to engage in the minimum level of consultation and accommodation required at the time of project approval. But if proponents want to avoid having their projects subsequently cancelled, obtaining the full consent of the affected Aboriginal peoples from the outset, even when the right is merely asserted, is the most prudent course of action.[22] Consent is typically secured through an Indigenous-industry agreement.

One might assume that consent need not be obtained from the Métis nation because it is incapable of satisfying the test for Aboriginal title. This assumption is a mistake. As Adam Gaudry and I have argued elsewhere, the arguments in favour of Métis title are compelling.[23]

Proponents seeking the certainty provided by Indigenous-industry agreements would do well to ensure the consent obtained from the relevant Aboriginal people is genuine. As Dwight Newman recognizes, Indigenous-industry agreements may be subject to legal challenge when members of the Aboriginal people disagree about their governance structure and about the terms of the agreement.[24] The principle of free, prior and informed consent can provide guidance to proponents who want to ensure the consent of Indigenous signatories to Indigenous-industry agreements is genuine in order to protect themselves from future legal challenges. Section 3 below analyzes the Métis Nation of Ontario's consultation procedures to show how these procedures ensure that consent given by the Métis Nation of Ontario to an Indigenous-industry agreement is truly informed. But first, Sections III(1) and III(2) discuss the first two sub-questions identified in the introduction, given that the third sub-question builds on issues raised by the first two.

III. Identifying Métis Rights-Holders to Whom the Duty to Consult and Accommodate Is Owed

1. *First Sub-Question: Who Qualifies as a Métis Rights-Holder?*

A section 35 Aboriginal right is held by an Aboriginal collective.[25] Although Aboriginal and treaty rights can be exercised or assigned to individuals, the rights-holder is the collective,[26] in contrast to the liberal paradigm in which the rights-holder is the individual.[27] *Powley* affirms the collective nature of Métis Aboriginal rights.[28] Because the right is held by the collective, the duty to consult and accommodate is owed to the collective as opposed to being owed to individuals.[29]

This brings us to the first sub-question of who qualifies as a rights-bearing Métis people. The Supreme Court of Canada in *Powley* answered this question by quelling the Métis-as-mixed approach according to which the term "Métis" refers to a race-based category, such that the Métis are merely a collection of individuals with mixed ancestry.[30] Instead, the Supreme Court in *Powley* adopted something closer to a nationhood approach, which holds that the term "Métis" refers "to distinctive peoples who, in addition to their mixed ancestry, developed their own customs, way of life, and recognizable group identity separate from their Indian or Inuit and European forebears."[31] In other words, the offspring of the initial unions between European men and First Nations women were individuals who merely possessed mixed European and First Nations ancestry.[32] But over the course of successive generations, a distinct Métis culture and collective identity emerged which was separate and distinguishable from either First Nations or European cultures.[33] To be rights-bearing, according to *Powley*, such collectives must have emerged prior to the effective imposition of European control.[34]

The Métis Nation of Ontario has made substantial progress towards identifying the areas in Ontario where a distinctive Métis people emerged who developed their own customs, traditions, and collective identity prior to European control. Since 2004—shortly after the release of the *Powley* decision—the Métis Nation of Ontario and the province of Ontario have worked collaboratively to identify seven historic Métis communities in Ontario who satisfy the requirements set out in *Powley* and outlined above.[35] The Métis Nation of Ontario cautions that the research underlying the recognition of these seven communities is not comprehensive, but rather is based on information available to date.[36] As research continues, these communities may be expanded and/or additional historic Métis communities in Ontario may be identified.[37]

Although various additional requirements must also be met before a Court will uphold a Métis right, the Métis Nation of Ontario's research provides a useful starting point for proponents seeking to identify a Métis rights-holder in Ontario.

As Jean Teillet notes, the only Métis rights-holder identified by Canadian courts is the Métis Nation of the Northwest[38] whose homeland extends into "much of the three prairie provinces, west into northern British Columbia, east into parts of Ontario, north into the Northwest Territories, and south into Montana and North Dakota"[39] but does not reach east of Ontario. Although many individuals have claimed to exercise Métis rights east of Ontario, all such claims have failed; courts have never recognized a Métis rights-holder east of Ontario.[40] Although the Court of Appeal of Newfoundland and Labrador affirmed that the Labrador Métis Nation was owed a duty to consult,[41] the Labrador Métis Nation subsequently changed its name to Nunatukavut, reflecting that it is an Inuit, not a Métis, people.[42]

2. *Second Sub-Question: What Is the Geographic Scope of the Métis Rights-Holder?*

The second sub-question asks: what are the geographic boundaries of the collective where the right can be exercised? On the one hand, some Métis advocates assert that the Métis rights-holder is the Métis nation.[43] That is, Métis people are entitled to exercise Métis rights throughout the homeland of the Métis nation.[44] On the other hand, governments have advocated for a narrow definition which limits a Métis rights-holder to "a site-specific physical settlement (village site and surrounding environs) that is local and fixed in nature"[45] or in other words, to "dots on a map around which boundary circles can be drawn (i.e., the 'hub and spoke' approach)."[46] The latter view results in limited and constricted exercises of rights. This issue is complicated by the current controversy between the Métis National Council and one of its Governing Members, the Métis Nation of Ontario, in which the Métis National Council asserts that the geographic scope of the Métis nation extends into only a portion of Ontario and does not include six of the seven historic Métis communities identified by the Métis Nation of Ontario and the province of Ontario.[47] In November 2018, the Métis National Council narrowly passed a resolution putting the Métis Nation of Ontario on probation for one year, and requiring it to comply with the Métis National Council's delineation of the geographic scope of the Métis homeland as a condition of lifting its probation.[48]

The courts have adopted a middle ground between the nationwide approach and governments' narrower hub-and-spoke approach by defining Métis rights-holders as being regional in scope.[49] The regional Métis collectives identified by courts span up to 35,000–45,000 square kilometres, and encompass thousands of Métis citizens.[50]

The courts' regional approach to identifying the boundaries of the Métis rights-holder suffers from two flaws which I analyze in the remainder of this section: the courts' approach is inconsistent, first, with the applicable constitutional text and second, with the broader jurisprudence on this topic. Thus, as Jason Madden recognizes, the regional Métis "communities" produced by the case law are legal fictions which fail to fully reflect historical or contemporary realities.[51]

a. Constitutional Text

The applicable constitutional text is section 35 of the *Constitution Act, 1982*, which recognizes and affirms the existing Aboriginal rights of the Aboriginal "peoples" and includes the Métis people among Aboriginal "peoples."[52] Thus, the written text stipulates that the rights-holder is a "people." As Larry Chartrand notes, however, the term "people" is almost entirely missing from the courts' discussion of the issue of how to identify the Métis rights-holder.[53] Instead, the term most often employed by courts when identifying the rights-holder is "community."[54] Courts' use of the term "community" is inexplicable, given the lack of textual foundation for it and the lack of equivalence between "people" and "community." While "people" generally connotes "nation," Chartrand explains that "community," from a western perspective, connotes "a static, preferably agrarian, local group as opposed to a semi-nomadic broad ranging kinship-based hunting community," the latter of which better corresponds to Métis social, legal, and political structures.[55] The Court provides no explanation for substituting "community" for "peoples" in its analysis.[56] This equivocation allows the Court to mask its departure from the textual authority that recognizes the rights-holder at the level of nationhood.[57]

b. Jurisprudence

The broader jurisprudence also supports the conclusion that the nation is the rights-holder. *Powley* allows for the possibility of identifying a "community" at a high level of generality: "a Métis community can be defined as a group of Métis with a distinctive collective identity, living together in the same geographic area and sharing a common way of life" as established by evidence of "shared customs, traditions, and a collective identity."[58] As Chartrand explains, this definition is potentially flexible enough to support the conclusion that the rights-holder should be defined as being national in scope.[59] The rights-holder is defined in terms of shared cultural markers such as customs, traditions, and a distinctive collective identity, all of which are consistent with nationhood.[60]

Moreover, the trial judge in *Powley* explicitly rejected the Crown's attempt to define the rights-holder in that case narrowly.[61] Instead, the trial judge adopted the regional approach by defining the "rights-bearing Métis community" as extending, at a minimum, "hundreds of kilometres to the east, north and west of Sault Ste. Marie, spanning almost 20,000 square kilometres on the Canadian side" and reaching into northern Michigan.[62] The Supreme Court of Canada upheld these findings.[63] The regional approach in *Powley*, however, is not a precedent for rejecting the nationwide approach, given that the issue of whether the rights-holder could be defined at a nationwide level was not at issue and so was not addressed.[64] Thus, as Madden concludes, it is a mistake for courts to try to replicate fictional regional *Powley* "communities" if the historical evidence supports a nationwide approach.[65]

This issue was raised squarely in the Tsilhqot'in Nation's claim to Aboriginal title, where the trial judge applied the factors set out in *Powley* for identifying the rights-holder.[66] The trial judge concluded that the proper rights-holder of both the claimed Aboriginal rights and title was the Tsilhqot'in people or nation—and not the individual bands or sub-entities making up the Tsilhqot'in Nation—because the shared language, customs, traditions, and historical experience required by the *Powley* test existed at the level of the larger nation.[67] In applying these factors, the trial judge looked to the people's own traditions and customs for self-identification.[68] The British Columbia Court of Appeal affirmed this approach.[69] The courts identified the nation as the rights-holder, despite the absence of any overarching social or political organization or decision-making body at the national level.[70] The trial judge concluded that requiring the rights-holder to have its own governance structure would be ethnocentric and would ignore Aboriginal peoples' own culture and norms.[71] The Court of Appeal added that even though Tsilhqot'in governance and decision-making structures traditionally existed at the level of smaller collectives, courts must not attempt to find modern counterparts of these smaller collectives. If courts were to insist that only the smaller collective with a clear governance structure was the rights-holder, then "no one would be able to claim Aboriginal rights on behalf of the Tsilhqot'in" given the fluidity of the Tsilhqot'in political structure.[72] A right without a right-holder is hollow. The province, "to its credit"—as the Supreme Court of Canada put it—did not pursue these issues at the Supreme Court of Canada.[73]

To summarize, the identification of a rights-holder requires cultural markers which are consistent with nationhood, but not necessarily a governance structure at the national level. Villages or bands could be, but are not necessarily, rights-holders.[74] The answer in any given case will depend on the rights-holder's own traditions, especially those pertaining to collective identification.[75] In at least one case, the evidence indicated that each of the smaller collectives who share a common language, culture, and history were the rights-holders.[76] In many more cases, courts have held that the nation is the rights-holder.[77]

The tests applied by the courts in the Tsilhqot'in Nation case support the conclusion that the geographic scope of the Métis rights-holder can be defined at a nationhood level. Granted, the seven historic communities jointly identified by the Métis Nation of Ontario and the province of Ontario seem to be defined at a regional level, perhaps because of the limits of currently available research[78] or perhaps to cohere with the current state of the jurisprudence recognizing regional Métis communities. But as mentioned above, the Métis Nation of Ontario acknowledges that eventually these communities may be expanded based on additional research.[79]

3. *Third Sub-Question: Who Is Entitled to Represent the Métis Rights-Holder for the Purpose of Consultation?*

The issue of delineating the geographic boundary of the rights-holder is distinct from the issue of determining who is entitled to represent the rights-holder for the purpose of consultation. For example, even if the rights-holder is the larger nation, a national level authority is not necessarily entitled or required to serve as the consultation representative.[80] This follows from the principle discussed above that a nation who is a rights-holder need not possess a governance or decision-making structure at the national level. For example, the British Columbia Court of Appeal concluded that even though the Tsilhqot'in Nation was the rights-holder, a smaller entity within the nation—the Xeni Gwet'in—was the custodian of the specific area at issue and thus held responsibility for administering and protecting the rights,[81] which presumably includes engaging in consultations. How, then, is the proper representative identified?

The jurisprudence on this issue is in its infancy.[82] The Supreme Court of Canada's guidance is minimal and some of the pronouncements of lower courts reveal inconsistencies. In his report to the Minister of Indigenous and Northern Affairs, Bryn Gray warned: "Determining who speaks for asserted or established rights-holders is a fundamental issue and this needs to be resolved on a priority basis."[83] For proponents wishing to overcome the ambiguity intrinsic to the duty to consult by entering into Indigenous-industry agreements, the certainty offered by such agreements will be a mirage if an authoritative representative of the rights-holder cannot be identified. As Newman explains, the potential obstacles to determining who speaks for a rights-holder correlate with the issue of how to obtain genuine consent.[84] To ensure a rights-holder has genuinely consented to an Indigenous-industry agreement, the representative signatory to the agreement must have the proper authorization of the rights-holder. The following propositions can be deduced from the existing jurisprudence and are discussed in turn below. First, a rights-holder can authorize a representative, including a corporation, to engage in consultation and enforce the duty to consult on its behalf. Second, the authorization need not be specific and it can be demonstrated by the governing documents of either the rights-holder or the representative. In most circumstances, the citizenry of the rights-holder likely need not be coextensive with the members of the representative. Third, courts are divided on whether consultation can be owed to overlapping sub-entities of the rights-holder.

The Métis Nation of Ontario's innovative approach to consultation complies with the existing jurisprudence, and even reconciles some of the jurisprudential inconsistencies. In so doing, the Métis Nation of Ontario serves as an exemplar for ensuring consent is informed.

a. A Rights-Holder Can Authorize a Representative to Engage in and Enforce Consultation

A rights-holder is entitled to authorize a representative to engage in consultation and enforce the duty to consult and accommodate in court. The Supreme Court of Canada explains in *Behn* that "an Aboriginal group can authorize an individual or an organization to represent it for the purpose of asserting its s. 35 rights."[85] The representative may take the form of a corporation.[86] Older, lower court decisions which prevented corporations from litigating section 35 rights did so on the ground that the corporation—as distinct from the collective which is the rights-holder—has no direct interest in the right.[87] Where corporations have been permitted to represent section 35 rights-holders, courts have relied on evidence that the rights-holder authorized the corporation to represent it.[88]

Allowing corporations to represent rights-holders is consistent with current practices of both First Nations and the Métis nation. With respect to First Nations, Section 3.b above showed that the legal entities created by legislation—band councils—are not necessarily rights-holders. Thus, First Nations sometimes incorporate entities to represent them at the nationhood level.[89] With respect to the Métis, for the most part, no analogue to the *Indian Act* exists.[90] Thus, most Métis governance structures necessarily operate as not-for-profit corporations or societies.[91]

b. Authorization Need Not Be Specific and It Can Be Demonstrated by the Governing Documents of Either the Rights-Holder or the Representative

What do courts look for when assessing whether an entity has been authorized to represent a rights-bearer? This issue has been considered only recently by lower courts, but not yet by the Supreme Court of Canada. In *Behn*, the Supreme

Court of Canada held that without authorization from the First Nation, individual members of that First Nation could not assert a breach of the duty to consult and accommodate.[92] The Court did not consider what would constitute sufficient evidence of authorization, because the appeal was from a decision on a motion to strike pleadings, and thus the Court was confined to the pleadings (which lacked an allegation of authorization).[93]

Authorization has been demonstrated in lower court decisions by the governing documents of either the representative or the rights-holder. Examples of the former include the preamble to an entity's memorandum and articles of association,[94] a corporation's constitution,[95] and a corporation's bylaws (suggested in *obiter*).[96] An example of the latter is the resolution of a band council to be represented by an incorporated society.[97]

Must the authorization specify the precise project in question or proponent to be consulted? How specific must the authorization be? In cases where courts accepted the authorization, the purpose identified was not especially specific: these authorizations referred to an entitlement to consultation regarding Aboriginal rights,[98] to promoting the interests and rights of the rights-holder,[99] to representation with respect to consultation protocols and accommodation agreements,[100] to advancing "constitutional, legal, political, social and economic rights," and to negotiating "agreements to advance and support the inherent right of self-government and self-determination."[101] In *Enge v Canada*, the Federal Court held that the general objects set out in the registered society's constitution authorizing it to represent its members' legal rights—including the right of self-government—was sufficient to allow it to commence an application alleging a breach of the duty to consult.[102] It was not necessary for the registered society to also obtain a resolution or any other membership approval specifically authorizing the application.[103] Thus, when the Alberta Court of Queen's Bench in *Fort Chipewyan Métis Nation of Alberta Local #125 v Alberta (Minister of Aboriginal Relations)* implies in *obiter* that the authorization should indicate the "specific purpose" of the representation,[104] it is out of step with prevailing jurisprudence.

The Métis Nation of Ontario's governance structure has been praised by Thomas Isaac, in his capacity as the Minister's Special Representative on Reconciliation with Métis, as an example of an entity with proper authorization to represent the rights-bearing people.[105] The legal entity that gives effect to the Métis Nation of Ontario's governance structure is the Métis Nation of Ontario Secretariat (the Secretariat), which is a corporation.[106] The Secretariat's Bylaws incorporate the Métis Nation of Ontario's *Statement of Prime Purpose*, which is the Métis Nation of Ontario's foundational constituting document and which provides that the Métis Nation of Ontario is the "representative body" of that portion of the Métis nation located within Ontario.[107] The "aims and objectives" of the Métis Nation of Ontario include, among other things, "to ensure that Métis can exercise their Aboriginal and Treaty rights."[108] The Secretariat, in turn, is the means by which the Métis Nation of Ontario's governance structure is given legal effect within the Canadian legal system: "It is the corporate and administrative arm of the Métis Nation of Ontario, which was created to represent and advocate on behalf of its registered citizens, and the Métis communities comprised of those citizens, with respect to their collective rights."[109] These statements are sufficient to authorize the Secretariat to represent the Métis Nation of Ontario for the purposes of consultation and negotiating Indigenous-industry agreements.

Must the membership of the representative entity be coterminous with the citizenry of the rights-holder? For example, in *Fort Chipewyan Métis Nation of Alberta Local #125 v Alberta (Minister of Aboriginal Relations)*, the Alberta Court of Queen's Bench rejected the corporation's claim to represent the rights-holder because the corporation had 173 members but the population of the rights-holder was between 350 and 1000 individuals, and the corporation claimed to represent not only its own members, but also the entire population of the rights-holder.[110] The Court held that "a corporate entity with a membership of less than one-fifth of the total population of [the rights-holder] cannot claim to be representative of the entire Aboriginal community for the purpose of asserting Aboriginal rights and seeking consultation."[111]

The answer to this question must depend on the context. Logic dictates that the population of the rights-holder need not be coterminous with the membership of the corporation when the authorization comes from the rights-holder's own governance processes (and not from the corporation's governing documents). Otherwise, the authorization itself would be superfluous.[112] Logic also dictates that the population of the rights-holder need not be coterminous with the membership of the corporation when the corporation represents only its own members.[113]

The coterminous population issue is not a concern for the Métis Nation of Ontario because it represents only its own members. The governance structure of the Métis Nation of Ontario's Secretariat includes 30 Community Councils which are subject to Community Charter Agreements between the Secretariat, the Métis Nation of Ontario, and the Community Council.[114] The Community Charter Agreements provide that each Community Council represents only those who are citizens of the Métis Nation of Ontario.[115] Pursuant to the Secretariat's Bylaws, the term "citizens" refers to the Secretariat's members.[116] Similarly, the *Métis Nation of Ontario Secretariat Act, 2015* affirms that the Secretariat represents "its registered citizens and the Métis communities comprised of those citizens."[117] Having a coterminous population can promote informed consent. Consent is informed when the different positions held by those being represented are available for consideration.[118] Entities who enter into Indigenous-industry agreements due to the duty to consult, and who claim to represent non-members, run the risk of failing to achieve this aspect of informed consent.

One might object that if an Indigenous government such as the Métis Nation of Ontario wants to serve as the authorized representative of the rights-holder, it must represent each and every Métis individual located within a given territory. However, this objection is not persuasive because it attempts to impose a static, Eurocentric conception of a "community" and it overlooks the doctrinal law, discussed above, which recognizes the fluidity of Indigenous governance structures.[119] A requirement that the rights-holder must encompass every individual within a given geographic area would deny the autonomy of Métis people to constitute and reconstitute themselves as they see fit.[120] As the British Columbia Court of Appeal stated, difficulties in identifying a rights-holder cannot "be allowed to preclude recognition of Aboriginal rights that are otherwise proven."[121] Thus it cannot be that only representatives who have the authorization of every single Métis individual within a given geographic area are entitled to consultation, because if this were the law, there would be no authorized representatives of Métis rights-holders. A right without a right-holder is hollow. As the majority in *R v Van der Peet* stated: "It would be entirely contrary to the spirit and intent of s. 35(1) to define aboriginal rights in such a fashion so as to preclude in practice any successful claim for the existence of such a right."[122] One might wonder about the logistics of two or more separate Métis rights-holders exercising Aboriginal rights within one and the same geographic area. This concern evaporates, however, when we recall that First Nations and Métis can have Aboriginal rights within one and the same territory and that doctrinal law allows for Aboriginal title to be held jointly by two or more Aboriginal peoples.[123] It is not unusual for two or more Indigenous peoples to coordinate their various legal orders within a shared space.[124] Canadian law refers to this unexceptional phenomenon as "overlapping Aboriginal claims," which give rise to a duty to consult more than one rights-holder in one and the same geographic area.[125]

c. Lower Courts Are Divided on Whether Consultation Can Be Owed to Overlapping Sub-Entities

How do courts determine whether the larger nation or a smaller sub-entity is entitled to be consulted? As discussed above in Section 3, the answer is not dictated by determining the geographic scope of the rights-holder. A rights-holder that exists at a national level is not necessarily entitled to consultation. Although the Tsilhqot'in Nation was the rights-holder, the Xeni Gwet'in, a smaller sub-entity, held responsibility for administering the rights in the area at issue.[126] This conclusion was grounded in the Tsilhqot'in Nation's own laws, as evidenced by their modern political structure.[127] Thus, Aboriginal peoples' laws—not the Crown and not proponents—determine who is entitled to be consulted. But what happens when both the larger national entity and the smaller entity claim to be owed consultation? Must the consultation engage every individual member or sub-collective of the rights-holder?

Although the Supreme Court of Canada in *Behn* established that the duty to consult is not owed to individuals but rather to the collective rights-holder, the Court has not yet considered whether the duty can be owed to both sub-entities—such as bands or Métis community councils and locals—and to the larger Aboriginal nation to which the sub-entity belongs.[128] Lower court decisions on this topic are inconsistent. In *FCMNA Local #125*, the Alberta Court of Queen's Bench held that it would be "a waste of resources for the

Alberta Crown to potentially have to consult with several separate organizations who state that they represent smaller or larger subsets of the same group in respect of the same interests and the same project."[129] In contrast, in *Nla'pamux Nation Tribal Council v Griffin*, the British Columbia Supreme Court held that "the government must discharge its duty to consult by taking reasonable steps to ensure that all points of view within a First Nation are given appropriate consideration."[130] The position of the band most directly affected by a proposed landfill project differed from that of the entity representing the nation to which the band belonged.[131] The provincial government implemented separate consultation processes with the band and with the entity representing the nation, which the Court concluded was appropriate.[132]

Even though the outcomes in these two decisions are inconsistent, their underlying policy values (efficiency vs. fully informed consultations) are not mutually exclusive, and have been reconciled within the Métis Nation of Ontario's consultation framework. By integrating the competing values from the divergent case law, the Métis Nation of Ontario's consultation framework ensures that their consent to any Indigenous-industry agreement resulting from the duty to consult is informed. The Métis Nation of Ontario has established a Lands, Resources and Consultations Branch (LRC Branch) which employs full-time staff who possess the scientific and technical expertise needed to support consultation.[133] The LRC Branch provides governments with a "one-window" approach to consultation with the Métis Nation of Ontario.[134] Governments can give notice of any proposed project or decision directly to the LRC Branch.[135] The LRC Branch then identifies the relevant sub-entities within the Métis Nation of Ontario's governance structure who should be consulted, coordinates their consultation activities, and provides administrative and technical support to those sub-entities.[136] The "one-window" approach means the onus is not on governments to attempt to determine which sub-entities need to be consulted, which in turn avoids duplication of government resources from consulting with overlapping entities. The LRC Branch also helps to ensure consent is informed by providing the expertise needed to analyze data and documents; it thereby ensures Métis Nation of Ontario citizens understand the consequences of proposed projects and government decisions.[137] Finally, a requirement of consent is that the "mechanism used to reach agreement must itself be agreed to by the Indigenous peoples concerned."[138] The LRC Branch helps to satisfy this requirement as it is a result of recommendations made by Métis Nation of Ontario citizens during province-wide consultations undertaken by the Métis Nation of Ontario in 2007–2008.[139] As such, it is part of a mechanism used to reach consent which was previously agreed to by the Métis Nation of Ontario.

A potential downside of a "one-window" or centralized approach like that of the LRC Branch—if not well executed—is it could result in consultation becoming siloed as opposed to ensuring all who are affected have an opportunity to participate in decision-making, as emphasized in *Nla'pamux Nation*. The Métis Nation of Ontario has developed an innovative solution to this dilemma within its governance structure in the form of Regional Consultation Protocols which are agreements between the Métis Nation of Ontario and the Community Councils located within each of the Métis Nation of Ontario's nine regions.[140] The Protocols establish Consultation Committees which include representatives from each of the relevant Community Councils. Consultation Committees are responsible for developing "a local and regional MNO citizen engagement plan" and for ensuring "all potentially affected MNO citizens are engaged and communicated with."[141] By coordinating consultation at both the local and regional level and across multiple Community Councils, Consultation Committees save governments from having to undertake this potentially duplicative work. At the same time, Consultation Committees help to ensure that consent to any Indigenous-industry agreement is informed by providing a mechanism to allow all affected Métis Nation of Ontario citizens to engage in the decision-making process and contribute their views.[142] Finally, like the LRC Branch, Consultation Committees are a result of recommendations made by Métis Nation of Ontario citizens during province-wide consultations undertaken by the Métis Nation of Ontario in 2007–2008.[143] As such, it functions as part of a mechanism for reaching consent which was agreed to by the Métis Nation of Ontario, and thus it serves to fulfill a requirement of consent.

IV. Conclusion

Proponents are incentivized to enter into Indigenous-industry agreements in order to overcome the legal ambiguity surrounding the duty to consult, including the possibility that projects which are initially approved could be cancelled when the right is subsequently established if the Indigenous nation did not initially consent to the project. To achieve the certainty desired by proponents, consent to an Indigenous-industry agreement should be free, prior, and informed. The Métis Nation of Ontario's consultation procedures help to ensure that consent is genuinely informed. The Métis Nation of Ontario Secretariat is a corporation that is sufficiently authorized to represent the Métis Nation of Ontario in consultations. The Secretariat does not claim to represent non-citizens of the Métis Nation of Ontario, which avoids the potential problem of consent being less than fully informed. The Métis Nation of Ontario's consultation framework also balances the competing values reflected in the jurisprudence, including efficiency and fully informed consent. Other Indigenous nations may find guidance from the various features of the Métis Nation of Ontario's consultation framework, such as its LRC Branch and its Consultation Committees.

Notes

1. I wish to recognize and thank Emma Baumann and Gabrielle Pellerin for their valuable research assistance. I also wish to acknowledge and thank Jason Madden and Megan Strachan for their insights in formulating the topic of this paper. Any errors are my own.

2. See Dwight Newman, "The Rule and Role of Law: The Duty to Consult, Aboriginal Communities, and the Canadian Natural Resource Sector" [2014] Macdonald-Laurier Institute Papers Series 12–13 [Newman, "Role of Law"].
3. Ibid 13; Dwight Newman, *Natural Resource Jurisdiction in Canada* (Lexis Nexis Canada 2013) 99.
4. See, for example, Emilie Cameron and Tyler Levitan, "Impact and Benefit Agreements and the Neoliberalization of Resource Governance and Indigenous-State Relations in Northern Canada" [2014] 93 Stud Polit Econ 29; Guillaume Peterson St-Laurent and Philippe Le Billon, "Staking Claims and Shaking Hands: Impact and Benefit Agreements as a Technology of Government in the Mining Sector" [2015] 2 Extr Ind Soc 590.
5. Natural Resources Canada, *Agreements Between Mining Companies and Aboriginal Communities or Governments* (Minerals and Metals Sector, Natural Resources Canada 2013) <www.nrcan.gc.ca/sites/www.nrcan.gc.ca/files/mineralsmetals/files/pdf/abor-auto/aam-eac-e2013.pdf>.
6. See Jason Madden, Zachary Davis, and Megan Strachan, "Recent Legal Developments on Métis Consultation in Alberta: A Case Summary of *MNA Local #125 v. Alberta*" (*Pape Salter Teillet LLP*, 7 March 2017) 3, 8 <http://albertametis.com/wp-content/uploads/2017/03/PST-LLP-Summary-MNA-125-Local-v-Alberta-Feb-2017-2.pdf>; See also *Mikisew Cree First Nation v Canada (Minister of Canadian Heritage)*, 2005 SCC 69 [34], [55] [*Mikisew Cree*]; *Rio Tinto Alcan Inc v Carrier Sekani Tribal Council*, [2010] 2 SCR 659 [40].
7. See Kerry Sloan, "Always Coming Home: Metis Legal Understandings of Community and Territory" (2016) 33 Windsor YB Access to Just 125; Chris Andersen, *"Métis": Race, Recognition, and the Struggle for Indigenous Peoplehood* (UBC Press 2014) [Andersen, *"Métis"*]; Sébastien Grammond and Lynne Proulx, "Finding Metis Communities" (2012) 32(1) Canadian Journal of Native Studies 33; D'Arcy Vermette, "Colonialism and the Process of Defining Aboriginal People" [2008] 31 Dalhousie LJ 21; Paul LAH Chartrand, "Defining the 'Métis' of Canada: A Principled Approach to Crown-Aboriginal Relations" in Frederica Wilson & Melanie Mallet, (eds), *Métis-Crown Relations: Rights, Identity, Jurisdiction, and Governance* (Irwin Law 2008) 27; Larry N Chartrand, "The Definition of Métis Peoples in Section 35(2) of the *Constitution Act, 1982*" [2004] 67 Sask L Rev 209; Catherine Bell, "Who are the Metis People in Section 35(2)?" [1991] 29 Alta L Rev 351.
8. See Thomas Isaac, *A Matter of National and Constitutional Import: Report of the Minister's Special Representative on Reconciliation with Métis: Section 35 Métis Rights and the* Manitoba Metis Federation *Decision* (June 2016) 21 <www.aadnc-aandc.gc.ca/eng/1467641790303/1467641835266>; Bryn Gray, *Building Relationships and Advancing Reconciliation through Meaningful Consultation: Report to the Minister of Indigenous and Northern Affairs* (May 30, 2016) 21 <www.aadn-caandc.gc.ca/eng/1498765671013/1498765827601> [Gray].
9. Those who are unable to read further without some guidance about the definition of "Métis" can read the text accompanying (n 30–34) in Section 3 below.
10. *Fort Chipewyan Métis Nation of Alberta Local #125 v Alberta (Minister of Aboriginal Relations)*, 2016 ABQB 713 [269] [*FCMNA Local #125*].
11. The third is the treaty context, which is not entirely analogous to the situation in which Aboriginal rights are asserted but not yet proven or admitted by the Crown: *Mikisew Cree* (n 6) [48].
12. *Constitution Act, 1982*, being Schedule B to the *Canada Act 1982* (UK), 1982, c 11.
13. *Haida Nation v British Columbia (Minister of Forests)*, 2004 SCC 73 [16], [18], [36] [*Haida Nation*].
14. Ibid [48].

15. Ibid [42].
16. *R v Sparrow*, [1990] 1 SCR 1075 [1113]–[1119] [*Sparrow*]. *Tsilhqot'in Nation v British Columbia*, 2014 SCC 44 [77], [80] [*Tsilhqot'in Nation*].
17. *Haida Nation* (n 13) [48], [40], citing *Delgamuukw v British Columbia*, [1997] 3 SCR 1010 [168] [*Delgamuukw*]; ibid *Tsilhqot'in Nation* [92].
18. See Karen Drake and Adam Gaudry, "'The lands … belonged to them, once by the Indian title, twice for having defended them …, and thrice for having built and lived on them': The Law and Politics of Métis Title" (2016) 54(1) Osgoode Hall Law Journal 1, 1.
19. *Tsilhqot'in Nation* (n 16) [17], citing *Haida Nation* (n 13) [25].
20. Ibid [92].
21. *Haida Nation* (n 13) [45].
22. See John Borrows, "Wise Practices in Indigenous Economic Development and Environmental Protection" 24.
23. Drake and Gaudry (n 18).
24. Dwight Newman, "Political Rhetoric Meets Legal Reality: How to Move Forward on Free, Prior and Informed Consent in Canada" (August 2017) Macdonald-Laurier Institute Papers Series 15 [Newman, "Legal Reality"].
25. *Behn v Moulton Contracting Ltd*, 2013 SCC 26 [30], [35] [*Behn*].
26. Ibid [33].
27. See Dale Turner, *This is not a Peace Pipe: Towards a Critical Indigenous Philosophy* (University of Toronto Press 2006) 13; Gordon Christie, "Law, Theory and Aboriginal Peoples" [2005] 2 Indigenous LJ 67, 81.
28. *R v Powley*, 2003 SCC 43 [24] [*Powley*].
29. *Behn* (n 25) [30]. See also *Beckman v Little Salmon/Carmacks First Nation*, 2010 SCC 53 [35].
30. *Powley* (n 28) 10.
31. Ibid [10]. See also *R v Blais*, 2003 SCC 44 [9]; *FCMNA Local #125* (n 10) [191]. But see Andersen, *"Métis"* (n 7) Ch 4.
32. See Jason Madden, "The Métis Nation's Self-Government Agenda: Issues and Options for the Future" in Frederica Wilson and Melanie Mallet (eds), *Métis-Crown Relations: Rights, Identity, Jurisdiction, and Governance* (Irwin Law Inc 2008) 323, 327 [Madden, "Self-Government Agenda"]; See also *Report of the Royal Commission on Aboriginal Peoples: Perspectives and Realities*, vol 4 (Canada Communication Group—Publishing 1996) 199–200 [RCAP, *Perspectives*], cited in *Powley* (n 28) [10].
33. *Powley*, ibid [10]–[11], 23; Madden, "Self-Government Agenda," ibid; RCAP, *Perspectives*, ibid.
34. *Powley*, ibid [10], [17], [18].
35. Métis Nation of Ontario, "Historic Métis Communities in Ontario" (*Métis Nation of Ontario*, 2019) <www.metisnation.org/registry/citizenship/historic-métis-communities/> [MNO, "Historic Métis Communities"].
36. Ibid.
37. Ibid.
38. Jean Teillet, *Métis Law in Canada* (Pape Salter Teillet LLP 2013) (loose-leaf 2017 supplement), Ch 1 [20].
39. Adam Gaudry and Karen Drake, "The Resilience of Métis Title: Rejecting Assumptions of Extinguishment for Métis Land Rights" in Yvonne Boyer and Larry Chartrand (eds), *Métis Rising* (UBC Press forthcoming in 2020) 2.
40. See Darryl Leroux, *Distorted Descent: White Claims to Indigenous Identity* (University of Manitoba Press 2019); Adam Gaudry and Darryl Leroux, "White Settler Revisionism and Making Metis Everywhere: The Contemporary Evocation of Metissage in Quebec and Nova Scotia" (2017) 3(1) Journal of Critical Ethnic Studies 116.

41. *Labrador Métis Nation v Newfoundland*, 2007 NLCA 75 [*Labrador Métis Nation*].
42. (n 38) Ch 1 [21].
43. See, for example, Jean Teillet and Carly Teillet, "Devoid of Principle: The Federal Court Determination That Section 91(24) of the Constitution Act, 1867 Is a Race-Based Provision" [2016] 13 Indigenous LJ 1, 11; See also Larry Chartrand, "The Constitutional Determination of a Métis Rights-Bearing Community: Reorienting the *Powley* Test" in Karen Drake and Brenda Gunn, *Renewing Relationships: Indigenous Peoples and Canada* (Native Law Centre 2019) 180 [Chartrand, "Métis Rights-Bearing Community"].
44. For the geographical scope of the Métis nation's homeland, see text accompanying (n 39).
45. Chartrand, "Métis Rights-Bearing Community" (n 43) 175; See also Jason Madden, "Métis Consultation and Accommodation: Answering The 'Who' Question" (March 2009) n 30 [unpublished, on file with the author] [Madden, "Answering The 'Who' Question"].
46. Ibid Madden, "Answering The 'Who' Question" [14], [18]–[19].
47. Clément Chartier, "Addressing the Integrity of the Historic Métis Nation Homeland: Report in Response to the Métis Nation General Assembly December 2017 Resolution on the Métis Nation of Ontario" (November 2018) 4 <http://www.metisnation.ca/wp-content/uploads/2018/11/MNO-Nov-2018-Report-Recommendations-appendices-final.pdf>.
48. Métis Nation of Ontario, "MNO responds to MNC resolutions" <http://www.metisnation.org/news-media/news/mno-responds-to-mnc-resolutions/>.
49. See Chartrand, "Métis Rights-Bearing Community" (n 43) 169; Madden, "Answering The 'Who' Question" (n 45) 17–18; Catherine Bell and Paul Seaman, "A New Era for Metis Constitutional Rights: Consultation, Negotiation and Reconciliation" (2015) 38 Man LJ 29 at 64–66.
50. See ibid Madden, "Answering The 'Who' Question" 18; See, for example, *R v Laviolette*, 2005 SKPC 70 [25]–[28]; *R v Belhumeur*, 2007 SKPC 114 [167]–[168]; *R v Goodon*, 2008 MBPC 59 [48]; The Alberta Court of Appeal in *R v Hirsekorn*, 2013 ABCA 242 [8], declined to address the question of the geographic scope of the Métis community, given its conclusion that no Métis community had sufficient presence in the area at issue prior to effective European control.
51. Ibid Madden, "Answering The 'Who' Question" 22; See also Teillet (n 38) Ch 1, 33–34.
52. (n 12).
53. See Chartrand, "Métis Rights-Bearing Community" (n 43) 171.
54. Ibid 172.
55. Ibid 171–72.
56. *Powley* (n 28) [11]–[12].
57. See Chartrand, "Métis Rights-Bearing Community" (n 43) 171.
58. *Powley* (n 28) [12], [23]. See also *FCMNA Local #125* (n 10) [197].
59. Chartrand, "Métis Rights-Bearing Community" (n 43).
60. But see Andersen, *"Métis"* (n 7) 17–20.
61. *R v Powley*, [1999] 1 CNLR 153 (OCJ) [68], [70] [*Powley Trial Decision*]; See also Madden, "Answering The 'Who' Question" (n 45) 14–15.
62. Madden, "Self-Government Agenda" (n 32) 14; See also *Powley Trial Decision* ibid [21], [26], [28]; Chartrand, "Métis Rights-Bearing Community" (n 43) 177.
63. *Powley* (n 28) [21], [26], [28].
64. See Madden, "Answering The 'Who' Question" (n 45) 15–16; Chartrand, "Métis Rights-Bearing Community" (n 43) 187; See also *Powley* ibid [12].
65. Madden, "Answering The 'Who' Question" ibid 16.
66. *Tsilhqot'in Nation v British Columbia*, 2007 BCSC 1700 [442], [444] [*Tsilhqot'in Trial Decision*].

67. Ibid [469]–[470].
68. Ibid [444], [471]–[472].
69. *Tsilhqot'in Nation v British Columbia*, 2012 BCCA 285 [149] [*Tsilhqot'in CA*].
70. Ibid [452]–[453].
71. Ibid [453].
72. *Tsilhqot'in Nation CA* (n 69) [146].
73. *Tsilhqot'in Nation* (n 16) [19]. As Kent McNeil explains, the conclusion that the Tsilhqot'in Nation was the rights-holder "was implicitly affirmed by the Court's declaration of the Tsilhqot'in Nation's Aboriginal title": Kent McNeil, "Aboriginal Title and Indigenous Governance: Identifying the Holders of Rights and Authority" (2016) 12(14) Osgoode Hall Law School Legal Studies Research Paper Series 44–45, 15–16 [McNeil].
74. *Tsilhqot'in CA* (n 69) [148]; *Kwicksutaineuk/Ah-Kwa-Mish First Nation v Canada (Attorney General)*, 2012 BCCA 193 [77].
75. See McNeil (n 73) 45–46.
76. *Ahousaht Indian Band v Canada (Attorney General)*, 2009 BCSC 1494 [287]–[365], rev'd in part on other grounds 2013 BCCA 300. See also McNeil (n 73) 46.
77. See ibid McNeil; *Tsilhqot'in Trial Decision* (n 66) [445]. For a list of decisions holding that the nation is the rights-holder, see *R v Bernard*, 2017 NBCA 48 [51].
78. See text accompanying (n 36).
79. MNO, "Historic Métis Communities" (n 35).
80. See John Borrows, "Wise Practices in Indigenous Economic Development and Environmental Protection" 11.
81. *Tsilhqot'in CA* (n 69) [154]. See also McNeil (n 73) 15.
82. See ibid McNeil 42.
83. Gray (n 8) 21.
84. Newman, "Legal Reality" (n 24) 15.
85. *Behn* (n 25) [30].
86. *Labrador Métis Nation* (n 41) [46]; See also *FCMNA Local #125* (n 10) [374], [389], [403].
87. *Campbell v British Columbia (Minister of Forests and Range)*, 2011 BCSC 448 [91], aff'd 2012 BCCA 274 [*Campbell*]; *FCMNA Local #125* ibid [371].
88. See, for example, *Labrador Métis* Nation (n 41) [46]. See also *FCMNA Local #125* ibid [403].
89. See, for example, *Red Chris Development Co v Quock*, 2014 BCSC 2399 [*Red Chris*].
90. The exception is the Alberta Métis settlements legislation: see Chartrand, "Métis Rights-Bearing Community" (n 43) 173.
91. Madden, "Answering The 'Who' Question" (n 45) 32.
92. *Behn* (n 25) [31].
93. *Behn* ibid [5], [31].
94. *Labrador Métis Nation* (n 41) [46].
95. *Enge v Northwest Territories (Department of Environment and Natural Resources, North Slave Region)*, 2013 NWTSC 33 [205]–[206] [*Enge v Northwest Territories*]; *Enge v Canada (Indigenous and Northern Affairs)*, 2017 FC 932 [101]–[103] [*Enge v Canada*].
96. *FCMNA Local #125* (n 10) [422].
97. *Red Chris* (n 89) [41].
98. *Labrador Métis Nation* (n 41) [46].
99. *Enge v Northwest Territories* (n 95) [206].
100. *Red Chris* (n 89) [41].
101. *Enge v Canada* (n 95) [102].
102. Ibid [102], [108].

103. Ibid [108].
104. *FCMNA Local #125* (n 10) [404].
105. Isaac (n 8) [14].
106. See *Métis Nation of Ontario Secretariat Act, 2015*, SO 2015, c 39 [*Secretariat Act*].
107. *Statement of Prime Purpose*, being "Appendix A" to Bylaws (n 116) 22 [*Statement of Prime Purpose*].
108. Ibid.
109. *Secretariat Act* (n 106) 1st preambular para.
110. *FCMNA Local #125* (n 10) [393].
111. Ibid [411]. See also *Campbell* (n 87) [153], [160]–[161].
112. This may explain why the court did not require coterminous populations in *Red Chris* (n 89) [41].
113. This may explain why the courts did not require coterminous populations in *Labrador Métis Nation* (n 41) [46], or in *Enge v Northwest Territories* (n 95) [205]–[206].
114. Métis Nation of Ontario Community Charter Agreement <www.metisnation.org/media/283015/kenora%20metis%20council%20community%20charter%20march%202011.pdf> [Community Charter Agreement].
115. Ibid 11th preambular para, s 3.2.
116. MNO Secretariat Bylaws (AGA Approved August 28, 2016) at ss 1, 2 <www.metisnation.org/media/653353/mno-bylaws-aug-29-2016-registered-aga-approved.pdf> [Bylaws].
117. *Secretariat Act* (n 106) 1st preambular para.
118. Andrea Carmen, "The Right to Free, Prior, and Informed Consent: A Framework for Harmonious Relations and New Processes for Redress" in Jackie Hartley, Paul Joffe, and Jennifer Preston (eds), *Realizing the UN Declaration on the Rights of Indigenous Peoples: Triumph, Hope and Action* (Purich Publishing Ltd 2010) 120.
119. *Tsilhqot'in CA* (n 69) [146], discussed above at text accompanying notes 71–72.
120. See Chartrand, "Métis Rights-Bearing Community" (n 43) 184; For a discussion of the Métis tradition of constituting and reconstituting jurisdiction-exercising collectives, see Adam Gaudry, *Kaa-tipeyimishoyaahk – "We are those who own ourselves": A Political History of Métis Self-Determination in the North-West, 1830–1870* (PhD dissertation, University of Victoria, Department of Indigenous Governance, 2014) [unpublished] Ch 3.
121. *Tsilhqot'in CA* (n 69) [151].
122. *R v Van der Peet*, [1996] 2 SCR [62] [*Van der Peet*].
123. *Delgamuukw* (n 17) [158].
124. See Signa A Daum Shanks, "The History and Promise of Shared Space in a Section 35 World" in Karen Drake and Brenda L Gunn, *Renewing Relationships: Indigenous Peoples and Canada* (Wiyasiwewin Mikiwahp Native Law Centre 2019).
125. See John Borrows, "Wise Practices in Indigenous Economic Development and Environmental Protection" 19; Dwight G Newman, *Revisiting the Duty to Consult Aboriginal Peoples* (Purich Publishing Limited 2014) 69–70.
126. *Tsilhqot'in CA* (n 69) [154]; See also McNeil (n 73) [15].
127. Ibid [152].
128. *Behn* (n 25) [31]. See also *Red Chris Development Co v Quock*, 2006 BCSC 1472 [15]–[16]; *Red Chris* (n 89).
129. *FCMNA Local #125* (n 10) [408].
130. *Nlaka'pamux Nation Tribal Council v Griffin*, 2009 BCSC 1275 [73] [*Nlaka'pamux Nation*]; See also McNeil (n 73) 37–38, 42.
131. *Nlaka'pamux Nation* ibid [4], [7], [44].
132. Ibid [75]; The Court of Appeal upheld this aspect of the decision: 2011 BCCA 78 [79], [81]; See also McNeil (n 73) n 132.

133. See Métis Nation of Ontario, "Lands, Resources & Consultation" <www.metisnation.org/programs/lands-resources-consultations/>.
134. I am indebted to Megan Strachan for this insight.
135. Consultation Agreement between the Métis Nation of Ontario and the Government of Canada, as represented by the Minister of Indian Affairs and Northern Development (July 31, 2015) s 5(b) <www.metisnation.org/media/652755/mno-canada-consultation-agreement-july-2015.pdf> [MNO-Canada Consultation Agreement].
136. Ibid ss 2(c), 2(e).
137. I am indebted to Megan Strachan for these insights regarding the benefits of the LRC Branch.
138. Carmen (n 118).
139. The Métis Nation of Ontario, *Towards a Consultation Framework for Ontario Métis—2007/08 Community Consultations What We Heard Report* (Métis Nation of Ontario 2008) 30–31 <www.metisnation.org/media/51968/towards_a_metis_consultation_framework.pdf> [*Consultation: What We Heard*]. I am indebted to Megan Strachan for this insight.
140. See, for example, Consultation Protocol—Lakehead/Nipigon/Michipicoten Traditional Territories (26 May 2012) s 2.8, 3.1(c) <www.metisnation.org/media/507393/mno%20consultation%20protocol%20-%20lakehead-nipigon%20(region%202).pdf> [Consultation Protocol].
141. Ibid 5.6(d), 6.1.
142. The principle that the MNO's "consultation processes must provide all Métis citizens the opportunity to participate and be heard" is also reflected in Métis Nation of Ontario, *Interim Statement of Principles on Métis Consultation and Accommodation and General Métis Framework for Consultation and Accommodation* (17 November 2008) 2 <www.metisnation.org/media/51971/mno_interim_framework_metis_consultation.pdf>. I am indebted to Megan Strachan for these insights regarding the benefits of the Métis Nation of Ontario's Consultation Committees.
143. *Consultation: What We Heard* (n 139) 22, 30. I am indebted to Megan Strachan for this insight.

Part III

Politics, Environment and Sustainability

8 The Contentious Politics of Impact and Benefit Agreements: A "Sons of the Soil" Conflict Perspective

Matthew I. Mitchell

I. Introduction

The growing international recognition of the environmental and social impacts associated with mining has led to important reforms in regulatory frameworks and measures to try to improve corporate-stakeholder relations. In response, there has been an upsurge of interest and debate surrounding the notion of Corporate Social Responsibility (CSR) as a framework for guiding mineral resource development.[1] According to Crowther, "[t]he broadest definition of corporate social responsibility ... is concerned with what is—or should be—the relationship between global corporations, governments of countries and individual citizens," whereas on a more localized level CSR concerns "the relationship between a corporation and the local society in which it resides or operates."[2]

The global push to improve relationships between proponents of natural resource extraction and local communities—notably, Indigenous peoples—has contributed to the development of a range of formal private contracts often termed "community development agreements" (CDAs) or "impact and benefit agreements" (IBAs). While such agreements are increasingly common in the Global South, IBAs in particular continue to play a much more prominent role in settler-state societies such as Canada, the United States, and Australia, where they have risen exponentially in recent decades.[3]

In concrete terms, IBAs can be defined as "confidential bilateral agreements, negotiated between mining corporations and aboriginal communities to address a multitude of adverse socio-economic and biophysical impacts that can arise from mining development."[4] Caine and Krogman echo the above in stating that "[d]espite the lack of a singular IBA definition, due in part to their context specificity and continually evolving nature ... they are commonly viewed as agreements that establish formal relationships between signatories, mitigate negative development impacts, and enhance positive development outcomes for Aboriginal communities."[5] Yet they critically note that although IBAs are contractual arrangements, they do not "fall under the purview of the state and thus fall within a historically uncontested, gray area of legality" sometimes referred to as "quasi-legal."[6]

The ambiguity and quasi-legal nature of IBAs highlights a fundamental feature of these agreements: they are a contested and often controversial form of governance. As such, while IBAs are heralded by some as a progressive tool for improving stakeholder relations in the extractive industries, others view their rise with suspicion and question the overarching value of IBAs. Rather than serve to mitigate or prevent conflict over natural resource development, there is cause for concern that IBAs could instead be a source of future unrest between mining proponents and Indigenous peoples. As O'Faircheallaigh[7] argues, the exclusion of Indigenous communities from key elements of the impact assessment process can create situations in which "communities have to deal with projects they have had no role in shaping, leading to conflict."

This paper expands upon recent literature on IBAs to examine the contentious politics around this emerging form of governance.[8] The paper breaks from previous studies, which have theorized IBAs from a "multilevel governance" perspective,[9] through the lens of anthropological performance theory[10] or via theories of neoliberalism.[11] Instead, it adopts a new conceptual and theoretical approach to study the potential *conflict* dynamics surrounding IBAs.

To do so, the paper employs a "sons of the soil" (SoS) conflict perspective to analyze the extent to which IBAs could serve to either fuel or prevent the outbreak of conflict. As discussed below, the concept of SoS is commonly used to explain Indigenous vs. migrant conflict over land, territory, resources, etc. throughout the Global South.[12] Yet as recent studies suggest, a SoS framework may also provide analytical insight for explaining conflict dynamics beyond the Global South in settler-state societies in the Global North.[13]

The paper draws upon recent developments in land use planning from the province of Ontario, Canada, to serve as an empirical illustration of the potential conflictual dimensions of IBAs. Specifically, it examines the government of Ontario's efforts to promote sustainable natural resource development in the northern regions of the province through the adoption of the Far North Act.[14] As I note below, this legislation could ultimately trigger a wave of IBAs in the context of future land use planning in the region. The significance of this development is further underscored by recent work, which suggests that the Far North Act could provide fertile conditions for future outbreaks of SoS conflict.[15] While the analysis herein is more exploratory than confirmatory, the findings underscore the critical need for more research on the conflictual dimensions surrounding IBAs.

The paper is structured as follows. The next section provides an overview and discussion of IBAs. In so doing, it identifies the origins and some of the contentious issues that relate to this emerging form of "private governance."[16] Section III briefly introduces the concept of SoS conflict and relates the framework's applicability to IBAs. Section IV then uses an empirical illustration through the case of the Far North Act in Ontario, Canada. This provides an opportunity to explore the link between the Far North Act and the potential conflict dynamics surrounding the potential increase of IBAs. Finally, the conclusion summarizes the arguments, identifies new directions for research, and outlines some wider policy implications for other settler-state societies.

II. Impact and Benefit Agreements: Cooperation, Controversy, and Critiques

While there has arguably been a need for CDAs for many decades now, such agreements have only recently gained ascendancy. A number of factors help explain this shift, including the increased capacity of local communities to mobilize, the growing national and international recognition of Indigenous rights, and the increased pressure on transnational corporations to operate with a "social license."[17] The significant rise of IBAs suggests that previous practices in resource extraction are no longer tolerated as meaningful consultation; and accommodation with Indigenous peoples is becoming a new norm.[18] In essence, IBAs are driven by the belief that "it is no longer acceptable to develop natural resources in such a way as to impose costs on those whose land is affected while the benefits are sent elsewhere."[19]

To explain the origins and appeal of IBAs we need to understand the broader legal context in which these agreements develop. For example, Gogal and others point to three legal requirements that help to explain the emergence of IBAs in the Canadian context: (1) the common law duty to consult and s 35 of the Constitution Act, 1982; (2) statutory requirements, including land claim or settlement agreements; and (3) regulatory requirements.[20]

The first requirement stems from the Supreme Court ruling on the legal duty of the Crown to consult Aboriginal peoples.[21] Although the Crown bears the legal responsibility to consult Aboriginal peoples, the authors note, "developers will likely be required to conduct the consultation as they are more knowledgeable of the project and its impacts."[22] Meanwhile, "statutory requirements" such as land claim agreements, oil and gas legislation, and environmental legislation now commonly require that proponents consult and engage affected populations in the development process. Finally, the authors note that "regulatory bodies generally require developers to consult with all stakeholders and mitigate the impacts from a project, which can lead to the negotiation of an IBA."[23] What is more, the adoption in 2007 of the *United Nations Declaration on the Rights of Indigenous Peoples*, notably its references to the concept of "free, prior, and informed consent" (FPIC) highlight the evolving landscape around the requirements for meaningful consultation.[24] In sum, this coalescing of legal factors helped create fertile conditions for the development of IBAs.

While the above highlights some of the main legal factors behind the growth of IBAs, there are additional forces behind their rise. For example, IBAs make good sense from a business perspective, as they align with corporate interests and arguably serve "to minimize risk and potential downstream project delays (i.e., costly litigation)."[25] These agreements can also provide proponents with an opportunity to secure the participation of local labour.[26] Finally, many argue these agreements can potentially reduce uncertainty in the development of natural resource projects. Writing about the mining sector, Fidler argues:

> Industry is aware that simply obtaining the requisite certificates, licenses and approvals to construct and operate a mine is only part of the overarching approval process. For the mining industry, which is time (commodity cycle) sensitive, it is imperative to have a social licence to operate and to ensure that business proceeds effectively with minimal uncertainty and opposition.[27]

As I argue below, this is a critical point given the evidence that *uncertainty* over property rights is a crucial factor behind many outbreaks of SoS conflict.[28]

Indigenous communities, for their part, have recently embraced IBAs. The rationale behind Indigenous support of IBAs includes "overcoming marginalization, strengthening regional economic and political sovereignty, and increasing control of resources to ensure regional benefit flows return to communities affected by development."[29] Many Indigenous communities have turned to IBAs to further aspirations and objectives that the Crown cannot or will not address. To quote Fidler, these agreements "can act as a layer of protection for Aboriginal rights, title and interests and can acknowledge issues Aboriginal peoples have that have thus far gone unaddressed by the Crown."[30] Owing to the high rates of unemployment, IBAs can also provide guaranteed employment opportunities for local Indigenous peoples who often reside in isolated and economically marginalized communities.[31] Finally, IBAs offer an improved alternative to the oft-criticized Environmental Assessment (EA) process which some have argued fails to adequately integrate Indigenous communities into the consultation process.[32] In sum, these factors explain why many Indigenous communities are increasingly eager to work with mining proponents to secure IBAs.

1. Controversy and Critiques Surrounding IBAs

Although IBAs may often serve to improve relations between mining proponents and Indigenous communities, many have voiced concerns over the rise of such agreements.[33] Despite recurring claims by stakeholders that IBAs often improve relations between mining proponents and Indigenous communities, after decades of implementation and hundreds of negotiated IBAs, there is little known about the actual success of IBAs.[34]

There are multiple critiques related to IBAs. Fidler and Hitch, for example, note that IBAs are perhaps weaker when compared with EA as IBAs tend to undermine the broader public interests related to environmental management in favour of prioritizing the interests of mining companies and local Indigenous communities.[35] Although one of the core objectives is to ensure that IBAs provide direct benefits to communities most affected by mineral development, there is also growing scepticism over how the actual benefits are distributed throughout the communities.[36] Finally, Fidler and Hitch point to another problematic feature of IBAs, namely, the (general) absence of the Crown in forging such agreements as "the Crown has the legal duty to promote reconciliation of aboriginal and non-aboriginal interests" and "to carry out consultation and, where appropriate, accommodation with aboriginal peoples."[37] As Peterson St-Laurent and Le Billon observe, the "instrumentalization of the industry's negotiation efforts by the government to partially fulfill their duty to consult exemplifies" the privatization of government functions while blurring the line between what falls within and beyond the legal purview of the state.[38]

Yet another concern relates to the power imbalance between mining proponents and Indigenous communities. This is nowhere more evident than regarding the issue of enforceability. While there is a great deal of time spent on negotiating business opportunities and key IBA provisions, there has been little focus on the enforceability of such agreements.[39] Caine and Krogman summarize this concern: "'Aboriginal peoples' inability to obtain legally binding agreements regarding the consequences for unmet industry promises represents one observable element of IBA negotiations in which the proponents have the power to avoid any specific sanctions."[40] There is a perception amongst many Indigenous communities that their sense of control or influence over the development of a given project is limited once exploration activities have begun. As such, IBAs "may be seen by Aboriginal groups as 'the best we can do,' given the perceived inevitability of the development and enormous wealth of the proponent."[41] Finally, given the uncertainty of obligations by government, and the wave of community consultants knocking at their door, many Indigenous communities are overwhelmed and thus often lack the capacity to participate in a meaningful way. This leads Caine and Krogman to conclude that IBAs can be a more attractive option "given that they allow more direct, face-to-face negotiation between one Aboriginal group and one company on key measurable benefits."[42]

Perhaps the most oft-cited concern over IBAs relates to the confidential nature of such agreements—a point to which I shall return. Given the private nature surrounding the negotiation of IBAs, they are difficult to access and consequently hard to evaluate.[43] Although Indigenous communities often request confidentiality clauses in IBAs—in order to prevent outsiders from gaining knowledge about specific land-based features on their territories, and to prevent Government funding agencies from knowing the amount of funds flowing from the IBA—these clauses present a number of significant concerns.[44] For instance, "there is a fundamental concern that IBAs may nurture injustice and hinder long-term sustainability if agreements are not procured in a manner that reflects the collective voice of the community."[45] These clauses could ultimately undermine democratic principles within Indigenous communities, as most community members are not able to engage in the decision-making process.

Furthermore, these clauses prevent Indigenous communities from learning from previous negotiations. This, in turn, means that they are not able to benefit from the useful precedents and learn from previous negotiations signed by other Indigenous groups.[46] To quote Caine and Krogman, Indigenous communities "are particularly disadvantaged in their negotiations with industry representatives who bring and incorporate valuable historical and collective corporate knowledge to the bargaining table through their lawyers and consultants."[47]

To summarize, while IBAs can serve as a novel governance tool when forged through a spirit of cooperation between industry proponents and Indigenous communities, they are not without controversy. As the above discussion highlights, there is clearly no shortage of critiques against their adoption and rising prominence. However, a key question remains: to what extent could the rising prominence of IBAs pave the way for future conflict between Indigenous communities and natural resource development proponents? The following section introduces the concept of SoS conflict to help answer this critically important question.

III. A "Sons of the Soil" Conflict Perspective

The concept of "sons of the soil" (SoS)[48] conflict has its origins in analyzing Indigenous vs migrant conflict over land, territory, and other resources in the Global South.[49] First introduced by Weiner as a framework for explaining native vs non-native ethnic violence in India's early post-independence period, the literature has recently expanded to explore conflict dynamics in more diverse geographical and political contexts.[50] As one influential study reveals, the historical scale of such conflicts is alarming as nearly one third of all "ethnic civil wars" fought between 1945 and 2008 can be described as SoS conflict.[51]

Notwithstanding the focus on ethnic conflict and civil war,[52] the outbreak of nativist violence and anti-immigrant sentiment in as wide ranging places as China, India, Israel, Sudan, former Soviet Republics, and various Organization for Economic Co-operation and Development countries, speaks to the global reach of such conflicts.[53] In so doing, this raises questions about the potential value of the SoS framework for explaining Indigenous vs non-Indigenous conflict beyond the Global South in settler-state societies such as Canada and elsewhere.

The standard definition of SoS conflict underscores the wider geographical and political relevance of this framework. According to Fearon and Laitin, SoS conflict can be summarized as follows:

> First, it involves conflict between members of a minority ethnic group concentrated in some region of a country, and relatively recent, ethnically distinct migrants to this region from other parts of the same country. Second, the members of the minority group think of their group as indigenous, and as rightfully possessing the area as their group's ancestral (or at least very long-standing) home.[54]

The above definition highlights the centrality of Indigenous claims to ancestral lands and the political significance of rootedness to territory. Moreover, it reveals the potential divisiveness of such claims. By virtue of having first-comer status, territorial claims are imbued with a moral dimension. The political symbolism of such attachment cannot be understated. In such a context, the arrival of non-Indigenous migrant populations can represent an existential threat to the survival of the legitimate "sons" of a given soil and thus constitute grounds for resisting outsiders.[55] This concept has clear relevance for explaining the potential for collective mobilization—and even violent conflict—in a settler-state context such as Canada. Although the country's Indigenous populations rarely self-define as "sons" of the soil, the French term commonly used to describe Canada's Indigenous peoples—*autochthone*—conjures the idea of attachment to soil.

In a more global attempt to decipher this emerging form of conflict, a recent survey of the literature highlights four enabling conditions or causal factors observed across a wide range of SoS conflicts.[56] These include: (1) increased economic competition and decline; (2) insecure and unenforceable property rights regimes; (3) political liberalization and competitive elections; and (4) horizontal inequalities. Though far from exhaustive, this list represents a critical set of factors behind many outbreaks of SoS conflicts.

To be sure, many of these factors are undoubtedly more relevant for explaining Indigenous and non-Indigenous conflict dynamics in the Global South where, for example, economic inequality and political liberalization and electoral competition are much more likely to be politically explosive.[57] As such, these factors arguably provide less insight into explaining prospects for conflict in settler-state societies in the Global North. Meanwhile, the concept of "horizontal inequalities" —the idea that growing overlapping group inequalities in economic, social, political, or cultural realms can coalesce to create violent group mobilization[58]—may offer some analytical purchase for analyzing SoS conflict beyond the Global South. After all, the economic, social, political, and cultural marginalization of Indigenous peoples has been a longstanding feature of settler-colonialism.

This brings us to the most compelling variable for explaining the potential escalation of SoS conflict in Canada and other settler-states in the Global North: the role of "insecure and unenforceable property rights regimes." Many scholars have underscored the link between competition over land and SoS conflict. Fearon and Laitin, for example, note that "sons of the soil facing competition from migrants for land appear to be particularly conflict prone—almost half have members involved in small scale guerrilla activity or more since 1980."[59] Territorial disputes and contested claims over territory are often relevant factors for understanding SoS conflicts in diverse contexts.[60] The ambiguous and contested nature of property rights regimes is common across these cases. This often enables political elites to mobilize supporters by instrumentalizing land grievances.[61] In a context of legal and political *uncertainty*, where weak and/or insecure property rights regimes reign, land can become a divisive issue pitting Indigenous populations against migrants. This perhaps explains why UNDRIP so emphatically advances the recognition and protection of Indigenous peoples' rights to their lands, and why FPIC is such a central component of the wider project to promote Indigenous rights at the global level.[62]

Though principally grounded in a broader review of SoS conflict in the Global South, these findings bear relevance to the Canadian context, notably, in relation to the rise of IBAs. This is because IBAs have become an increasingly prominent tool to try to overcome uncertainty around land rights. Given the enduring uncertainty and contested claims surrounding Indigenous rights to land in many settler-state societies such as Canada, a SoS framework may thus provide a useful framework for analyzing the prospects for nativist violence.[63] To be clear, there are obvious limitations to applying this framework to the Global North. First, and foremost, the socio-political conditions for reaching high thresholds of violent SoS conflict are arguably absent in settler-state societies such as Canada. Moreover, the escalatory dynamics commonly associated with SoS conflict would undoubtedly play out differently in cases characterized more by contested natural resource development than by contentious state-sponsored population settlements.[64] However, this should not preclude us from considering and theorizing the prospects of conflict and the role of IBAs in a political context such as northern Ontario. After all, as noted below, this region is home to Indigenous groups that have previously demonstrated their ability and willingness to mobilize against controversial resource developments.[65]

IV. An Empirical Illustration: The Far North Act in Ontario, IBAs, and SOS Conflict

1. *The Far North Act in Ontario, Canada*[66]

In July 2008, Dalton McGuinty, then Premier of Ontario, Canada, announced the launching of the Far North Land Use Planning Initiative. The core objective of the initiative was the development of community-based land use plans which would ultimately: (1) identify key areas that could be used to promote environmentally sustainable economic opportunities; and (2) ensure that large amounts of land are protected in the Province's Far North region. In developing these community-based land use plans, Ontario's Ministry of Natural Resources (MNR) promised to work in tandem with the region's many Indigenous groups. The MNR boldly declared that Indigenous groups would be able to "express what types of economic development activities they are interested in" as the "planning process for the Far North will be based on respect and a strong working relationship with First Nations."[67]

In order to give the plan legal weight, the government of Ontario passed *Bill 191: An Act with respect to land use planning and protection in the Far North.* Commonly referred to as The Far North Act (the Act), the Bill provides for the first time in Ontario's history a requirement to seek First Nations approval of land use plans on public land.[68] Though somewhat diverse in its goals, the core objectives of the Bill are as follows:

> The purpose of this Act is to provide for community-based land use planning in the Far North that, (a) sets out a joint planning process between the First Nations and Ontario; (b) supports the environmental, social and economic objectives for land use planning for the peoples of Ontario that

are set out in Section 5; and (c) is done in a manner that is consistent with the recognition and affirmation of existing Aboriginal and treaty rights in section 35 of the *Constitution Act, 1982*, including the duty to consult.[69]

Noteworthy here, is the reference in part (c) to the recognition of Aboriginal treaty rights, including the duty to consult.[70] While the Act does not go so far as to include language or requirements in line with the principle of FPIC, it nonetheless breaks new ground. This is the result of entrenching the doctrine of the duty to consult within the Act itself. As we shall see, this dimension of the Act has a clear connection with IBAs. By institutionalizing the requirement of consultation with Indigenous peoples, the Act could serve to trigger a rapid upsurge of new IBAs in future land use planning within the region.

Notwithstanding the government's—and some environmental groups'—enthusiasm about the Bill, the general sentiment is that the legislation is fundamentally flawed.[71] For example, both of the provincial-level opposition parties strongly condemned the Bill, arguing that the legislation would generate future uncertainty, disruption and even civil disobedience.[72] Numerous Indigenous groups have offered similar condemnations, many of which relate to the central critique that they were not meaningfully consulted in the development of this legislation.[73] In addition, there is widespread concern that the Act gives the Government final say over land use planning.[74] Unlike the doctrine of FPIC, which is often interpreted as granting Indigenous peoples a veto to prevent resource developments, the Act affords such groups much more limited rights related to consultation.

The statements of key Indigenous leaders captures the heated opposition to this legislation. According to Grand Chief Stan Beardy of Nishnawbe Aski Nation (NAN), who represents 49 communities under Treaties 5 and 9: "NAN First Nations and Tribal Councils do not and will not recognize this legislation on our homelands. We will continue to uphold our Aboriginal and Treaty rights and jurisdiction over our land. The real fight is just beginning."[75]

The tone of this statement speaks to the tension surrounding the Act in Ontario and the prospect for future conflict over resource development. In so doing, this underscores the importance of the following questions: could implementation of the Act create fertile conditions for an explosion of new IBAs as a means to overcome concerns that this legislation limits Indigenous decision-making power? In such politically sensitive contexts, could IBAs provide a tool for mitigating future conflict between Indigenous groups and stakeholders or ultimately pave the way for future outbreaks of SoS conflict? It is to these questions that we now turn the analysis.

2. IBAs in Canada and Beyond: A Source of Cooperation or Conflict?

The brief overview of the contentious politics surrounding the Act in Ontario illustrates the need for more meaningful consultation with Indigenous peoples.

From this perspective, the rise of IBAs may offer an improvement to past practices of natural resource governance in the Canadian context and beyond. Reviewing the positives of IBAs, Alcantara and Morden identify a number of potential advantages for Indigenous communities:

> Such agreements are flexible, dynamic and are negotiable within relatively short time frames, all without requiring major institutional reforms to the federal system or constitutional order ... These agreements may also bolster Indigenous claims to Aboriginal or treaty rights in a territory because they constitute a kind of formal recognition on the part of the mining company of an Indigenous group's right to exercise control over a given territory ... IBAs provide both substantive and symbolic value to Indigenous groups, and accord them governance space not otherwise provided by the Canadian federation in the formal distribution of powers.[76]

On the surface, the above points suggest that IBAs could serve to overcome some of the deficiencies built into the Act; the most relevant being that the Act is perceived by Indigenous groups as granting them little actual control in decision-making. Based on this logic, IBAs may be an antidote to a natural resource governance model characterized by interventionist government. On deeper analysis, however, there is cause for concern that notwithstanding some of the obvious benefits to IBAs, these agreements may contain the seeds of future (SoS) conflict.

The concept of Horizontal Inequalities provides some insight for explaining the prospects for IBA-related SoS conflict. As this framework argues, increased overlapping group inequalities across economic, social, political, or cultural domains can combine to mobilize identity groups who feel aggrieved. This connects with the idea of power asymmetries that feature prominently across the development of many IBAs. As Peterson St-Laurent and Le Billon remind us, "it is not uncommon for Aboriginal communities to enter the discussion over a mining project with limited knowledge, capacity and resources, placing them in a position of inferiority in terms of negotiation power."[77] The authors add: "[c]onflicts are particularly frequent when structures of power are unequally distributed and local communities' rights over development paths are limited."[78] Given the power imbalance between natural resource proponents and Indigenous groups, the cards are stacked in favour of the former. As one recent analysis on IBAs suggests, "[i]ntrinsic in IBAs is a potential for power asymmetries."[79] This power asymmetry can fuel the perception amongst Indigenous community members that IBAs disproportionately benefit stakeholders, often to the detriment of the local Indigenous community. As such, real—or perceived—increases in inequality can provide a spark for fierce opposition towards development and potentially even trigger violent resistance.

The idea of "legitimacy" is a related concept that connects IBAs with the potential for conflict. Writing about the implications of IBAs as an emerging form of multilevel governance, Alcantara and Morden contend that "[i]n the absence of formal institution-building, the question of who can legitimately speak on behalf of a government or community may be altogether skipped, and the legacy impact of existing institutional configurations may be profound."[80] This is a critical point as it underscores the idea that the formal decision to enter into an IBA does not necessarily mean that such an agreement is perceived as legitimate in the eyes of all community members. This is illustrated in the case of the Victor Diamond Mine (VDM) IBA in northern Ontario. As one study concludes: "[o]ur analysis of the VDM IBA affirms the concerns over the confidentiality of IBAs, but frames those concerns in relation to legitimacy considerations. The lack of transparency in relation to the IBA undercuts the procedural legitimacy of the arrangement, which was viewed as remote and opaque by the community."[81] This has implications for understanding the potential for conflict: while IBAs are partly intended to act as a legitimizing tool for development of natural resource projects, they may enjoy little legitimacy amongst an Indigenous population and instead raise suspicions and deepen cleavages.

How might IBAs come to be perceived as legitimate and what might this do to mitigate potential conflict over these agreements? It is worth quoting Craik and others at length to shed light on this question:

> Understanding the underlying factors that can lead to IBAs being viewed as legitimate by affected First Nation communities has strong potential, in our view, to improve the effectiveness of these arrangement to achieve their objectives, including the ongoing relationship between the resource sector and Indigenous groups and the broader public goal of reconciliation. In this regard, we have indicated that attention must be paid to matters such as the transparency of the arrangement, the form of participation in the negotiation and management of the agreement and the coherence between the substantive obligations and the broader normative environment in which IBAs are embedded.[82]

In other words, IBAs should be forged in a spirit of open consultation and cooperation.

This brings us to the final, and arguably, most significant concern related to the contentious politics of IBAs: the extent to which their lack of transparency may serve to heighten instead of reduce uncertainty over rights and access to land. The above discussion clearly captures the point that there are serious concerns surrounding the lack of transparency in the negotiation of IBAs.[83] Alcantara and Morden, for example, point to the confidential nature of IBAs, citing the impact this has on "the ability of Indigenous groups to examine and leverage other agreements," the impediment to share knowledge of the agreement with community members, and its creation of "political challenges."[84] One such challenge is that this prevents Indigenous groups from being able to engage in "various legal and regulatory processes (such as environmental impact assessment hearings, court challenges, and so on) and/or direct action aimed at halting a project."[85]

With the closure of these channels for critique and contestation, the likelihood of violent resistance to projects may increase. The uncertainty that this breeds is a key factor in outbreaks of SoS conflict. To reiterate, the literature highlights how insecure and enforceable property rights regimes can be a main driver behind SoS conflicts. Although the core objective of IBAs is to reduce uncertainty and provide guarantees, the confidential nature of these agreements can be a recipe for developing mistrust. As Craik and others argue, transparency is imperative in developing "IBAs since greater openness provides Indigenous communities with a basis for assessing the fairness of proposed arrangements."[86] Without meaningful and informed engagement and consultation on the part of a wide range of community members, the legitimacy of IBAs can be called into question. Herein lies the potential for SoS conflict, as efforts to move projects forward on the basis of approved IBAs may be met with fierce resistance if some members in the community challenge the entire premise and legitimacy of this private contract.

V. Conclusion

In concluding their assessment of the place of IBAs in resource governance in Northern Canada, Cameron and Levitan note: "[w]hen compared to past practices, where Indigenous peoples gained almost no benefits from extraction on their lands, IBAs surely represent an improvement."[87] As the above discussion reveals, IBAs offer an alternative form of private governance and many appealing features when juxtaposed against the longstanding status quo in Indigenous-state relations. Yet to view IBAs as a panacea for the governance of natural resource development in Indigenous territories is to fail to recognize some of the potential perils associated with these agreements. To quote Cameron and Levitan once more, the improvements wrought by IBAs must be weighed against the many concerns "among northern Indigenous leaders that IBAs are merely a 'quick fix' whose primary function is to secure consent for projects with significant long-term effects" and "that IBAs absolve the Crown of its responsibility to consult and accommodate Indigenous peoples."[88]

This paper adds to the list of concerns by advancing a new argument and approach that builds on emerging research on the contentious politics of IBAs. In basic terms, the central argument is that IBAs can heighten the possibility of SoS conflict in settler-state societies such as Canada. While the paper itself is more exploratory than confirmatory, it nonetheless identifies some of the common factors found across other cases of SoS conflict that may be present in the natural resource governance landscape in Canada. This is illustrated through the brief discussion of the Act in Ontario. To be clear, the paper is not intended to be predictive nor to suggest that conflict is likely to reach the threshold of violence experienced in high profile cases of SoS conflict.[89] The key objective instead is to shed light on some of the overlooked and potentially conflictual dimensions of IBAs. Despite some limitations in its applicability to a political context such as Northern Ontario, there is clearly demonstrated value in adopting a SoS conflict framework beyond the Global South.

One thing is certain: more research is needed to decipher the political implications of IBAs. As Peterson St-Laurent and Le Billon argue, research must be undertaken "to examine conflicts and possible court cases around IBAs to help reveal tensions and governance failure."[90] This could in turn "unveil Aboriginal groups' relative agency and mobilization of IBAs as part of economic and political autonomy strategies, and determine the context in which it is likely to exercise positive effects on the outcomes."[91] Given the opacity and the lack of transparency surrounding IBAs, this might be a tall order in light of the challenges associated with securing information on these agreements. As one recent study laments: "private IBAs are typically governed by strictly upheld confidentiality conditions. This fact presents a research challenge and makes a comprehensive overview of the content of IBAs impossible."[92] In an evolving political landscape in which FPIC continues to gain traction, the significance of these questions is bound to increase.

Despite the theory-driven nature of the paper, the insights from the case of Ontario and wider analysis on the contentious politics of IBAs highlight some clear policy implications. Central among these is the need for a more sustained and engaged role for the state in the development of IBAs. The selective absence of the state and shift to private forms of governance serves to absolve the state from many of its responsibilities.[93] While there are some obvious benefits to reconfiguring Indigenous-state relations, the increased role of industry does little to address the power asymmetries that often inform the drafting of IBAs. As one study concludes: "Although framed as a morally and politically appropriate shift away from paternalism, the neoliberalization of Indigenous state relations and state involvement in northern resource extraction risks ushering in new forms of dependency, even while it is rightly celebrated by Indigenous northerners as a rejection of longstanding, deeply colonial relations."[94]

This argument is echoed by a leading expert on IBAs who argues: "State authorities must be included in the equation, because despite its withdrawal from many areas of regulation that affect extractive industries, the state retains the power to make fundamental decisions in relation to approval and management of extractive projects."[95] What is more, the state must also play a critical role in mitigating the outbreak of conflict, given its monopoly on the use of violence and thus its responsibility to ensure and enforce security. After all, the consequences of future SoS conflict between Indigenous peoples and natural resource proponents could prove disastrous for many settler-state societies engaged in long overdue though politically charged reconciliation processes.

Notes

1. Heledd Jenkins, "Corporate Social Responsibility and the Mining Industry: Conflicts and Constructs" (2004) 11(1) Corporate Social Responsibility and Environmental Management 23; David Vogel, *The Market for Virtue: The Potential and Limits of Corporate Social Responsibility* (Brookings Institution Press 2005); Hevina S. Dashwood, "Canadian Mining Companies and Corporate Social Responsibility: Weighing the Impact of Global Norms" (2017) 40(1) Canadian Journal of Political

Studies 129; Archie B. Carroll, "A History of Corporate Social Responsibility: Concepts and Practices" in Andrew Crane and others (ed) *The Oxford Handbook of Corporate Social Responsibility* (Oxford University Press 2008) 19.
2. David Crowther, "The Maturing of Corporate Social Responsibility: A Developmental Process" in David Crowther and Nicholas Capaldi (ed) *The Ashgate Research Companion to Corporate Social Responsibility* (Ashgate 2008) 22.
3. Guillaume Peterson St-Laurent and Philippe Le Billon, "Staking Claims and Shaking Hands: Impact and Benefit Agreements as a Technology of Government in the Mining Sector" [2015] 2 The Extractive Industries and Society 590, 594–595.
4. Courtney Fidler and Michael Hitch, "Impact and Benefit Agreements: A contentious issue for environmental and aboriginal justice" (2007) 35(2) Environments 49, 50.
5. Ken J. Caine and Naomi Krogman, "Powerful or Just Plain Power-Full? A Power Analysis of impact and benefit agreements in Canada's North" (2010) 23(1) Organization and Environment 76, 80.
6. Ibid.
7. Ciaran O'Faircheallaigh, "Shaping Projects, Shaping Impacts: Community-Controlled Impact Assessments and Negotiated Agreements" (2017) 38(5) Third World Quarterly 1181, 1182.
8. Peterson St-Laurent and Le Billon (n 3); Ciaran O'Faircheallaigh, "Extractive Industries and Indigenous Peoples: A Changing Dynamic?" (2013) Journal of Rural Studies 30; Ciaran O'Faircheallaigh, "Community Development Agreements in the Mining Industry: An Emerging Global Phenomenon" (2013) 44(2) Community Development 222 [Ciaran O'Faircheallaigh]; Neil Craik, Holly Gardner and Daniel McCarthy, "Indigenous-Corporate Private Governance and Legitimacy: Lessons Learned from Impact and Benefit Agreements" (2017) 52 Resources Policy 379 [Neil Craik, Holly Gardner and Daniel McCarthy].
9. Christopher Alcantara and Michael Morden, "Indigenous Multilevel Governance and Power Relations" (2017) 7(2) Territory, Politics, Governance.
10. Philippe Hanna, Esther Jean Langdon and Frank Vanclay, "Indigenous Rights, Performativity and Protest" [2017] 50 Land Use Policy 490.
11. Emilie Cameron and Tyler Levitan, "Impact and Benefit Agreements and the Neoliberalization of Resource Governance and Indigenous-State Relations in Northern Canada" [2014] 93 Studies in Political Economy 25.
12. Myron Weiner, *Sons of the Soil: Migration and Ethnic Conflict in India* (Princeton University Press 1978); James D. Fearon and David D. Laitin, "Sons of the Soil, Migrants and Civil War" (2011) 39(2) World Development 199 [James D. Fearon and David D. Laitin]; Isabelle Côté and Matthew I. Mitchell, "Elections and 'Sons of the Soil' Conflict Dynamics in Africa and Asia" (2016) 23(4) Democratization 657; Catherine Boone, "Sons of the Soil Conflict in Africa: Institutional Determinants of Ethnic Conflict over Land" [2017] 96 World Development 276 [Catherine Boone].
13. Isabelle Côté and Matthew I. Mitchell, "Deciphering 'Sons of the Soil' Conflicts: A Critical Survey of the Literature" (2017) 16(4) Ethnopolitics 333 [Isabelle Côté and Matthew I. Mitchell]; Isabelle Côté, Matthew I. Mitchell and Monica Duffy Toft, *People Changing Places: New Perspectives on Demography, Migration, Conflict, and the State* (Routledge 2018) [Isabelle Côté, Matthew I. Mitchell and Monica Duffy Toft].
14. Bill 191, *An Act with Respect to Land Use Planning and Protection in the Far North*, 1st Sess, 39th Parl, Ontario, 2010 (assented to 25 October 2010), SO 2010, c 18.
15. Isabelle Côté and Matthew I. Mitchell, "The Far North Act in Ontario, Canada: A Sons of the Soil Conflict in the Making?" (2018) 56(2) Commonwealth & Comparative Politics 137.
16. Neil Craik, Holly Gardner and Daniel McCarthy (n 8).
17. Ciaran O'Faircheallaigh (n 8) 227.

18. Fidler and Hitch (n 4) 50.
19. Caine and Krogman (n 5) 76, 80.
20. Sandra Gogal, Richard Riegert and Joann Jamieson, “Aboriginal Impact and Benefit Agreements: practical considerations” (2005) 43(1) Alberta Law Review 43 129,130.
21. See Dwight G. Newman, *Revisiting the duty to consult Aboriginal peoples* (Purich Publishing 2014) for a comprehensive analysis of the concept of the duty to consult.
22. Gogal and others (n 20) 133.
23. Ibid 140.
24. Mauro Barelli, “Free, Prior and Informed Consent in the aftermath of the UN Declaration on the Rights of Indigenous Peoples: Developments and Challenges Ahead” (2010) 16(1) The International Journal of Human Rights 1; On the applicability and challenges surrounding FPIC in the Canadian context, see Ken S. Coates and Blaine Favel, *Understanding FPIC: From Assertion and Assumption on “Free, Prior and Informed Consent” to a New Model for Indigenous Engagement on Resource Development: Aboriginal Canada and the Natural Resource Economy Series* (Macdonald-Laurier Institute 2016).
25. Fidler and Hitch (n 4) 57.
26. Caine and Krogman (n 5) 81.
27. Courtney Fidler, “Increasing the Sustainability of a Resource Development: Aboriginal engagement and negotiated agreements” (2010) 12(2) Environment, Development, and Sustainability 233, 237.
28. Isabelle Côté and Matthew I. Mitchell (n 13).
29. Caine and Krogman (n 5) 80–81.
30. Fidler (n 27) 237.
31. Gogal and others (n 20) 147.
32. Ciaran O’Faircheallaigh, “Environmental Agreements, EIA Follow-Up and Aboriginal Participation in Environmental Management: The Canadian Experience” (2007) 27(4) Environmental Impact Assessment Review 319, 322–325; Peterson St-Laurent and Le Billon (n 3) 593.
33. Fidler and Hitch (n 4); Caine and Krogman (n 5); Cameron and Levitan (n 11); Peterson St-Laurent and Le Billon (n 3); Neil Craik, Holly Gardner and Daniel McCarthy (n 8).
34. Caine and Krogman (n 5); O’Faircheallaigh (n 7).
35. Fidler and Hitch (n 4) 66.
36. Ibid 63.
37. Ibid 52.
38. Peterson St-Laurent and Le Billon (n 3) 596.
39. Gogal and others (n 20) 157.
40. Caine and Krogman (n 5) 84.
41. Ibid 86–87.
42. Ibid 87.
43. O’Faircheallaigh (n 7).
44. Caine and Krogman (n 5) 86.
45. Fidler and Hitch (n 4) 66.
46. Ibid 64.
47. Caine and Krogman (n 5) 85.
48. SoS conflicts are commonly referred to as “conflicts of autochthony.” Though similar, the latter often describes conflicts from sub-Saharan Africa: Morten Bøås and Kevin Dunn, *Politics of Origin in Africa: Autochthony, Citizenship and Conflict* (Zed Books 2013); Quentin Gausset, Justin Kenrick and Robert Gibb, “Indigeneity and Autochthony: A Couple of False Twins?” (2011) 19(2) Social Anthropology, 135–142 provides a thoughtful analysis on the distinction between the notions of “indigeneity” and “autochthony.”

49. James D. Fearon and David D. Laitin (n 12); Isabelle Côté and Matthew I. Mitchell (n 13).
50. Peter Geschiere, *The Perils of Belonging: Autochthony, Citizenship, and Exclusion in Africa and Europe* (University of Chicago Press 2009); James D. Fearon and David D. Laitin (n 12); Matthew Mitchell, "Insights from the Cocoa Regions in Côte d'Ivoire and Ghana: Rethinking the Migration-Conflict Nexus" (2011) 54(2) African Studies Review 54 123; (n 48); Isabelle Côté, "Horizontal Inequalities and Sons of the Soil Conflict in China" (2015) 17(3) Civil Wars 357; Isabelle Côté, Matthew I. Mitchell and Monica Duffy Toft (n 13).
51. Fearon and Laitin (n 12) 200.
52. For a critique of the focus on the ethnic nature of these conflicts and on the category of civil wars, see Isabelle Côté and Matthew I. Mitchell (n 13).
53. Isabelle Côté, Matthew I. Mitchell and Monica Duffy Toft (n 13).
54. James D. Fearon and David D. Laitin (n 12) 200.
55. For a gendered analysis of the concept of "sons of the soil," see Isabelle Côté and Limingcui Emma Huang, "Where are the Daughters? Examining the Effects of Gendered Migration on the Dynamics of 'Sons of the Soil' Conflict" (2020) 43(10) Studies in Conflict and Terrorism.
56. Isabelle Côté and Matthew I. Mitchell (n 13).
57. Henrik Urdal, "People vs Malthus: Population Pressure, Environmental Degradation, and Armed Conflict Revisited" (2005) 42(4) Journal of Peace Research 417; Kathleen Klaus and Matthew I. Mitchell, "Land Grievances and the Mobilization of Electoral Violence: Evidence from Côte d'Ivoire and Kenya" (2015) 52(5) Journal of Peace Research 622 [Kathleen Klaus and Matthew I. Mitchell].
58. Frances Stewart, "Horizontal Inequalities and Conflict: An Introduction and some Hypotheses" in Frances Stewart (ed) *Horizontal Inequalities and Conflict: Understanding Group Violence in Multiethnic Societies* (Palgrave Macmillan 2018) 3.
59. James D. Fearon and David D. Laitin (n 12) 201.
60. Pål Kolstø and Blakkisrud Helge, "Yielding to the Sons of the Soil: Abkhazian Democracy and the Marginalization of the Armenian Vote" (2015) 36(12) Ethnic and Racial Studies 2075; Isabelle Côté, "Internal Migration and the Politics of Place: A Comparative Analysis of China and Indonesia" (2014) 15(1) Asian Ethnicity 111; Catherine Boone (n 12).
61. Kathleen Klaus and Matthew I. Mitchell (n 57).
62. Sheryl Lightfoot, *Global Indigenous Politics: A Subtle Revolution* (Routledge 2016).
63. See J. Andrew Grant and others, "A Historical Institutionalist Understanding of Participatory Governance and Aboriginal Peoples: The Case of Policy Change in Ontario's Mining Sector" (2014) 95(4) Social Science Quarterly 978 for a study on the institutional and legislative uncertainty in the area of mining in Canada (notably, the Province of Ontario).
64. See Côté and Mitchell (n 15).
65. Ian Ross, "First Nation pushes back against 'Ring of Fire' mine, rail project" (*Northern Ontario Business,* 26 January 2010) <https://www.northernontariobusiness.com/industry-news/mining/first-nation-pushes-back-against-ring-of-fire-mine-rail-project-366517>.
66. This section is an abbreviated and revised version of Côté and Mitchell (n 15) 144–147.
67. Ministry of Natural Resources, "The Far North land use planning initiative" <http://www.mnr.gov.on.ca/en/Business/FarNorth/2ColumnSubPage/266509.html> accessed on May 4, 2011.
68. Ibid.
69. (n 14).
70. See Newman (n 21) for a comprehensive analysis on the doctrine of the duty to consult.

71. Tanya Talaga, "Ring of Fire a chance to remake, or ruin, the North" (*The Toronto Star*, 27 March 2010) <http://www.thestar.com/news/insight/article/785429–ring-of-fire-a-chance-to-remake-or-ruin-the-north> accessed on 27 March 2010 (Talaga 2010a); Tanya Talaga, "Liberals push through Far North bill despite First Nations outcry" (*The Toronto Star*, 23 September 2010) <http://www.thestar.com/news/sciencetech/environment/article/865509–liberals-push-through-far-north-bill-despite-first-nations-outcry> accessed on 5 May 2011) (Talaga 2010b); Tanya Talaga, "Stop Far North Act or Face Conflict: First Nations" (*The Toronto Star*, September 14, 2010) <http://www.thestar.com/news/canada/article/860957–stop-far-north-act-or-face-conflict-first-nations> accessed on May 5, 2011).
72. Talaga 2010a (n 71).
73. Holly L. Gardner and others, "The Far North Act (2010) consultative process: A new beginning or the reinforcement of an unacceptable relationship in Northern Ontario, Canada?" (2010) 3(2) The International Indigenous Policy Journal 1 provide an extensive critique of the consultation process for the development of Bill 191.
74. Talaga 2010b (n 71).
75. Nishnawbe Aski Nation, September 23, 2010, NAN Releases Statement on the Passing of Third Reading of Bill 191—The Far North Act. Media Release. Retrieved from <http://www.nan.on.ca/article/nan-releases-statement-on-the-passing-of-third-reading-of-bill-191–the-far-north-act-638.asp>.
76. Alcantara and Morden (n 9) 12.
77. Peterson St-Laurent and Le Billon (n 3) 597.
78. Ibid 591.
79. Alcantara and Morden (n 9) 12.
80. Ibid.
81. Neil Craik, Holly Gardner and Daniel McCarthy (n 8) 385.
82. Ibid 387.
83. Cameron and Levitan (n 11); Peterson St-Laurent and Le Billon (n 3); Alcantara and Morden (n 9).
84. Alcantara and Morden (n 9) 8.
85. Cameron and Levitan (n 11) 34.
86. Neil Craik, Holly Gardner and Daniel McCarthy (n 8) 386.
87. Cameron and Levitan (n 11) 48.
88. Ibid.
89. James D. Fearon and David D. Laitin (n 12); Isabelle Côté and Matthew I. Mitchell (n 12).
90. Peterson St-Laurent and Le Billon (n 3) 599.
91. Ibid.
92. Alcantara and Morden (n 9) 7.
93. Peterson St-Laurent and Le Billon (n 3) 591.
94. Cameron and Levitan (n 11) 46.
95. O'Faircheallaigh (n 7) 1190.

9 Impact Benefit Agreements, Transparency, and Sustainability

Jason MacLean

In this chapter I examine the relationship of impact benefit agreements (IBAs) to environmental assessment processes, and IBAs' *potential* to serve as living laboratories of sustainability. I begin by discussing the critically important role that IBAs play regarding Indigenous rights and interests in Canada, a role that is all the more important owing to the failure of recent environmental law reform efforts to meaningfully advance the aspirations of the United Nations Declaration on the Rights of Indigenous People (UNDRIP) and reconciliation, let alone sustainability. Next, I briefly discuss sustainability as a form of experimental knowledge in order to explore the sustainability-enhancing potential of IBAs. I argue, however, that the lack of transparency surrounding IBAs' terms and outcomes undermines their ability to promote environmental protection and sustainability. I conclude by advocating for carefully tailored public disclosure of IBAs' terms and performance data to ensure IBAs conduce to the broadest possible environmental benefit.

I. Environmental Law Reform's Failures, IBAs' Futures

In Canada there are few statutes that facilitate Indigenous peoples' development and conservation of natural resources in a manner that promotes their own interests, including sustainability.[1] As Borrows argues, "[a] people's self-determination is strongest when their lands and people are physically healthy and self-sustaining and can act in post-colonial ways."[2] Canada's environmental protection and natural resource laws, however, "are not attentive to Indigenous self-determination in structuring Canada's wider policy framework."[3]

In 2012, the situation worsened substantially, as federal environmental protection laws were systematically attenuated.[4] These amendments had the effect of making it easier still for the Canadian government to develop lands in respect of which Indigenous peoples may lay claim on the basis of Aboriginal title, rights, or treaty protections.[5]

In 2016, after a change of government at the federal level, the Minister of Environment and Climate Change convened an expert panel to review and restore Canadians' trust in the government's environmental assessment (EA) processes. The Expert Panel for the Review of Environmental Assessment Processes (Expert

Panel), as it was called, solicited input from Canadians—including Indigenous peoples, environmental groups, environmental assessment practitioners, academics, industry representatives, and members of provincial and federal regulatory agencies—and held public hearings across the country.

In its final report, *Building Common Ground: A New Vision for Impact Assessment in Canada*, the Expert Panel summarized the views of Indigenous peoples in respect of environmental protection thus:

> Indigenous Peoples bear a disproportionate burden of development impacts. There is widespread belief that current processes fail to adequately account for Indigenous constitutional rights. Indigenous Groups across the country express a lack of trust in current EA processes, and there is a lack of confidence in past environmental assessment decisions. EA processes are viewed as being based on flawed planning, misinformation, mischaracterization of Indigenous knowledge and Aboriginal and treaty rights, and opaque decision-making. Many Indigenous Groups decide not to participate in EA processes, while others create their own parallel or independent assessment processes. Instead of advancing reconciliation, EA processes have increased the potential for conflict, increased the capacity burden on under-resourced Indigenous Groups and minimized Indigenous concerns and jurisdiction.[6]

Enter IBAs. Although private and confidential bilateral agreements between Indigenous groups and industry proponents, IBAs often contain provisions notionally designed to mitigate adverse environmental effects and, in so doing, assist in mitigating and accommodating impacts to Indigenous interests and rights.[7] Absent the adequate participation of Indigenous peoples in federal and provincial EA processes and natural resource decision-making more generally, IBAs have emerged as *the* principal mechanism by which Indigenous communities seek to negotiate environmental protections.[8]

Because IBAs are private bilateral agreements, however, the Expert Panel presumed that the role of government should be limited to ensuring that Indigenous communities are made aware—through the exercise of EA processes—of the full impacts of a project *prior* to negotiating an IBA.[9] This would be a marked departure from the usual practice in Canada, whereby IBAs are typically negotiated before the completion of the applicable EA processes. This, in turn, implicates the application of Free, Prior, and Informed Consent (FPIC) pursuant to UNDRIP. "To reflect FPIC," the Expert Panel observed, "all Indigenous Peoples who are impacted by a project have the right to provide or withhold consent. While Indigenous Peoples have the right to say no, the Panel believes this right must be exercised reasonably."[10]

The Expert Panel concluded its discussion of IBAs in relation to EA on an unusually—and, it turns out, unduly—optimistic note. "Going forward," the Expert Panel predicted, "IBAs will continue to provide Indigenous communities direct engagement with the proponent and an opportunity to shape the development of their traditional lands and to maximize potential benefits."[11] According to the Expert Panel, improved EA processes "may mean that Indigenous Groups will no longer need to rely solely on proponents to provide environmental protections, mitigations and opportunities for follow-up and monitoring." [12]The Expert Panel thus decided "not to make a recommendation regarding Impact Benefit Agreements."[13]

Following the release of the Expert Panel's final report, however, the federal government issued a short and sparsely detailed "Environmental and Regulatory Reviews Discussion Paper"[14] setting out a loosely connected set of ideas and once again inviting the public's input. The government's discussion paper effectively resiled from the Expert Panel's vision of the future of EA in Canada, including its recommendations in respect of sustainability and Indigenous peoples. In early 2018, the federal government tabled Bill C-69, which, among other things, was designed to repeal and replace the *Canadian Environmental Assessment Act 2012* with a new *Impact Assessment Act* (*IAA*).[15]

The *IAA* is mostly silent, however, on both UNDRIP and FPIC (and, for that matter, consent); UNDRIP merits a mention only in the *IAA*'s Preamble. Moreover, the *IAA* provides for an unduly narrow definition of Indigenous jurisdiction; only Indigenous groups having modern self-government agreements or EA powers conferred under other federal statutes are recognized as "jurisdictions" pursuant to the *IAA*. While the *IAA* contemplates an early planning phase for assessments, that phase—subject to the possible development of further, clarifying regulations and guidelines—will be shaped predominantly by proponents, who will be responsible for providing an initial project description and notice; Indigenous groups may well be unable to participate meaningfully—if at all—in this crucial, path-dependent phase of the government's new EA regime.[16]

Incidentally, these deficiencies might have been *partially* cured by the inclusion in the *IAA* of a regional EA regime. Regional assessments have the potential of identifying baseline cumulative impacts already experienced and understood by Indigenous peoples against which multiple projects can be assessed in a manner better suited to recognizing and implementing treaty rights than Canada's subsisting project-by-project assessment model. As the Expert Panel explained, regional assessment "can play a major role in managing cumulative impacts on matters of federal interest in an airshed, watershed or other regionally defined area. Regional assessments may therefore play an important role in addressing cumulative impacts on Indigenous communities and their ability to exercise their constitutionally protected Aboriginal and treaty rights."[17]

However, while the *IAA* mentions regional assessment, it does not define it, let alone mandate its use under any circumstances; its use is entirely a matter of ministerial discretion, and future governments may construe this option narrowly or ignore it altogether.

All of which strongly suggests that, contrary to the optimism expressed by the Expert Panel, proponent-driven IBAs are likely to remain the predominant governance mechanism affording Indigenous communities an opportunity to vindicate their rights and interests in sustainable resilience and self-determination.

This renders the Expert Panel's decision not to make recommendations regarding the reform of IBAs a sorely missed opportunity. Compounding the Panel's unfortunate choice is its unsubstantiated assertion that, because IBAs are private bilateral agreements, the government—and by implication, the public—has no role to play in their governance. Two compelling objections to this presumption immediately present themselves.

First, the rights in respect of which Indigenous communities seek recognition and accommodation through IBAs are in significant part constitutional: their source, other than in inhering in Indigenous peoples' own legal orders, is section 35 of the *Constitution Act, 1982*.[18] Indigenous rights and interests implicated by IBAs also sound in treaties, including legal disputes regarding their proper interpretation.[19] These rights are plainly a matter of public concern.

Second, the resource-based rights and interests that Indigenous peoples seek to vindicate through IBAs implicate broad public-interest issues of environmental protection and sustainability. As the Expert Panel observed, "Indigenous Peoples bear a disproportionate burden of development impacts."[20] This matter of environmental injustice is itself a necessary and sufficient reason to enhance the environmental governance features of IBAs. But owing to their cumulative nature, most such impacts are not limited to Indigenous communities, and cannot be effectively monitored and mitigated by either Indigenous communities or industry proponents. Rather, such impacts have broader, cumulative effects on the environment. Even if framed in terms of legal rights and interests falling within the inherent jurisdiction of Indigenous peoples' autonomous legal orders, the negative environmental externalities attendant to resource development can take the form of transboundary—*international*—pollution.[21] The environmental protection and sustainability measures of IBAs, which are discussed in greater detail below, implicate matters of broad public interest.[22]

Given the public importance of IBAs, and the Expert Panel's decision not to discuss options for their improvement, this chapter explores the strengths, weaknesses, and possibilities for reform of IBAs through the lens of sustainability. The first step in this exploration is a brief discussion of the concept of sustainability operationalized as experimental "learning by doing."

II. Sustainability as Experimental Knowledge

Sustainability remains a contested concept.[23] The Expert Panel's overarching recommendation that EA must "lead to decisions that are based on the five pillars of sustainability (environment, economy, social, cultural and health)"[24] was met with skepticism and strident criticism.[25] Sustainability, however, is an eminently workable law and policy tool. In relation to environmental impact assessment, sustainability encompasses both the positive and adverse effects of development in five broad "pillar" areas—environmental, economic, social, cultural, and health—in addition to their interactions.[26] Particular emphasis is placed on long-term cumulative effects and lasting wellbeing, and progress is achieved through improvements in: (1) socio-ecological system integrity; (2) livelihood sufficiency;

(3) intragenerational equity; (4) intergenerational equity; (5) resource maintenance and efficiency; (6) transparent and democratic governance; (7) precaution, prevention, and adaptive management; and (8) immediate and long-term integration of gains in each of these dimensions.[27]

This definition arises out of decades of Canadian deliberation and experimentation.[28] For some time now, experimentation—learning by doing—has been understood as crucial to facilitating the transition to sustainability.[29] Learning through participation in environmental impact assessments has emerged not only as a key means of identifying and strengthening the potential for lasting ecological, economic, and social wellbeing,[30] but also as a useful avenue for additional research and research-based practice aimed at incorporating and elaborating on the understandings, capacities, and motivations of multiple stakeholders across industry and resource sectors.[31] The public dimension of sustainability as experimental learning-by-doing is paramount:

> Mandatory monitoring and public reporting of effects in comparison with effects predictions, and of the effectiveness of responses to emerging problems and opportunities, will be essential to encouraging learning outcomes that are lasting and applicable beyond a single case. In this regard, an important facilitating step will be the establishment of an easily accessed, well-organized and searchable electronic library (or linked set of libraries) on environmental assessment case materials, including documentation of impact predictions and monitoring findings, records of decisions and justifications, and associated cases in law. *If made available to all, such a resource could be used by all parties in the assessment community to improve future project and strategic level assessments and decisions over time and to identify needs and opening[s] for improvements to assessment law, regulation and policy.* Regularly updating and upgrading guidance material and reviews of individual regime performance and progress towards *upward harmonization within and across jurisdictions* will also be required.[32]

The paramount importance of publicly available and assessable data to sustainability experiments,[33] and the potential of IBAs as such, is illustrated by an innovative action research initiative provisionally described as "Low-Carbon Energy Transition Learning Projects." Coordinated by Sustainable Canada Dialogues (SCD), a national network of interdisciplinary climate scholars, these co-learning projects seek to accelerate the transition to sustainable, low-carbon energy use.[34] Specifically, SCD's co-learning projects aim to (1) stimulate transformative low-carbon energy transition experiments, which are defined as initiatives led by proponents—be they provinces, Indigenous groups, on-the-ground businesses, municipalities, public-private partnerships, non-profit organizations—to instigate iterative "learning cycles" encompassing project design, implementation, evaluation, and readjustment; (2) stimulate co-learning to broaden and scale-up low-carbon energy initiatives via the establishment and coordination of a pan-Canadian transition experiment learning network; and (3) support the co-design of low-carbon energy policy options with Indigenous, federal, provincial, territorial, and municipal policymakers using transparent, publicly available data and evidence-based methodologies.[35] Structured this way, sustainability experiments can facilitate co-learning about socioeconomic change, including the scaling-up of successful initiatives; promote capacity-building; "de-risk" low-carbon innovation; and serve as a potentially transformational citizen outreach and engagement tool.[36] To fulfill their promise, the results of these experiments must be made public in an accessible form.

As envisioned by SCD's co-learning projects initiative, the aggregation of lessons learned could be supported through an online portal whereby project proponents can access evaluation tools as well as record their final project evaluations. This data, in turn, could then be made widely accessible to encourage further knowledge creation through the involvement of not only the broader research community, but also stakeholders and proponents of sustainability experiments, who can "adopt, adapt, and scale-up relevant technologies, practices, and business models. Such real-time knowledge sharing can build pride, show change is happening on the ground, and reinforce the notion that groups and individuals can actually make a difference."[37]

SCD's co-learning projects initiative is but one illustrative example of the experimental and solutions-based practice of sustainability research.[38] In the next section of this chapter, I discuss the opportunities and obstacles associated with utilizing IBAs to similarly contribute to our working knowledge of sustainability.

III. IBAs as Living Laboratories of Sustainability

IBAs are not merely private, bilateral agreements negotiated by resource development proponents and Indigenous groups. IBAs can also be thought of as potentially innovative—if presently imperfect—sustainability experiments. IBAs are concerned not only with resource access and financial benefits, but also much broader considerations, including: (1) special operating practices for environmental and cultural protections; (2) business and employment opportunities; (3) training and capacity-building; and (4) diverse community benefits.[39] Moreover, IBAs can help fill the governance gap discussed above. As the Expert Panel observed, "in the absence of adequate government consultation and accommodation, IBAs are utilized to secure additional mitigation and monitoring of impacts."[40] As one IBA practitioner argues, "[b]ecause of their progressive and creative environmental terms, this body of private agreements constitutes a new level of environmental management beyond provincial and federal regulatory regimes."[41]

Many IBAs, for example, contemplate the direct integration of Indigenous ecological knowledge into day-to-day project management. This can serve as an especially effective sustainability tool where baseline Indigenous ecological knowledge is established at the outset of a project, and subsequently utilized as a benchmark for safeguarding the sustainability of traditional hunting, fishing, trapping, and plant harvesting activities.[42] In most resource development contexts, baseline studies founded on local Indigenous ecological knowledge are sorely needed to precisely quantify contaminant levels prior to the initiation of new projects.[43] Baseline studies are especially important where there has been previous industrial activity in order to establish where a new project proponent's environmental responsibility begins.[44] As the Expert Panel observed, however, "current EA legislation does not require the integration of this knowledge [...] in EA, there continues to be almost exclusive reliance on western science in decision-making."[45]

IBAs can, and sometimes do, additionally stipulate that project operations *exceed* regulatory standards (e.g., enhanced water quality standards in ecologically sensitive areas; special, site-specific protections for medicinal plants not otherwise protected by legislation).[46] IBAs are also capable of establishing lifecycle project monitoring and fulfilling the largely unrealized potential of adaptive management.[47] In these ways, some IBA practitioners argue, IBAs are capable of offering "a more localized and refined layer of environmental management."[48] Some practitioners argue that IBAs confer considerable collective benefits: "Environmental protection measures common to many [IBAs] benefit not only First Nations whose rights and interests are affected by a project. *They contribute to better environmental management, the protection of biodiversity and the sustainability of natural resource development for the benefit of all.*"[49]

IBAs have enormous *potential* to serve as living laboratories of sustainability supportive of Indigenous rights. The striking difference between the nature of sustainability experiments discussed in the previous section and IBAs, however, is the confidential nature of IBAs. Absent publicly available and accessible information about both the environmental and cultural protection terms of IBAs and their on-the-ground applications, IBAs cannot facilitate the kind of experimental, learning-by-doing knowledge critical to the promotion of sustainability.[50]

The problems posed by the lack of publicly available and accessible data about IBA terms and, particularly, their on-the-ground environmental outcomes, are compounded by what appears to be the standard use of boilerplate contractual language that is, at least insofar as IBA environmental management and protection provisions are concerned, highly discretionary. Consider the following three provisions, which appear to be commonplace in Canadian IBAs:

> THE COMPANY will implement the management and mitigation measures required by regulatory instruments relating to the Project and use *reasonable efforts* to minimize or prevent adverse impacts of the Project.
>
> THE COMPANY commits to *consider* traditional ecological knowledge (TEK) delivered by the FIRST NATION in relation to the Project.
>
> THE COMPANY agrees to *include* FIRST NATION representation on an adaptive management advisory committee to be established by THE COMPANY in respect of the Project.[51]

Consistent with the highly discretionary nature of such commitments, neither TEK nor adaptive management is typically—if ever—binding on a project proponent's IBA Implementation Committee; the same holds in respect of IBAs implemented through a Joint Implementation Committee that includes representation from the Indigenous group designed to make recommendations to the proponent's management function.[52] Taken together, the lacuna in respect of IBAs' environmental management terms and their on-the-ground implementation outcomes significantly limits the contribution that IBAs could otherwise make to the understanding and promotion of sustainability.

In the next section, the arguments for and against IBA confidentiality are canvassed, and law reforms are proposed that are capable of simultaneously addressing the legitimate grounds of limited and carefully circumscribed IBA confidentiality while also allowing for the public dissemination and use of IBAs' environmental terms and outcomes.

IV. IBA Law Reform: Sunshine for Sustainability

Many Indigenous groups and project proponents alike maintain that IBAs should remain confidential and free from governmental regulation.[53] IBAs, these groups insist, are private bilateral agreements that, outside of the modern treaty context, should not be subject to regulation.[54] Proponents in particular argue that, because IBAs regularly contain commercially sensitive information such as financial contributions, employment commitments, and contracting commitments, they are specifically designed to be confidential as between the proponent and the Indigenous group.[55]

Some Indigenous groups also favour the confidential nature of IBAs because they fear—not unduly—a reduction in their federal funding were the financial terms of IBAs to become public. Indigenous groups are not incorrect to raise concerns about the potential use of IBA terms to counter their rights and interests. In the treaty rights case of *Yahey v British Columbia*,[56] for instance, the province of British Columbia sought an order for the production of documents from the Blueberry River First Nations, including "impact agreements with industrial proponents."[57] British Columbia based its motion for disclosure of the First Nations' IBAs negotiated with industry proponents on the argument that those First Nations have benefited from and acquiesced to industry development, and cannot at the same time argue that such development has breached their rights under Treaty 8.[58] The British Columbia Supreme Court (BCSC) ordered production of the IBAs entered into by the Blueberry River First Nations, holding that "[t]his is a novel legal argument in the context of a treaty infringement claim that raises novel legal issues, particularly with respect to the cumulative impacts on the exercise of treaty rights."[59] The BCSC further found that "these documents are pertinent to its [the Province's] pleading that Treaty 8 foreshadowed change and that the Province has managed that change honourably."[60]

Other Indigenous groups, however, argue that IBAs ought to be regulated and made publicly available and accessible to enable Indigenous communities to learn from each other.[61] Were IBAs not confidential, a body of environmental management best practices could be developed from the ground up.

Transparency around IBAs terms and outcomes would allow for the negotiation of IBAs capable of providing optimal benefits to Indigenous groups, and would ensure that the consent of community members is obtained.[62] As one leading IBA practitioner notes, "[t]here are hundreds of [IBAs] that have been negotiated [in Canada] over the past 10–15 years. Many of these agreements fly 'under the radar.'"[63] This hampers both their enhancement as well as their potential to promote sustainability more broadly, and strongly suggests the need for public disclosure in order to facilitate standard-setting and best practices: "all parties and the interests of sustainable development would benefit from standards or requirements, tailored to each sector [...] There are a few examples of requirements in legislation and Treaties. In general, these requirements appear to lead to more stable and mutually beneficial [IBAs] than in situations where there are no requirements."[64]

Regarding public disclosure, the connection to EA is once again instructive. The Expert Panel made two recommendations that bear on this issue. First, and generally, the Expert Panel recommended that monitoring and follow-up information about the effects of natural resource projects should be made publicly available. As the Expert Panel explained:

> One clear benefit to posting monitoring data publicly is the potential for that data to be taken into account in subsequent IAs [impact assessments], for example in the evaluation of cumulative effects. Over time, this would lead to a significant increase in the availability of IA-related data that could be drawn upon in other studies, eliminate some of the burden of data collection and increase the accuracy of impact prediction.[65]

The Expert Panel further explained that local community involvement in monitoring is a critical component of its effectiveness. Accordingly, the Expert Panel recommended that EA be reformed so as to ensure that monitoring and follow-up programs "provide opportunities for affected Indigenous Groups and local communities to be involved and to influence results and decisions on the need for adaptive management."[66]

As discussed throughout this chapter, however, the Expert Panel's law reform recommendations were largely ignored by the federal government; the *IAA* has been characterized as a missed opportunity, and with respect to Indigenous peoples' participation in assessment processes in particular, one commentator aptly noted that "the fog persists."[67]

For the foreseeable future IBAs will remain *the* mechanism for Indigenous communities to "negotiate environmental protections that are absent in the regulatory process."[68] While the Expert Panel was hopeful that EA law reform would mean that Indigenous communities would no longer need to rely solely on proponents to provide environmental protection, mitigation, and opportunities for monitoring and follow-up, and thus chose not to make law reform recommendations in respect of IBAs,[69] plainly such reforms remain necessary. But what form should such reforms take?

The Expert Panel's recommendations concerning the EA mechanisms of follow-up and monitoring provide a useful starting point. The Expert Panel recommended that "all monitoring and follow-up data, including raw data, results and any actions taken to address ineffective mitigation, be posted on a public registry."[70] The Expert Panel additionally recommended that "the results of inspections be promptly available to the public. An annual report of compliance with [project approval] conditions should be published in a public registry."[71]

A similar registry should be established for IBAs, subject to the lessons learned and associated best practices arising out of the design and use of EA registries.[72] The perfect registry, as true for IBAs as for EAs, "would be an organic and adaptive entity—one that grew with the availability of project information; it would be open to all, inclusion of material would be a requirement of proponents and relevant agencies. It would be complete; information would be posted in easily accessible formats and would be readable for broad audiences."[73]

Notwithstanding objections raised by proponents and some Indigenous groups, there is nothing inherently private about IBAs. In fact, IBAs are subject to the federal *Extractive Sectors Transparency Measures Act*.[74] In any event, arguable concerns about the disclosure of *financial* information are beside the point. Paramount to the promotion of environmental protection and sustainability is the disclosure of *environmental management* terms and those terms' associated performance data. The ideal IBA registry would ensure the prompt verification of reported data concerning the *effectiveness* of measures implemented to prevent or mitigate adverse environmental effects and to positively contribute to long-term sustainability. However, because the effectiveness of existing public registries in Canada and abroad is limited by "the protection of commercial and industrial information, intellectual property rights, protection of personal data, and public security and defence,"[75] in order to ensure effective reporting of monitoring, compliance, and effectiveness data, it is critically important that an IBA registry treat proponent-generated information as presumptively public and available, subject to a narrow legal requirement obligating proponents to establish a countervailing confidentiality interest.[76] As the Expert Panel explained in respect of EAs, such transparency requirements enable "sunshine compliance" at a low cost.[77] Crucially, they would also facilitate the kind of experimental, learning-by-doing approach to promoting sustainability discussed here.

Similarly, the ideal public IBA registry must also be developed in such a way as to ensure compliance with article 31 of UNDRIP, which recognizes the rights of Indigenous peoples to maintain, control, protect, and develop their cultural heritage, as well as "the manifestations of their sciences, technologies and cultures, including human and genetic resources, seeds, medicines, knowledge of the properties of fauna and flora [...] their intellectual property over such cultural heritage, traditional knowledge, and traditional cultural expressions."[78]

More generally, measures designed to unlock the sustainability-enhancing potential of IBAs must also contribute to a "just transition" to sustainability. As envisaged by SCD's co-learning projects initiative discussed above, sustainability transition experiments should recognize reconciliation with Indigenous peoples as a crosscutting objective. SCD's conceptualization of a just transition in respect of low-carbon energy experiments provides a useful frame for understanding the role IBAs could play in promoting both sustainability and reconciliation:

> Reconciliation entails recognizing Indigenous experts and elders as legitimate knowledge holders and participants, a structuring factor of the proposed management structure and research activities. In contrast to Indigenous peoples being the recipients of new low-carbon technologies produced externally, Reconciliation demands that Indigenous participation throughout the low-carbon energy transition be equitable and result in the repositioning of Indigenous peoples as drivers of a low-carbon energy transition that also leads to employment, technological transfer and full participation in public-private partnerships. Renewable energy projects have already enabled Indigenous partnerships, providing communities with new sources of funding and a transition away from diesel.[79]

V. Conclusion: FPIC and the Future of IBAs

The confidential nature of IBAs not only undermines Indigenous peoples' and all other Canadians' rights and interests in respect of environmental protection and sustainability, but it also exacerbates the absence in some—perhaps many—instances of Indigenous groups' full, prior, and informed consent to IBAs. This is particularly problematic in the broader context of the failed environmental law reforms discussed throughout this chapter. Consider the Expert Panel's finding about the negotiation of IBAs in respect of project environmental assessments:

> Indigenous Groups noted that Impact Benefit Agreements are often signed before an assessment is completed and the full knowledge of all impacts, including cumulative impacts, is available. Some Indigenous Groups do not want to discuss [IBAs] until they are fully informed of a particular project's impacts, *but they feel pressure, often in the absence of adequate government consultation, to agree to IBAs before a project is approved.*[80]

As the Expert Panel correctly concluded, this standard practice raises serious concerns related to UNDRIP's principle of FPIC. More pointedly, this standard practice arguably amounts to a form of economic-*cum*-environmental duress.[81]

Compounding this dubious practice is the standard use of contractual language designed to avoid disputes (e.g., certainty clauses) and channel disputes that nevertheless arise in respect of IBAs to private and confidential forms of alternative dispute resolution (e.g., mandatory mediation and arbitration clauses). Consider the following "certainty clause" from a Canadian IBA:

> In consideration for the obligations to be performed by THE COMPANY under this Agreement, the FIRST NATION acknowledges, covenants and agrees on its own behalf and on behalf of its Members and/or their respective heirs, successors or legal representatives that:

the FIRST NATION has been adequately consulted concerning the Project, including its potential socioeconomic and environmental effects and its impact on the Rights of the FIRST NATION;

the impacts of the Project on the Rights of the FIRST NATION have been adequately assessed and accommodated;

this Agreement, the Environmental Assessment Process and other regulatory processes relating to the Project provide opportunities to mitigate the potential adverse impacts of the Project;

this Agreement is entered into in full and final satisfaction of any present or future claim by the FIRST NATION for any infringement by the Project of the Rights of the FIRST NATION;

the FIRST NATION consents irrevocably to the Project and to granting each Authorization necessary for the Project;

the FIRST NATION will not, and will make all reasonable efforts to ensure that its Members do not, engage in any action that might frustrate, delay or stop THE COMPANY from proceeding with and implementing the Project, including challenging or opposing the granting or validity of an Authorization in any Proceeding on any grounds.[82]

"Certainty" of this kind is at the very core of the bargain of an IBA from the perspective of project proponents. Such certainty clauses are typically accompanied and reinforced by dispute resolution clauses mandating mediation and/or binding arbitration.[83]

The use of such sweeping clauses, which are not unlike the kinds of "rights deletion schemes"[84] and "litigation avoidance clauses"[85] typical in boilerplate consumer contracts, not only raises serious questions about the enforceability of IBAs, but it also further calls into question the ability of IBAs to vindicate the rights and interests of Indigenous peoples, including the promotion of sustainability. Analogously, the Supreme Court of Canada argues that as far as the relationship between access to justice and the rule of law is concerned, "[i]n some circles, private arbitration is increasingly seen as an alternative to a slow judicial process. But private arbitration is not the solution since, without an *accessible public forum* for the adjudication of disputes, the rule of law is threatened and *the development of the common law undermined*."[86]

So it goes for public interest matters of Indigenous rights and interests, including sustainability. Not unlike justice, sustainability must not only be done, it must also be *seen*—and learned from—to be done. Accordingly, contractual terms that serve to vitiate Indigenous peoples' consent as well as further remove IBAs from public scrutiny should be deemed unenforceable as contrary to the public interest.

Situated at the nexus of natural resource and energy development, Indigenous rights and interests, and environmental protection, IBAs have enormous potential to serve as living laboratories of sustainability, on-the-ground experiments yielding vital information about how we might more sustainably and more justly pursue economic development. Yet the confidential nature of IBAs' environmental terms and the complete absence of publicly available and accessible information about IBAs' environmental *outcomes* significantly limit the contribution that IBAs are capable of making to the promotion of sustainability. We may soon know more about the specific terms and conditions of IBAs because of legislative (e.g., the *Extractive Sectors Transparency Measures Act*) and judicial (e.g., treaty rights litigation) pressures for their disclosure. However, without further law-and-policy reform, either in respect of IBAs themselves or in the broader form of shared governance arrangements between Canadian and Indigenous governments with respect to economic development and environmental protection, we will remain in the dark about the sustainability outcomes of IBAs. And we will all be poorer for it.

Notes

1. John Borrows, *Freedom and Indigenous Constitutionalism* (University of Toronto Press 2016) 177 [Borrows]. A notable exception is the *Indian Oil and Gas Act*, RSC 1985, c I-7, complemented by the *First Nations Oil and Gas and Moneys Management Act*, SC 2005, c 48.
2. Borrows (n 1) 175.
3. Ibid 179.
4. Meinhard Doelle, "CEAA 2012: The End of Federal EA As We Know It?" (2012) 24 Journal of Environmental Law and Practice 1.
5. Borrows (n 1) 178.
6. Expert Panel for the Review of Environmental Assessment Processes, *Building Common Ground: A New Vision for Impact Assessment in Canada* (Government of Canada 2017) 26–27 [Expert Panel].
7. Ibid 35.
8. Ibid.
9. Ibid.
10. Ibid 29.
11. Ibid 35.
12. Ibid.
13. Ibid.
14. Government of Canada, "Environmental and Regulatory Reviews Discussion Paper" (Government of Canada June 2017) <https://www.canada.ca/en/services/environment/conservation/assessments/environmental-reviews/share-your-views/proposed-approach/discussion-paper.html>.
15. Bill C-69, An Act to enact the Impact Assessment Act and the Canadian Energy Regulator Act, to amend the Navigation Protection Act and to make consequential amendments to other Acts. Bill C-69 was enacted in June 2019.
16. For initial commentaries on the *IAA* in respect of its recognition of Indigenous rights and interests in EA processes, see, for example, Sara Mainville, "The Ghost of the Harper OmniBus Legislation Continues on with Bill C-69" (*Olthuis Kleer Townshend LLP*, February 2018) <http://www.oktlaw.com/ghost-harper-omnibus-legislation-continues-bill-c-69/>; David V. Wright, "Indigenous Engagement and Consideration in the Newly Proposed *Impact Assessment Act*: The Fog Persists" (*ABlawg*, 27 February 2018) <https://ablawg.ca/2018/02/27/indigenous-engagement-and-consideration-in-the-newly-proposed-impact-assessment-act-the-fog-persists/> [Wright, "Indigenous Engagement"].
17. Expert Panel (n 6) 76.
18. *The Constitution Act*, 1982, being Schedule B to the *Canada Act 1982* (UK), 1982, c 11, s 35.

19. IBAs are at the core of a dispute concerning alleged violations and competing interpretations of Treaty 8 in British Columbia. The province argues that Treaty 8 itself foreshadows changing conditions, and that it has managed that change honourably. This case is discussed below in connection with the confidential nature of IBAs. The background of the treaty rights dispute is described in *Yahey v British Columbia*, 2017 BCSC 899.
20. Expert Panel (n 6) 26.
21. As explained above, cumulative effects in respect of a given airshed or watershed may be registered in areas of overlapping and shared federal, provincial, territorial, and Indigenous rights and interests (ibid 76).
22. The *IAA* also disappoints in respect of its operationalization of the concept of sustainability. Most problematically, the *IAA* fails to mandate sustainability-based assessments and decisions, reverting instead to an opaque and discretionary "public interest" test.
23. See, for example, Jason MacLean, Meinhard Doelle and Chris Tollefson, "Polyjural and Polycentric Sustainability Assessment: A Once-in-a-Generation Law Reform Opportunity" [2016] 30 Journal of Environmental Law and Practice 35.
24. Expert Panel (n 6) 20–21.
25. For a discussion of this reaction to the Expert Panel's sustainability recommendations, see Jason MacLean and others, "A plan that promotes environmental sustainability" (30 May 2017) Policy Options <http://policyoptions.irpp.org/magazines/may-2017/plan-promotes-environmental-sustainability/>.
26. Martin Olszynski and others, "Sustainability in Canada's environmental assessment" (5 September 2017) Policy Options <http://policyoptions.irpp.org/magazines/september-2017/sustainability-in-canadas-environmental-assessment-and-regulation/>. See also Martin Olszynski and others, "Strengthening Canada's Environmental Assessment and Regulatory Processes: Recommendations and Model Legislation for Sustainability" (18 August 2017) <https://t.co/6WxDKmclBE> [Olszynski and others, "Strengthening Canada's Environmental Assessment"].
27. Olszynski and others, "Strengthening Canada's Environmental Assessment" (n 26).
28. See, for example, Robert B. Gibson, Meinhard Doelle and A. John Sinclair, "Fulfilling the Promise: Basic Components of Next Generation Environmental Assessment" [2016] 29 Journal of Environmental Law and Practice 252.
29. Ibid 268.
30. Ibid.
31. Ibid 269.
32. Ibid [emphasis added].
33. Transparent data systems capable of providing credible and timely information showing environmental, social, and economic changes are crucial, not only to sustainability experiments, but also to the achievement of sustainability more generally, including the UN's 2030 Sustainable Development Goals. See, for example, Jessica Epsey, "The missing ingredient for a better world: data" (2019) 571 Nature 299.
34. The "Low-Carbon Energy Transition Learning Projects" initiative is a work in progress. For more information, see Sustainable Canada Dialogues <http://www.sustainablecanadadialogues.ca/en/scd/workinprogress>.
35. "NRCan Follow-Up Questions for Sustainable Canada Dialogues to Guide Policy Discussions on the Proposed Energy Transition Experimentation Program." Unpublished manuscript on file with the author.
36. Ibid 2.
37. Ibid 3. For further discussion of this policymaking approach, see Jason MacLean, "Regulatory Capture and the Role of Academics in Public Policymaking: Lessons from Canada's Environmental Regulatory Review Process" (2019) 52(2) UBC L Rev 479, 539–547.

38. For a discussion of similar examples drawn from China and India, see Junguo Liu and others, "On knowledge generation and use for sustainability" (2019) 29(2) Nature Sustainability 80.
39. See, for example, Krista Robertson, "A New Deal" (*Canadian Bar Association British Columbia Bar Talk*, 1 August 2016) <https://www.cbabc.org/BarTalk/Features/In-this-Issue/August-2016/A-New-Deal> [Robertson, "A New Deal"]; Krista Robertson, "Impact Benefit Agreements—Not Just About the Money" presentation made to The Emerging LNG Industry and Aboriginal Relations Workshop (May 2014).
40. Expert Panel (n 6) 94.
41. Robertson, "A New Deal" (n 39).
42. Ibid.
43. Irene Sosa and Karyn Keenan, "Impact Benefit Agreements Between Aboriginal Communities and Mining Companies: Their Use in Canada," (*Canadian Environmental Law Association*, October 2001) 15, <http://www.cela.ca/sites/cela.ca/files/uploads/IBAeng.pdf>.
44. Ibid.
45. Expert Panel (n 6) 28. The Expert Panel defines Indigenous traditional ecological knowledge—commonly referred to as TEK—as "a subset of Indigenous knowledge which pertains specifically to the environment" (ibid 33).
46. Robertson, "A New Deal" (n 39).
47. Olszynski and others, "Strengthening Canada's Environmental Assessment" (n 26).
48. Robertson, "A New Deal" (n 39).
49. Ibid [emphasis added].
50. Confidentiality similarly limits scholarship on IBAs, rendering the academic literature on IBAs increasingly self-referential. This point was made by Ciaran O'Faircheallaigh in his keynote address to the conference out of which this essay collection arises: Ciaran O'Faircheallaigh, "Negotiated Agreements and Indigenous Peoples: Opportunities and Challenges," Keynote Address, Law and Politics of Indigenous-Industry Agreements, October 13, 2017, University of Saskatchewan College of Law.
51. Confidential IBA, provided via confidential personal communication dated October 6, 2017 [Confidential IBA] [emphasis added]. I have removed the names of the proponent (for which I have substituted THE COMPANY) and the specific First Nation (for which I have substituted FIRST NATION) in order to preserve confidentiality, and as a precondition of accessing this IBA in the first place. Based on this and other IBAs that I have accessed, these and the other contractual terms discussed in this chapter appear to be representative of IBAs generally.
52. Robertson, "A New Deal" (n 39).
53. Expert Panel (n 6) 94.
54. Ibid.
55. See, for example, John Olynyk, Keith B. Bergner and Lana Shipley, "Disclosure of Private Impact Benefit Agreements Ordered in BC Treaty Right Infringement Case" (*Lawson Lundell LLP Project Law Blog*, 29 January 2018) <https://www.lawsonlundell.com/project-law-blog/disclosure-of-private-impact-benefit-agreements-ordered>.
56. *Yahey v British Columbia* 2018 BCSC 123 (CanLII).
57. Ibid [4].
58. Ibid [40].
59. Ibid [43].
60. Ibid [44].
61. Expert Panel (n 6) 94.
62. As noted by the Expert Panel, ibid, some participants in the Panel's hearings suggested that the confidential nature of IBAs is not conducive to community

resilience because their negotiation is prone to being a leadership-driven process that proceeds without the consent of community members.

63. Woodward & Company, "Benefit Sharing Agreements in British Columbia: A Guide for First Nations, Businesses, and Governments" (*Ecosystem-Based Management Working Group*, no date) viii, <http://www.woodwardandcompany.com/wp-content/uploads/pdfs/4487_benefit_sharing_final_report_-_updated.pdf>.
64. Ibid.
65. Expert Panel (n 6) 70.
66. Ibid.
67. Wright, "Indigenous Engagement" (n 16).
68. Expert Panel (n 6) 35.
69. Ibid.
70. Ibid 70.
71. Ibid 71.
72. See, for example, Kevin Hanna and Bram Noble, "The Canadian Environmental Assessment Registry: Promise and Reality" (2011) 25(4) UVP-report 222.
73. Ibid 222.
74. *Extractive Sector Transparency Measures Act,* SC 2014, c 39, s 376. The Act came into force on June 1, 2015, but only payments made after June 1, 2017 are potentially captured. See Keith B. Bergner and John Olynyk, "ESTMA Update: Reporting Requirements Apply to Aboriginal Governments Effective June 1, 2017" (*Lawson Lundell LLP Project Law Blog,* 30 May 2017) <https://www.lawsonlundell.com/project-law-blog/estma-update-reporting-requirements-apply-to-payments-to-aboriginal-governments-effective-june-1-2017>. While payments made pursuant to IBAs must be disclosed, the IBAs themselves need not be. Nothing in the Act, however, specifically precludes fuller disclosure.
75. Lisa F. Odparlik and Johann Koppel, "Access to information and the role of environmental assessment registries for public participation" (2013) 31(4) Impact Assessment and Project Appraisal 324, 330.
76. Olszynski and others, "Strengthening Canada's Environmental Assessment" (n 26) 15.
77. Expert Panel (n 6) 71.
78. UN General Assembly, *United Nations Declaration on the Rights of Indigenous Peoples: resolution adopted by the General Assembly,* 2 October 2007, A/RES/61/295, <https://www.refworld.org/docid/471355a82.html>.
79. "Government of Canada Networks of Centres of Excellent Letter of Intent (LOI) Application Form" (14 November 2017) 5, unpublished manuscript on file with the author. For an excellent introduction to the "just transition" concept and the broader environmental justice literature from which it originates, see Ryan Holifield, Jayajit Chakraborty and Gordon Walker (eds), *The Routledge Handbook of Environmental Justice* (Routledge 2018).
80. Expert Panel (n 6) 94 [emphasis added].
81. Economic duress, as an excuse for non-performance of a contract, is established by demonstrating the presence of impermissible pressure that leaves a party with no practical alternative but to agree. See, for example, John D. McCamus, *The Law of Contracts* (Irwin Law 2012) 385–402.
82. Confidential IBA (n 51).
83. The virtually universal inclusion of such dispute resolution clauses in IBAs helps explain why there are no reported judicial decisions concerning alleged breaches of IBAs in Canada. See, for example, Krista Robertson, "'Peace is not the absence of conflict but the ability to deal with it': Dispute Resolution Clauses in IBAs—First Nations Perspective," presentation made to the Pacific Law and Business Institute, Aboriginal Impact and Benefit Agreements: Negotiation and Implementation, March 5–6, 2015.

84. Margaret Jane Radin, *Boilerplate: The Fine Print, Vanishing Rights, and the Rule of Law* (Princeton University Press 2013) 16.
85. Julie E. Cohen, "Law for the Platform Economy" [2017] 51 U.C. Davis Law Review 133, 179.
86. *Hryniak v Mauldin*, [2014] 1 SCR 87 [26] [emphasis added].

10 The Relationship between Indigenous-Industry Agreements and Environmental Assessment: Enhanced Credibility and Collaboration, or Undermining the Project Review Process?

Bram Noble

I. Introduction

Environmental assessment (EA) is one of the most widely practiced environmental management tools in the world. Since first introduced in 1970 in the United States, some form of EA is now required in 191 member nations of the United Nations[1]—either through national legislation or by way of international conventions, agreements, and protocols.[2] Despite jurisdictional differences, EA is fundamentally a deliberative process for identifying and evaluating the potential environmental and social impacts of a proposed development, and determining the strategies for managing adverse impacts and creating or enhancing positive ones.[3] In principle, EA ensures that affected interests, including the public and Indigenous peoples, and regulatory decision-makers are aware of the range of potential impacts associated with a project and the efficacy of impact mitigation and benefits commitments such that informed decisions can be made about a project's acceptability.

Indigenous-industry agreements, in contrast, such as impact and benefit agreements, environmental agreements, mutual benefits agreements, or socio-economic agreements are private, bilateral arrangements between an industry proponent and (usually) an affected Indigenous group. With few exceptions, governments are not directly involved in the development and negotiation of these agreements.[4] O'Faircheallaigh explains that such agreements typically include negotiated measures to mitigate adverse project impacts, and to ensure that Indigenous peoples benefit from project contracting and employment opportunities.[5] For Indigenous communities, Indigenous-industry agreements provide, among other things, assurance of benefits from development they may not otherwise receive.[6] For proponents, Indigenous-industry agreements provide some level of guaranteed support for a project, especially during the EA review and licensing process.[7]

Indigenous-industry agreements are now common practice in the resource sector, and for most companies and Indigenous communities they are an accepted part of doing business.[8] According to the Mining Association of Canada, since the mid-1970s more than 300 agreements have been negotiated across Canada for mining projects alone.[9] O'Faircheallaigh reports that agreements are also increasingly being negotiated in many developing countries, such as Peru, Bolivia, and Papua New Guinea.[10] Such agreements can provide Indigenous communities affected by development with benefits that the EA process simply cannot deliver—and in some cases, was never intended to deliver.[11] That said, the relationship between EA and Indigenous-industry agreements remains a contested one. Privatizing mitigation and negotiations about the acceptability of a project's impacts may undermine the deliberative value of the public EA process, and compromise the knowledge base on which development consent is given regulatory decisions made.[12]

Much has been written about the value of Indigenous-industry agreements with respect to the impacts and benefits that accrue to Indigenous peoples, but there has been only limited analysis of the relationship between privately negotiated agreements, the public EA process, and Indigenous peoples' free, prior and informed consent (FPIC) to project development.[13] The 2017 Expert Panel commissioned by the Minister of the Environment and Climate Change—which reviewed federal EA in Canada and made recommendations for reform that led to the changes made through Bill C-69 and the adoption of the *Impact Assessment Act* in place of the *Canadian Environmental Assessment Act, 2012*—acknowledged the increasing role of negotiated agreements. But the Expert Panel chose not to make a recommendation regarding Indigenous-industry agreements, or how they should be treated under federal EA law.[14] This is notwithstanding previous calls from industry for increased clarity of the role of agreements in the context of the overall process for the assessment, approval, and regulation of project developments.[15]

This paper steps back from recent debates about the value-added of Indigenous-industry agreements for Indigenous peoples. It examines the merit of such agreements from the perspective of 'good practice' EA as an open, informed, and accountable process for identifying, assessing, consenting to, and finding ways to manage the potential impacts of proposed resource development projects. The subject is approached from the perspective of EA scholarship, and draws on the author's experience from the field as an EA practitioner and consultant, both for project proponents and Indigenous communities.

The sections that follow first provide a primer on EA, highlighting its fundamental purpose, state of practice, and rationale for the emergence of privately negotiated Indigenous-industry agreements as an adjunct to EA. This is followed by an analysis of the relationship between EA and Indigenous-industry agreements. Attention is focussed on the sequencing of agreements in the planning, decision-making, and impact management process, along with the implications for credible EA. The paper concludes by highlighting the reforms needed to improve the Indigenous-industry agreement-EA relationship.

II. Environment Assessment

Environmental assessment is a planning and decision-support tool intended to minimize or avoid adverse environmental effects before they occur, and to incorporate environmental factors into decision-making. However, expectations about EA vary considerably. Cashmore explains that for some, EA is a scientific exercise designed to test hypotheses and generate new understandings about the functioning of environmental systems and how they respond to human perturbations. For others, EA is a means to empower local communities to make decisions and chart their own course in terms of resource development and self-governance.[16] Arguably, the *practice* of EA reflects neither of these norms; rather, the EA process brokers knowledge or, more realistically, provides information about the likely impacts of a proposed undertaking and how best to manage them.[17]

Environmental assessment is informed by science and technology, and by the knowledge and insight gained through the participation of the potentially affected Indigenous communities, public interests, and other experts. It is fundamentally a means to ensure that at least some forethought and foresight are given to proposed development projects before they become a reality. Over the short term, EA is intended to: ensure that environmental and socioeconomic factors are explicitly addressed in decision-making; to improve the design of a proposed development undertaking; to anticipate, avoid, minimize, or offset potentially adverse effects; to ensure a proponent's accountability and compliance with relevant laws and regulations; and to provide a fair, meaningful, and transparent process for public participation in the development process.[18]

Systems of EA vary internationally, and across Canada, but the EA process is usually triggered when a proponent submits a project application indicating an intent to develop.[19] The designated government agency then determines whether, and to what extent, a formal EA is required.[20] At this stage, it is expected that a project proponent has already begun engagement with those Indigenous communities or interests potentially affected by the project; however, practice varies considerably and the meaningfulness and extent of early engagement has traditionally been at the discretion of the project proponent. If an EA is required, terms of reference are issued for the assessment, based on input from the proponent, regulators, and the public. The project proponent is normally responsible for conducting the assessment of the project's potential impacts, and identifying impact management strategies. This is followed by a technical and public review of the impact statement and, in some cases, a formal public hearing—usually reserved for large, complex, or highly controversial projects[21]. A decision is then made by the responsible government authority as to whether the project should proceed and, if so, under what conditions. If approved, certain impact management plans and monitoring and reporting strategies must be implemented.

Environmental assessment can be a lengthy, heavily regulated, and adversarial process, depending on the project's characteristics, political interests, and whether the project proponent engaged with potentially affected Indigenous communities early in the process. Most EA applications across the country, however, are for routine undertakings with known mitigation measures, generating little to no concerns from affected communities. It is the large, politically contested and controversial resource mega-projects that receive the most attention.[22] Consider for example the proposed Site C Clean Energy Project in British Columbia, Canada—a proposal by BC Hydro to construct a dam and hydroelectric generating station on the Peace River to provide up to 1,100 megawatts of capacity and over 5,000 gigawatt hours of energy each year to the province's electricity system. The project drew significant opposition from Treaty 8 First Nations, including criticism from the national chief of the Assembly of First Nations over permits being issued for the project's construction despite ongoing First Nations protests. National Chief Bellegarde characterized the situation as forcing First Nations to court because the regulatory system is not designed to consider Indigenous rights *before* decisions are made.[23] Site C, and other projects like Kinder Morgan's Transmountain pipeline expansion, are the projects that tend to shape public understanding and perception of the EA process, and ones that can either strengthen or weaken relationships between industry, the Crown, and Indigenous peoples.

Participation during the EA process is intended to ensure that those who have a vested interest in a project—or those whose lands, rights, and values are potentially affected—have an opportunity to contribute to project planning and assessment, thus facilitating the exchange of knowledge, values, and information required for informed decision-making.[24] The interests addressed in EA are primarily the shared interests of society regarding the maintenance of an acceptable level of environmental quality, which may, at times, be traded off against social or economic gain.[25] The status of Indigenous peoples in EA can thus be problematic.[26] Indigenous peoples in EA are often viewed as one of many interest holders, alongside developers, regulators, environmental groups, and affected non-Indigenous communities and land owners who also play a role in the EA process.[27] Under most EA systems there is no *guarantee* that Indigenous traditional knowledge, interests, or concerns will determine, or even shape, EA decision-making processes and outcomes.[28] Papillon and Rodon explain that EAs create the space for debating with proponents the environmental and social impacts of a project, but they offer limited opportunities for Indigenous peoples to shape the decision-making process in light of these debates.[29]

Indigenous-industry agreements have emerged as a potential instrument, and often a legally binding one, to fill this void. They have *de facto* become an important mechanism for proponents to secure Indigenous consent to a project.[30] Bradshaw and Wright describe such agreements as a "convenient and practical way of addressing the duty to consult and accommodate legislation … as well as supporting FPIC principles."[31] The growing popularity of Indigenous-industry agreements is directly related to the growing dissatisfaction amongst Indigenous groups about their ability to shape, and benefit from development projects; coupled with the resulting frustration for project proponents when such grievances are aired as EA approvals and certificates are being sought.[32]

Indigenous-industry agreements are designed to minimize negative project impacts and ensure that Indigenous communities obtain benefits from development, thus helping to reduce or eliminate conflict and facilitate project approval—especially if negotiated in advance of the EA process.[33] Emphasis is most often on cultural, social or economic aspects, such as guaranteeing employment, local contracting, infrastructure investment, or revenue sharing opportunities.[34] Increasingly, however, agreements are also addressing biophysical impact mitigation, such as wildlife or habitat protection (e.g., Mary River Project Inuit Impact and Benefit Agreement; Meadowbank Mine Inuit Impact and Benefit Agreement), as well as longer-term environmental monitoring provisions (e.g., Athabasca Working Group 2004)—issues typically at the core of regulatory EA review and public approval processes.[35]

III. Environment Assessment and Industry-Indigenous Agreements: An Awkward Coupling

Indigenous-industry agreements are private instruments; EA is a public process. In principle, they can be conceptualized as parallel processes on parallel tracks, and as distinct processes with different objectives.[36] In practice, however, as agreements expand to capture biophysical impact mitigation and monitoring, and as EA expands to include social and cultural impact considerations, the lines between the two processes are becoming increasingly blurred. Indigenous-industry agreements are not meant to replace regulatory EA, but do they undermine it?

The timing of Indigenous-industry agreements relative to the EA process may have significant implications for EA and its role as a deliberative process for impact identification and management for informed, public decision-making. There are three basic windows when agreements are negotiated: (1) prior to EA commencement, during the early pre-project planning stages; (2) during the EA process, in parallel to impact assessment and mitigation planning and decision-making; and (3) post-EA, focussed primarily on impact management and monitoring (Figure 10.1).

These are not mutually exclusive—a negotiation process may commence pre-EA, but not be finalized until post-EA. Each of these windows of opportunity is briefly discussed below. The examples referred to are to illustrate the range of practice, and the different relationships between IIAs and EA. There is no intent to evaluate specific agreements or their meaningfulness to either the proponents or to the communities by way of benefits creation or conflict resolution.

1. Pre-EA Agreements

Agreements are often negotiated before EA commencement, or very early in the project design and application process.[37] There are many benefits to early negotiation; arguably the most significant is *certainty* provisions. For project

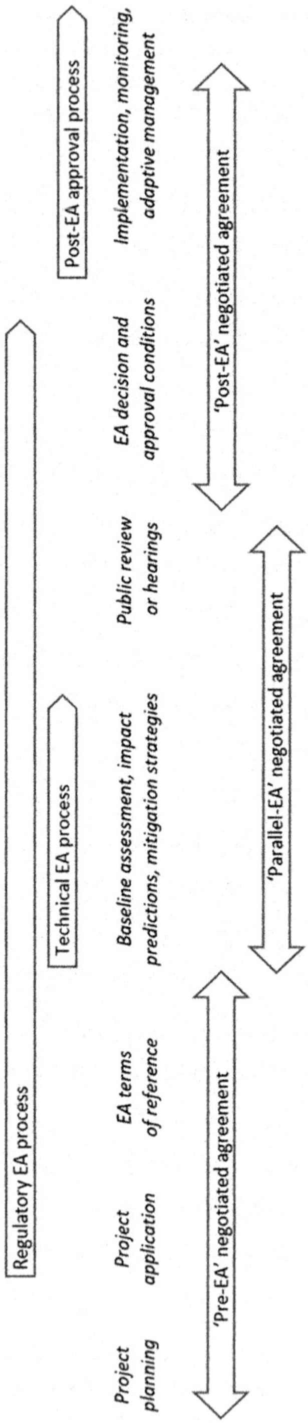

Figure 10.1 Timing of Indigenous-industry agreements relative to a typical/conceptual EA process.

Source: Prepared by author

proponents, Indigenous-industry agreements provide certainty (often legally binding) that the affected Indigenous community will consent to the project, or at least not publicly challenge it or air grievances during the EA process.[38] For communities, such *prior* engagement in pre-EA agreement-making provides an opportunity to exert influence over project design and mitigation strategies, and offers greater leverage to secure more favourable benefits from a project.[39] An Indigenous community may have no reason to support or enable a project without first coming to an agreement on the benefits it will receive[40]. In the case of the Orca sand and gravel mine in northeast Vancouver Island, British Columbia, for example, a pre-EA agreement between the project proponent, Polaris Materials Corporation, and the 'Na̲mg̱is First Nation provided the First Nation with power to veto the project up to the conceptual design stages of the mining operation.[41] This agreement paved the way for the Orca Sand and Gravel Limited Partnership, with the 'Na̲mg̱is obtaining a 12 percent interest in the project.[42]

Negotiated in advance of the EA process, however, agreements materialize under considerable uncertainty for the Indigenous community, and the community is less *informed* about the project's final design, potential impacts, and the efficacy of impact mitigation strategies. Negotiations unfold without the benefit of the knowledge generated through the public EA review process, including knowledge about environmental baseline trends, ecological limits or thresholds, and predicted or modelled future conditions, and in absence of knowledge about regulatory standards or requirements for impact management. Less information is available, to both parties, to inform the terms of negotiation.[43] Certain terms of an agreement may be open to renegotiation subject to new knowledge that emerges during the regulatory EA process, or they may provide additional compensation to cover any unforeseen impacts associated with a project, but this is not always the case.[44] Should new concerns arise during the EA process that may be deemed significant and adverse, communities may be bound by the agreement to not demonstrate opposition to the project.

The EA process relies on the information filed on the public record. Noble and Udofia argue that agreements negotiated pre-EA may limit the information that is available: (i) to other potentially affected communities, so as to understand the distribution of impacts and whether impacts and impact management strategies are equitable; (ii) to review panels who make recommendations to decision-makers about the significance of impacts and appropriateness of a proponent's mitigation strategies, and who may also commission independent expert reviews to determine the adequacy of those strategies; and (iii) to decision-makers who must weigh all available public, proponent, and expert-based information and make a determination of whether the project is in the public interest—including the interest of the communities directly affected.[45] The confidential nature of Indigenous-industry agreements can undermine the purpose of a public EA review process, and be detrimental to the Indigenous community should agreed-upon mitigation solutions be inadequate to address the full range and magnitude of a project's impacts.[46]

Pre-EA agreements can also raise serious concerns regarding the nature of the expressed consent, most notably its *free* and *informed* nature.[47] Although most often approached in terms of the relationship between Aboriginal communities and the Crown, there is concern that negotiated agreements may undermine the deliberative value of EAs for the negotiating community. Privatized negotiations tend to bypass fully informed community-based deliberations.[48] Confidentiality and non-disclosure requirements often imposed by project proponents can tie the hands of Aboriginal organizations and their ability to share information with their community members, or with other parties when involved further negotiations.[49]

In the case of the Galore Creek coal mine, in British Columbia, for example, Nova Gold's early negotiations with the Tahltan First Nation was instrumental in defining how the Tahltan and the proponent would collaborate to achieve EA approval.[50] Negotiations commenced in 2004, during the EA pre-application phase, with the agreement coming into effect part way through the EA process.[51] The agreement assured certain benefits to the Tahltan, in return for the Tahltan's public support during the EA process. The agreement was part of a larger negotiating process between the Tahltan Nation Council, developers, and the province, involving only a small negotiating team and in absence of the opportunity for broader community deliberations.[52] The result was fractions within the Tahltan community and accusations that the process did not respect the community voice. Agreements can deliver significant benefits to communities, but they can limit the opportunity for broader and informed debate during the EA process about the merits of a proposed development.

2. *Parallel-EA Agreements*

Simultaneous EA and agreement negotiation provides an opportunity for both processes to leverage information and input. In principle, the knowledge and concerns raised during the EA process can immediately inform and influence agreement-making, and vice versa.[53] In practice, however, the two processes may be in conflict given that they serve two different functions. The Voisey's Bay nickel mine project in northern Labrador is a commonly cited example of where the EA process and agreement negotiation overlapped. A focal point of the case is often the benefits the negotiated agreement provided to Inuit women.

O'Fairchellaigh reports that in the Voisey's Bay case, the negotiation process was inclusive of Inuit women, and that women effectively influenced the negotiation of the project's impact and benefit agreement.[54] Cox agrees, but suggests that the confidentiality of the negotiations also disadvantaged women who were also engaged during the parallel EA process.[55] Women could effectively leverage the EA process to have their concerns heard during the negotiation process, but the conflict between the EA and the negotiation process negatively influenced the ability of the EA process itself to establish concrete commitments. The project proponent often referred to the agreement as the solution to concerns raised during the assessment, but the ongoing negotiations meant that the details of mitigation strategies or commitments were confidential and thus not available to the public EA process. Cox thus argues that the ability of a project proponent to refer to confidential negotiations, but without providing details, as a solution to addressing concerns raised during parallel EA processes is problematic.[56]

Parallel EA and Indigenous-industry agreement negotiation allows a proponent to make undisclosed commitment to address concerns—commitments that have yet to be bounded by an agreement—and avoid putting those commitments to the public acceptability test during the EA process. In principle, the processes should be mutually supportive. In practice, the confidential nature of agreements may prevent the open flow of information such that both processes equally benefit from the other. Industry, Indigenous groups, governments, and the public require a clearer understanding of the appropriate boundary between negotiated agreements and EA processes.

The Canadian experience is in sharp contrast to the Greenlandic context, where impact assessment leads to an impact and benefit agreement with communities before a project can gain approval.[57] Greenlandic negotiated agreements, referred to as impact benefit agreements, are tri-lateral agreements between a company, community, and government and are required for projects subject to social impact assessments under Greenland's *Mineral Resources Act*.[58] Negotiations do not commence until after a draft impact assessment report has been produced by the proponent, along with a white paper documenting public comments and concerns that have emerged during consultation, as well as the proponent's responses.[59] The proponent's draft impact statement contains a benefit and impact plan, detailing how impact mitigation strategies and strategies to enhance local opportunities from development will be implemented. This information informs the impact benefit negotiation process. The agreement must be signed prior to project approval, but the agreement may require modifications to the proponent's proposed benefit and impact plan identified in its impact statement. The social and economic content of agreements are similar to Canada, setting such conditions as local labour and contracting commitments, infrastructure investment, training and education, protection of social values and traditions, and long-term capacity building.[60]

3. Post-EA Agreements

There are clear benefits to post-EA Indigenous-industry agreement negotiation. After a proponent has filed its project impact statement, but before impact management plans and monitoring programs are implemented, negotiations can proceed based on much greater certainty about anticipated impacts and mitigation. Community members may be more informed about a project and its potential impacts and benefits, including knowledge about baseline conditions and limits, cumulative effects, regulatory approval conditions, and proponent commitments. Post-EA agreements can also respond to shortcomings of EAs, by strengthening the requirements for follow-up, monitoring, and management of impacts through, for example, the development of participatory monitoring or impact management programs.[61]

However, negotiated post-EA, agreement-making is late in the project planning cycle—therefore there may be less opportunity for Indigenous communities to leverage benefits. The EA process itself also cannot benefit from any issues that may have emerged when negotiating the agreement, assuming such information is shared openly, and there is limited to no ability through the agreement to influence the types of mitigation or impact compensation measures that may become part of *EA approval* conditions.[62] In some instances, agreements negotiated post-EA have been described as "comfort monitoring" with no formal mechanism to influence project mitigation or decision-making.

For example, Noble and Birk report on an impact management agreement in northern Saskatchewan, signed between the uranium mining industry and seven communities in the Athabasca basin, to monitor the off-site impacts of uranium mining activity. Monitoring is conducted by the community, based on community-appointed monitors.[63] Data are analyzed by independent laboratories and results reported back to the community. The agreement was separate from the EA regulatory process and came after dozens of EAs had already been completed and projects approved. In this regard, Noble and Fidler explain that the agreement was designed to reassure communities that impacts identified in the EAs are being appropriately managed—even though monitoring data generated by communities are not directly comparable to those generated under regulatory-based monitoring programs.[64] The agreement does serve to build trust between the communities and the proponent, but there is no formal mechanism under the agreement for the community to stop mining operations, as in the case of Polaris Materials Corporation and the 'Na̲mg̲is First Nation; or directly influence mitigation practices should effects be detected.

That said, it is possible that the EA process itself can lend credibility to post-EA agreements or related programs and ensure influence over project mitigation and impact management actions. Consider, for example, Northcliff Resources Ltd.'s Sisson tungsten-molybdenum project, an open pit mining operation northwest of Fredericton, New Brunswick, on the traditional territory of the Maliseet First Nations. Northcliff signed a capacity funding agreement with the St. Mary's First Nation, Woodstock First Nation, and the Assembly of First Nations Chiefs of New Brunswick to support their participation during the EA process. The project was eventually approved by New Brunswick's Minister of Environment and Local Government in 2015, subject to 40 conditions. One of these conditions included the establishment of an environmental and socioeconomic effects monitoring program, and that the proponent strike an agreement with the First Nations to ensure ongoing capacity funding to participate in the development, planning, and implementation of the program.[65]

IV. Conclusions

There are many examples from practice where Indigenous communities have been meaningfully engaged in EA processes, and shaped not only the EA and decision outcome, but also continue to shape project impact management practices post-EA approval.[66] However, these cases are more the exception than the norm and increasingly Indigenous communities are challenging the adequacy of EAs to address their rights and interests. The solution, in part, has been to turn to privately negotiated agreements between project proponents and the affected Indigenous group to address concerns about the project, to leverage benefits from the project, to provide greater certainty regarding project approvals, and to obtain Indigenous people's consent to the project.

Such agreements do provide many benefits and opportunities to both communities and proponents that EAs cannot deliver, but they may also risk undermining the deliberative nature of EAs, informed consent, and informed regulatory decision-making when negotiated prior to the EA process and when the content of the agreement is not transparent. Four recommendations are presented below regarding the nature and timing of Indigenous-industry agreements relative to the EA process.

First, the timing of agreement-making during the EA process is critical to its role in facilitating informed EA *and* informed consent. Indigenous communities, through EA processes, need to be aware of the full impacts of a project before negotiating agreements.[67] Agreements may help support FPIC principles,[68] but when negotiated in advance of the EA process the Indigenous community entering the agreement are not fully aware of the potential adverse impacts of the project being proposed, whether the compensation provided through the agreement is sufficient to accommodate for those effects, and whether agreed-upon mitigations fall short of those that would be required anyway through the project regulatory review and approval process. To be considered an expression of FPIC, and not to undermine public EA debate, the preferred timing for negotiating or ratifying an agreement may be later in the EA stages—after a proponent's impact statement is submitted but before EA approval or certificates are issued. Communities still retain leverage to negotiate benefits, but they also benefit from greater certainty about the project's potential impacts, public and community concerns, mitigation design, and desired benefits.

Second, environmental impact mitigation strategies included in Indigenous-industry agreements also need to be transparent and made available to review panels and regulatory decision-makers as part of the public deliberations that inform EA processes. Any commitments regarding the mitigation or offsetting of environmental impacts that may have an impact on Aboriginal health or socioeconomic conditions, physical and cultural heritage, or the use of lands for traditional purposes, where such traditional uses and locations are not considered confidential, should be disclosed and available to regulatory decision-makers as it weighs the proponent's commitments and determines approval conditions. Non-disclosure of such matters may result in incomplete information about project impacts, and about the adequacy of the proponent's mitigation commitments—commitments that may prove inadequate to address potential cumulative impacts or impacts that extend beyond the scope of the Indigenous community. Privately negotiated impact mitigation limits information sharing and opportunities for proponents, communities, and decision-makers to learn from those projects that have come before.

Third, details concerning commercial interests or a community's financial gain (e.g., royalty regimes, contracting) may very well remain confidential from the public EA process, and from regulatory decision-makers. However, sufficient details should be shared with members of the Indigenous community to ensure a degree of transparency, but at the same time being cautious to protect the financial interests of the community. Agreements that are negotiated or implemented in complete absence of a community's knowledge of their content are not consistent with the notion of free and informed consent and can undermine the deliberative value of a public EA process.[69]

Fourth, the EA process must provide a lever to ensure that Indigenous-industry agreements include provisions that communities have the capacity to engage and the ability to influence impact management actions, post-EA approval, should adverse impacts be detected. Many recently negotiated agreements include environmental protection and monitoring measures that capture the entire lifecycle of a project.[70] In the absence of clear EA approval conditions, however, there is risk that agreements or post-EA monitoring activities provide no more than comfort monitoring for potentially affected communities—or are focussed on indicators that are unrelated to *actual* project-induced stress or that do not trigger regulatory response.

In conclusion, greater emphasis needs to be placed on strengthening the EA process such that Indigenous-industry agreements are no longer the default mechanism for meaningfully engaging Indigenous communities in resource development, and for securing development consent. Much can be achieved by way of early engagement in pre-EA project planning, before the regulatory process begins, which may reduce the need for Indigenous groups to rely solely on privately negotiated agreements. However, even in jurisdictions such as Canada where early engagement is a legislated requirement of EA,[71] there is no resolution as to the relationship between Indigenous-industry agreements and the EA process in terms of timing or transparency. Arguably, Indigenous-industry agreements do have a meaningful role to play in development planning and Indigenous people's consent, but they do not replace the importance of public deliberation through the EA process and they certainly must not undermine it.

Notes

1. Richard Morgan, "Environmental Impact Assessment: The State of the Art" [2012] 30 Impact Assessment and Project Appraisal 5.
2. For example: Convention of Environmental Impact Assessment in a Transboundary Context (adopted 15 February 1991, entered into force 10 September 1997) 1989 UNTS 309, art 2[2]; Protocol on Environmental Protection to the Antarctic Treaty (adopted 14 January 1998, entered into force 4 October 1991) 2941 UNTS, art 8.
3. Morgan (n 1).
4. Parliamentary Information and Research Service, Norah Kielland, *Supporting Aboriginal Participation in Resource Development: The Role of Impact and Benefit Agreements Publication* (In Brief), Publication No. 2015-29-E (Library of Parliament 2015).

5. Ciaran O'Faircheallaigh, "Shaping Projects, Shaping Impacts: Community-Controlled Impact Assessments and Negotiated Agreements" [2017] 38 Third World Quarterly 1181, 1189 [O'Faircheallaigh].
6. Agreements vary but they often include provisions for royalties or revenue sharing, employment, economic development, infrastructure investment, and environmental and socio-cultural protection arrangements. See Lindsay Galbraith, Ben Bradshaw and Murray Rutherford, "Towards a Supraregulatory Approach to Environmental Assessment in Northern Canada" [2007] 25 Impact Assessment and Project Appraisal 27, 28 [Galbraith, Bradshaw, and Rutherford].
7. Courtney Fidler, "Increasing the Sustainability of a Resource Development: Aboriginal Engagement and Negotiated Agreements" [2010] 12 Environment Development and Sustainability 233 [Fidler].
8. Marcello Veiga, Malcolm Scoble and Mary McAllister, "Mining with Communities" [2001] 25 Natural Resources Forum 191.
9. Mining Association of Canada, "Aboriginal Affairs" (*The Mining Association of Canada*, 2019) <http://mining.ca/our-focus/aboriginal-affairs> accessed 21 March 2018.
10. O'Faircheallaigh (n 5) 1189.
11. Rarely do EAs deal with such matters as project ownership or revenue sharing arrangements. See discussions on the scope and constraints of agreements in the context of EAs in Bram Noble and Aniekan Udofia, *Protectors of the Land: Toward an Environmental Assessment Process that Works for Aboriginal Communities and Developers* (Macdonald-Laurier Institute 2015) [Noble and Udofia].
12. Martin Papillon and Thierry Rodon, "Proponent-Indigenous Agreements and the Implementation of the Right to Free, Prior, and Informed Consent in Canada" [2017] 62 Environmental Impact Assessment Review 216 [Papillon and Rodon].
13. Philippe Hanna and Frank Vanclay, "Human Rights, Indigenous Peoples and the Concept of Free, Prior and Informed Consent" [2013] 31 Impact Assessment and Project Appraisal 146 [Hanna and Vanclay]; Ciaran O'Faircheallaigh, "International Recognition of Indigenous Rights, Indigenous Control of Development and Domestic Political Mobilisation" [2012] 47 Australian Journal of Political Science 531; Irene Sosa and Karyn Keenan, *Impact Benefit Agreements Between Aboriginal Communities and Mining Companies: Their Use in Canada* (Canadian Environmental Law Association 2001).
14. Expert Panel for the Review of the Environmental Assessment Process, "Building Common Ground: A New Vision for Impact Assessment in Canada" (Minister of Environment and Climate Change 2017) 28 <http://eareview-examenee.ca/> accessed 12 July 2019 [Expert Panel].
15. In a formal letter to Neil McCrank on the Northern Regulatory Improvement Initiative, the Mining Association of Canada, the Prospectors and Developers Association of Canada, and the Northwest Territories and Nunavut Chamber of Mines requested that the federal government develop immediately an official policy on the nature, scope and purpose of impact and benefit agreements. For further discussion see Tyler Levitan, *Impact and Benefit Agreements in Relation to the Neoliberal State: the case of Diamond Mines in the Northwest Territories* (Carlton University 2012) 104.
16. Matthew Cashmore, "The Role of Science In Environmental Impact Assessment: Process and Procedure Versus Purpose in the Development Theory" [2004] 24 Environmental Impact Assessment Review 403, 407.
17. Maria Rosario Partidário and William Sheate, "Knowledge Brokerage—Potential for Increased Capacities and Shared Power in Impact Assessment" [2013] 39 Environmental Impact Assessment Review 26; Aud Tenney, Jens Kværner and Karl Idar Gjerstad, "Uncertainty in Environmental impact Assessment Predictions: The Need for Better Communication and More Transparency" [2006] 24 Impact Assessment and Project Appraisal 45.
18. Noble and Udofia (n 11) 5.

19. For an overview of a typical EA process, including roles of the proponent and regulators, see Bram Noble, *Introduction to Environmental Impact Assessment* (3rd edn, Oxford University Press 2016) [Noble].
20. Provisions vary by jurisdiction. At the Canadian federal level, under Bill C-69, *An Act to enact the Impact Assessment Act and the Canadian Energy Regulator Act, to amend the Navigation Protection Act and to make consequential amendments to other Acts*, 1st Sess, 42nd Parl, 2019 (assented 21 June 2019), sec 2 [Bill C-69], EA is required only for certain "designated projects" that are prescribed on a project list, and that affect matters for which there is federal jurisdiction. Provincially in Saskatchewan, under *The Saskatchewan Environmental Assessment Act*, RSS 1978, e 10.1, s 2d, for example, EA is required on a case-by-case consideration based on project characteristics and local environmental context.
21. The minority of projects reviewed at the Canadian federal level are assessed by review panel, which includes those projects with the potential for significant adverse impacts, projects that are multi-jurisdictional in nature, projects that adversely impact Indigenous rights, or projects that are involve a life-cycle regulator. See Bill C-69 (n 20) s 36, 43.
22. Bram Noble, *Learning to Listen: Snapshots of Aboriginal Participation in Environmental Assessment* (Macdonald Laurier Institute 2016) 7 [Noble]. See also Marla Orenstein, *What now? The Fate of Projects: a Review of Outcomes from the Federal EA Approval Process* (Canada West Foundation 2018) for an overview of the number of projects submitted for EA review in Canada at the federal level.
23. Perry Bellegarde, "Site C Dam Approval Another Violation of First nations Rights" (*The Star* 28 September 2016) <http://www.afn.ca/uploads/files/parliamentary/ceaa.pdf>.
24. Noble and Udofia (n 11) 8.
25. Alastair Craik, "Process and Reconciliation: Integrating the Duty to Consult with Environmental Assessment" (Osgoode Legal Studies Research Paper Series 2016) <http://digitalcommons.osgoode.yorku.ca/olsrps> accessed 18 April 2018.
26. Papillon and Rodon (n 12).
27. Aniekan Udofia, Bram Noble and Greg Poelzer, "Meaningful and Efficient? Enduring the Challenges to Aboriginal Participation In Environmental Assessment" [2017] 65 Environmental Impact Assessment Review 164.
28. Ciaran O'Faircheallaigh, "Environmental Agreements, EIA Follow-Up and Aboriginal Participation In Environmental Management: The Canadian Experience" [2007] 27 Environmental Impact Assessment Review 319.
29. Papillon and Rodon (n 12).
30. Ibid.
31. Ben Bradshaw and Adam Wright, "Review of IBA Literature and Analysis of Gaps In Knowledge, Gap Analysis Report #9" (*Resources and Sustainable Development In the Arctic* 2013) 10. <http://yukonresearch.yukoncollege.yk.ca/resda/projects/gap-analysis/> accessed 12 July 2019 [Bradshaw and Wright].
32. Hanna and Vanclay (n 13).
33. O'Faircheallaigh (n 5).
34. Bram Noble, and Jasmine Birk, "Comfort Monitoring? Environmental Assessment Follow-Up Under Community-Industry Negotiated Environmental Agreements" [2011] 31 Environmental Impact Assessment Review 17 [Noble and Birk].
35. Bradshaw and Wright (n 31).
36. Fidler (n 7) 237.
37. Expert Panel (n 14).
38. Noble (n 19). See also Dwight Newman and Levi Graham, "Indigenous-Industry Agreements, Legal Uncertainty, and Risk Allocations", in Ibironke T. Odumosu and Dwight Newman (eds.), *Indigenous-Industry Agreements, Natural Resources, and the Law* (Routledge 2021) on the scope of certainty achieved and limits on it.

39. Bram Noble and Courtney Fidler, "Advancing Indigenous-Community Corporate Agreements: Lessons from Practice In the Canadian Mining Sector" [2011] 4 Oil, Gas and Energy Law Intelligence [Noble and Fidler].
40. Ben Bradshaw "Impact and Benefit Agreements" (Submission to the Expert Panel "Lets Talk EA" Consultation Process 2016) <www.letstalkea.ca/developing-the-vision/news_feed/section-3?posted_first=true&wbdisable=true> accessed 26 March 2018.
41. Noble (n 22) 12.
42. Natural Resources Canada, "Partnership Agreements: ORCA Sand and Gravel Project—British Columbia" (*Government of Canada* 2010) <www.nrcan.gc.ca/mining-materials/publications/aboriginal/bulletin/8820> accessed 2 October 2018.
43. Ginger Gibson and Ciaran O'Faircheallaigh, *IBA Community Toolkit: Negotiation and Implementation of Impact and Benefit Agreements* (Walter and Duncan Gordon Foundation 2010) [Gibson and O'Faircheallaigh].
44. Sandra Gogal, Richard Riegert and JoAnn Jamieson, "Aboriginal Impact and Benefit Agreements: Practical Considerations" [2005] 43 Alberta Law Review 129.
45. Noble and Udofia (n 11) 14.
46. Courtney Fidler and Michael Hitch, "Impact and Benefit Agreements: A Contentious Issue for Environmental and Aboriginal Justice" [2007] 35 Environments 49. On issues concerning the confidentiality of such agreements, see also Jason Maclean, "Impact Benefit Agreements, Transparency, and Sustainability", in Odumosu-Ayanu and Newman (eds.) (n 38); Thomas Isaac and Arend J.A. Hoekstra, "Canadian Law and Realpolitik Regarding Indigenous-Industry Agreements" in Odumosu-Ayanu and Newman (eds. (n 38).
47. Papillon and Rodon (n 12).
48. Ibid.
49. Kevin O'Reilly, "Impact and Benefit Agreements: Tools for Sustainable Development?" (2000) 25(4) Northern Perspectives 1.
50. Fidler (n 7).
51. Noble and Fidler (n 39).
52. Ibid.
53. Gibson and O'Faircheallaigh (n 43).
54. Hanna and Vanclay (n 13).
55. David Cox, *Environmental Impact Assessment and Impact Benefit Agreements: The Participation of Aboriginal Women at Voisey's Bay mine* (McMaster University 2013) 50.
56. Ibid 57.
57. Anne Hansen, "Offshore Oil Exploration and Impact Assessment in Greenland" [2016] 4 Northern Public Affairs 61.
58. Indigenous-industry agreements are largely voluntary in Canada, except under modern land claims agreement such as Articles 8, 9 and 26 of the Nunavut Land Claims Agreement. See also Isaac and Hoekstra (n 46).
59. Bureau of Minerals and Petroleum, *Guidelines for Social Impact Assessments for Mining Projects in Greenland* (BMP Greenland 2009).
60. Ibid.
61. Galbraith, Bradshaw, and Rutherford (n 6).
62. Gibson and O'Faircheallaigh (n 43).
63. Noble and Birk (n 34).
64. Noble and Fidler (n 39).
65. Noble (n 22) 13.
66. Ibid 11.
67. Expert Panel (n 14).
68. Bradshaw and Wright (n 31).
69. Papillon and Rodon (n 12).
70. Bradshaw and Wright (n 31).
71. Bill C-69 (n 20).

Part IV

Jurisdictional Case Studies

11 Contesting Indigenous-Industry Agreements in Latin America

Charis Kamphuis[1]

I. The Context for Indigenous-Industry Agreements in Latin America

The principle that resource extraction should only occur on Indigenous land after a process of free, prior and informed consultation with affected communities first made its appearance on the international legal stage in the 1989 *International Labour Organization (ILO) Convention concerning Indigenous and Tribal Peoples* (*Convention 169*).[2] Since then, this principle has become ubiquitous, endorsed in many statements of international law, in constitutions and/or constitutional jurisprudence around the world and in the policies of investors and corporations. The related principle that consultation must occur "in order to obtain the free, prior and informed consent" of affected Indigenous peoples has continued to gain acceptance since its articulation in the 2007 UN *Declaration on the Rights of Indigenous Peoples* (UNDRIP).[3] In a 2013 survey of norm development in this area, Special Rapporteur for the Rights of Indigenous Peoples James Anaya concluded there is a general rule in international law that extractive activities should not take place on the territories of Indigenous peoples without their free, prior and informed consent.[4] Notably though, the precise meaning of the right to consent remains controversial.[5]

Latin American countries have been at the forefront of these global developments. Of the countries that have ratified *Convention 169* worldwide, approximately two-thirds (15) are Latin American.[6] Since 2011, four countries in the region, Bolivia, Ecuador, Colombia, and Peru, have developed legislation to regulate Indigenous peoples' right to consultation.[7] Attention to these rights instruments is not surprising given that many Latin American states claim sovereignty over a land base that is also inhabited and claimed by Indigenous peoples.

This land is also the site of some of the richest mineral and petroleum deposits in the world. Most Latin American countries have adopted a political economy of resource extraction consistent with neoliberal economic globalization.[8] This refers to the use of domestic law to attract and facilitate foreign investment, the use of international economic law to protect foreign investors from certain state decisions, and the use of corporate law and tax law to enhance companies' profits and locate them outside of the countries where they operate. This framework has enabled the intensification of foreign-owned mineral extraction in Latin America over the last 20 years.[9]

In this context, it stands to reason that resource companies are increasingly pursing benefit agreements with affected communities. Many have espoused the "business case" for respecting human rights and community agreements.[10] The idea is that agreements improve profitability by securing social stability for specific projects. Notably, Industry-community agreements are primarily formed outside of formal state-led consultation processes. This is due to the fact that consultation-related legislation in Latin America has focussed exclusively on regulating the state's consultation process with affected Indigenous communities. The relationship between these state-led processes and Industry-community agreements in Latin America is further explored below.

Yet resource-related social conflicts remain endemic.[11] In 2015, 185 environmental defenders were assassinated across 16 countries around the world.[12] Mining was the industry most linked to violence and four of the top five countries with the worst incidence of violence were Latin American: Peru, Brazil, Nicaragua, and Colombia.[13] Another study of the reports of violence and criminalization in Latin America in relation to Canadian mining operations found that between 2000 and 2015 there were 44 deaths and 403 injuries across 13 countries in incidents involving 28 different companies.[14]

This background reveals that over the last 20 years, a curious state of affairs has emerged. The Indigenous right to consultation has been widely endorsed *in tandem* with the intensification of resource extraction on Indigenous land and the proliferation of violent resource-related conflicts.[15] In making this observation, my intent is not to undertake a full examination of this phenomena and potential explanations.[16] Rather, it is to frame a more narrow set of arguments and inquiries in relation to the formation of Indigenous-industry benefit agreements in this context.

In part II of this chapter, I survey the contributions of scholars who share my concern that the legal and social contexts that inform the formation of Indigenous-industry agreements in Latin America are problematic. This body of research raises serious questions about whether Indigenous-industry "agreements" formed in these conditions could possibly rest on any meaningful notion of consent. This supports the proposition that it is likely that many Indigenous-industry agreements in Latin America lack legitimacy and perhaps legality.

I make this point in order to focus on a narrower set of questions as we face the aftermath of the proliferation of agreements under present circumstances. What happens when a community mobilizes in order to challenge the legality of a past agreement, such as by contesting the idea that it actually consented? What if the company and/or the state holds up a document with signatures from past community leaders that allegedly represent consent? If the company and the state are unresponsive to a community's concerns, can it resort to the courts?

In part III, I explore these questions by referring to Peru as a case study. I begin by summarizing the main features of the legal frameworks that inform the formation of Indigenous-industry agreements in Peru. I complete this section by sharing the experience of San Andres de Negritos, a community that is challenging the constitutionality of agreements with Yanacocha Mine in Peruvian courts. This experience illuminates interesting opportunities, as well as potential procedural obstacles, when it comes to challenging illegitimate agreements in Latin America.

While this chapter is framed in relation to relevant literature on Latin America as a region, it adopts Peru and the Negritos litigation as a useful case study. Peru shares many familiar challenges with other Latin American countries. Its democratic present is marked by deep problems with the rule of law, extreme social inequality, entrenched economic dependency on foreign resource extraction, and endemic and violent social conflicts. At the same time, Peru has a history of recognition, regulation, litigation, law reform, and political mobilization in relation to Indigenous rights. It also has one of the largest Indigenous populations in Latin America and was the first country in the region to regulate the right to consultation.

Significantly, many key features of Peru's constitution and procedures are also commonly shared by other Latin American countries. All of these factors make Peru and the Negritos case an important site for examining the possibility of legal challenges to Indigenous-industry agreements in the region. In the conclusion, I explore the significance of this research for ongoing normative developments in relation to Indigenous peoples' right to consultation, consent, and the formation of Indigenous-industry agreements.

II. Critical Research on Consultation and Consent in Latin America

Writing in 2010, David Szablowski observed a dearth of knowledge about the effective implementation of Indigenous peoples' right to consent, and in particular, about the institutional arrangements required to give this principle concrete meaning in different contexts.[17] In Szablowski's view, where Indigenous communities lack legal rights to resources and must settle "for what they think they can get in the circumstances," this falls short of consent.[18] After referring to developments in public international law, private transnational regimes, and corporate policy, he concluded that "FPIC is everywhere discussed, but it is not much of an exaggeration to say that it is practised virtually nowhere."[19] Moreover, Szablowski expressed concern that if power imbalances remain unaddressed, consent could become a double-edged sword for Indigenous peoples. As a partial remedy to this, Szablowski argued that "informed" consent must infuse the contractual relationship between industry and communities with fiduciary obligations, thereby requiring a departure from the classical liberal approach to consent.[20]

These assertions raise questions about Indigenous-industry agreements. In his 2013 report, Anaya articulated a normative standard for evaluating the legitimacy of these agreements. Specifically, he described the legal conditions that enable consent to a proposed project "on equitable and just terms."[21] His framework captures two issues: first the wider legal and negotiating context within which the agreement is formed, and second, the substance of the agreement itself.

With respect to the first issue, Anaya argued that the protection of basic civil rights (including the right to oppose projects without repression and criminalization) is a pre-condition for the formation of legitimate agreements. However, the wider context must also include regulatory regimes that recognize and protect Indigenous peoples' rights and apply sanctions for violations.[22] Anaya also addressed the negotiation dynamic itself, stating that consultation procedures should ameliorate power imbalances. To this end, he asserted that States should establish mechanisms for ensuring that Indigenous peoples have adequate negotiation capacity.[23]

Having established these contextual conditions, Anaya identified the fundamental characteristics of "rights-centred equitable agreements." In his view, these agreements must safeguard rights and/or mitigate the impact of resource development on rights.[24] As a preferred model, agreements should also ensure genuine long-term partnership such that Indigenous peoples participate in project decision-making and benefits as well as regulatory control.[25] According to Anaya, this substantive standard for agreements is required by international human rights law.

Furthering Anaya's framework, Elisa Morgera has argued that Anaya's principle of equitable benefits-sharing has received insufficient attention among international human rights bodies and experts.[26] Morgera advocates for an expansion of Anaya's argument through cross-fertilization between international human rights law and environmental law. She argues that a combined doctrinal reading of these areas supports a positive concept in international law of equitable benefit-sharing. Morgera argues that this principle is a substantive right that is integral to Indigenous peoples' rights connected to natural resources.[27]

In pursuing this line of doctrinal development, Morgera and Anaya explicitly cast their approach as a remedy to the potential pitfalls of agreement-making. Morgera refers to the risk that benefits-sharing becomes a mere financial transaction, reinforcing advantages of the powerful and legitimizing loss of resources by the vulnerable.[28] Anaya similarly specified that agreements should not result from "undue pressure," access to basic services should not be conditioned upon acceptance of extractive projects, and State and company officials should guard against the manipulation or intimidation of Indigenous leaders.[29] Notably, Szablowski, Morgera, and Anaya all connect these developments in human rights law in relation to Indigenous consultation and consent, and the formation of Indigenous-industry agreements. They all elaborate on the fundamental proposition that human rights law should come to bear in some way on these private agreements.

In spite of their concerns, these authors provide little guidance with respect to the matter of how questionable agreements might be reviewed on substantive or procedural grounds if disputes arise.[30] Lack of attention to this issue is of concern in light of the fact that many of consent's pitfalls are indeed materializing in practice.[31] Anthropologists Riccarda Flemmer and Almut Schilling-Vacaflor studied forty-five state-led consultation processes in Bolivia and Peru, all undertaken in accordance with recent Indigenous consultation legislation. In 2015 they concluded that the implementation of this right is abysmally distant from the ideals of human rights advocates working on norm development at the international level.[32]

Flemmer and Schilling-Vacaflor found that the terms of consultations, including procedures, timelines, scope/issues, and information were largely imposed by the State. Consultations suffered from serious power asymmetries, enormous information and knowledge deficiencies, and intercultural inadequacies.[33] Notably, consultations were often overloaded with a wide range of community concerns not directly related to the extractive project in question. Finally, these researchers observed that the resulting agreements were weak, lacked follow up mechanisms, and key provisions were subsequently disregarded.[34]

Drawing on these findings, Flemmer and Schilling-Vacaflor argue that Bolivia and Peru lack the preconditions necessary to ensure that their pioneering consultation laws fulfil their rights protecting promise. In both countries, the State has implemented consultations without changing the status quo: Indigenous communities do not have a decisive say in extraction activities; they lack continuous channels for political participation; their basic social and economic needs are not met; and broader Indigenous rights to land, territory and political power are ignored. These authors observed that without these pre-conditions, consultations can have disempowering or exacerbating effects.[35]

A 2018 comprehensive study by lawyer Ana Layva of the 38 consultation processes undertaken in Peru in relation to proposed mining and hydrocarbon projects since the enactment of Peru's consultation regulations found numerous serious deficiencies with these processes, mirroring many of the findings in the Flemmer and Schilling-Vacaflor study.[36] Leyva observed that Indigenous participants in the consultations had a profound lack of knowledge about the basic functions of the state, the legal obligations of companies, and their rights.[37] She also found that consultations took place *after* the state had already made all, or nearly all, key decisions about the project.[38] As a result, state-community agreements had extremely little, if any, relevance to protecting the rights of the communities in relation to the proposed project.[39] Rather, agreements simply duplicated the existing legal obligations of both the state and the company and merely catalogued the communities demands for public services or to resolve historic grievances.[40] In only one case, with independent legal support were communities able to secure some direct economic benefits.[41]

Colombian legal scholar César Rodríguez Garavito has also undertaken detailed fieldwork in this area, mostly in Colombia but also in Ecuador, Chile, and Peru.[42] He found that consultations are highly procedural/technical, are primarily focussed on monetizing anticipated harms, and are plagued by endemic miscommunications (sometimes intentionally produced by company and State officials). Perhaps most significantly, Rodríguez Garavito found that the conditions of negotiation are often so coercive (physically and economically) and asymmetrical that free participation and consent are not possible in practice.[43]

He argues that where agreements are formed, communities' substantive claims are diluted and the terms of agreements create new dependencies (on experts and companies), internal divisions, and conflicts.[44]

On the basis of these findings, Rodríguez Garavito concluded that consultation is the new device for the assimilation of Indigenous peoples and the legitimation of a global economy predicated on "accumulation by dispossession."[45] He argues that, in practice, consultation is reduced to a formal procedural right (due process and free contract), based on the "liberal fiction" of formal equality ("a level playing field"), ignoring questions of power, self-government, and the material conditions necessary for genuine deliberations.[46]

These observations from the field are further supported by a comparative textual study of consultation laws in Bolivia, Peru, Colombia, and Ecuador. In this study, Peruvian academic Patricia Urteaga-Crovetto tracked how technicalities and procedures work to diminish the political significance of the rights in question. She identifies four groupings of technicalities: (1) the definition of the right to consultation; (2) the subjects of the right; (3) the subject matters to be consulted; and (4) timelines. Urteaga-Crovetto also recorded reports of manipulation to obtain agreements with communities in Colombia and Peru.[47]

This textual analysis of consultation laws, in combination with observations from the field, support Peruvian legal theorist Roger Merino Acuña's theoretical critique of consultation regimes in Latin America. He argues that the mainstream rationale for the Indigenous right to consultation, as a mechanism to reduce the barriers to investment created by social conflicts (i.e., "the business case"), reveals its roots in the colonial legality and capitalist political economy of classical liberalism.[48] In opposition to this, he calls for recognition of territory and self-determination as foundational rights, beyond liberal colonial legality.[49] He further argues that negotiations must be permitted to fundamentally question the "extractivism model" itself.[50]

Robert Coulter extends this critique to address the related right to free, prior, and informed consent.[51] He argues that its current conception is fatally flawed in that it fundamentally presumes agreement to an act that would otherwise violate Indigenous rights. Referring to UNDRIP, Coulter argues that consent has been reduced to a procedural right that, rather than safeguarding substantive rights, simply permits Indigenous peoples to negotiate the financial terms of rights violations. In Coulter's view, the right to consent has diverted attention from Indigenous peoples' fundamental substantive right of self-determination, which includes the right to govern, own, control, and benefit from Indigenous lands and resources.[52] He asserts that the concept of consent is so poorly defined that is it practically useless and that, due to these limitations, "some form of monitoring is needed to guard against abuse, fraud, corruption and dishonourable dealings."[53]

Like Coulter, Nathan Yaffe advocates for independent third-party monitoring of Indigenous-industry agreements.[54] Yaffe bases this recommendation on his analysis of the Indigenous consent policies of various private sectors actors, including companies, the International Council on Mining and Metals (ICMM) and the International Finance Corporation. His analysis includes a case study, featured by the ICMM, of an agreement between mining company Newmont and a community in Suriname.[55] Yaffe concluded that the private sector's approach to Indigenous consent is often purely or predominately commercial and presumes a "thin, liberal, individualistic lens."[56] He argues that the private sector's dominant role in pursuing benefit agreements is thus "radically altering" consent's normative foundations in the right to Indigenous self-determination.[57] He cautions that this should raise alarms about the "experiment of corporate-controlled" Indigenous consent processes.[58]

In sum, the research reviewed uses five different approaches to the topic of Indigenous consultation and agreement-making: (1) international law normative interpretation; (2) fieldwork data collection; (3) regulatory analysis; (4) corporate policy analysis; and (5) theoretical critique. Fieldwork in the region has documented how present institutional conditions have exacerbated or failed to ameliorate profound power disparities and information gaps. In general, these researchers' findings apply equally to consultations/negotiations and agreements undertaken by either private or public officials. These conclusions are bolstered by the findings of researchers focussed on law and policy analysis.

Notably, these researchers agree that there are few examples *in practice* of agreements that meet human rights standards. They also commonly assert that classical liberal contractual approaches to consent risk legitimatizing inequitable agreements that may leave communities worse off. Several conclude that the Indigenous right to consent must be rooted in self-determination *in practice*, and that more radical transformations of the legal, political, and economic context are necessary to achieve "equitable rights-centred agreements."

III. Legal Challenge to Illegitimate Indigenous-Industry Agreements in Peru

The body of research reviewed above supports the conclusion that, under present conditions, agreements between Indigenous peoples in Latin American and industry actors are rarely, if ever, a product of meaningful, legitimate, free, prior, and informed consultation and consent. This section conveys the experience of the Peruvian Campesino Community San Andres de Negritos and its attempts to challenge the legality of so-called agreements with Yanacocha Mine. It begins with an overview of the complex legal framework in Peru in relation to Indigenous-industry agreements. It then presents the Negritos Community's experience as a case study of the dynamics of illegitimate agreements. Finally, this section describes the pathway to challenging such agreements in Peruvian courts, as well as the obstacles and opportunities that the Negritos Community has encountered.

1. *Legal Framework*

There are approximately 7,267 Campesino (Andean) and Native (Amazonian) Communities in Peru.[59] Many (but not all) of these communities acquired communal title during the agrarian reform years. Thus, the governance of

Indigenous-Industry agreements in Peru is intertwined with two main issues: (1) the status of Campesino and Native Communities vis-a-vis international and national laws recognizing Indigenous rights; and (2) the legal terms that govern the acquisition of surface and resource rights to communally titled land by investors. An array of constitutional provisions, statutes, and case law constitute the matrix of positive state law in this area. This includes: 1970s and 1980s agrarian reform laws, the Constitution, neo liberal foreign investment laws beginning in the 1990s; and a handful of Indigenous rights statutes and case law, emerging after the turn of the millennium.[60]

Agrarian reform laws declared in 1969 that Peru's Indigenous peoples would thereafter be called Campesino or Native Communities.[61] Subsequent laws recognized these communities as legal persons, with special cultural characteristics, self-governing institutions, communal property, and political and economic autonomy. This included a statutory provision, constitutionalized in 1979, that communal property can only be alienated with a vote of 2/3 of the community. However, Alberto Fujimori's government halted communal titling programs and rewrote the Constitution in 1993, removing the 2/3 vote rule. Fujimori introduced laws to promote foreign investment in resources, particularly on communally held land, and subsequent governments have continued on this path. This includes facilitating the conversion of communal title to individual title and expediting agreements between companies and communities.[62]

Following unprecedented violent conflicts between police and Indigenous protesters opposed to pro-foreign investment reforms, the Peruvian government passed Indigenous consultation legislation in 2011.[63] Notably, this regime excludes consultations led by private companies and does not mention Indigenous-industry agreements. Critically then, proponent-led agreements with communities in Peru remain essentially unregulated.

Peru's consultation legislation ultimately omitted many provisions demanded by Indigenous organizations.[64] One of its most controversial aspects is its narrow definition of Indigenous peoples. The onus is on communities to "objectively" prove their Indigeneity by, *inter alia*, showing that they: are the direct descendants of populations that inhabited the country at the time of colonialism; have maintained their social, economic, cultural, and political institutions; have maintained an Indigenous language; and reside in their ancestral territory.[65] These criteria are inconsistent with international instruments and are widely criticized.[66] Peru's restrictive definition excludes most Campesino and Native Communities and it is widely believed that the exclusion of Campesino Communities is due to their proximity to mining projects.[67]

For the majority of Campesino and Native communities who hold communal title but do not have a state-recognized right to consultation, applicable laws create enormous pressure to agree to resource development in ways that are likely inconsistent with agrarian reform laws and the Peruvian constitution.[68] For example, Peru has passed legislation permitting the sale of land or other private agreements between communal property holders and private actors with only a bare majority of votes of the communities' executive leadership in attendance at any given meeting.[69] Peru has also strengthened expropriation laws in favour of mineral tenure holders.[70] For example, after a company solicits the expropriation of communal land, Campesino or Native Communities have 15 days to meet with the company and come to an agreement. If this does not happen, the relevant ministry has full discretion to approve the expropriation.[71] Added to this, Peruvian law severely constrains the available compensation amount, including for communally held land.[72] These coercive legal conditions form the context within which Campesino and Native communal titleholders, not recognized as Indigenous by the Peruvian state, are left to negotiate land-related agreements with the private sector.

The situation is only marginally better for the 55 Indigenous peoples that Peru recognized under the 2011 consultation law.[73] Peru's consultation laws impose short and strict timeframes, including a maximum of 120 days for the formal consultation process.[74] The process begins informally when state authorities believe a decision may directly affect an identified Indigenous community.[75] The authority then meets with identified communities "to inform them of the proposed Consultation Plan."[76] Once the Consultation Plan and the proposed state measure to be consulted about are published, the process formally begins. Communities have 30 days to designate their representatives and between 30 and 60 days to review information about the proposed decision.[77] This is followed by the internal evaluation phase, where communities have 30 days to make an internal decision.[78] If the community disagrees, the maximum time for "intercultural dialogue" is 30 days[79] before the state makes a final decision.[80]

In Leyva's study she found that the majority of consultations were completed between 49 and 90 days.[81] Incredibly, the time between the information meeting and the internal decision was often extremely short. Sometimes these two events were separated by only a few days or even occurred on the same day.[82] In other words, in practice, communities took very little time to evaluate the proposed measures.

Where an agreement is reached between the Peruvian government and an Indigenous community, the regulations make it enforceable against both parties. However, the law makes no reference to remedies for a possible failure on the part of the state to appropriately consult or comply with an agreement. There is a Permanent Multisectoral Commission with a narrow mandate to follow up on agreements reached in consultation processes. Notably, the Commission is not independent; rather its membership consists entirely of state representatives, and primarily members of the Executive.[83]

In terms of jurisprudence, the Constitutional Court of Peru recognized in 2007 that certain Indigenous rights recognized in international law are incorporated directly into the Constitution.[84] Following this, the Court decided eight Indigenous rights cases, primarily between 2008 and 2010. In this case law, the Court has recognized that Indigenous communities have the right to communal property, the right to free, prior, and informed consultation—and in some cases consent—and finally the right to equitably benefit from resource extraction that impacts their land and livelihood.[85]

These jurisprudential advances have some important limitations.[86] Significantly, the Constitutional Court has declined to provide guidance with respect to the definition of Indigenous peoples in Peru. Moreover, the litigants have primarily been non-governmental organizations (NGOs) seeking constitutional review of foreign investment laws on behalf of all Indigenous peoples in Peru. At present, the Negritos case (described below) is the only case before the Court that raises the substantive rights of a specific community in relation to a proposed resource project, and further seeks to challenge the constitutionality of a so-called agreement. The decided cases have also not touched on other key issues like the remedy for failure to consult appropriately or for deficient or fraudulently obtained consent.[87] This sparse case law is notable given that Campesino and Native Communities' rights were constitutionally recognized in Peru in 1979 and noting that international Indigenous rights norms were first incorporated into Peru's constitution in the early 1990s. Clearly there is a significant gap between the articulation of norms/rights on one hand, and access to the courts on the other.[88]

This description of Indigenous peoples' consultation rights in Peru would not be complete without a reference to civil rights issues. Recall that in Anaya's framework, respect for civil rights is a basic pre-condition for right-centred agreements. In other words, the legitimacy of Indigenous-industry agreements cannot be analyzed in isolation from the circumstances that communities will face if they oppose a project. The history of numerous environmental conflicts in Peru indicates that when communities oppose projects, companies and state officials alike often fail to effectively manage the situation.[89] Like elsewhere in Latin America, leaders who are critical of proposed projects are often harassed, threatened, or even harmed. When communities protest, they are often met with force by police operatives in the employ of the company.[90]

The criminalization of dissent in Peru has extended to international advocates who work with mine-affected communities. In a troubling 2017 case, Jen Moore, a Canadian NGO worker, was detained and permanently banned from returning to Peru after she showed a documentary film depicting conflicts between the Canadian company Hudbay and affected communities.[91] Peruvian authorities rationalized their decision by arguing that Moore is a threat to public order.[92] Significantly, some Campesino Communities in the area of Hudbay's operations have signed land transfer and benefit agreements with the company and others are under pressure to do so. At the same time, public security forces, employed by Hudbay, have responded violently to community members protesting the proposed mine.[93] The Peruvian government's actions to ban Moore mean that "agreements" between Hudbay and local communities will likely be signed without the presence of human rights observers.

This review of key laws that apply to communally held (or claimed) land in Peru complements the broader critiques of Indigenous consultations described in the previous section. While Peru's consultation regime has significant deficiencies, many Campesino and Native communities with communal title are excluded from its application entirely. As such, general resource and land laws apply to these Communities and they must deal directly with private companies, under aggressive timelines and extra-ordinary power asymmetries. Moreover, regardless of a community's legal status as Indigenous or not, agreements negotiated with industry are entirely unregulated. Finally, critics of proposed projects often face criminalization, threats and possible harm. All of this confirms that, under current conditions, there are serious risks that benefit agreements with Indigenous communities in Peru will fail to meet basic criteria for legitimacy or even legality.

2. The Dynamics of Illegitimate Agreements

The experience of the Campesino Community San Andres de Negritos offers some insight into how illegitimate agreements with industry may form and come to be subsequently challenged. Although the story of the Negritos Community's contemporary dispossession began decades ago, its struggle to challenge an illegitimate agreement with foreign owned Yanacocha Mine is very much a story of the present. Moreover, the Negritos Community's experience reveals some of the legal barriers that may arise in this context. Given the dynamics of the consultations taking place in Latin America and the concomitant risk of illegitimate agreements, the Negritos experience remains highly relevant.

The Negritos Community acquired title to its land pursuant to agrarian reform legislation and a 1974 presidential declaration granting it communal title to 14,375 hectares. However, shortly after the arrival of Yanacocha Mine to the area, in 1993 and 1995 the Community allegedly consented to transfer title to approximately 1400 hectares of its land to the company in exchange for approximately $US 48,000. This arrangement was reflected in two different documents signed by company and community representatives after the company had officially requested the expropriation of the Community's land.[94] Yanacocha quickly mortgaged a portion of the transferred property (609 hectares) to international banks, for loans totalling $85 million. The Negritos Community alleges that the documents that underlie these transfers were signed by a handful of corrupt community leaders, that community members were misinformed, bribed or extorted into signing ancillary documents, and that the Community as a whole was never properly consulted or even informed of these dealings, much less its rights in applicable domestic and international law.[95]

The Negritos Community's gradual turn to the law began a decade after these events, in tandem with a general rise in Indigenous and Campesino protest, rights consciousness, and growth in civil society organizations in Peru and across Latin America. Campesino protests against Yanacocha began in 2004, and in 2006 a Negritos community leader opposed to the mine was assassinated by hitmen and a protestor was killed by Yanacocha's security forces.[96] In spite of this, Negritos community members persisted and raised the money necessary to collect volumes of documents from various government ministries. Emboldened by the contents of these documents, they appealed to the company and various public officials and administrative decision-makers for recognition of their grievances, but to no avail. Finally, in 2011, with the support of *pro bono* lawyers, the Negritos Community presented its claim before a court of first instance, alleging that its communal property had been transferred without proper consultation, without free and informed consent, and that the payment made in return was grossly unfair and inequitable.

While the underlying facts of the Negritos case took place in the early to mid-1990s, the literature reviewed in the previous sections demonstrates that many communities in Peru continue to face similar power asymmetries. Like the Negritos Community, they lack: awareness of their rights; independent advice; access to credible and accessible information about proposed projects; and previous experience with the courts. Communities also often face coercive conditions, including poverty, social exclusion, and threats of violence if they oppose proposed projects. Like the Negritos case, at present agreements and access to land are often procured by: dividing and misleading community members; disregarding or actively subverting broad consultation; and/or choosing to negotiate secretly with leaders that support the company.

As in the Negritos case, there continues to be significant risk that industry-Indigenous agreements will, at worst, be obtained through corruption, extortion or dishonesty, and at best, that communities will negotiate agreements without fully understanding applicable laws, as well as social and environmental consequences. All of this makes the Negritos Community's litigation instructive, as it explores the practical question of how a potentially unconstitutional or otherwise illegally obtained agreement between a foreign company and an Indigenous community (communal titleholder) might be challenged in court on the basis of constitutional and international Indigenous rights principles.

3. Challenging Illegitimate Agreements in the Courts

As indicated, in 2011 the Negritos Community launched a constitutional challenge to two agreements with Yanacocha Mine, signed in the early to mid-1990s. Under Peru's Constitutional Procedural Code, an *amparo* is the single cause of action available to defend Campesino and Native constitutional rights in these circumstances.[97] In principle, it allows for a kind of judicial review of Indigenous-industry agreements. This is possible due to three important features of Peruvian constitutional law. First, the *amparo* allows communities to request a remedy for alleged violations of Campesino and Native rights already explicitly recognized in the Constitution and domestic legislation. Second, communities can bolster their claims by referring to international Indigenous rights principles that are directly incorporated into Peru's constitution and therefore legally binding. Third, the *amparo* allows communities to bring their claim directly against a private party's acts or omissions, such as for example those of a resource company. These features of Peruvian constitutional law are similar in a number of other Latin American countries and suggest that the *amparo* cause of action could capture Indigenous-industry agreements more broadly in the region.[98]

Since presenting its *amparo* action, the Negritos Community has faced many delays and obstacles both inside and outside of the courtroom.[99] Defendant Yanacocha responded by immediately objecting to the admissibility of the Community's claim. However, only one objection prevailed at both first and second instance, namely that the claim is outside of the required limitation period. This refers to the provisions of the Code that require a claimant to bring an *amparo* claim within 60 days from the time that the claimant (1) became *aware* of the rights violation; and (2) is *able* to bring the claim. The Code also recognizes exceptions to this general rule, including where the alleged rights violating actions are ongoing, or where the alleged violations are the result of omissions.

In 2015, an appeal court held that the 60-day limitation period began on the precise date in the mid-1990s when a handful of Community leaders signed the agreements with Yanacocha. The court reasoned that the Negritos Community must have known about the land transfers due to the fact that the company filed the change in title in the public registrar and given that community members could plainly observe the mine's subsequent operations on formerly communal land. It characterized the Community's constitutional concerns about the agreement as a convenient excuse. The court also refused to consider an equitable interpretation of the limitation period rule, in light of community members' lack of knowledge of their substantive and procedural rights, and of the nature and consequences of the agreement with Yanacocha. The court also declined to consider the argument that the impugned agreements represent ongoing violations and/or omissions with respect to the Community's rights, thereby triggering an exception to the limitation period. On this basis, the court refused to consider the Community's claim on the merits.

In doing so, the appeal court adopted a formalistic view of consent whereby the sole fact of the signatures on the agreement documents triggered the 60 days limitation period. This reasoning ignored the fact that the Community's central substantive allegations in the case are precisely that its land titles were transferred to the company without its informed consent, on the basis of misinformation, falsehoods or extortion, and in some cases without its knowledge. In other words, the court's approach to consent in the limitation period context explicitly ignored social and cultural facts and context that informed the so-called agreements. Rather, the court expected the Community to interact with Yanacocha like a sophisticated legal actor, fully aware of, and able to act on, its procedural and substantive rights. The Negritos Community is challenging the appeal court's decision on these points in Peru's Constitutional Court.

IV. Conclusion: Equitable Rights-Centred Oversight Mechanisms

This chapter reviewed literature evaluating the regulation of the Indigenous right to consultation in various Latin American countries, as well as the implementation of this right on the ground. Building on this, it offered an account of the Peruvian legal context in order to establish the relationship between state-led consultations under statute, and unregulated Indigenous-industry agreements. With this background, I have argued that the legal and social conditions in many Latin American countries generate a serious risk that Indigenous communities will accept agreements with resource companies in the absence of full information and knowledge of the meaning and significance of the agreement, without a variety of human rights safeguards, and sometimes as a result of illegal tactics or coercion.

The Negritos Community's efforts to challenge agreements with Yanacocha have uncovered an avenue for judicial scrutiny of allegedly unconstitutional agreements. Peru's constitutional order contains three key features that make this possible: (1) it recognizes Campesino, Native and Indigenous Peoples' communal rights; (2) it incorporates certain internationally recognized Indigenous rights; and (3) it allows rights violations claims to be brought directly against a company. These features are also part of the legal system of a number of other Latin American countries. This framework is interesting in that it subjects private contracts to constitutional scrutiny and the standards vested in constitutionalized Indigenous rights.[100]

However, the social and legal dynamics of the Negritos case underscore that communities may need time to marshal a court challenge to an unfair agreement. While the applicable limitation period in Peru's Procedural Code is short, the rule arguably requires a claimant to have the knowledge and capacity to bring a claim. Moreover, the Code provides certain exceptions to the rule. In principle this would give the courts discretion to take a claimant's circumstances into account. However, in the Negritos case the courts to date have favoured an extraordinarily narrow interpretation of the limitation period rule.

The observations and findings in the Negritos case study merit analysis in relation to the research reviewed in part II of this chapter. The Negritos Community's experience reveals that the inequities, power asymmetries, and improprieties that underlie illegitimate agreements also prevent communities from launching litigation in a timely fashion. Thus, notwithstanding the existence in principle of potential legal avenues for judicial scrutiny of Indigenous-industry agreements, in practice the formal equality logic of liberal contract law may work to bar Indigenous challenges to past agreements with industry. There is an important continuity between the failure to address questions of social context and power in the conceptualization and implementation of the rights to consultation and consent, and the failure to address these same issues in the procedural rules that function as gatekeepers to substantive judicial scrutiny of Indigenous-industry agreements.

This observation is important for those seeking to develop emancipatory normative and practical approaches to Indigenous consultation and consent. As stated, the literature reviewed in this chapter has critiqued the ways in which these rights are being articulated and implemented in Latin America. The Negritos case study adds to this critique, revealing that normative developments in this area have also failed to consider the procedural obstacles to defending the right to an equitable rights-centred agreement, including in the courts. In particular, they have failed to articulate the rules that should govern how communities might challenge the legitimacy of past agreements on substantive or procedural grounds.

Current social and legal dynamics in Latin America indicate that this is not a small oversight. There is a clear need for mechanisms capable of independently scrutinizing the validity of benefits agreements against the normative criteria of substantive Indigenous rights. Such mechanisms must safeguard against formalistic and exclusionary approaches to consent, as exemplified by the Negritos case. These mechanisms must adopt equitable and contextual approaches to substantive *and* procedural questions. In short, Anaya's concept of equitable rights-centred agreements must be accompanied by the development of equitable rights-centred causes of action, limitation periods, and normative standards for scrutinizing Indigenous-industry agreements after the fact.

As companies continue under present conditions to pursue benefits agreements with Indigenous peoples in Latin America, there are problems and there will be more problems with these agreements. In the absence of specialized oversight mechanisms, courts will often be the only forum for ensuring the legitimacy and legality of past agreements. However, judicial oversight will only be possible if civil procedures enable communities to access the courts in practice. At stake is communities' ability to operationalize substantive Indigenous rights principles to remedy past and ongoing violations enshrined in so-called "agreements."

Notes

1. I thank Nnaemeka Ezeani, Judith Acevedo Paz and Carlos Alberto Quispe Davila very much for research assistance and to the reviewers for their comments.
2. *International Labour Organization (ILO) Convention concerning Indigenous and Tribal Peoples* (27 June 1989) C169 (entered into force 5 September 1991) art 15(2).
3. United Nations Declaration on the Rights of Indigenous Peoples, GA Res 61/295, UN Doc A/RES/61/295 (13 September 2007), 46 ILM 1013 art 32(2).
4. James Anaya, "Report of the Special Rapporteur on the rights of indigenous peoples: Extractive industries and indigenous peoples" [1 July 2013] GA, 24th Sess, UN Doc A/HRC/24/41 [27] [Anaya, "Extractive Industries"].
5. See for example David Szablowski, "Operationalizing Free, Prior, and Informed Consent in the Extractive Industry Sector? Examining the Challenges of a Negotiated Model of Justice" [2010] 1(2) Canadian Journal of Development Studies 111, 116 [Szablowski]; *Saramaka People v Suriname* [12 August 2008] IACHR Series C No 185 IHRL 3058 [134]; James Anaya, "Report of the Special Rapporteur on the Rights of Indigenous Peoples" [6 July 2012] GA, 21st Sess, UN Doc A/HRC/21/47 [65] [Anaya, "Report"].
6. See "Ratifications of C169—Indigenous and Tribal Peoples Convention, 1989 (No. 169)" (International Labour Organization, 2017) <http://www.ilo.org/dyn/normlex/en/f?p=1000:11300:0::NO:11300:P11300_INSTRUMENT_ID:312314>.
7. Patricia Urteaga-Crovetto, "Implementation of the Right to Prior Consultation in the Andean Countries: A Comparative Perspective" (2018) 50(1) The Journal of Legal Pluralism and Unofficial Law 7, 8 [Urteaga-Crovetto].

8. Fábio De Castro and others, *The Extraction and Conservation of Natural Resources in South America: Recent Trends and Challenges* (Centre for Latin American Research and Documentation (CEDLA) 2014) <http://www.cedla.uva.nl/50_publications/pdf/cuadernos/cuad27.pdf> 6–7.
9. Economic Commission for Latin America and the Caribbean (ECLAC), *Foreign Direct Investment in Latin America and the Caribbean* (LC/G.2680-P 2016) 107.
10. OECD, *OECD Guidelines for Multinational Enterprises* (OECD 2011) <http://www.oecd.org/daf/inv/mne/48004323.pdf> [40].
11. Inter-American Commission on Human Rights, *Criminalization of the Work of Human Rights Defenders* (OROEA/Ser.L/II.Doc.49/15 2015) [48]–[50].
12. "On Dangerous Ground: The Killing and Criminalization of Land and Environmental Defenders Worldwide" (*Global Witness*, 20 June 2016) <https://www.globalwitness.org/en/campaigns/environmental-activists/dangerous-ground/> 5.
13. Ibid 8.
14. Shin Imai, Leah Gardner and Sarah Weinberger, "The 'Canada Brand': Violence and Canadian Mining Companies in Latin America" (Osgoode Legal Studies Research Paper No 17, 17 December 2016) <https://poseidon01.ssrn.com/delivery.php?ID=501005104009101082109016002113098095100069023042044044077006004127070088101093000100124100057006057063050085115015083086016080033035092028083004001073000095124024119022054020004079088126096029115079081121094019065025028065126066005011115101101013066031&EXT=pdf>.
15. Rodríguez Garavito asks: "How is this coexistence of order and chaos (this coexistence of the utmost legal formalism and the most extreme violence) possible?": César Rodríguez-Garavito, "Ethnicity.gov: Global Governance, Indigenous Peoples, and the Right to Prior Consultation in Social Minefields" [2010] 18 Indiana Journal of Global Legal Studies 1, 4–5 [Garavito]; Also see Roger Merino Acuña, "The politics of extractive governance: Indigenous peoples and socio-environmental conflicts" [2015] 2 The Extractive Industries and Society 85 [Merion Acuña].
16. Roger Merino Acuña, "Critical Human Rights and Liberal Legality: Struggling for 'The Right to Have Communal Rights'" (2013) 3(3) Philosophy Study 246; Umut Özsu, "Neoliberalism and Human Rights: The Brandt Commission and the Struggle for New World" [2018] 81 Law and Contemporary Problems 139; David Kennedy, "The International Human Rights Regime: Still Part of the Problem?" in Ole Windahl Pedersen (ed), *Examining Critical Perspectives on Human Rights* (Cambridge University Press 2013).
17. Szablowski (n 5) 116.
18. Ibid 120.
19. Ibid 127.
20. Ibid 124–125.
21. Anaya, "Extractive Industry" (n 4) [41].
22. Ibid [41]–[46]. Anaya mentions three other pre-conditions related to: (1) state-driven strategic planning regarding resource use; (2) company due diligence; and (3) extraterritorial regulation by companies' home states ([47]–[57]).
23. Anaya, "Report" (n 5) [67].
24. Anaya, "Extractive Industries" (n 4) [73]–[77].
25. Anaya stated that benefits should include direct financial benefits and compensation for adverse effects, determined in proportion to what Indigenous peoples provide in return, including access to land and resources, as well as what they may give up, including alternatives for future development.
26. Elisa Morgera, "Under the Radar: Fair and Equitable Benefit-Sharing and the Human Rights of Indigenous Peoples and Local Communities Connected to Natural Resources" [2017] BENELEX Working Paper No 10, 2–3, 9–10.

27. Ibid 8.
28. Ibid 6.
29. Anaya, "Extractive Industries" (n 4) [24]–[25].
30. Ibid [78].
31. Also see: "El derecho a la consulta previa, libre e informada de los pueblos indígenas" (*Due Process of Law Foundation*, 2011) <http://www.dplf.org/sites/default/files/1301596126.pdf>; Amanda Fulmer and others, "Indigenous Rights, Resistance and the Law: Lessons from a Guatemalan Mine" (2008) 50(4) Latin American Politics and Society 91.
32. Riccarda Flemmer and Almut Schilling-Vacaflor, "Unfulfilled Promises of the Consultation Approach: The Limits to Effective Indigenous Participation in Bolivia's and Peru's Extractive Industries" (2016) 37(1) Third World Quarterly 172; Also see: Deborah Delgado-Pugley, "Contesting the Limits of Consultation in the Amazon Region: On Indigenous Peoples' Demands for Free Prior and Unformed Consent in Bolivia and Peru" [2013] 43 Rev Gen 151 [Delgado-Pugley].
33. Ibid 7, 8.
34. Ibid 10–11.
35. Ibid 12. For another study that concluded that agreements with industry left communities in Peru worse off, see: Glenn H. Shepard Jr., "Compensation to Native Communities of the Lower Urubamba by the Camisea Consortium: Impacts, Benefits and Failures" (*Academia*, November 2017) <https://www.academia.edu/36453472/Compensation_to_Native_Communities_of_the_Lower_Urubamba_by_the_Camisea_Consortium_Impacts_Benefits_and_Failures?auto=download>.
36. Ana Leyva, *Consúltame de Verdad: Aproximación a un balance sobre consulta previa en el Perú en los sectores minero e hidrocarbonífero* (Oxfam June 2018) [Leyva].
37. Ibid 53.
38. Ibid 65–6, 68.
39. Ibid 21, 55–6.
40. Ibid 21, 55, 67, 69–70; The CooperAcción/Oxfam study also cites similar findings made by Peru's Ombudsperson in 2016: ibid 53.
41. Ibid 24.
42. Garavito, (n 15). This research included 88 interviews along with participant observation.
43. Ibid 37.
44. Ibid 39. Notwithstanding this, Rodríguez Garavito believes that the right to consultation can have an emancipatory effect when its procedures are used strategically to challenge or postpone resource extractive projects or introduce legal innovations that help address communities' substantive concerns: ibid 12, 40–42.
45. Ibid 6, 22–23; Garavito (n 15) builds on David Harvey, "The 'New' Imperialism: Accumulation by Dispossession" [2004] 40 Socialist Register 63.
46. Ibid 16, 22–23.
47. Urteaga-Crovetto (n 7) 18–20. Also see Elizabeth G. Salmon, "The Struggle for Laws of Free, Prior, and Informed Consultation in Peru: Lessons and Ambiguities in the Recognition of Indigenous Peoples'" [2013] 22 Pac Rim L & Pol'y J 353, 356 [Salmon].
48. Roger Merino Acuña, "Prior Consultation: Law and the Challenges of the New Legal Indigenism in Peru" (2014) 4(1) Hendu 19, 22–26. According to Acuña, one feature of this legality is its insistence that certain people must be sacrificed in favour of the national interest and the alleged economic benefits for all. Also see: ibid Salmon 354.
49. Merino Acuña (n 16) 23–24.
50. Ibid 85, 90.
51. Robert T. Coulter, "Free, Prior, and Informed Consent: Not the Right it is Made Out to Be" (University of Colorado Law School Conference on Free, Prior and Informed Consent: Pathways for a New Millennium, 31 October 2013)

unpublished. Also see: Robert T. Coulter, "The Law of Self-Determination and the United Nations Declaration on the Rights of Indigenous Peoples" [2010] 15 UCLA Journal of International Law & Foreign Affairs 1.

52. Ibid 3.
53. ibid 2 (emphasis original).
54. Nathan Yaffe, "Indigenous Consent: A Self-Determination Perspective" (2018) 19(2) Melbourne Journal of International Law 39.
55. Ibid 27.
56. Ibid 4–5.
57. Ibid 37.
58. Ibid 4–5.
59. Instituto del Bien Común, Centro Peruano de Estudios Sociales, *Directorio 2016 Comunidades Campesinas del Perú: Sistema de Información sobre Comunidades Campesinas del Perú (Instituto Del Bien Comun* 2016) 10 <http://www.ibcperu.org/wp-content/uploads/2017/06/DIRECTORIO-DE-COMUNIDADES-CAMPESINAS-DEL-PERU-2016.pdf>. This includes 6,138 Communities in the costal and Andean regions and 1,129 in the Amazonian region. Of these, a total of 5,137 have official recognition and communal title.
60. For a full description of the relationship between these legal frameworks, see Charis Kamphuis, "Litigating Indigenous Dispossession in the Global Economy: Law's Promises and Pitfalls" (2017) 14(1) Brazilian Journal of International Law 165 [Kamphuis, "Litigating Indigenous Dispossession"].
61. Salmon (n 47) 372.
62. For a detailed account of the transition from agrarian reform laws to pro-investment laws, see: Kamphuis, "Litigating Indigenous Dispossession" (n 65).
63. Law on the Right of Consultation of Indigenous Peoples Recognized in Convention 169 of the International Labour Organization (L 29785) 2011.
64. See: Delgado-Pugley (n 35); Salmon (n 51) 385–7; Claire Wright, "Indigenous Mobilisation and the Law of Consultation in Peru: A Boomerang Pattern?" (2014) 5(4) International Indigenous Policy Journal 1, 8.
65. Directive No 03-2012/MC adopted by Ministry of Culture, Ministerial Resolution No 202-2012-MC (2012) art 7.1.
66. The ILO Committee of Experts has criticized Peru's approach to defining Indigenous peoples. For just one example, see: ILO, Committee of Experts on the Application of Conventions and Recommendations, "*Indigenous and tribal peoples: Observations of Peru, Indigenous and Tribal Peoples Convention, 1989 (No. 169),*" ILC.100/III/1A (ILO: 2011), 794–795.
67. Delgado-Pugley (n 35) 169; Leyva (n 40) 38–39.
68. For a full analysis of this issue: Kamphuis, "Litigating Indigenous Dispossession" (n 60).
69. Álvaro Másquez Salvador and Juan Carlos Ruiz Molleda, "Gobierno aprueba norma que consagra intromisión en autonomía de Comunidades Campesinas" (*Instituto de Defensa Legal: Justicia Viva*, 15 January 2015) <http://www.justiciaviva.org.pe/notihome/notihome01.php?noti=1526>*; Juan Carlos Ruiz Molleda,* "¿El sexto paquetazo normativo? La aprobación de los DL N° 1192 y N° 1210" (*Instituto de Defensa* Legal: Justicia Viva, 1 October 2015) <http://www.justiciaviva.org.pe/blog/el-sexto-paquetazo-normativo-la-aprobacion-de-los-dl-n-1191-y-n-1210/>.
70. Legislative Decree No 1192 as modified by Legislative Decree No 121 (2015). The law exempts Indigenous peoples from its expropriation provisions (but not Campesino Communities).
71. General Mining Law (Supreme Decree No 014-92-EM) 1992, art 37. The only constraint on the exercise of the state's discretion to approve a company's request to expropriate communal land is "public necessity" or the "national interest."

72. Compensation for expropriation of communal land can only be valued in terms of its commercial value, fixed by the value of any existing improvements and crops being cultivated *at the time* that the expropriation is solicited: Legislative Decree No 1192 (n 77) art 13.1.
73. Ministry of Culture, Base de Datos de Pueblos Indígenas u Originarios, Lista de pueblos indígenas u originarios <https://bdpi.cultura.gob.pe/pueblos-indigenas>. Leyva finds that the state recognizes approximately half of all Campesino and Native Communities as Indigenous: Leyva (n 36) 67.
74. Supreme Decree No 001-2012-MC, Regulation of Law No 29785, *Law for the right of Indigenous and original peoples to prior consultation, recognized in Convention 169 of the International Labour Organization* (2012) art 24.
75. Ibid art 14.
76. Ibid art 15.
77. Ibid arts 10, 18.1. For any community not initially included, or for a state decision for which consultation was not planned, communities have only 15 days after the publication of a consultation plan and/or administrative decision to request that they be included in the consultation process: art 9.
78. Ibid art 19.7.
79. Ibid art 20.6.
80. Ibid arts 23, 11–15.
81. Leyva (n 36) 57–58.
82. Ibid 57–58, 68.
83. Ibid 15.
84. STC No 00007-2007-PI/TC (19 June 2007) [36].
85. Pedro P. Grández Castro, "Sobre el Emergente Derecho Constitucional Indígena en el Espacio Interamericano: Notas Sobre el Derecho a la Consulta Desde la Experiencia Peruana" in *XII Congreso Iberoamericano de Derecho Constitucional* (Universidad Externado de Colombia 2015) 373 [Grández Castro].
86. Some scholars argue that Peru's Indigenous consultation jurisprudence falls short of the standards established by international law: Grández Castro, ibid.
87. Kamphuis, "Litigating Indigenous Dispossession" (n 60).
88. For references to literature on this gap and barriers to accessing justice in Peru: Salmon (n 47) 367, 373.
89. Anthony Bebbington and others, "Anatomies of Conflict: Social Mobilization and New Political Ecologies of the Andes" in Anthony Bebbington and Jeffery Bury (eds), *Subterranean Struggles: New Dynamics of Mining, Oil and Gas in Latin America* (University of Texas Press 2013).
90. Charis Kamphuis, "Foreign Investment and the Privatization of Coercion: A Case Study of the Forza Security Company in Peru" [2011] 37 Brooklyn Journal of International Law 529, 548; EarthRights International et al, *Convenios entre la Policía Nacional y las empresas extractivas en el Perú* (Peru, 2019) <https://drive.google.com/file/d/1tNTEp6aVg-sz_X__L39MNqwSIpvqT7iG/view>.
91. John Dougherty, "InvestigativeMEDIA releases online version of Hudbay Minerals documentary 'Flin Flon Flim Flam'" (*InvestigativeMEDIA*, 31 December 2015) <http://www.investigativemedia.com/investigativemedia-releases-online-version-of-hudbay-minerals-documentary/> [Dougherty].
92. "Comunicado Minister No 008—2017" (*Minister of the Interior*, 22 April 2017) <https://www.mininter.gob.pe/content/sobre-la-situaci%C3%B3n-migratoria-irregular-de-una-ciudadana-canadiense-y-un-norteamericano>.
93. See Dougherty (n 91).
94. One was an "expropriation agreement" and the other was an "easement agreement." It is widely recognized that under Peru's mining laws, a mining easement is tantamount to an expropriation: see Kamphuis, "Litigating Indigenous Dispossession" (n 60).

95. For a full description of the Negritos case, including the complex series of events that took place in relation to these agreements and land transfers, as well as the Community's turn to the law and its legal arguments: see ibid.
96. See Charis Kamphuis, "Foreign Mining, Law and the Privatization of Property: A Case Study from Peru" (2012) 3(2) Journal of Human Rights and the Environment 217, 239.
97. Omar Cairo Roldán, "El panorama general del proceso de amparo en el Perú" (2008) 3(8) Palestra Tribunal Constitucional: Revista de doctrina y jurisprudencia 153, 157.
98. Peru's *amparo* is similar to that of Brazil, Colombia, Dominican Republic, Ecuador, Guatemala and Nicaragua: Allan-Randolph Brewer-Carías, *Constitutional Protection of Human Rights in Latin America: A Comparative Study of Amparo Proceedings* (Cambridge University Press 2008) 139.
99. See Kamphuis "Litigating Indigenous Dispossession" (n 60).
100. For an excellent analysis of the relationship between public law/judicial review and the private law of contracts: Roger Arturo Merino Acuña, "La Tutela Constitucional de la Autonomía Contractual. El Contracto Entre Poder Público y Poder Privado" in *El Derecho Civil Patrimonial y Derecho Constitucional* (Gaceta Jurídica 2009) 43; Roger Arturo Merino Acuña, "Legitimando el Abuso en el Contrato: El Pleno Casatorio Sobre Transacción Extrajudicial y los Contratos Contaminados" [2010] Actualidad Civil y Procesal Civil, Normas Legales 221.

12 Is This Really Benefit Sharing? Understanding Current Practices Around Community-Industry Agreements Tied to Land Investments

Kaitlin Y. Cordes, Tehtena Mebratu-Tsegaye, and Sam Szoke-Burke[1]

I. Introduction

Communities located near land investments for agricultural and forestry projects increasingly interact with investors who seek to sign a range of agreements with them. In theory, this is a positive development: guidelines for responsible land investments urge greater benefit-sharing with, and participation by, land users and project-affected communities, including through the negotiation of agreements between the investor and affected communities or their members. Increased use of community-industry agreements in this context follows patterns seen in the extractive industries, as such agreements, particularly between Indigenous groups and industry, often form an essential component of extractive project design and implementation in some countries. Yet little analysis has been undertaken to date on actual community-industry agreements linked to land investments. This gap in analysis leaves stakeholders without a clear understanding of existing practices, and without evidence-based guidance for improving future agreements.

This chapter highlights the "state of play" around community-industry agreements tied to land investments for agricultural and forestry projects, and provides recommendations on how such agreements, and practices around them, could be improved. It is based on an examination of 42 community-industry agreements tied to land investments in eight countries (Cameroon, Democratic Republic of the Congo, Indonesia, Liberia, Madagascar, Senegal, Sierra Leone, and South Sudan).[2] In addition, the chapter draws from desktop research, including a review of multiple investor-state contracts for land investments that create requirements related to affected communities, as well as from discussions with stakeholders working with communities affected by land investments. While community-industry agreements differ dramatically—including in composition of the parties, with community parties to the agreements including

Indigenous or "native"[3] peoples, as well as rural peoples who do not identify as Indigenous—a close analysis of the agreements collected for this research reveals a number of commonalities. Many of the commonalities are instructive when considering ways to improve or refine future agreements to maximize the benefits realized by project-affected communities while minimizing their risks. Recommendations in this chapter also draw from the much larger body of research on community-industry agreements concluded in the extractive industries.

Part II of the chapter considers how community-industry agreements fit within the broader legal frameworks governing land investments, and how such agreements may serve as a mechanism for benefit sharing. Part III provides an overview of the community-industry agreements examined for this chapter, focussing on the text of the agreements, supplemented by accounts of actual practice.

Based on those observations, and drawing where appropriate from best practices included in guidelines and/or used for community-industry agreements in the extractive industries, Part IV provides substantive and process-oriented recommendations that can be used to avoid common pitfalls and to improve future community-industry agreements tied to land investments.

II. Community-Industry Agreements in Context

Land investments are governed by a complex set of legal frameworks; community-industry agreements should be considered in this context. The domestic legal framework is the primary source of applicable legal rules regulating land investments. International law is also relevant. International human rights law, which imposes obligations on governments and creates responsibilities for investors, requires that rights are respected, protected, and fulfilled, including in the context of investment projects. International investment law may also be relevant to foreign (or sometimes even domestic) investments in land via applicable international investment treaties. Additionally, for foreign investments, the laws of the home country may set out applicable requirements with extraterritorial reach.[4]

In addition to national and international laws, contracts also govern land investments in many countries. Particularly in parts of Africa and Asia, investor-state contracts are often used to transfer land to investors, to reach agreement on what types of incentives will be offered to investors, and/or to otherwise delineate certain rights and obligations related to a land investment. In some places, community-industry agreements are used instead of, or in addition to, investor-state contracts. For example, in contexts where communities own the land and have the right to lease or otherwise transfer use rights to investors, community-industry agreements may be used to effect the transfer. Alternatively, where communities do not have the ability to transfer rights in land, communities and investors may wish to supplement investor-state contracts with their own agreements in order to govern or guide their relationship, or aspects of it. Approaches may also vary within the same country, depending for example on the type and/or location of land being transferred, the type of investor, or the size of the investment.

In addition to potential differences within and between countries, practices may also evolve. Changing practices may be particularly likely in countries where governments are taking steps to recognize the legitimate tenure rights of their citizens or to implement the Voluntary Guidelines on the Responsible Governance of Tenure of Land, Fisheries and Forests in the Context of National Food Security ("Voluntary Guidelines") (See, for example, efforts in Senegal to use a "lease-sub-lease" approach that navigates existing legal restrictions to provide a greater role to communities in leasing land to investors[5]). This wide range of legal contexts and approaches to contracting for land investments means that community-industry agreements themselves differ considerably, as described in Part III.

This chapter focusses on community-industry agreements without distinguishing whether the community members party to the agreements are Indigenous or non-Indigenous. Although the distinction can be helpful in signaling the nature of an individual or group's relationship with and rights to land, and their right to free, prior, and informed consent,[6] the distinction is less relevant to the chapter. The chapter is primarily based on a textual analysis of agreements, with consent and consultations considered only in the very narrow context of the descriptions of consultation processes included in community-industry agreements.

As the agreements analyzed for this chapter fall on a spectrum of legitimate tenure rights, a detailed analysis and overlay of the international and domestic laws applicable to each relevant jurisdiction is beyond the scope of the chapter. Instead, the authors' recommendations are grounded in the best practice of consulting all peoples whose legitimate tenure rights may be affected by an activity.

III. State of Play: What Do These Community-Investor Agreements Look Like?

This chapter uses the term "community-industry agreement" to refer to a contract or agreement between a community (or its representatives) and an investor seeking to carry out an agricultural or forestry project on or near land that is owned, used, or claimed by a community or its members, either communally or individually.[7] The 42 community-industry agreements analyzed for this chapter are diverse in objectives, functions, and detail,[8] and can be described as occupying a spectrum. At one end are "pure lease agreements" that involve a transfer of rights to use land, with the investor compensating landowners or the community financially for use of their land. At the other end of the spectrum are agreements that offer "development benefits" to a community, essentially in exchange for cooperating with the investment, even when the community does not have the power to control allocation of the land required for the investment. Many of the agreements analyzed fall somewhere in the middle of this spectrum. For example, the community may have some, but not full, control over the allocation and use of land, or the investor may offer a mixture of financial and development-related inducements.

Where any agreement is located on this spectrum depends in part on the land governance system in place. In countries where the government leases the land directly to an investor, the community-industry agreements tend to focus on the provision of development benefits in exchange for cooperation. The most common types of benefits seen in these agreements relate to job creation in the affected communities, the development of health- or education-related facilities, and promises to improve infrastructure, including the repairing of roads and building of water wells. In countries where communities are able to lease land directly to an investor, the community-industry agreements are closer to the "pure lease agreement" end of the spectrum. Given the range of objectives, as well as ambiguity regarding the legal status of some of the community-industry agreements reviewed, we use the term "agreements" rather than "contracts" for the remainder of this chapter.

Assessing agreements is an exercise fraught with challenges. There is only so much that the words within the "four corners" of an agreement can explain. Without embedding assessments of agreements within the larger context of relevant domestic legal frameworks, the true meaning or implications of particular provisions may be lost. Moreover, reading community-industry agreements without this context, and without reference to investor-state contracts and other documents relating to the underlying investment, makes it impossible to ascertain how many new obligations or responsibilities are being placed on parties via the agreements. Without further research beyond the documents themselves, one cannot know whether actions described in the document actually took place, how the document is being or will be implemented in practice, or—for any unsigned agreements—whether such agreements were ever finalized and signed. Given these challenges, any assessment of agreements that relies primarily on analyzing the documents—such as the one undertaken for this chapter—will be limited.

Yet despite these caveats, assessing existing agreements provides important insights into current practices around community-industry agreements tied to land investments. Such assessments allow scrutiny of the types of agreements into which communities and investors are entering, and permit a deeper understanding of how such agreements may affect the rights and obligations of, and relationships between, those actors. To the extent that communities and investors continue to use such agreements, this type of assessment also helps to provide recommendations for how those agreements, and practices around them, can be improved. The general observations gleaned from this particular exercise also sound a cautionary note for all stakeholders interested in ensuring that communities' rights are protected in the context of land investments: the research shows that community-investor agreements alone should not be expected to lead to improved outcomes on the ground.

This section first considers the extent to which evidence of consultative processes or legal support for communities is found in the community-industry agreements reviewed. It then examines some of the provisions purporting to benefit communities.

1. *Community Engagement and Access to Legal Support*

Just under half of the community-industry agreements reviewed mention community engagement processes either before or during negotiations of the agreement, as discussed further below. In addition, twelve agreements reviewed reference legal support accessed by the community representative(s).

Although provisions acknowledging engagement processes or legal support provide useful information, analysis of the text cannot fully explain the circumstances in which an agreement was concluded. The absence of such provisions does not preclude the possibility that participatory processes were used; conversely, where participatory processes are mentioned, it is impossible to ascertain from the text the quality of such processes and whether they served their intended purpose. For example, while the involvement of land governance committees suggests that community members may have been involved in decision-making, there is no way to tell whether the governance structures used were actually representative of the groups or community they purport to represent.

This section first discusses evidence of participatory mapping, before turning to evidence of other types of engagement at the negotiation stage. It then looks at whether and how the agreements reviewed mention legal support used by the community in negotiating the agreement.

a. Evidence of Participatory Mapping

Participatory mapping of community lands relevant to the investment is explicitly mentioned in both of the Indonesian agreements reviewed, and eleven of the Liberian agreements reviewed.[9] One participatory mapping process described in a Liberian agreement includes explanations that community representatives—including town chiefs, women's leaders, and youth leaders—had identified the lands that could *not* be developed by the company and includes community members' signatures evincing the participatory mapping process.[10] The Indonesian agreements allow the parties to invite witnesses to observe the mapping of land to be used by the company.[11]

b. Evidence of Consultation at the Negotiation Stage

Some agreements refer to the participation of land or forestry governance committees or of particular groups, such as women or youth, in the negotiation of the agreements. Others refer to consultations related to the agreement's conclusion.

For example, many of the Liberian agreements reviewed contain provisions suggesting that consultative processes were used. These agreements all take the form of either "social agreements" (which are required by Liberian law in the context of timber production, and which are meant to document, among other things, the financial benefits that communities are to receive) or provisional MOUs (mostly focussed on benefits to communities tied to underlying investor-state deals for agricultural investments). In the Liberian agreements that note consultative processes, specific provisions describe direct negotiation of the agreements between the affected communities and the company. The social agreements, for example, typically include the criteria used to elect a community forest development committee to represent the community in such dealings.[12] Eleven out of the sixteen Liberian agreements reviewed clearly state that the free, prior, and informed consent of relevant communities was sought and given in relation to the transfer of land referenced in the agreement.[13] One MOU also includes a provision that community members were satisfied that the land that remained in their control was sufficient for their needs, which perhaps was included to counter any potential claims that the communities were left without adequate fertile lands to safeguard their livelihood.[14] In addition, in fourteen of the sixteen Liberian agreements reviewed, members of the community, members of committees representing the community, or individuals representing different groups in the community (including women's leaders, youth leaders, and elders) are signatories to the agreements.[15]

Another example of an agreement that includes details of consultative processes is the *clause sociale* of a *cahier des charges* from the Democratic Republic of the Congo.[16] This agreement details who was involved in the negotiation process, with each negotiator's signature included at the bottom of each page. The document also mentions that the agreement was a result of three days of negotiation between the parties, which included: alignment of project budgets with the needs of communities; the presentation, identification, and validation of the mandates of the representatives in the negotiations; and the formation of management committees and monitoring committees.

In contrast, multiple agreements reviewed either include no indications of, or remain unclear regarding, the use of participatory or consultative processes. For example, twelve of the fourteen Sierra Leonean lease agreements analyzed were signed by the chiefdom council and, in some cases, other "men of note," without explicit inclusion of landowning families as signatories.[17] As mentioned above, these characteristics do not necessarily mean that participatory processes were not used in the conclusion of the leases. Indeed, under Sierra Leonean domestic law, the chiefdom council is empowered, as custodian or trustee of the land,[18] to assent to such agreements on behalf of landowning families. However, discussions with community stakeholders in dozens of communities that host land investments in Sierra Leone reveal that it is common for land to be leased without landowning families' knowledge, participation, or consent—meaning that the participation of a chiefdom council does not, on its own, indicate a participatory process.

c. Legal Support and Legal Costs During or after the Negotiation Process

Most agreements reviewed do not indicate whether the community's representative had received any legal support in the negotiation and conclusion of the agreement. The Sierra Leonean agreements reviewed were unique in this regard: twelve out of the fourteen Sierra Leonean agreements reviewed included warranties given by the traditional leaders who signed the agreements that they had taken expert legal advice on the terms.[19] Including a warranty of this kind does not necessarily indicate equality between negotiating parties in terms of quality and impartiality of legal advice received, but does imply an awareness of generally existing power imbalances at the negotiating table, and of the potential lack of access to legal support by community representatives entering into agreements.

Almost none of the agreements reviewed mention responsibility for legal costs related to the agreement once concluded. Two agreements from Senegal, however, do address the issue in divergent ways. One agreement states that both parties are required to pay for arbitration fees equally; interestingly, however, it also notes that in the case of "resistance, contestation or abusive opposition" compelling the rural community to engage a "substantive procedure" in which the admissibility and the merits of the case are judicially and permanently recognized, the entirety of the reasonable costs, including lawyers' fees, will be borne by the company.[20] Another agreement includes a provision noting that if legal action is required to clarify or enforce the terms of the agreement, the party requesting such clarification or enforcement shall bear the legal fees and all accompanying costs arising from the claim. This is problematic, as it could create a strong disincentive for community members to attempt to clarify or enforce their rights and obligations under the agreement using legal processes.[21]

2. *Rent and Social-Benefit Provisions*

All of the community-industry agreements reviewed include at least one provision purporting to benefit the community—such as a commitment to pay rent or compensation, or to provide benefits like jobs or infrastructure. The lease agreements reviewed, for example, include provisions on lease rent, and many also list other benefits. Benefits in the non-lease agreements reviewed focus primarily on social infrastructure or services, physical infrastructure, and/or employment.

Many of the "social benefit" provisions have been drafted in a concerning manner. As discussed below, these provisions are often vague, caveated, or lack the detail to be truly enforceable or operationalized. By contrast, provisions designed to protect the rights of an investor are often stated with clarity. This general imbalance raises questions about whether social-benefit clauses have been deliberately drafted to avoid creating concrete rights and obligations to which liability can meaningfully attach. While there may be legitimate reasons for an investor to seek to include caveated or imprecise language, the resulting disparity in how provisions are drafted could affect whose rights are protected and whose are ignored.

Vague or caveated drafting related to social benefits also creates the possibility of a divergence of expectations between the company, whose lawyers will likely identify when a vague clause does not create an enforceable obligation for the investor to do or refrain from doing something, and the community, which may expect to receive certain benefits or protections mentioned in the agreement. If the company's behavior does not meet community expectations (even where the company fully complies with the agreement), such perceived and/or actual failure by a company could cause a breakdown in trust between a company and a community, and lead to community grievances and opposition.

This section first discusses how the agreements reviewed address (when applicable) lease rent, royalties, and method of payment. It then examines provisions related to social benefits, including social and physical infrastructure as well as employment provisions.

a. Lease Rent, Royalties, and Method of Payment

The price to lease agricultural land varies between the agreements reviewed. In some contexts, the price depends on the type of farmland being acquired; in most cases, the price was very low. Those from Sierra Leone, for example, set annual rents that were much lower than the government's recommended rent, which had been set in a policy pre-dating the conclusion of all Sierra Leonean agreements reviewed.

In addition to rent, multiple agreements mention royalties or other types of monetary compensation. For example, ten agreements from Sierra Leone include a royalty provision under which a percentage of net profits is to be paid into a community development fund controlled and managed by the paramount chief, members of parliament, councilors, and company representatives (as well as, in one agreement, representatives of landowners).[22] Some profit-sharing clauses include caveats that make payment of a community's share in the profits conditional on that share being greater than the amount of lease rent paid.

In addition, some of the agreements reviewed stipulate how the lease rent or royalty will be spent or distributed. For example, some agreements say that money can be spent for the purpose of funding development projects,[23] or is to be split multiple ways between landowners and traditional and other authorities.[24]

Many agreements reviewed either do not include details of rent payment mechanisms, or provide details of mechanisms that have the potential to create challenges in practice. A problematic payment mechanism found in half of the Sierra Leonean agreements reviewed, for example, requires that rent owed to a large number of landowners be paid to a local authority, or into one communal account with three signatories (a tribal authority along with two landowner representatives).[25] This sort of payment mechanism creates a risk that the payments will not reach all intended beneficiaries, even where some or all of the signatories to the account were appointed directly by the community. Although these agreements do not protect the landowning beneficiaries from the risk of funds being spent or distributed inappropriately, seven of the agreements reviewed do protect the company against this risk, requiring the community to indemnify the company with respect to claims relating to rent distribution once the company has paid into the relevant communal account.[26]

b. Social Benefits and Infrastructure Development

As noted above, the provisions around social benefits in the agreements reviewed are usually vague and often qualified. In a Madagascan agreement, for example, the company agrees to set up a health centre, schools, and training facilities, amongst other things.[27] Apart from the vague nature of the commitments (which fail to specify, for example, who would be responsible for financing and administering the institutions' ongoing operations), the clause contains a major caveat that such activities would be undertaken "where it is necessary for implementation of the project." This caveat makes it likely that the company would have complete discretion in determining when such activities are necessary. Similarly, in twelve Sierra Leonean lease agreements, the company agrees to reasonably assist in providing and supporting education initiatives (or similar language).[28] This language leaves at the companies' discretion the extent of support constituting reasonable assistance. Without a commitment to confer certain benefits in a non-discretionary manner, or clear and appropriate guiding principles for the exercise of such discretion, it is unlikely that such provisions could be successfully enforced by community members. Similarly weak language was found in a Cameroonian agreement: the company agrees to provide certain social benefits "where practicable," and to "contribute" to schools, without detail regarding to which schools the company will contribute, the nature of the contribution, or the time frame for delivering on this commitment.[29]

Another example of commitments that may have limited benefits for the community involves promises to build physical infrastructure that will primarily benefit the company's operations. For example, the majority of the Liberian agreements reviewed include commitments to build and improve road and bridge infrastructure "as part of"—and presumably only when needed for—the company's operations under the concession. Many of the agreements also note that "this will provide repairs to roads to the direct benefit of communities," but do not provide information on whether communities have any say in which roads are repaired. This may mean that the company could repair a road or bridge needed for its operations, and claim that the repairs constitute part of its contribution of social benefits. Several agreements, however, do identify specific roads or areas with roads to be repaired.[30] To the extent that the communities were involved in identifying those roads or areas, such specification in the agreement might help ensure a closer match between community and company expectations, and could make it easier for the communities to monitor whether the companies comply with their commitments. On the other hand, specifically identifying roads limits the community's ability to obtain repairs to other infrastructure as needed.

In contrast to these vague or potentially unenforceable social commitments, an agreement from the Democratic Republic of the Congo includes more detail, with the company agreeing to finance the development of one school and one medical centre in a specific stated location, and committing to provide local transportation to every person in circumstances specified in the agreement.[31] While this provision could benefit from an even higher degree of specificity to aid enforceability—in particular, time frames for development of the facilities, and greater detail on what the company commits to finance (and whether this includes financing staff on an ongoing basis)—it represents an improvement on the heavily discretionary provisions seen in the vast majority of agreements reviewed.

c. Job Creation

Individuals and communities that own, use, or claim land on which a company's operations are to take place often consider meaningful employment as a key reason to agree to investment in their lands. It is therefore no surprise that over half of the investor-community agreements analyzed mention employment of local workers.

The type and quality of employment commitments, however, vary in the agreements reviewed. An agreement from Cameroon, for example, promises employment priority for indigenes of the particular area in which it is operating.[32] Similar provisions are seen in twelve of the Liberian agreements reviewed, with slightly broader wording that prioritizes employment of communities affected by the company's operations.[33] In twelve Sierra Leonean agreements, companies' commitments are even broader, and include efforts to employ local people with requisite qualifications and skills over expatriates.[34] Because "local person" in the context of the agreement is not defined, the companies could (and in practice, many do) employ workers from communities unrelated to the land on which their businesses operate; this has been a common source of discontent.

A shared feature of the majority of agreements reviewed is an absence of detail regarding the type of jobs that will be provided beyond describing jobs as either "skilled" or "unskilled." Many of the unskilled jobs offered by an agribusiness are seasonal; failure to communicate this to community members (with such understanding reflected in the agreement) may lead to the disappointment of those who eagerly await steady employment and income. Similarly, none of the agreements reviewed contain indications of the scale of employment opportunities available, with the exception of one agreement stating that the company's operations will employ "several thousand full time permanent employees."[35] (Incidentally, it has been reported that this provision has not been honoured, and that the numbers of locally employed people fell far below several thousand.[36])

3. *Other Issues*

Several other aspects of the agreements reviewed raise particular concerns, but do not fall into the broader categories listed above. They are described briefly below.

a. Breach of Agreement and Dispute Resolution

Twelve of the agreements reviewed, all land leases from Sierra Leone, contain provisions that allow for land to revert back to the landowners when rent payments are in arrears for a certain number of days, as long as notice has been given to the company and/or a reasonable amount of time has passed to rectify the breach.[37] Such a reversion is not automatic. Rather, the chiefdom council as lessors can trigger the reversion by re-entering the land. This type of provision incentivizes the company's timely payment of rent, and provides the community with a point of leverage to ensure compliance by the company with the agreement. In practice, however, the benefit of such leverage may be undermined if traditional leaders fail to invoke such a provision. In most of these twelve agreements, 21 days is the standard cure period, although some agreements contain longer periods or include additional conditions, such as requiring that the amount of lease rent in arrears total at least US$15,000 to trigger the community's right to re-enter the land.[38]

None of the agreements reviewed contain similar reversion clauses based on the company's failure to deliver other social benefits or comply with any other obligations under the agreement. This represents a missed opportunity for increasing the tools available to the community to hold the investor to the terms of the agreement. Separately, when related investor-state contracts exist, *host states* could also seek to incentivize company compliance with social benefits commitments by reserving their right to terminate the related investor-state contract in the event of the company's failure to deliver the social benefits outlined in the community-industry agreement.[39] Of course, such a provision in an investor-state contract would only benefit the community if the government were inclined to invoke such a right in practice.

To the extent that the community-industry agreements reviewed contain provisions on dispute resolution, they envisage local options for the final mode of dispute resolution—including resort to local courts or local arbitration in accordance with local law—with the exception of two agreements. One agreement, which is from Senegal but governed by French law, requires any dispute arising out of the agreement that cannot be settled amicably to be heard by the International Chamber of Commerce in Paris, France and to be conducted in English.[40] Similarly, a draft lease agreement from Sierra Leone requires any dispute arising out of the lease to be resolved by final and binding arbitration in London.[41] These outlier provisions raise obvious accessibility concerns, and reduce the likelihood that communities and their representatives could feasibly engage with the designated dispute procedures.

b. Confidentiality Clauses

Four of the agreements reviewed contained confidentiality clauses. There may be instances where community members themselves wish to keep details regarding promised benefits confidential from those outside the community: for instance, to minimize tensions with or resentment from neighbouring communities, or to prevent the diversion of government-provided social services due to the community's new source of income. Yet confidentiality clauses may limit communities' options in receiving informed support from civil society allies or the media in the event that the company does not comply with the agreement. At the very least, confidentiality clauses should not preclude the sharing of information within a community.

One confidentiality clause reviewed explicitly prohibits disclosure of the agreement, unless required by law.[42] This express prohibition could narrow the strategies available to the community if it subsequently seeks to protect its interests. Such confidentiality clauses also prevent communities from sharing their agreements with other communities that may benefit from learning about the content and operation of other agreements.

Three other agreements contain broader confidentiality clauses. One agreement prohibits either party from disclosing any information relating to the business of the other party, except insofar as disclosure is necessary for the work of each party in the investment project.[43] This provision is potentially skewed in favour of the company, given that the community may not have any "work" to do under the project. The agreement also sets out that wrongful disclosure can be remedied by injunctive relief requiring the party not to disclose specific information or to return to the other party all documents and information. Another agreement is even broader, restricting disclosure of "all the information end [sic] details." This clause applies to landowners and a landowners association, but not to the company itself.[44] An additional agreement focusses on non-disclosure of the agreement and information contained within the agreement, although providing exceptions for parties' advisors, for disclosure required by law or by order of court, and for disclosure that may be agreed by the parties.[45] This agreement also potentially broadens the disclosure prohibition to "any information of any nature whatsoever which is not in the public domain," as well as restricts parties from making public announcements regarding the transactions referred to in the agreement. These broad confidentiality clauses could be interpreted expansively to prohibit disclosure of the agreement itself, as well as information regarding the company's performance under, and any breaches of, the agreement. This in turn could hamper each community's ability to conduct advocacy regarding any failure by the company to comply with the agreement.

IV. Recommendations

This section provides recommendations that are primarily aimed at communities, communities' advocates, and companies, but may also be of interest for host governments, development partners, and other stakeholders.[46]

Recommendations draw from the community-industry agreements reviewed,[47] as well as from the authors' experience and field work. Where relevant, they also refer to international best practice related to land investments and to community-industry agreements concluded in the extractive industries. Indeed, the recommendations described below largely reflect the much larger body of research on extractives-related community-industry agreements. Of course, there are fundamental differences between agricultural projects and extractives projects, as well as between their related community-industry agreements. For instance, the impacts and project economics of such investments can differ dramatically. Another difference arises in the objectives of community-industry agreements. As noted above, the objectives of community-industry agreements tied to land investments can vary significantly: approximately one-third of the agreements reviewed for this research could be considered central project documents because they transfer rights to use land for company operations. In the extractive industries, on the other hand, community-industry agreements are largely, although not exclusively, ancillary to investor-state contracts.

Despite these differences, lessons from the extractive industries are relevant in reflecting on ways to improve community-industry agreements around land investments. One critical question relates to whether "contractual" arrangements between communities and investors should even be emulated in the agricultural and forestry sector, or whether different approaches of securing rights and benefits should be considered and advanced. As noted in ICCM guidance, the most effective community-industry agreements in the extractive sector are not considered "static legal documents," but rather a framework to govern the relationship between communities and companies.[48] Given the less frequent use of community-industry agreements in the agriculture and forestry sectors to date, there is an opportunity for practitioners to reflect on whether such agreements would be better reframed as binding frameworks that are revisited over time to adjust for evolving conditions, and, if so, how that could be successfully implemented in practice. The answers might be highly context-specific, requiring nuanced approaches for different types of agreements. Agreements transferring rights to agribusinesses to access and use land for long-term operations, for example, might necessarily require that certain rights and obligations remain static for the duration of the agreements.

1. *Consultations and Support in the Context of Negotiations, and Documentation Thereof*

Unless legal support, capacity building, and other resources are available, communities should strongly consider not negotiating an agreement with a company, especially where the proposed agreement would transfer interests in land or create obligations for the community. Legal and other types of support for communities considering such agreements are necessary to ensure that agreements represent the interests of the community and align with their expectations. The availability of capacity building and other support can also help communities negotiate agreements in accordance with robust and inclusive community decision-making processes. Support can also help communities to access and understand information relating to a project, such as the outcome of impact assessments, in advance of deciding whether to enter into an agreement.

Host governments and companies should implement programs and strategies to make legal and other support available to communities, in ways that guarantee the independence of such support. Innovative efforts have been undertaken in some places to strengthen communities' access to legal support in the context of land investments. For example, in Liberia and Sierra Leone, early warning and legal hotlines have been piloted to support communities that have been approached by investors interested in land-related dealings.[49] Host governments and other stakeholders could consider establishing similar programs to support the legal needs of communities in the context of potential investment; this would align with guidance documents such as the Voluntary

Guidelines, which suggest that governments capacitate rights-holders to know their rights and exercise them effectively in consultations. Such efforts could be supplemented by initiatives to ensure that communities have the financial resources that they need to engage appropriate legal and technical support; for example, under Sierra Leone's National Land Policy, the government is meant to implement a legal assistance fund that will support communities, land owners, and land users negotiating with land investors.[50]

Communities and companies should ensure that any consultative and participatory processes carried out before the negotiation of an agreement are documented in the agreement, and that the agreement includes community members as signatories or witnesses. Documenting consultative and participatory processes and their outcomes in the final agreement helps to illustrate that the agreement was entered into with the support of the wider community. Lessons learned from the extractives sector suggest that the success of community-industry agreements depends in large part on "the methods and techniques" used to develop them.[51] Including community members as signatories or witnesses to agreements that impact their rights also helps to indicate that agreements took their interests into account, although it does not automatically safeguard against exploitative agreements, or even guarantee that signatories understood what they signed.

As seen in some of the Liberian agreements reviewed, agreements could include explicit provisions that set out the identity and authority of the negotiators and signatories to the agreement (ensuring that all relevant rights-holders are signatories), as well as provisions that describe the nature of the involvement of project-affected communities in consultations and negotiations.

Agreements could also document any participatory mapping processes that were used to determine the area of land to be allocated to an investment, as evidence that such practices were carried out. Participatory mapping allows communities to take part in identifying the exact location of land to be used for company operations, and helps to establish a common understanding. When communities are not involved in the mapping process, they are less likely to know the size or boundaries of land to be used.

2. Creating Clear, Detailed, Time-bound Obligations

Communities and companies should ensure that agreements are drafted in clear language, with detailed and time-bound obligations. In general, social-benefit provisions within community-industry agreements would benefit from a higher degree of specificity. Such provisions should not give the company discretion to, at a later date, decide the nature and extent of the benefits to be provided to the community. Rather, benefits should be negotiated and clearly articulated in the agreement. Communities can work to make company's obligations clearer and more enforceable by requiring that agreements: set time frames for carrying out relevant activities; specify minimum amounts of spending on benefits or of revenue that will be shared with the community, as well as the basis on which those amounts will be calculated; and include detail on the parameters of what the company is required to provide for the committed benefits.

3. Compensation and Monetary Benefit Sharing

Communities and companies should work towards agreements that include adequate payments and compensation, and could consider, where appropriate, including profit-sharing arrangements. Improving the payments and compensation that communities or individuals receive is critical to improving the terms of most community-industry agreements. Mechanisms to support stronger negotiations by communities and more equitable payment terms include: technical support for communities or individuals in valuing land, in assessing the true costs of leasing the land, and in ascertaining the value and limitations of offered benefits; legal support to communities or individuals in the negotiation process; and the opportunity to actually negotiate the rent and compensation numbers, rather than receiving those numbers from the company as a fait accompli. In no case should lease rent or land use compensation fall below the amounts suggested by government policy (as seen in the Sierra Leonean agreements). At the same time, so long as such policies do not limit lease rents, government recommendations should be considered simply as a floor below which rents should not go.

In addition to lease rent and other social benefits offered, profit-sharing mechanisms could also be included. While such mechanisms offer potential benefits for communities, they also can be used exploitatively and as a mechanism to shift greater risk onto communities. Communities considering such mechanisms should carefully assess the benefits and costs of such mechanisms. They also should seek support in negotiating favourable terms and equitable risk-sharing, and in creating safeguards to ensure that they will still receive a baseline amount of compensation, rent, or other benefits that are not tied to profits.

Communities and companies should agree on payment mechanisms that ensure that rent and other compensation, including shared profits, will be allocated equitably and spent in ways that directly benefit community members and contribute to community-driven development. Payment mechanisms that concentrate access to funds, particularly regarding land lease rent or land use compensation, in the hands of a small number of community representatives do little to mitigate the risk of the potential illicit diversion of funds. When faced with a very large number of community member beneficiaries, the community and the company should work together to design the most appropriate mechanism for disbursing and receiving payments. In some cases—especially where land is not communally held, and individual community members or families have formally or customarily recognized tenure rights, and when the community-industry agreement takes the form of a pure lease agreement—the most appropriate mechanism may be for each beneficiary to receive their share of payment. In other cases, where land is communally held, a representative and inclusive community development committee may be formed, with representatives from traditional leadership, as well as women, youth, and other subgroups, to determine how funds can be most effectively put towards the community's development.

Companies' attempts, seen in some of the agreements reviewed, to avoid liability for diversion of payment through indemnity provisions are onerous and should be avoided. Such provisions apportion the risk that such funds will be diverted or misspent entirely to the community beneficiaries; they also do not address the structural deficiencies that exacerbate such risks, such as ill-designed methods of payment that fail to account for local politics. Instead of seeking an indemnity, companies should seek methods of payment that will ensure that the funds get to the intended beneficiaries.

V. Conclusion

Community-industry agreements have the potential to assist in better aligning land investments with respect for the rights of landowners and land users. They can encourage meaningful communication between the community and the investor, allowing project-affected people to articulate their priorities while supporting investors in managing expectations through concrete time-bound commitments. Importantly, they can help translate a community's prioritized needs, and an investor's promises, into legally binding obligations.

Yet analysis of the agreements reviewed for this chapter reveals that community-industry agreements, as they have been drafted in most agreements to date, are failing to realize this potential. To realize their potential, community-industry agreements for land investments must: (a) establish, with clarity and certainty, the enforceable rights and obligations of each party with respect to the use of land; (b) be negotiated on a level playing field with adequate and equitable consideration or benefits; and (c) provide each party with a means to access remedy should one party breach the terms of the agreement in a material way.

Of course, even the most clear and certain agreement—drafted after an equal, thorough, and participatory negotiation, and including enforceable rights, obligations, and mechanisms to incentivize compliance—will not always translate into better practices on the ground. Agreements do not guarantee increased respect for the rights of project-affected communities or increased access to benefits from land investments. Moreover, the efficacy of a well-drafted community-investor agreement will also depend on the integrity and accessibility of enforcement mechanisms.

The findings of this chapter sound a cautionary note: as currently used, community-investor agreements are unlikely to lead to more equitable sharing of benefits with communities affected by land investments. This does not mean that they cannot be improved, however. And despite their limitations, in some contexts, a well-drafted agreement has the potential to improve understandings between the community and the investor, to sharpen investor's obligations and strengthen communities' rights, and to serve as a tool for communities to enforce promises made to them by investors at the outset of a project.

Notes

1. The authors are extremely grateful for the research support provided by Lauren Waugh during her time serving as an LLM Fellow at the Columbia Center on Sustainable Investment.
2. While the agreements surveyed come from seven African and one Southeast Asian country, questions around community-industry agreements—particularly benefit agreements—have arisen around the world, including in the global North. See Lila Katz Barrera-Hernandez and others, *Sharing the Costs and Benefits of Energy and Resource Activity: Legal Change and Impact on Communities* (1st ed, Oxford University Press 2016). Published agreements available at: openlandcontracts.org.
3. For example, for the purpose of land tenure in the provinces of Sierra Leone where many of the agreements reviewed for this research are from, "natives" and "non-natives" are distinguished on the basis of patrilineal affinity with indigenous Sierra Leoneans. See Ade Renner-Thomas, *Land Tenure in Sierra Leone* (AuthorHouse 2010) 7–9.
4. The interactions between these various legal frameworks, and obligations under them, is beyond the scope of this chapter. For further discussion of interactions between international law, domestic law, and investor-state contracts in the context of land investments, see Kaitlin Y. Cordes, Lise Johnson, and Sam Szoke-Burke, "Land Deal Dilemmas: Grievances, Human Rights, and Investor Protections" (*Columbia Center on Sustainable Investment*, March 2016) <http://ccsi.columbia.edu/files/2016/03/CCSI_Land-deal-dilemmas.pdf>.
5. World Bank, "World Bank Finances Senegal's Agribusiness Plans to Boost its Food Production and Jobs; Will Also Help the Wider Sahel Region" (*World Bank*, 19 December 2013) <http://www.worldbank.org/en/news/press-release/2013/12/19/world-bank-senegal-agribusiness-sahel>.
6. As codified in international law and set out in international guidelines, for e.g., *International Labour Organization (ILO) Convention concerning Indigenous and Tribal Peoples* (27 June 1989) C169 (entered into force 5 September 1991); United Nations Declaration on the Rights of Indigenous Peoples, GA Res 61/295, UN Doc A/RES/61/295 (13 September 2007).
7. For purposes of this chapter, "investor" and "company" are used interchangeably.
8. For this research, we collected as many community-industry agreements for land investments as we could find, both through searches for publicly available contracts (including on OpenLandContracts.org) as well as through our network of contacts working on land investments. Land investments are often opaque, and documents governing them are often not publicly available—particularly at the time that this research was conducted. For this reason, we were limited in the number of documents available for analysis. Some of the agreements reviewed are now available on OpenCommunityContracts.org. A few caveats about the 42 agreements that we did analyze: one agreement reviewed was labeled as "draft" and did not contain signatures. Four other agreements also did not contain signatures, and thus may not constitute the final version of the agreement; some may never have been finalized. Some of the agreements reviewed were also described as "provisional," although noted to be binding until superseded by a final version.
9. See, for example, Memorandum of Agreement between Agronusa Investama and Sajingan Kecil Hamlet Community (Indonesia, 2008) [MOU Agronusa Investama]; Provisional Memorandum of Understanding and Social Agreement between Zoloken and Golden Veroleum (Liberia, 17 December 2013).
10. Memorandum of Understanding between Equatorial Palm Oil Company, Tarlo Town, Blayah Town, Nuhn Town and Qlakpojelay (Liberia, 2016).
11. MOU Agronusa Investama (n 9); Memorandum of Agreement between Wilmar Sambas Plantation Co and Senujuh Village (Indonesia, 2008).

12. See, for example, "Social Agreement Negotiations Guide Liberia" (*Client Earth, May 2017*) <https://www.documents.clientearth.org/wp-content/uploads/library/2017-05-03-social-agreement-negotiations-guide-liberia-coll-en.pdf>.
13. See, for example, Memorandum of Understanding and Social Agreement between Golden Veroleum Liberia and Tartweh-Drapoh (Liberia, 2014).
14. Memorandum of Understanding and Social Agreement between Golden Veroleum Liberia and Jarbo (Liberia, 2014).
15. See, for example, Provisional Memorandum of Understanding and Incorporation Social Agreement between Numopoh Community and Golden Veroleum (Liberia) Inc (28 April 2014). (Agreement features over 750 signatures).
16. Kapopo Alunda, "Cahier des charges présenté au gouvernement de la RD Congo. Groupe Mai-Mai Kapopo. Division des Hauts-Plateaux. Etat-Major commandement" (2 January 2011), unpublished document on file with the Rift Valley Institute ["Cahier des charges"].
17. See, for example, Lease Agreement between West Africa Agriculture Limited and Maforki Chiefdom (Sierra Leone, 2011) [Lease Agreement West Africa Agriculture Limited].
18. *The Provinces Land Act*, Ch 122; *The Local Government Act*, 2004 [No. 1 of 2004].
19. See, for example, Lease between Aristeus Palm Oil Limited and the Chiefdom Council of Sorogbema (Pujehun District) (Farm Land Grab, 9 August 2011) <https://www.farmlandgrab.org/post/view/22699-sierra-leone-lease-between-aristeus-palm-oil-limited-and-the-chiefdom-council-of-sorogbema-pujehun-district>; Lease Agreement, Redbunch Ventures (SL) Ltd, Barri Chiefdom (Sierra Leone, 2011) [Lease Agreement Redbunch].
20. Agreement Protocol between Senethanol SA and the Rural Community of Fanaye (Senegal, 2011).
21. "Contrat d'exclusivité pour l'utilisation de terre, Agroafrica (Norvége) et Kounkane" (*Farm Land Grab*, 7 March 2008) <https://www.farmlandgrab.org/post/view/14253-contrat-d-exclusivite-pour-i-utilisation-de-terre-entre-agroafrica-norvege-et-kounkane-senegal> [Contrat d'exclusivité pour l'utilisation de terre].
22. See, for example, Lease Agreement between West Africa Agriculture Number 2 Limited and Makpele Chiefdom (Sierra Leone, 22 June 2012) art. 2.6.
23. Memorandum of Understanding and Social Agreement between Golden Veroleum Liberia and Tarjuowon (Liberia, 2014).
24. Draft Lease Agreement, Addax, Sierra Leone (Unsigned) [Draft Lease Agreement Addax].
25. See, for example, Lease Agreement between West Africa Agriculture Limited and Sorogbema Chiefdom (Sierra Leone, 2011).
26. See, for example, Lease Agreement West Africa Agriculture Limited (n 17).
27. Farming Contract, Varun Agriculture Sarl, Associations of 13 Plains in the Sofia region (Madagascar, 2009) [Farming Contract Varun Agriculture].
28. See, for example, Lease Agreement West Africa Agriculture Limited (n 17); Lease Agreement between Sierra Leone Agriculture and Bureh, Kasseh Maconteh Chiefdom (Sierra Leone, 2010) [Lease Agreement Sierra Leone Agriculture].
29. Memorandum of Understanding between SG Sustainable Oils Cameroon Ltd and Nguti (Cameroon, 2010) [MOU SG Sustainable Oils].
30. Provisional Memorandum of Understanding and Social Agreement between Nitrian Community and Golden Veroleum, Liberia (Liberia, 30 September 2014); Provisional Memorandum of Understanding and Social Agreement between Numopoh Community and Golden Veroleum, Liberia (Liberia, 28 March 2014); Provisional Memorandum of Understanding and Social Agreement between Tartweh-Drapoh Chiedom and Golden Veroleum, Liberia (Liberia, 11 October 2014).
31. "Cahier des charges" (n 16).
32. MOU SG Sustainable Oils (n 29).

33. See, for example, Social Agreement between the Euro Liberia Logging Company and River Gee Counties (Liberia, 2011).
34. See, for example, Lease Agreement Redbunch (n 19).
35. MOU SG Sustainable Oils (n 29).
36. Greenpeace Africa, "SGSOC'S Social Investments: A Cemetery of Broken Promises" (*Greenpeace*, 15 December 2016) <https://www.greenpeace.org/africa/en/publications/493/sgsocs-social-investments/>.
37. See, for example, Lease Agreement Sierra Leone Agriculture (n 28).
38. Draft Lease Agreement Addax (n 24).
39. Land Title Agreement between Central Equatoria State and Tree Farms Sudan Ltd, Annex (Community Support Program Agreement) Lease Agreement, Tree Farms Sudan Ltd, Central Equatoria State (Sudan, 2008).
40. Contrat d'exclusivité pour l'utilisation de terre, Agroafrica (n 21).
41. Draft Lease Agreement Addax (n 24).
42. Ross Béthio, "Convention Strategique West Africa Farms—Ngnith" (*Farm Land Grab*, 1 April 2011) <https://www.farmlandgrab.org/24967>.
43. Contrat d'exclusivité pour l'utilisation de terre (n 21).
44. Farming Contract Varun Agriculture (n 27).
45. MOU Liberia (n 13).
46. For further guidance on negotiating community-industry agreements, see Rachael Knight and others, "Community-Investor Negotiation Guide 1: Preparing in Advance for Potential Investors" (*Namati, Columbia Center on Sustainable Investment*, September 2018) <https://namati.org/resources/community-investor-negotiation-guide-1-preparing-in-advance-for-potential-investors/>; Sam Szoke-Burke and others, "Community-Investor Negotiation Guide 2: Negotiating Contracts with Investors" (*Namati, Columbia Center on Sustainable Investment*, September 2018) <http://ccsi.columbia.edu/work/projects/guidance-for-communities-interacting-with-investors>.
47. As the agreements reviewed were from a small sample size of eight countries, some recommendations may require adaptation to fit particular country contexts.
48. "Good Practice Guide: Indigenous Peoples and Mining" (*International Council on Mining and Metals*, 2010) <http://icmm15ipg.interactiveinvestor.com.au> 40.
49. Ali Kaba and Chelsea Keyser, "Leasons from the Field: Holding Leaders Accountable and Ensuring Community Participation in Land Transactions" (Namati Publications, 2014) <https://namati.org/resources/lessons-from-the-field-holding-leaders-accountable-and-ensuring-community-participation-in-land-transactions/>.
50. This example and others are further discussed in Sam Szoke-Burke and Kaitlin Y. Cordes, "Innovative Financing Solutions for Community Support in the Context of Land Investments" (*Columbia Center on Sustainable Investment*, March 2019) <http://ccsi.columbia.edu/files/2019/03/CCSI-Innovative-Financing-report-Mar-2019.pdf>.
51. Sunrita Sarkat and others, "Mining Community Development Agreements-Practical Experiences and Field Studies" (*The World Bank*, June 2010) <https://womin.org.za/images/the-alternatives/free-prior-and-informed-consent/World%20Bank%20-%20Mining%20Community%20Development%20Agreements%20-%20Field%20Studies.pdf>.

13 Enhancing the Benefits of Local Content in Extractive Industry Agreements: Legal Approaches and Trends in Frontier Extractive Jurisdictions

Damilola S. Olawuyi

I. Introduction

This chapter provides a multijurisdictional analysis and survey of local content requirements (LCRs) in frontier oil, gas, and mining jurisdictions, especially Canada, Australia, United Kingdom, Nigeria, Saudi Arabia, and Qatar, six countries that are home to significant portions of the world's extractive resources.[1] It also examines how LCRs can be clarified and aligned to deliver mutually reinforcing outcomes for governments, industry, and host communities.

Indigenous-industry agreements specifically aim to increase the direct participation of, and economic value to, Indigenous peoples in the exploration, development, and production of extractive resources found in their lands and territories.[2] Yet, in many parts of the Middle East and Africa (MEA) region, while some communities self-identify as "native or Indigenous communities," this nomenclature remains unrecognized in domestic laws.[3] For example, the Nigerian constitution does not specifically recognize any group as Indigenous, rather it contains human rights provisions that apply equally to all Nigerians.[4] Furthermore, all MEA countries, except Central African Republic, have yet to ratify the *1989 International Labour Organization (ILO) Convention concerning Indigenous and Tribal Peoples in Independent Countries*,[5] while Kenya, Republic of Congo, and Cameroon are the only MEA countries to have adopted domestic legislation that mention or recognize minority or Indigenous groups.[6] This lack of formal recognition of Indigenous peoples means that unlike in Canada and Australia, where tailored Indigenous-industry contracts are widely adopted, in much of the MEA region, as well as in the United Kingdom, the relationships between extractive companies, Indigenous or host communities, and governments are often addressed in legislation, regulations, guidelines, bidding practices and generic extractive agreements, such as production sharing contracts (PSCs), or mining development agreements (MDAs). Despite the variance in contexts and conceptualization of the term "Indigenous," one increasingly common approach adopted by resource rich countries across the world to maximize the direct benefits of extractive industry investments to Indigenous or host communities is through the introduction of LCRs in extractive industry agreements and legal frameworks. Extractive industry agreements in this chapter therefore refer to agreements that specify the commitments and relationships between companies, governments, and Indigenous or host communities with respect to extractive activities and projects. These include generic petroleum or mining contracts, as well as community development agreements (CDAs), Indigenous-industry agreements, and associated agreements.

Over the last decade, LCRs—contractual provisions, laws, and policies that require extractive companies to give priority to nationals or locals, Indigenous communities, domestic companies and locally produced material, in the procurement of goods and services used for petroleum and mining operations—have grown in prominence across the world.[7] LCRs have become even more important in resource rich countries following the global fall in oil prices and ensuing economic recession.[8] Generally, LCRs are designed to increase the degree of subnational or local benefits from an extractive investment or project, beyond what it would be in the absence of such policies, through the promotion of local employment, skills development, and national industry participation.[9] Economic benefits may include employment of locals or Indigenous peoples, procurement of goods and services from companies resident in the host country, development of enabling infrastructure, improvement of skills and capacity of local businesses, and expansion of endogenous technological capabilities.[10] For example, in Canada, specifically in Saskatchewan, Newfoundland, and Nova Scotia, LCRs have included contractual obligations that 35% of all goods and services are to be sourced from Indigenous-owned businesses.[11] Similarly, in 2019, Qatar's national oil company, Qatar Petroleum, launched its Localization Program for Services and Industries in the Energy Sector (TAWTEEN), which sets the target of localizing Qatar's oil and gas supply chain to provide growth opportunities for local small and medium enterprises.[12] Also, in 2015, Saudi Arabia's national oil company, Saudi Aramco, launched its In Kingdom Total Value Add (IKTVA) program, aimed at driving, measuring, and monitoring the "added value" brought to the Kingdom by a contractor.[13] Similarly, in 2012, the United Kingdom's UK Offshore Wind Industry Council (OWIC) approved an aspirational target of achieving 50% UK content in offshore renewable energy projects by 2020.[14]

While LCRs provide important policy tools for maximizing the degree of local benefits from the extractive sector, LCRs could also provide a basis for international oil companies (IOCs), service companies, and investors to negotiate some level of freedom to procure goods and services on the basis of cost, availability, and quality.[15] If carefully negotiated, LCRs can provide a basis for IOCs and Indigenous or host communities to negotiate mutually beneficial terms that could address social, economic, and environmental concerns of extractive production in Indigenous or host communities.[16]

However, despite its potential benefits, LCRs can also lead to misalignment between governments, IOCs, and Indigenous or host communities, especially in countries with unclear and unspecific legal frameworks on LCRs.[17] For instance, in Canada and Australia, while LCRs specify the portion of total expenditures that must be comprised of locally sourced goods and services, procurement procedures are frequently not well established.[18] Consequently, different interpretations and approaches have emerged in extractive industry agreements. For example, what qualifies as a local supplier or an Indigenous-owned business? What amounts to sufficient local content? To what extent can the host government participate in, or exercise control and influence in, the IOCs procurement process? And is there a requirement for the IOC to report or submit its local content and procurement plans to the joint management committee for approval prior to extractive operations? If so, what should such report demonstrate? While governments, industry, and Indigenous communities have developed a range of LCRs that deal with aspects of these questions, clear and comprehensive best practices have yet to emerge.[19]

Lack of clarity and resulting misalignment in understanding and expectations between Indigenous communities and IOCs on the meaning, nature, scope, and methodology for implementing, measuring, and reporting local content performance could result in significant legal risks to investors.[20] These risks could result in regulatory fines, penalties, or even allegations of corruption and/or material breach of the Indigenous-industry agreement, all of which may trigger a loss of the exploration and production (E&P) licence or contract. Misalignment of LCRs can also lead to distraction in Indigenous-industry relationships, disruption in E&P operations, and potentially costly formal dispute resolution. To mitigate and eliminate legal risks relating to the application and implementation of LCRs, there is need for governments, industry, and Indigenous communities to evolve clear, realistic, and collaborative LCRs that minimize contentions and ineffectiveness. As a previous comprehensive study rightly concluded, there is a clear need for more research that brings together the "effectiveness of different local content policies and practices in different contexts."[21] This chapter aims to fill this gap.

This chapter develops a multijurisdictional profile of how LCRs have been addressed in extractive industry agreements in Canada, Australia, United Kingdom, Nigeria, Saudi Arabia, and Qatar. It then discusses the need for a collaborative approach in the design and implementation of LCRs. The chapter is divided into five sections. After this introduction, Section II examines LCRs and practices in the surveyed countries, outlining the main drivers of LCRs in those countries. Section III outlines the main approaches to LCRs in the surveyed countries. Section IV unpacks the main legal risks and debates surrounding the design and implementation of LCRs, especially how misaligned LCRs may affect Indigenous-industry relationships. Section V discusses the four elements of a collaborative approach to LCRs: clear regulatory frameworks; institutional support; cooperative contractual terms; and performance communication. The chapter concludes in Section V.

II. Drivers of LCRs in Frontier Extractive Jurisdictions

There are five key drivers of the increased adoption of LCRs in frontier extractive jurisdictions. First is the desire by host governments to increase the capabilities and competencies of the Indigenous workforce over time.[22] LCRs proceed from the premise that Indigenous workforce and Indigenous-owned industries should over time develop the capacities to supply the goods, services, and human resources needed to drive the extractive industry value chain by substituting locally produced goods for imported goods, and create more local employment by substituting domestic labour for imported or foreign-based labour. LCRs therefore emphasize the need for IOCs to adopt practices that foster the development of qualified domestic workforce over the term of the extractive contract. All of the surveyed regimes therefore mandate IOCs to prepare plans and programs for training and educating nationals during the term of the contract. The aim is to ensure that domestic capabilities of the local workforce are enhanced over time.[23]

A second driver is the desire to create a level playing field for local businesses, specifically businesses owned and controlled by traditional owners (TOs) or Indigenous communities (ICs), to participate in exploration activities.[24] Without creating a level playing field for new or emerging local industries and workforces to participate and compete with international suppliers of goods and services, the cycle of excessive dependence on foreign goods and services may never be broken.[25] LCRs are designed to ensure that local industries are given a full, fair, and reasonable chance to compete with foreign suppliers. For example, the ultimate goal of the Australian Industry Participation (AIP) Framework is to provide "full, fair and reasonable opportunity for Australian industries to participate in significant public and private sector activity."[26] The *Australian Jobs Act 2013* requires project proponents of all major projects to prepare and implement an AIP plan that outlines how the project proponent will provide full, fair, and reasonable opportunity to Australian industry to supply goods and services to the project.[27] Similarly, the Saudi Arabia IKTV program emphasizes the goals of creating a level playing field for local participation, by adopting uniform evaluation processes in sourcing services and materials; and promoting uniform access to project information for local suppliers.[28]

A third driver of LCRs is the desire to maximize economic benefits to citizens through job and employment opportunities.[29] All of the surveyed regimes mandate IOCs to give priority to the employment to suitably qualified nationals and in more specific cases, like Canada and Australia, preferential employment of TOs and ICs are stipulated.[30] By mandating the preferential employment of nationals and/or TOs and ICs, the aim is to create opportunities for domestic employment, thereby contributing to growth in income, capacity development of local stakeholders, and overall increased economic growth of a resource rich region. Local employment is consistently one of the topmost concerns of nationals, TOs and ICs, and often a central issue behind disputes, grievances, and conflicts.[31] More local jobs could result in more support for extractive projects, help improve company-community relations, and enable IOCs to obtain and retain social licence to operate.[32]

A fourth driver is the desire to improve endogenous technological capacity in resource-based countries and communities. All of the surveyed contracts mandate IOCs to give preference to locally manufactured equipment and machinery when their price, quality, time of delivery, and other terms are comparable to internationally available ones. They also include requirements to bring some level of technology or perform research and development (R&D) in the country so that local companies can perform competitively by using latest state-of-the-art technology, or benefit from technology transfer.[33] Mandating IOCs to utilize locally made technology in extractive operations could directly reduce the importation of technology. It could also compel IOCs to establish or invest in technologies and facilities for local manufacturing plants.[34] For example, some IOCs operating in Qatar have opened a technology venture arm of their operations in order to speed up the development and deployment of innovative technologies that could complement oil and gas exploration activities.[35] By opening up technology ventures, IOCs can facilitate domestic production and availability of technologies required for oil and gas exploration.

A final driver is that LCRs are also utilized to mitigate and manage social and political risks that may result from rising local expectations for better and more equitable distribution of wealth and authority.[36] Despite the diverse programs designed to increase the direct financial flows of oil wealth to nationals, TOs, and ICs (through direct cash payment and/or subsidy programs) host communities may demand greater economic participation, such as employing nationals in key operating positions.[37] By introducing detailed LCRs, countries can ensure that access to the control of extractive operations is evenly distributed amongst the several interest groups and tribes across the country. For example, the Qatar PSC stipulates that the Deputy Manager of the petroleum operation shall be an individual appointed by the national oil company.[38] Such a provision allows the host country to at all times control and ensure that a greater spectrum of the society take part in and influence extractive projects.

Despite the clear and uniform overall policy objectives of LCRs, the implementation and enforcement approaches in the surveyed extractive jurisdictions vary. Some countries such as Australia and Nigeria provide comprehensive legislation that specify the scope, content, and enforcement of LCRs, while LCRs in countries such as Canada, Qatar, and Saudi Arabia are often stipulated in extractive industry contracts. While the diversity of approaches in implementing LCRs is by itself not a problem, it could result in misalignments and contentions if not properly negotiated and clarified. Essentially, an IOC, especially those with multiple operations across the world, must carefully understand the nature of LCRs from one country to another. The next section provides a survey of the fundamental themes on LCRs found in industry contracts, legislation, and guidelines in the surveyed countries.

III. Approaches to LCR Implementation in Frontier Extractive Jurisdictions

Surveying extractive industry agreements and legislation in Canada, Australia, the United Kingdom, Nigeria, Saudi Arabia, and Qatar reveals five key variations in approaches to LCRs. These variations are: (1) the source of local content obligations; (2) the definition of local; (3) the local content threshold; (4) the role of government and/or national oil companies in the procurement processes; and (5) the monitoring/institutional coordination for LCRs.

1. The Source of the Local Content Obligations

Extractive countries have adopted two main approaches to codifying LCRs the legislative approach and the contractual approach. Under the legislative approach, obligations relating to LCRs are expressly stipulated in legislation, regulations, government directives, and guidelines. For example, countries such as Nigeria and Australia, have enacted comprehensive legislation on local content, therefore providing clarity on the meaning, nature, and scope of LCRs applicable to petroleum operations.[39] While the legislative approach provides certainty and clarity of expectations between government, industry, and Indigenous stakeholders, it provides limited opportunities for the negotiation of LCR terms on a case-by-case basis. For instance, while the threshold stipulated in the legislation could be workable for a project, it could turn out to be irrelevant or inappropriate for another project.

Under the contractual approach, obligations relating to LCRs are located in extractive industry contracts, such as MDAs, PSCs, CDAs, and Indigenous-industry agreements such as Indigenous land use agreements (ILUAs) and impact benefit agreements (IBAs). In this case, LCRs are not established in legally binding local content legislation and regulations.[40] For example in Canada, the United Kingdom, Saudi Arabia, and Qatar, LCRs are often laid down, on a case-by-case basis, in extractive industry agreements that stipulate industry and Indigenous community expectations with respect to employment of local communities, TOs, and ICs. Such agreements also clarify expectations with respect to capacity development, training, and procurement of goods and services from Indigenous-owned businesses. Similarly, contracts adopted in Qatar and Saudi Arabia contain extensive provisions on LCRs. While the contractual approach provides flexible opportunities for industry and Indigenous or host communities to negotiate LCRs on case-by case basis, the scope and content of such requirements change very quickly. For instance, projects can be delayed due to demands by TOs and ICs requesting for the renegotiation of LCRs. Similarly, in Saudi Arabia, LCRs have been expanded in routine guidelines released by the national oil company.[41] For example, centralized guidelines on local content, product mandating, and procurement procedures contained in the Saudi IKTV program introduce additional layers of obligations with respect to employment, product sourcing, training, and total in-country expenditure, all of which could alter the profitability or otherwise of a petroleum operations for an IOC.

There are two main reasons why countries may choose not to enact local content legislation. The first is that countries, such as Canada, that are members of the World Trade Organization (WTO) are under obligations not to deviate from non-discrimination obligations ("national treatment" and "most-favoured nation" obligations), under which foreign companies cannot be forced to buy from local suppliers or hire local service suppliers if a better alternative in terms of price or quality exists abroad.[42] While some WTO members, such as Australia, have introduced carefully worded LCRs that are in line with the WTO clause, others have in line with this obligation followed the cautious approach of not specifying any legislative obligation on LCRs. The second reason is extractive jurisdictions with limited legislative experience and/or practice, generally favour the flexibility provided by the contractual approach.[43] For example, Nigeria and Australia, who have mature and robust E & P sectors, have codified decades of best practices in legislative instruments. Whatever the reasons, lack of legislative clarity and uniform framework on the scope of local content obligations could result in uncertainty and indeterminacy for an IOC operating in these jurisdictions.

The relative strengths and legal risks in both the legislative and contractual approaches can be leveraged through a collaborative and hybrid approach. For instance, Australia has increasingly adopted a hybrid approach that includes a mix of legislative and contractual provisions on LCRs. Under the hybrid approach, LCRs are comprehensively codified in local content legislation which spells out and clarifies the minimum threshold with respect to employment of TOs, procurement of goods and services from TO-owned businesses, and the provision of training in all extractive projects in Australia. To avoid legal risks related to uncertainty and misalignment with respect to the level and timeframe of local content to be achieved, tailored provisions on timelines, reporting, and project requirements are then negotiated on a project-by-project basis between industry and Indigenous stakeholders. Such contractual clarity is provided in ILUAs and state agreements that are frequently utilized in Australia.

2. *The Definition of "Local"*

All of the surveyed regimes emphasize local content, whether in terms of priority or preference for local goods, services, consumables, works, or enterprises.[44] However, several of these countries do not exactly define the term "local."[45] There are therefore widespread variations in the categories of people and entities that could come under the broad conceptualization, and must be given priorities, as locals. Generally, Qatar and Saudi Arabia contextualize "local" in terms of nationals and companies owned or majority controlled by nationals.[46] In terms of employment, these countries expressly aim to ensure that qualified nationals are given first consideration in matters of employment and that adequate provision is made for the training of nationals on the job. "Local" in these countries therefore refers to nationality, rather than the locality or region where E&P activities take place.

Canada, the United Kingdom, Nigeria, and Australia adopt a more expansive definition of "local" that includes services by locally registered firms and entities and the employment of local workers, which includes Indigenes, nationals, and residents.[47] "Local" in this case refers to the subnational jurisdiction, locality, or region where extractive activities take place, as opposed to nationality or citizenship of the provider of good, services or labour. In Canada and Australia, IBAs often specify that TOs and ICs in the locality or region where E&P activities take place must be given preferential opportunities for employment.[48]

This distinction is indeed very important and could be a legal risk point if not properly clarified and handled. Generally, in resource-based communities, relationships between IOCs, Indigenes, nationals, and expatriate workers could be very fragile due to consistent agitations for more direct participation of TOs and ICs in running extractive operations.[49] While LCRs designed to give special recognition and priority to ICs and TOs may provide a mechanism for addressing this fragility, it could be a legal risk point for IOCs in situations whereby it is difficult to find a right fit for the required goods, services or labor from the available pool of nationals.[50] Also, conceptualizing "local" in terms of nationality or Indigenous-owned businesses could result in project delays and higher costs for the IOCs where locally made goods are not immediately available or available at much higher costs. However, the benefits of maintaining social stability in a resource-bearing community and, more broadly, the impetus to retain a social licence to operate that such a strategy would bring about may be more important for an IOC than the loss to be occasioned by these tradeoffs.

A more flexible model to managing such tradeoffs is found in the Qatari PSC which provides that the Contractor shall, *when possible*, give first consideration or preference to locally manufactured or locally available goods.[51] This provides some flexibility for an IOC to consider other categories of locals if the IOC so decides for operational reasons, or in cases when suitably qualified nationals or service providers are not available.

3. Local Content Threshold

Extractive countries adopt a mix of flexible and mandatory approaches to specifying local content thresholds that must be demonstrated or met by an operator or licence holder. For example, in Qatar the minimum level of "local content" to be achieved for each category of goods and services is not expressed as a percentage or with a timeframe, rather, the obligation is simply to give priority to services, materials, equipment, consumables, and other goods when their price, quality, time of delivery, and other terms are comparable.[52] The Qatari PSC adopts flexible language by stating that the Contractor shall, when possible, select contractors who are nationals of the State of Qatar or companies which are majority owned by Qatar nationals.[53] The Qatari PSC also notes that in purchasing goods for petroleum operations Contractor shall, when possible, give preference to locally manufactured or locally available goods so long as their technical specifications, quality, and time of delivery and services are comparable to internationally available ones.

However, while local content obligations are flexible and without mandatory thresholds in Qatar, in Saudi Arabia, Canada, and Australia a percentage threshold of local content that must be met, and the timeframe is expressly set out. For example, the Saudi Arabia IKTV Program places an obligation on contractors to achieve 70% local content by the year 2021 (70 by 21 threshold).[54] It also plans to raise the export of Saudi-made energy goods to 30% by 2021.[55] Similarly, in IBAs adopted in Canada, especially in the provinces of Saskatchewan, Newfoundland, and Nova Scotia, LCRs have included contractual obligations that 35% of all goods and services are to be sourced from Indigenous-owned businesses.[56] Also, under the Australian legislation, project proponents of all major projects with a capital expenditure of $500 million or more, including projects in both the mining sector and the petroleum sectors, must prepare and implement an Australian Industry Participation (AIP) plan.[57] ILUAs in Australia have also stipulated that at least 40% of workforce at the mine will be comprised of Local Aboriginal People.[58]

The flexible preference approach is arguably a more straightforward approach that allows an operator to align the implementation of LCRs with prevailing realities. This flexibility is particularly important for operators to maintain quality when locally manufactured goods or services are unavailable or more expensive to source. The flexible approach also reduces legal risks relating to non-compliance with employment or LCR thresholds and offers IOCs opportunities to align product sourcing and procurement practices with their existing operations and market conditions in other countries.

4. *The Role of the State*

The role of governments in setting LCRs varies from one jurisdiction to another. In Canada for example, IOCs are required to consult and engage with Indigenous communities to privately negotiate and evolve maximum local benefits.[59] Such negotiated terms are often codified in tailored and project-specific Indigenous-industry agreements, such as CDAs, IBAs, and ILUAs that are designed to capture the specific needs and aspirations of Indigenous communities. However, in Nigeria, the United Kingdom, Qatar, and Saudi Arabia, LCRs are often stipulated and mandated in legislation, guidelines, and generic extractive contracts.[60] These mandated thresholds are often set by government agencies or the national oil companies and may not widely reflect the specific aspirations and realities of subnational communities and vulnerable groups who are affected the most by extractive activities and projects. The need for a negotiated approach to evolving LCRs cannot be overemphasized.[61] Despite debates on the efficacy of negotiated approaches to extractive industry agreements, LCRs are likely to be more realistic and effective if they are designed with the Free, Prior, and Informed Consent (FPIC) and involvement of Indigenous or host communities who are most affected by such LCRs.[62]

Government and national oil company participation in procurement processes varies across the surveyed countries. While LCRs may specify the portion of total expenditures that must be comprised of locally sourced goods and services, procurement procedures are frequently not well established. In Canada for example, the contractor has the flexibility to design and implement its own procurement processes and procedures, so far as they comply with LCRs stipulated in applicable contracts and are based on generally accepted standards in the international petroleum industry.[63] What constitutes international best practice, especially when there is a dispute relating to compliance with LCRs, may however be subject to debates and complex ligation. Furthermore, in some regimes, government must be informed after the fact through yearly statements, audits, or mandatory performance plans that demonstrate compliance with LCRs and procurement requirements (i.e., Saudi Arabia, Australia); in others, procurement plans must be submitted prior to the commencement of petroleum operations.[64] A variation arises where the national oil company or a management committee is directly involved in advisory capacity. (i.e., Qatar) and, in more extreme cases, government must be informed and may participate in procurement activities above certain financial thresholds (i.e., Nigeria).[65]

Understanding the variations in the designated role of national or provincial authorities in the procurement processes is critical to avoiding disputes and contentions. As governments increasingly seek to exercise some form of influence in the contractor's procurement process to ensure total value in terms of local content, it is important for IOCs to clarify, from the outset, the level of government involvement in the process. Government participation in procurement processes, as a way of monitoring LCRs and transparency, could particularly pose significant risks and delay for extractive operations, especially in countries where government approval processes could be slow and bureaucratic. Government participation in procurement processes should be avoided by IOCs willing to achieve efficiency in extractive operations.

5. *Monitoring, Reporting, and Institutional Coordination*

While LCRs have been increasingly adopted in frontier extractive jurisdictions, approaches to supervising and monitoring compliance with LCRs vary. Only very few countries have established institutions or mechanisms for monitoring and enforcing such requirements. In Australia for example, the Australian Industry Participation Authority is charged with monitoring and promoting compliance with LCRs in the Australian Jobs Act 2013, as well as advising and assisting persons in relation to their obligations under the Act.[66] Similarly, in Saudi Arabia, Saudi Aramco directly evaluates and monitors the "added value" brought to the Kingdom by a supplier.[67] Furthermore, the Nigerian local content legislation establishes the Nigerian Content Development and Monitoring Board (NCDMB), which is mandated to oversee, monitor, and implement the LCRs in the Nigerian legislation.[68]

However, some of the surveyed countries have not established focal agencies for local content monitoring and enforcement. In Canada and Qatar, for example, there is no focal institution or agency on local content. Typically, in contracts utilized in Canada and Qatar a management committee established to oversee the entire contract assesses LCRs. The scope and methodology on how LCRs are to be assessed or measured, by Indigenous or host communities, IOCs, or by the government therefore varies on a contract-to-contract basis. The lack of a standardized approach to local content monitoring and enforcement makes it difficult for host communities to effectively assess and obtain remedies for non-compliance with LCRs. Remedies for non-compliance will in such cases depend on dispute resolution mechanisms established in the applicable industry contract. One of the shortcomings of resolving disputes on LCRs is that while some courts or arbitral tribunals may provide expansive definitions and interpretations of LCRs in Indigenous-industry contracts, some other courts may not do so.[69] Countries can address the indeterminacy of the contractual approach to LCR implementation by establishing robust legislative requirements that mandate oil, gas, and mining companies to submit periodic reports and plans in LCRs to designated focal institutions or agencies.

Measuring and quantifying value-add is difficult without robust institutions and mechanisms for effective monitoring and enforcement. In addition to promoting public awareness and reducing uncertainty on the scope of LCRs, a focal local content unit or agency can coordinate and spearhead the development of a standard approach to LCRs. Such an agency can also guide operators and investors in formulating and developing petroleum operations or projects that are in line with the country's national vision; and more specifically that can result in real, measurable, and long-term local benefits. A local content agency can also monitor and investigate companies in relation to their compliance with local content requirements. For example, the Nigerian NCDMB has clear statutory powers to prescribe penalties of at least 5% of the project sum on any entity that fails to comply with LCRs.[70] Fines levied by the NCDMB are paid into a Local Content Development Fund dedicated to training and supporting local enterprises. From the perspective of an IOC, such clear institutional approach reduces ambiguities and surprises with respect to LCR enforcement and implementation. From government and policy standpoints, it ensures that LCRs are indeed actually monitored and enforced such that they can result in real and quantifiable benefits in the long run.

While a number of countries have recognized LCRs in their regulatory frameworks, a coherent set of best practices has yet to emerge. The diverse LCR regimes, and the unclear scope of local content obligations, raise several legal risks and uncertainties for an IOC, a very small portion of which can be managed through traditional contractual documentation. Furthermore, in several of the surveyed countries, there have been concerns over failure to adequately provide opportunities for local communities to take part in and influence decision making processes on what constitutes success in terms of local content and "in-nation" value addition. In order to minimize contentions and legal risks relating to LCR implementation and enforcement, it is important to provide a framework for collaboration and active stakeholder participation in defining and setting LCRs. The next section discusses the need for a collaborative approach between host communities, national authorities, and IOCs to minimize legal risks and contentions relating to LCRs.

IV. Mitigating Legal Risks Relating to LCRs: The Need for a Collaborative Approach

Whatever regulatory approach taken, whether contractual or legislative, the most important factor to successfully advance local content benefits in host communities is to ensure a collaborative and multi-stakeholder approach to setting and implementing LCRs.[71] Rather than approach LCRs from a compliance, punitive or mandatory project requirement mindset, that demand more local content or introduce more punitive enforcement measures, national authorities could adopt a collaborative approach based on clear, transparent, and attainable LCRs with adequate institutional support for IOCs to achieve those goals.[72]

The collaborative approach to LCRs provides a practical template for national authorities and private actors to ensure FPIC in the allocation and utilization of benefits and resources in extractive activities and projects.[73] FPIC in international law requires national authorities and private actors to respect, protect, and fulfil the rights of Indigenous communities to meaningfully participate in decisions directly impacting their lands, territories, and resources.[74] FPIC underlines the idea that consent to extractive projects must be freely given, obtained prior to implementation of activities, and founded upon an understanding of the full range of benefits and challenges resulting from the activity or decision in question.[75]

Indigenous communities have the right to fully understand the local content benefits that could result from an extractive activity, and be able to take part in and influence decision-making processes relating to the delivery of such benefits. "Free" in the FPIC framework implies no coercion, intimidation, or manipulation in decision making processes.[76] "Prior" implies that consent and approval of host communities must be sought in advance of any authorization or commencement of extractive operations.[77] "Informed" refers to the full disclosure of the intent, scope, and benefits of the projects and policies, most especially local content benefits. "Consent" means that the final decision of host communities with respect to in-community value and LCRs must be collectively granted or withheld.[78]

A collaborative approach to LCRs provides a chance for national authorities, host communities, and IOCs to cooperatively clarify and agree upon what constitutes success in terms of local content and "in-nation" value addition in accordance with FPIC tenets. Local content objectives must be specific, measurable, and achievable to avoid ambiguities and misalignments. Rather than adopting a rigid and inflexible approach, a collaborative approach that clarifies the expectations of governments and host communities, while providing the IOC with the flexibility to develop its local content plans and procurement procedures, could achieve greater results. Also, rather than stipulating blanket and unrealistic timeframes, countries, in defining LCRs and ambitions, must recognize that the timeframe for delivering in-country value may vary from project to project and could be affected by political and other factors not envisaged during contract negotiation.

Secondly, there is a need for countries to establish clear, transparent and comprehensive contractual frameworks that provide guidelines on LCRs. Despite the politics and debates associated with Indigenous-industry agreements, they provide more collaborative and multi-stakeholder opportunities to codify the local benefits, opportunities, and terms of engagement with Indigenous or host communities. Rather than lump or place community benefits in generic extractive industry agreements which are hardly prepared with the participation of Indigenous or host communities, tailored and negotiated agreements, such as CDAs and IBAs, can provide clear and specific frameworks for elaborating project-specific commitments between the project developer and host communities on how to address, implement, and maximize LCRs. Such tailored contracts should, amongst other things, provide clear definitions of key concepts such as local, local content, local company, project sum, and in-country value.[79] There is also a need to clearly identify the skills, competencies, technologies, and economic activities that a country wants to improve or build upon as part of local content implementation. Such clear definitions will reduce ambiguities with respect to the scope and content of LCRs. A clear local content agreement or framework can also address overlap and limitations in other domestic legislation that could hinder the successful implementation of LCRs.[80] For example, procurement laws that have elaborate provisions on procurement procedures may hinder the coherent implementation of LCRs. They also may result in misalignments and risks if they do not clarify if such procedures apply in the extractive sector. The adoption of clear and specific contracts on local content could provide opportunities for a country to harmonize LCRs with existing laws to avoid overlap and mismatch.

Thirdly, to provide adequate institutional support for IOCs to achieve LCRs and goals, it is important to establish a focal institution, committee, or administrative unit that will coordinate the design, approval, and implementation of local content plans across the life cycle of a project. While such focal institution can be established as a supervisory committee of a petroleum contract, a more long-term approach is to establish a national local content agency or unit that will oversee LCRs in multiple sectors of the economy. Apart from serving as a one-stop-shop that will streamline the approval processes for local content implementation, such an institution would also provide methodologies and tools for operators to report and monitor their compliance with LCRs so as to minimize contentions and disputes. By empowering and establishing a focal institution on projects, investors across multiple sectors can obtain relevant information and develop a standardized approach to tracking, monitoring, and complying with LCRs.

One of the outstanding elements of the Qatari, Saudi, and Australian local content regimes is that they establish reporting obligations, fixed key performance indicators (KPIs), and measuring metrics that mandate suppliers to provide quarterly status updates and annual reporting on the scope and level of compliance with LCRs. Periodic reporting of targets, accomplishments, and strategies provides a collaborative opportunity for all parties to mutually evaluate the feasibility and efficacy of LCRs and to explore approaches that can improve performance and deliver shared wins.[81] Timely and effective communication can reduce the likelihood of contentions and disputes as it allows both parties to explore if, and how, a company is achieving LCRs. KPIs could also provide a basis for renegotiating or amending LCRs when set targets that may be difficult to achieve.

V. Conclusion

LCRs are likely to be more realistic and effective if they are designed with FPIC and involvement of Indigenous peoples and host communities who are likely to be most affected by projects. Maximizing in-nation benefits and value from resource extraction activities cannot be achieved by mere legislative or contractual provisions. There is a need to forge greater partnerships and industry-wide collaboration between national authorities, IOCs, and Indigenous communities in the design, implementation, and enforcement of LCRs. As can be seen from countries such as the United Kingdom, Australia, and Nigeria that have achieved some measure of success in implementing LCRs, governments must go beyond merely stipulating LCRs. Governments should create the right regulatory framework and institutions that allow Indigenous peoples and host communities to play more active roles in clarifying and establishing the meaning, nature, scope, and methodology for implementing, measuring, and reporting local content performance.

A collaborative approach to LCRs, built on FPIC, stakeholder cooperation, and shared values between government, Indigenous communities, and investors, and propelled by supportive institutions, can allow all stakeholders to set realistic and achievable local content goals. National authorities can provide appropriate institutions that bring together stakeholders from Indigenous communities, IOCs, and service providers amongst others to periodically set, review, and evaluate progress made in advancing local content goals for extractive projects.

With respect to practical strategies and tools for implementing a collaborative framework for LCRs, further research and field consultation is needed. This research is necessary to determine and compile industry-wide best practices on how to revamp procurement practices, tender pre-qualification processes, prequalification, contractor rosters, and tender advertisement processes to create a level playing field for local industries in the award of contracts.

Notes

1. The extractive industry consists of people, companies, and activities involved in removing petroleum and mineral resources from the earth. Examples of extractive processes include oil and gas exploration, solid mineral mining, dredging, and quarrying. See: Damilola Olawuyi, *Extractives Industry Law in Africa* (Springer 2018) 1–5 [Olawuyi]. For a summary of the strengths of the six surveyed countries in the extractive sector, see BP Statistical Review of World Energy (65th ed, BP June 2016) *20* <https://www.bp.com/content/dam/bp/pdf/energy-economics/statistical-review-2016/bp-statistical-review-of-world-energy-2016-full-report.pdf>.
2. Ibironke T. Odumosu-Ayanu, "Indigenous Peoples, International Law, and Extractive Industry Contracts" [2015] 109 AJIL Unbound 220, 221.
3. This chapter does not delve into debates as to whether Indigenous peoples exist in the MEA region, as well as in the United Kingdom. See: African Commission on Human and Peoples' Rights, *Indigenous Peoples in Africa: The Forgotten Peoples? The African Commission's work on Indigenous peoples in Africa* (International Work Group for Indigenous Affairs 2006) 9–11 (ACHPR 2006), stating that one of the key challenges is the widespread misconception across African countries that the term "Indigenous"

is not applicable in Africa as "all Africans are Indigenous." See also: Minority Groups International, "World Directory of Minorities and Indigenous Peoples-United Kingdom" (*Welsh* August 2018) <https://www.refworld.org/docid/49749c8cc.htm>. See also Madawi al-Rasheed, "The Shia of Saudi Arabia: A Minority in Search of Cultural Authenticity" (1998) 25(1) British Journal of Middle Eastern Studies 121.

4. Chapter IV of the Nigerian Constitution fails to recognize distinct rights of minority, tribal, or Indigenous groups. Section 21 refers to the protection of "Nigerian culture," while Section 10 emphasizes that Nigeria is a secular state. See *Constitution of the Federal Republic of Nigeria*, 1999 Cap C-23, LFN 2004.
5. International Labour Organization (ILO) Convention Concerning Indigenous and Tribal Peoples in Independent Countries, 27 June 1989, C169 art 15(2) (entered into force 5 September 1991) [Convention 169].
6. ACHPR 2006 (n 3).
7. See: Damilola Olawuyi, "Local Content and Procurement Requirements in Oil and Gas Contracts: Regional Trends in the Middle East and North Africa" (2019) 37(1) Journal of Energy and Natural Resources Law 93 [Olawuyi, 2019]; Per Heum and others, "Policy and Regulatory Framework to Enhance Local Content: Yardsticks and Best Practice" (2011) SNF Working Paper No. 02/11 <https://openaccess.nhh.no/nhh-xmlui/handle/11250/166346>.
8. Ibid Olawuyi, [2019] 94.
9. Silvana Tordo and others, *Local Content Policies in the Oil and Gas Sector* (World Bank 2013).
10. Michael Levett and Ashley E. Chandler, *Maximizing Development of Local Content across Industry Sectors in Emerging Markets* (Center for Strategic and International Studies 2012) 1–3.
11. See for example: Article 4 of the Hibernia Southern Extension Benefits Agreement, requiring operators to provide full and fair opportunity to businesses and individuals in Newfoundland and Labrador, to participate in the supply of goods and services and in employment opportunities arising from petroleum operations <http://www.nr.gov.nl.ca/nr/energy/petroleum/offshore/projects/hse_benefits_agreement.pdf> [Hibernia Southern Extension Benefits Agreement]; see also: Government of Saskatchewan, "2015 Northern Benefits Summary - Saskatchewan Mine Surface Lease Agreements" <http://cvmpsk.ca/wp-content/uploads/2015-Northern-Benefits-Summary-Mine-Surface-Lease-Agreement-Final-June-2016.pdf>; see also: s. 45 of *the Canada–Newfoundland and Labrador Atlantic Accord Implementation Act*, SC 1987, c 3).
12. Qatar Petroleum, "Qatar Petroleum to Launch the Localization Program for Services and Industries in the Energy Sector" (*Tawteen*, 8 January 2019) <https://www.tawteen.com.qa/News-Media/Press-Releases/News-Qatar-Petroleum-to-launch-the-Localization-Pr>.
13. In Kingdom Total Value Add (IKTVA) Program, <https://www.iktva.sa/introduction/> [IKTVA].
14. Renewable UK, "Offshore Wind Industry Investment in the UK: 2017 Report on Offshore Wind UK Content" (Offshore Wind Programme Board 2017) 1–2 <https://cdn.ymaws.com/www.renewableuk.com/resource/resmgr/publications/Offshore_Wind_Investment_V4.pdf>.
15. IKTVA (n 13).
16. Ana Maria Esteves, Bruce Coyne and Ana Moreno, "Local Content Initiatives: Enhancing the Subnational Benefits of the Oil, Gas and Mining Sectors" (2013) Natural Resource Governance Institute <https://resourcegovernance.org/sites/default/files/Sub_Enhance_Benefits_20151125.pdf>.
17. Trade Arabia, "Big boost to Saudi industries as Aramco to double local market sourcing" (*Trade Arabia*, 1 December 2015) <http://tradearabia.com/news/IND_295936.html>; R Darling, *Beyond Taxation: How Countries Can Benefit from the Extractive Industries through Local Content* (NRevenue Watch Institute 2011) 1–10.

18. Damilola Olawuyi, "Legal Strategies and Tools for Mitigating Legal Risks Associated with Oil and Gas Investments in Africa" (2015) 39(3) OPEC Energy Review 247 [Olawuyi, 2015]; Damilola Olawuyi and Trent Mercier, "Local Content and Procurement Requirements in Frontier African Oil and Gas Jurisdictions—One Size Does Not Fit All" (*Norton Rose Fulbright*, 9 December 2015) <http://www.insideafricalaw.com/blog/local-content-and-procurement-requirements-in-frontier-african-oil-and-gas-jurisdictions-one-size-does-not-fit-all>.
19. See also Olawuyi and Mercier, ibid.
20. Legal risks refer to the risk of financial, reputational, or investment loss; legal liability; or dispute settlement costs to a company or institution that may arise from defective contractual arrangements or transaction. Roger McCormick, *Legal Risk in the Financial Markets* (2nd ed, Oxford University Press 2010) 1–3; see also Olawuyi, "Legal Strategies and Tools" (n 18).
21. Esteves, Coyne, and Moreno (n 16).
22. Thomas Muller and Monika Schitzer "Technology Transfer and Spillovers in International Joint Ventures" (2003) Munich Discussion Paper, 2003(22) <https://www.econstor.eu/bitstream/10419/104125/1/lmu-mdp_2003-22.pdf> [Muller and Schitzer]; Michael Levett and Ashley E. Chandler (n 10) 1–3.
23. See for example Art 23 State of Qatar Model Development and Production Sharing Agreement of 2002; IKTVA (n 13); *The Nigerian Oil and Gas Industry Content Development Act* 2010, Cap. N124A, LFN 2004 [NOGICDA, 2010].
24. Section 3 of *Australia's Traditional Owner Settlement Act 2010* (Vic) defines TOs as "a group of Aboriginal persons who authorise certain Indigenous Land Use Agreements under the Native Title Act, or native title holders"; Hibernia Southern Extension Benefits Agreement (n 11) art 4.
25. See Tordo (n 9); Warner, Manzano, and Anouti (n 17) 115–117.
26. Under Section 3 of the AIP National Framework, full, fair and reasonable opportunity is defined as follows: "*Full*: Australian industry has the same opportunity afforded to other global supply chain partners to participate in all aspects of an investment project (e.g., design, engineering, project management, professional services, IT architecture); *Fair*: Australian industry is provided the same opportunity as global suppliers to compete on investment projects on an equal and transparent basis, including being given reasonable time in which to tender; and *Reasonable*: tenders are free from non-market burdens that might rule out Australian industry and are structured in such a way as to provide Australian industries the opportunity to participate in investment projects", Nick Minchin and others, "Australia Industry Participation National Framework" (2011) <https://www.industry.gov.au/sites/default/files/australian-industry-participation-national-framework.pdf> [Nick Minchin and others].
27. *The Australian Jobs Act, 2013,* C2013A00069.
28. IKTV (n 13).
29. According to a recent report, 48% of UK offshore projects now go to UK companies. Renewabe UK (n 14).
30. Article 2.3 and 2.4, Management Plan of *Argyle Diamond Mine Participation Agreement—Indigenous Land Use Agreement between Argyle Diamond Limited and Argyle Diamond Mine Pty Ltd; Traditional Owners for the Mine Area; and Kimberley Land Council Aboriginal Corporation* stating that Argyle aims to have Local Aboriginal People comprising at least 40% of its workforce at the Mine by the time underground operations commence and maintaining that level until cessation of production operations. See also Section 15 of the Gorgon Gas Processing and Infrastructure Project Agreement (Schedule 1 to the Barrow Island Act 2003), stating that Joint Venturers shall use labour available within Western Australia, and specifically from Pilbara; Art. 23 State of Qatar Model Development and Production Sharing Agreement of 2002; IKTVA (n 13); See also Articles 4–5 of the Collaboration Agreement between the Northern Village of Pinehouse and

Kineepik Metis Local Inc. and Cameco Corporation and Areva Resources Canada Inc., December 12, 2012.

31. Jesse Ovadia, *The Role of Local Content Policies in Natural Resource-Based Development* (Österreichische Forschungsstiftung für Internationale Entwicklung 2015) 37–38.
32. World Bank, "Human Capital for the Oil, Gas and Minerals Industries (English)" Science, Technology, and Skills for Africa's Development 1–4 <http://documents.worldbank.org/curated/en/406101468202451878/Human-capital-for-the-oil-gas-and-minerals-industries>.
33. See for example Article 4.4 B of the Hibernia Southern Extension Benefits Agreement (n 11) requiring the project proponent to contribute a total of CDN$10 million to one or more education and research oriented legacy projects within three years of first commercial production; see also Section 4 of the AIP National Framework: Nick Minchin and others (n 26).
34. Muller and Schitzer (n 22); Amy Glass and Kamal Saggi, "The Role of Foreign Direct Investment in International Technology Transfer" in Amitava Krishna Dutt and Jamie Ros, *International Handbook of Development Economics* (Edward Elgar 2008).
35. For example, IOCs such as Conoco Philips, General Electric, Shell, and ExxonMobil have opened up technology innovation centers and programs at the Qatar Science and Technology Park. See: Qatar Science and Technology Park, "ConocoPhillips Water Sustainability Centre" (2019) <https://qstp.org.qa/companies/conocophillips/>.
36. See M. Cook and H. Mahdavy, "The Pattern and Problems of Economic Development in Rentier States: The Case of Iran" in M. Cook, *Studies in the Economic History of the Middle East: From the Rise of Islam to the Present Day* (Oxford University Press 1970) 435–436.
37. Chris Hanlin, *The Drive to Increase Local Procurement in the Mining Sector in Africa: Myth or Reality?* (MMCP Discussion Paper No. 4, Making the Most of Commodities Programme (MMCP), 2011).
38. Art. 23 Development and Production Sharing Agreement of 2002, State of Qatar.
39. See NOGICDA, 2010 (n 23); See also *The Australian Jobs Act 2013* (n 27) which requires project proponents in mining and petroleum sectors in Australia to prepare and implement an Australian Industry Participation Plan.
40. In the UK for example, although there is no legislation mandating LCRs in the extractive sector, IOCs are encouraged to give fair and favourable consideration to UK registered companies. See Patrick Smith, "UK minister hints at local content requirement" (*WindPower Offshore*, 11 June 2014) <https://www.windpowermonthly.com/article/1298415/uk-minister-hints-local-content-requirement>.
41. See IKTVA (n 13).
42. Under the General Agreement on Tariffs and Trade 1994 (GATT 1994) and the Agreement on Trade-Related Investment Measures (TRIMS), WTO members may not apply any domestic measure that discriminates against foreign products or that leads to quantitative restrictions, such as local content requirements: <https://www.wto.org/english/tratop_e/invest_e/invest_info_e.htm>.
43. See Esteves, Coyne and Moreno (n 16) 12–13.
44. See (n 38).
45. On the importance of clarifying the meaning of "local," see Chilenye Nwapi, "Defining the 'Local' in Local Content Requirements in the Oil and Gas and Mining Sectors in Developing Countries" (2015) 8(1) Law & Development Review.
46. Often described as the "Saudisation" or the "Qatarisation" policy, the aim of nationality focussed local content policies is to increase local skills and competencies and thus enable the progressive coverage of roles, respectively by Saudi or Qatari personnel; See IKTVA (n 13).

47. See (n 38) and Renewable UK (n 14).
48. See (n 38).
49. World Bank, *Human Capital for the Oil, Gas and Minerals Industries* (World Bank Group 2014).
50. Ibid. See also Olawuyi (n 1) 233–258.
51. See Art. 23 (2) of the Qatari PSC (n 38).
52. Ibid.
53. Ibid.
54. IKTVA (n 13).
55. Ibid.
56. See Article 4 of the Hibernia Southern Extension Benefits Agreement (n 11).
57. Australian Jobs Act 2013 (n 27) s 8.
58. Management Plan of Argyle Diamond Mine Participation Agreement-Indigenous Land Use Agreement (n 30).
59. On the duty to consult, see Dwight G. Newman, *Revisiting the Duty to Consult Aboriginal Peoples* (Purich Publishing 2014). See also Ken J. Caine and Naomi Krogman, "Powerful or Just Plain Power-Full? A Power Analysis of Impact and Benefit Agreements in Canada's North" [2010] 23 ORG. & ENV'T 76, 77.
60. While not applicable to the petroleum sector, Section 116 of *The Nigerian Mineral and Mining Act 2007* introduces the mandatory conclusion of Community Development Agreements (CDAs) between mining companies and their host communities as a condition precedent to commencement of mining operations.
61. On the importance of multi-stakeholder approach, see Ibironke Odumosu-Ayanu, "Governments, Investors and Local Communities: Analysis of a Multi-Actor Investment Agreement Framework" (2014) 15 (2) Melbourne Journal of International Law 473.
62. For a critical view of the negotiated model, see David Szablowski, "Operationalizing Free, Prior, and Informed Consent in the Extractive Industry Sector?: Examining the Challenges of a Negotiated Model of Justice" [2010] 30 Can. J. Deve. Stud. 111, 112.
63. Hibernia Southern Extension Benefits Agreement (n 11) art 4.
64. See (n 38).
65. The Nigerian legal framework provides for government participation in all local procurement where the estimated value exceeds 10 Million Naira (approximately $50,000); See NOGICDA, 2010 (n 23); also Production Sharing Contract between Nigerian National Petroleum Corporation and Gas Transmission and Power Limited, Energy 905 Sunera Limited and Ideal Oil and Gas Limited (2007).
66. The Australian Jobs Act 2013 (n 27).
67. IKTVA (n 13).
68. NOGICDA, 2010 (n 23) s 4.
69. Esteves, Coyne and Moreno (n 16) 12–13.
70. NOGICDA, 2010 (n 23) s 4.
71. See Odumosu-Ayanu (n 61).
72. For excellent discussions of the utility of a collaborative approach to regulation, see S. Shapiro and R.S. Rabinowitz, "Punishment versus Cooperation in Regulatory Enforcement: A Case Study of OSHA" [1997] 49 Administrative Law Review 713. See also A. Perrault, K. Herbertson and O. Lynch, "Partnerships for Success in Protected Areas: The Public Interest and Local Community Rights to Prior Informed Consent (PIC)" (2007) 19(3) Georgetown International Environmental Law Review 477.
73. See J. Ruggie, "United Nations Guiding Principles on Business and Human Rights: Implementing the United Nations 'Protect, Respect and Remedy' Framework" (2011) UN Document A/HRC/17/31 (21 March 2011), [8]–[12]; See also United Nations Environment Program (UNEP), *UN-REDD Programme Guide-*

lines on Free Prior Informed Consent (UNEP, 2012) 11–12 [UNEP], stating that states are required to consult Indigenous peoples as well as forest-dependent communities in good faith regarding matters that affect them.

74. See arts 1, 12, 20, 27, 30, 32 of the United Nations Declaration on the Rights of Indigenous Peoples (UNDRIP) A/RES/61/295, adopted 2 October 2007; also art 1 of both the International Covenant on Civil and Political Rights and the International Covenant on Economic, Social and Cultural Rights (ICESCR); arts 6, 7, 16, 22 of the International Labour Organization's *Convention on Indigenous and Tribal Peoples in Independent Countries—169/1989.*
75. S. Anaya, "Indigenous Peoples' Participatory Rights in Relation to Decisions about Natural Resource Extraction: The More Fundamental Issue of What Rights Indigenous Peoples Have in Lands and Resources" (2005) 22 Arizona Journal of International and Comparative Law 7.
76. See UNEP (n 73) 7.
77. Ibid.
78. Ibid.
79. Nwapi (n 45).
80. Ibid.
81. See for example, Byron Sparkes, "Local Content Development in Newfoundland and Labrador" (*Newfoundland and Labrador Oil and Gas Industries Association*) <http://www.mun.ca/econ/more/events/Bryron_Sparks_Nor_M2017.pdf> identifying lack of measurement, reporting and communication as a key challenge for advancing LCRs in Newfoundland and Labrador, Canada.

14 Indigenous Land Use Agreements in Australia: A Vehicle for Economic Prosperity or an Empty Gesture?

Franklin Gaffney

I. Introduction

With growing international recognition of Indigenous rights and interests and the increasing use by resource companies of the "social licence to operate" as a policy instrument to mitigate for community engagement and corporate sustainability, many resource companies now invest considerably in agreement-making with Indigenous communities to secure, in the words of Chris Salisbury, Chief Executive of Rio Tinto Iron Ore (RTIO), "*the privilege to operate*"[1] on their traditional lands.

Facilitated by governments who provide the legislative mechanisms for the orderly and timely granting of mining interests that are critical to the industry, resource companies negotiate a range of compensation and benefit-sharing arrangements with Indigenous communities over the traditional lands on which they operate. As Professor Ciaran O'Faircheallaigh states "[i]f an assessment of agreement outcomes indicates that they are not generating significant benefits for Indigenous people, this would threaten a substantial political and economic status quo"[2] and would call into question the legitimacy of the land access regime on traditional lands that has underpinned the success of the Australian resource industry in the 21st century.

Conscious of the need to maintain public support for the policy framework that forms the basis for the Australian resource industry's access to traditional lands in Western Australia, in June 2018, the Western Australian government announced that "one of the strengths of the WA [Western Australia] resources sector is that we are including the Indigenous community in the success of the industry and that is very important."[3] This paper examines this assertion and explores whether agreement-making between Pilbara-based Aboriginal people in Western Australia and the resource companies who operate on their traditional lands, is having the desired impact.

The paper does this in four parts. The first part summarises the native title landscape in the Pilbara region of Western Australia where resource companies and local Aboriginal people have been negotiating native title agreements since the introduction of the legislative agreement-making arrangements in 1998. The second and third parts examine the native title agreement implementation and monitoring processes, with particular attention on the training, employment, and business development (known as economic participation) obligations contained in those agreements and examine the importance of the legal enforceability of those obligations to achieving the parties' objectives. The last part draws on these together, reiterating some of the complexities of agreement implementation and securing enforceability of obligations, and then summarizes the key issues that practitioners should consider when negotiating these obligations.

II. Overview of the Native Title Landscape in the Pilbara

Twenty-five years has elapsed since the enactment of the *Native Title Act 1993* (Cth) (the NTA) by the Australian Commonwealth Parliament. The passage of the legislation followed intense public debate surrounding the historic decision in *Mabo v Queensland* (No. 2),[4] where the High Court of Australia upheld a claim to rights of possession, occupation, use, and enjoyment of the Murray Islands under a communal native title sourced in the Meriam people's pre-sovereignty laws and customs. The controversy surrounding the passage of the NTA has not subsided, with amending legislation being introduced nearly every two years since 1993 to, among other things, mitigate the consequences of judicial interpretation or advance a change in policy direction.

Amendments enacted in 1998[5] introduced a new vehicle for potential advancement of a native title claim group's economic and social wellbeing through agreements with third parties such as resource proponents, pastoralists, or governments. This new agreement-making model, replacing the existing agreement-making model which was only available to native title holders but not claimants,[6] sought to balance broad policy objectives whilst creating a legislative instrument that provided certainty for resource projects that was legally enforceable.[7]

Parties can now avail themselves of a range of agreement-making models provided under the NTA. The model most widely used, known as section 31 agreements (also referred to as Future Act agreements) stem from the native title claimants' procedural rights, including their right to negotiate,[8] which arise once their native title determination application is registered by the Registrar of the National Native Title Tribunal (the statutory body charged with responsibility for registering native title determination applications and agreements made pursuant to the agreement-making model enshrined in the NTA). The ambit of the Future Act agreement-making model is limited to granting access rights to undertake a proposed future act (such as the granting of a mining lease or compulsory acquisition of native title rights and interests) and heritage protection associated with the proposed future act. Future Act agreements can also contain compensatory components. Unlike the other agreement-making streams under the NTA, Future Act agreements do not require the native title claim group's "authorization"[9] and can be approved by a majority of the group's named applicants.

The other agreement-making scheme provided for by the NTA is Indigenous Land Use Agreements (ILUAs). Unlike Future Act agreements, ILUAs offer parties more flexibility and can include a broader range of interests. ILUAs can address past and intermediate acts, as well as future acts. Some ILUAs include provisions which displace the future act process under the NTA in its entirety. ILUAs can also address issues of land access, compensation for the loss or impairment of native title rights and interest, and the surrender of native title rights and interests.

Under these statutory agreement-making models, Pilbara-based resource companies have, as at September 2018, negotiated with local native title groups nearly 80 ILUAs, over 7,000 Future Act Agreements, and various ancillary agreements and deeds[10] covering an area of nearly 500,000 km^2 in Western Australia. These agreements underpin over 100 mining projects with production value in 2016–2017 of $85.9 billion AUD that comprised 48% of Western Australia's exports, the largest exporter of iron ore in the world.[11] A further $103 billion AUD worth of resource projects are estimated to be in the pipeline.

This take-up rate led the former President of the NNTT, Mr Graeme Neate, to opine that it demonstrates the resource industry's embrace of the agreement-making model and the flexibility enshrined within it.[12] Many in the resource sector now view the model as one of the key steps to getting major Western Australia resource projects to fruition "quickly."[13]

1. *The Trade-Off: Are the Benefits Materializing?*

The prevalence of ILUAs in the Pilbara has also seen the establishment in the region of twenty-one Aboriginal corporations and related native title charitable trusts to manage the compensatory elements of the agreements. The compensation is intended to mitigate or recompense Aboriginal people for loss of resources or the ability to access country to exercise cultural practices after a company has secured tenure. Ideally, the amount of compensation should be commensurate to the value of a loss both in economic and intangible terms.[14] Such assessment is "a complex, but essentially an intuitive, one"[15] with "the compensation being assessed by reference to the spiritual and usuf ucturary significance of the area of the affected land."[16]

Pilbara-based Aboriginal corporations, with average annual revenue in 2016–2017 of $6.98 million AUD derived predominantly from the royalty payments received by the associated native title charitable trusts, are responsible for ensuring that the native title parties comply with their agreement obligations. Amongst other things, they are also responsible for monitoring the implementation of the resource companies' obligations and the development of community-based capacity building programs.

The native title charitable trusts, on the other hand, oversee the management of royalty payments received by native title parties which, since 2013, exceed $1.1 billion AUD.[17] Professional trustee companies, such as the Mutal Trust, Australian Executor Trustees and Perpetual, manage the funds on behalf of the native title charitable trusts. These funds are held under various arrangements, though in most cases there are "future funds," "direct benefit trusts" and "discretionary charitable trusts" which support the provision of member programs in the areas of hardship, lore and culture, education, health and funeral assistance. Generally speaking, 50% of the funds are held in "future funds," 30% of the funds are used to support their Aboriginal corporations and the development of member programs, and the balance is distributed to native title beneficiaries twice yearly. The distribution of native title royalty payments to native title beneficiaries is exempt from income tax and can, for senior beneficiaries (those 50 years or older), exceed $100,000 AUD per annum.[18]

A few resource companies and Aboriginal corporations, such as Fortescue Metals Group and Manungurra Aboriginal Corporation in the Northern Territory, question the transformational impact of these royalty payments, asserting that monetary compensation entrenches reliance on "mining welfare" viewed as "sit-down money"[19] and "can pose challenges for achieving lasting positive outcomes."[20] Where the royalty payments "far outweighs what they get from welfare, people don't work: [instead] they get welfare and royalties."[21] They contend that the transformational impacts of agreement-making are contained in the benefit packages that as part of the project create investments and add value to the local Aboriginal community and individuals. These benefit packages "constitute the extra things that developers can offer as a result of opportunities created by the development"[22] like training, employment and business development opportunities (known as the "economic participation obligations").[23]

Putting to one side the benefits or otherwise that may arise from royalty payments being in the native title trusts, to obtain the agreement of native title claim groups for projects to proceed, resource companies and the native title parties statutory appointed and government funded Native Title Representative Bodies, Yamatji Marlpa Aboriginal Corporation (YMAC) in the Pilbara, promote the positive impact of economic participation obligations have on native title groups as "life changing economic opportunities"[24] offered by mining and the realization of those opportunities as a "critical part of the socio-economic transformation of Indigenous people."[25]

III. The Challenge to Meet the Commitment

With just over 7,700 Aboriginal people living in the Pilbara, and an unemployment rate at nearly 25%, the 2016 Census showed that only 907 Pilbara-based Aboriginal people had identified being employed in the resources industry.

In the case of the native title holders, a sub-group of the Pilbara-based Aboriginal population, the statistics associated with their levels of employment are not collated by governments or most resource companies. In an exception to the rule, however, RTIO having negotiated 9 ILUAs with native title groups to support its 16 mines in the Pilbara, and with after tax earnings in 2017 exceeding $US6.5 billion AUD, only managed to employ 163 native title holders in its Pilbara operations during the same period.[26]

The low levels of employment support the view expressed by prominent Pilbara Aboriginal Elders that government and resource companies' policies and practices directed at their communities in the region are about establishing consent for the projects to progress uninterrupted at least as much, if not more, than delivering economic benefits for Pilbara Aboriginal people.[27]

The minister responsible for native title issues in the Western Australian government, Ben Wyatt MLA, appeared to grasp the gravity of the issue. Speaking at the annual native title conference in Perth in 2017, he told industry representatives in attendance that having now negotiated their native title agreements with native title holders in the Pilbara, which in turn had benefited the resource companies and the Western Australian economy, "the challenge to maximise socio-economic opportunity for traditional owners in regional communities is one of the most pressing issues"[28] now facing his government. One year from that speech, his ministerial colleague, Bill Johnston MLA, with portfolio responsibility for the resource industry, stated that the Western Australian government's priorities had changed and that "[*w*]e very much think one of the strengths of the WA resources sector now is that we are including the Indigenous community in the success of the industry and that is very important."[29]

The difficultly of sourcing, training, and placing local Aboriginal workers into employment in the resource sector is by no means easy. To better understand why the employment outcomes promised to local Aboriginal people are not being achieved, this paper now turns to consider two critical factors of the agreement-making model that make the challenge more confronting:

1 the nature and content of the economic participation obligations negotiated in exchange for resource companies securing land access and proceeding with their projects; and
2 the implementation and monitoring of those obligations on the part of resource companies to bring about the desired outcomes.

1. Key Aspects of the ILUA Regime

The NTA provides for different types of ILUAs.[30] The majority of ILUAs negotiated by resource companies in the Pilbara are known as "*area agreements*" and "*claim wide agreements.*" These agreements involve securing tenure for a specific tenement, resource project, or for a company's entire current and future mining operations. Once an agreement is registered as an ILUA with the NNTT it can be contractually binding for up to 100 years and approve all mining operations within that period,[31] in one case estimated to be at least 30 new mines.[32]

Negotiating ILUAs covering Pilbara resource projects has become a highly technical and resource intensive exercise with native title claim groups' negotiating committees providing strategic direction to YMAC to conduct negotiations on their behalf. Generally speaking, members of the native title claim group only get to hear the terms of the proposed ILUA at the statutorily convened "authorization" meetings for the purpose of entering into the ILUA on their behalf. This practice raises important concerns as to whether those in attendance have exercised their free, prior, and informed consent when approving the agreement in that they may not have been provided with a copy of the relevant agreement to review beforehand, or have had the terms of the agreement sufficiently explained to them prior to exercising their right to vote at the statutorily convened meeting.[33] The statutory "authorization" process identifies no requirements directed towards explaining the terms of agreement or the parties' obligations, only that:

a all reasonable efforts must have been made to ensure that all persons who hold or may hold native title in relation to the area covered by the agreement have been identified; and
b all persons so identified must have authorized the making of the agreement.[34]

It is implied that attendees would not approve the agreement unless the terms of the agreement were sufficiently explained to them and they understood the impact of the agreement and their decision to approve it. In some cases however, as in the recent controversial Adani mining development in Queensland illustrates, the statutorily appointed NTRB—the Queensland South Native Title Service—left it to Adani Mining representatives to explain parts of the proposed ILUA to attendees.[35]

The registration of ILUAs also has other critical implications that depart from general contractual principles and impact on the enforceability of the obligations and, therefore, the intended transformational impact of the agreements:

a In a departure from the common law principle of privity of contract, all persons holding native title in relation to any land or waters in the area covered by an ILUA are contractually bound by the obligations, irrespective of whether they are parties to the agreement.[36] Accordingly, future generations of native title claim group members have to comply with the agreement's obligations.
b Unlike other statutory agreements in Australia involving a specific group of people,[37] little is known about the content of ILUAs. The agreements usually contain confidentiality obligations and the statutory disclosure requirements for registering them do not require the disclosure of their substantive provisions. This lack of transparency has raised questions about the assessment and monitoring of the impact of the benefits,[38] and consequently, the potential for corrupt practices to arise, disputing the validity of the assertion regarding the agreements' "transformative" effect on local Aboriginal people.

a. The Economic Participation Obligations

While championing the transformational effects that mining can provide to native title groups, resource companies inevitably argue in agreement negotiations that they are not in a position to guarantee employment opportunities because:

a members of the group may not have sufficient skills to perform the duties safely, especially in an industry where occupational health and safety is a priority for employers;
b the company is not aware of the numbers, contact details, precise skills and experience of native title group's members; and

c commencing mining operations are dependent on many factors including, statutory and business approvals, and the price of the commodity.

Depending on the negotiating leverage and evidence that native title parties can muster during the negotiations, the uncertainties more often than not lead the parties' legal representatives to negotiating positions where the resource companies commit to provide employment and training opportunities using their "reasonable endeavours," "all reasonable endeavours" or—for the reasons examined below—begrudgingly concede to using their "best endeavours."

The following examples of clauses are typically found in many ILUA agreements in the Pilbara:

Example 1

> Miner intends to conduct its Project Operation in the Project Area in such a manner as to maximize employment of and training opportunities for the XXX people. The Miner will use its reasonable endeavours to promote the employment of XXX people at the Project Operations in the Project Area.

Example 2

> On the commencement of Mining Operations, each Participant will use its best endeavours to employ at least six appropriately qualified Claimants in connection with its activities on the Project Area.

And Example 3

> The Proponent is committed to the principle of providing meaningful employment, training and contracting opportunities to members of the Claimant in connection with its operations in the Agreement Area. To achieve this commitment, the Proponent agrees to the following provisions:
>
> The Proponent will use its best endeavours to employ members of the Claimant at its operations in the Agreement Area.
>
> The Proponent will require its contractors to adopt a pro-active policy in relation to the employment of members of the Claimant in connection with its activities on the Agreement Area.
>
> Every 2 months, the Proponent will notify the Claimant of any employment opportunities in connection with its activities on the Agreement Area.
>
> The Proponent will include members of the Claimant who are employed by the Proponent in on the job training programmes undertaken by the Proponent.

b. How Reasonable Is Reasonable?

While the parties' legal representatives craft wording to accommodate the uncertainty, native title parties are often unaware of the practical effect of these compromises and have little appreciation of the legal meaning of these terms.

The reality is that the common meaning of these terms can be very different from the meanings the courts have given them. Indeed, the judicial meaning of these terms varies across jurisdictions.

From the viewpoint of the Aboriginal corporations responsible for holding the resource companies to account for their commitments, most native title claim groups believe that the words mean what they say, or as expressed by Lawrence J in the UK decision of *Sheffield District Railway v Great Central Railway*,[39] over 100 hundred years ago:

> best endeavours means what the words say; they do not mean second-best endeavours … the words mean that [the promisor] must, broadly speaking, leave no stone unturned …[40]

There is also the common perception among the native title groups that the term *best endeavours* conveys a stronger requirement on the resource company than *reasonable endeavours*, and that *all reasonable endeavours* fits somewhere on the spectrum between the two terms.

When told that of the negligible difference between the respective phrases in Australian courts,[41] native title parties are disappointed though not surprised by the development, considering the historical absence of Australian judicial interpretation that supports Aboriginal wellbeing. When the Australian stance is compared to the clear distinction in terminology provided by the English courts,[42] litigants are left to apply the principles of contractual interpretation and seek to lead evidence which can demonstrate to quote the High Court of Australia in *Electricity Generation Corporation v Woodside Energy Ltd* (the Woodside case): "what a reasonable businessperson would have understood those terms to mean … [I]t will require consideration of the language used by the parties, the surrounding circumstances known to them and the commercial purpose or objects to be secured by the contract."[43]

The question arises as to whether the Woodside decision changes the approach to determine the application of *the reasonable endeavours* clause. The express entitlement of Woodside to take into account "all relevant commercial, economic and operational matters" was critical to it being able to make a commercial decision not to supply Verve with additional gas at the price stipulated under their gas supply agreement, without breaching its obligation to use reasonable endeavours to supply the additional gas.

The case serves to illustrate that endeavour-based clauses that require consideration of the resource companies' own commercial interest, to the exclusion of those of the native title parties in deciding whether to perform the obligation, should be resisted if the intent of the agreement is to see the "*socio-economic transformation of Aboriginal people's lives.*"

If the deal, however, is in fact that a resource company should have discretion as to whether they will perform the obligation, rather than that they should be excused for imperfect performance, the drafting should reflect that.

The second issue that the Woodside case left hanging was whether, in cases of contractual interpretation, the express terms must be ambiguous before evidence of surrounding circumstances may be led. As highlighted, the court described the tasks of interpreting commercial contracts as requiring "... consideration of the language used by the parties, the surrounding circumstances known to them and the commercial purpose or objects to be secured by the contract."[44] While the decision does not depart from established principles of contractual interpretation, it serves to reinforce the importance of including express qualification on the scope of resource company's obligation to use reasonable endeavours so as to ensure that those qualifications may be taken into account in determining what is reasonable in the circumstances.

Assuming that a court is called upon to interpret the resource company's *reasonable endeavours* in the context of implementing the economic participation obligations, and the court is prepared to take account of the "*genesis of the transaction*" and hear evidence as to the commercial intent of the agreement as championed by the resource companies—to provide employment opportunities for local Aboriginal people—the next threshold issue faced by the native title parties is to establish what *reasonable endeavours* the resource companies have taken to employ local Aboriginal people.

In this context, the Court is likely to consider such factors as:

a any internal standards that the parties have agreed to guide the interpretation of the obligation;

b in the absence of any internal standards, what a "reasonable business person" working in the resource industry in the Pilbara would have understood those terms to mean. With the proliferation of ILUAs in the last 5–8 years in the Pilbara whose number is now approaching 70, it would be reasonable to anticipate that evidence would exist of what measures the companies have taken to implement their obligations; and

c any commitments, understandings or statements that the resource companies (or their advisers) gave to the native title groups regarding the implementation of the obligations during the negotiations.

To make matters more difficult for the native title parties, resource companies do not volunteer any detailed information about what measures they take to implement their obligations. While companies, such as RTIO, have commenced releasing annual "Communities Review" newsletters as part of their social licence to operate, the information in these publications relate to their operations throughout Western Australia and are not confined to the Pilbara where they have their mining operations.

To gain government approval to commence mining operations, many resource companies commit to develop Local Participation Plans and Community Development Plans.[45] These plans are meant to include strategies to address local participation in resource projects, including providing employment opportunities for local Aboriginal people. However, until the recent decision by the Office of the Information Commissioner,[46] neither the resource companies nor the government were required to publicly disclose the information and this inhibited native title groups from developing a greater understanding of what efforts would constitute "reasonableness," or to use the plans and annual reports in courts.

While the plans are intended to benefit the Pilbara community, the resource companies and government claimed they were private contracts between the State and the company and reporting on their progress was not in the public interest because it would have an adverse effect of the business and commercial affairs of the company, never mind that the intention of the plans is to generate community benefits. With an eye on their potential use in litigious proceedings by native title parties, resource companies also submit that disclosure of the plans and accompanying annual reports would prejudice the future supply of the information to the government.[47]

Despite the barriers faced by native title groups when collating evidence to enforce the obligations, successive governments reassured native title parties that they may "be able to continue to avail themselves of certain general law remedies while an ILUA is registered, notably for damages and specific performance."[48]

Accordingly, it is left to the native title groups to obtain any information they can about the resource companies' attempts to implement their economic participation obligations through the mechanisms, if any, established in the ILUAs to monitor the implementation of the agreements.

IV. Monitoring the Implementation of Benefits

There is growing evidence that agreement obligations are "either not put into effect at all or do not bring about the results intended by the parties."[49] To reinforce the view that effective processes and structures are not being put in place to implement the obligations, a prominent mining sector adviser involved in more than 150 native title negotiations claims that poor implementation processes is one of the significant reasons why the promises of "jobs and contract targets have not been delivered in most jurisdictions and agreements."[50]

The resource industry is aware of these shortcoming and in its 2016 publication, *Why agreements matter: How to guide*, the RTIO cautioned against ignoring the significance of implementation when it stated that "a common oversight [in agreement making] is to focus on content without thinking about the resource that will be required during implementation."[51]

That is not to say that discussion on implementation is absent during the negotiations, but it is limited. More importantly, as the RTIO publication alludes to, the people who negotiate the agreements are not the same people charged with responsibility to implement the agreements and this disconnect is now coming to the fore.[52]

1. Governance Arrangements

A common governance model contained in most ILUAs involves the establishment of participatory monitoring mechanisms with "shared responsibility" for successful delivery of outcomes. These are often referred to as "joint," "relationship," or "implementation" committees consisting of company and native title claim group representatives who are meant to meet during the implementation of the ILUA.

Depending on the nature of the agreement and life of the project, committees may meet on an annual, half-yearly, or quarterly basis. In one extreme example, the ILUA provided that the relationship committee meet annually and cease to exist after the fifth anniversary of the agreement, even though the company continues to operate, engage employees, and tender contracting opportunities on the native title claim group's traditional lands.

Likewise, the capacity and resources that the companies are prepared to invest in the implementation and monitoring of the agreement obligations vary significantly. With the downturn in the resources industry in 2013, companies implemented cost-cutting measures such as the cancellation of implementation committee meetings and reduction in the number of staff assigned to manage the implementation and monitoring of obligations, significantly impacting their implementation. In many cases, the measures imposed continue in place despite Pilbara-based resource companies commanding nearly 40% of the global iron ore market.[53]

When implementation committee meetings do occur, the adopted governance arrangements vary significantly across the industry. With the exception of a few resource companies prepared to distribute agendas and reports prior to meetings to allow committee members to prepare, most resource companies rely on verbal reports or PowerPoint presentations. At these meetings the resource companies are often seen by native title parties as "just ticking a box" where there is "no accountability."[54] The meetings generally last no longer than one to two hours and most of the time is devoted to "relationship building" where resource company representatives enquire about developments occurring in the Aboriginal community and seek useful intelligence on heritage surveys commissioned by their competitors.

2. Membership of Implementation Committees

Despite the establishment of monitoring mechanisms premised on participatory governance arrangements, native title members on implementation committees are often ill-equipped to effectively represent their members' interests. In most cases, the native title claimant group's corporation (whose establishment is contractually required under the ILUA regime) is not operational for at least 24–36 months after the registration of an ILUA due to resourcing, capacity, governance, and legitimacy hurdles that need to be overcome for sustainable operation. For the same reasons the representatives of native title claim groups on implementation committees are unlikely to have the capacity to monitor the implementation of the obligations for at least two years after the agreement is registered.

Membership of the implementation committees is a hotly contested issue within native title groups, because committee members are entitled to significant financial and non-financial rewards. Consisting of between four and six native title representatives, the committee members are entitled to sitting fees, travel allowances, and in many cases, annual visits to capital cities. These payments can be significant, between $500 and $1000 per day/meeting, especially where meetings occur on mining sites or in regional towns and centres away from committee members' normal place of residence.

To mitigate the potential for intra-group conflict over the financial benefits associated with committee membership, a common resolution to the issue is that membership of the various committees, corporation boards, and trusts is spread across different families, as decided by those attending the Aboriginal corporation's annual general meeting.

Outside the receipt of royalty compensation payments, becoming a member of the implementation committee is viewed as the easiest avenue to access financial benefits because there is scant community accountability associated with the committees' work and, unlike the Aboriginal corporations and native title charitable trusts, there is no regulatory oversight of the committee's work or eligibility criteria for appointment. If eligible for appointment, directors on Aboriginal corporations and native title charitable trusts are required to be financially literate and comply with the various statutory duties and obligations as outlined in the *Corporations (Aboriginal and Torres Strait Islander) Act 2006* (Cth) (CATSI Act)[55] and the *Australian Charities and Not-For Profit Commissions Act 2012* (Cth) (ACNC Act).

More importantly, the non-financial benefits of committee membership can indirectly lead to significant financial rewards for the family members on the committees. The absence of fiduciary obligations on committee members and the non-existence of the prohibition on "related-party benefits" found in the CATSI Act[56] and ACNC Act,[57] means that committee members often take advantage of the advanced notice they receive about employment and contracting opportunities. These opportunities are shared with family members, rather than the wider native title group. If shared through social media and periodic newsletters to reach the wider membership of the native title group, this often occurs after the deadline.

Significantly also, in many cases, the implementation committee members are not the same working group members involved in the negotiations that led to the ILUA and therefore lack the "corporate knowledge" behind the negotiations and the commitments made to secure agreement. Moreover, directors of native title corporations and the associated charitable trusts are often required to undergo basic governance training within one year of their appointments to the boards; in the case of the implementation committees, no compulsory training is required.

The lack of accountability, both at community level and statutorily, has resulted in committee members often being chosen from the older generation of native title group members (in some cases respected Elders and senior law men and women), who for historical reasons, have had little exposure to commercial dealings, working on mining projects, participating in negotiations, and are in poor health. The fees, allowances, and travel benefits they receive for attending committee meetings are viewed by their family members as supplementing the Elders' royalty compensation payments and State pension.

The compounding of these issues has led Transparency International Australia to identify the likelihood of self-interest, nepotism, and corruption occurring during the implementation of ILUAs as being "high" risk.[58] The potential increases if resource company representatives are prepared to manipulate committee members.

V. Conclusion

The challenge of placing Pilbara-based Aboriginal people into employment in resource projects in the Pilbara cannot be underestimated. A lack of employment history, poor educational, health, and housing outcomes together with successive governments' ineffectual responses to deal these issues, has unsurprisingly shifted the focus of the native title holders on to the resource industry to provide them with opportunities to improve the socio-economic wellbeing of their communities.

Governments provide resource companies with the mechanisms to win over native title holders' hearts and minds that bring their projects to fruition "quickly." At the same time, governments legislate to bypass many of the common law safeguards developed over the centuries and intended to foster commercial arrangements. The consequences for these policy decisions are now coming to the fore. Poor transparency in the ILUA agreement-making model and the lack of accountability for its outcomes are evidenced by the highly questionable employment statistics for Pilbara-based Aboriginal people in resource projects.

Lawyers, acting on instructions from the resource companies, have ensured through clever drafting techniques that their clients are unlikely to be held accountable and liable for the failure to comply with the promises made. For their part, governments—while acknowledging that the promised benefits may not have materialized—appear reluctant to step-in and impose conditions on an industry that plays a significant role in the economy.

To address the issue of enforceability and accountability of economic participation obligations in Indigenous-industry agreements—particularly in countries without extensive histories of working in, or collaborating with, the industry—lawyers representing Indigenous groups should ensure the agreements contain internal standards that establish how resource companies are expected to comply with each obligation, particularly where they insist that the obligations contain caveats such as "reasonable endeavours" and "best endeavours."

These standards could focus on stakeholder engagement strategies and activities that promote the company in the community as a workplace that supports Indigenous employment; work-readiness programs for Indigenous people, particularly the skill-set required to obtain employment with the company; and recruitment strategies and activities that encourage Indigenous employment with the company. Additional standards could centre on cultural competency training for all new employees and refresher training for existing employees every few years and mentorship programs as well as policies and procedures supporting Indigenous employees to meet their cultural obligations. As far as supervisors, managers, and executive level employees are concerned, key performance indicators could concentrate on attracting, retaining, and promoting Indigenous employees; designing preferential strategies that encourage greater participation of Indigenous employees on workplace committees and forums; instituting recognition awards for Indigenous engagement, support and achievement in the workplace and community; quantifying the monetary value that should be set aside to support Indigenous employment and engagement strategies; and periodic reporting to implementation committee, senior management, and at board level that tracks the implementation of the agreement obligations.

Without the revenues they receive from resource companies operating in the Pilbara, governments cannot deliver on the promises they make to the electorate. Making up just over 15% of the Pilbara population, Aboriginal people lack the legal, political, and economic capacity to effect change that will lead to improvements in their socio-economic wellbeing. Their native title agreements will not effect the change they seek; their parliamentarian representatives lack the political will to initiate the change needed; and their representative bodies continue to promote the perceived positive virtues of the agreement-making model. As long as these elements maintain the status quo, native title holders will continue to sit back and watch others reap the benefits from the resources on their native title lands.

Notes

1. Rio Tinto, "Iron Ore's landmark Indigenous employment result" (15 January 2018). <https://connect.riotinto.com/content/news/article/5a5c4a9f76012095a89368bd>.
2. Ciaran O'Faircheallaigh, "Evaluating agreements between Indigenous peoples and resource developers," in Marcia Langton and others (eds), *Honour Among Nations? Treaties and Agreements with Indigenous People* (Melbourne University Press 2005) 303, 308–309.
3. Brad Thompson, "Mining leases in limbo as Christian Porter rejects native title fix" (*The Australian Financial Review*, 17 June 2018) <www.afr.com/business/mining-leases-in-limbo-as-attorney-general-rejects-native-title-quick-fix-20180616-h11h5l>.
4. (1992) 175 CLR 1.
5. *Native Title Amendment Act 1998* (Cth).
6. The old section 21 agreements under the NTA did not allow parties to contract out of other procedural requirements of the NTA, such as the "right to negotiate" and governments were also required to be a party to the section 21 agreement.
7. G. Neate, "Indigenous Land Use Agreements: Some legal issues," paper presented at the Native Title Forum 2001, 1. It should be noted that only agreements that are lodged and meet the registration requirements under the NTA are called ILUAs, and therefore attract the type of certainty and enforceability conferred by registration under the NTA.
8. NTA (n 5) s 31(1)(b).

9. In the context of ILUAs, authorization is the process by which all persons who hold or may hold native title within the area of the ILUA decide whether or not to make the agreement.
10. Predominantly Trust Deeds which outline sub-fund arrangements associated with the payment of royalties.
11. Western Australia is the largest iron ore producer and exporter in the world, accounting for 37% of global production. Iron ore accounted for 48% of the value of Western Australia's exports in 2016–2017 and is expected to contribute $4.6 billion AUD in royalty payments to the West Australian government—see Department of Jobs, Tourism, Science and Innovation, "Western Australia Iron Ore Industry Profile," (*Government of Australia*, November 2017) <www.jtsi.wa.gov.au>.
12. Neate (n 7) 2: former NNTT President Graeme Neate asserts that the "flexibility of ILUAs is illustrated by the agreements registered and lodged for registration."
13. ABC News, "RIO Tinto signs huge $2b native title deal" (*ABC*, 5 June 2011) <www.abc.net.au/.../rio-tinto-signs-huge-2b-native-title-deal/2743734>.
14. NTA (n 5) s 51. The criterion for determining compensation in s 51 is by reference "just terms." The NTA, however, does not prescribe any particular framework for the determination of the compensation payable, save that in the circumstances of this application by the operation of s 51(4).
15. *Alan Griffiths and Lorraine Jones on behalf of the Ngaliwurri and Nungali Peoples v Northern Territory of Australia (No3)* [2016] FCA 900 [302].
16. *Northern Territory v Mr A. Griffiths (deceased) and Lorraine Jones on behalf of the Ngaliwurru and Nungali Peoples* [2019] HCA 7 [163].
17. Based on an analysis of the information disclosed, Pilbara native title charitable trusts are required to disclose annually to the Australian Charities and Not-for-Profit Commission since reporting commenced in 2013.
18. For a general discussion on the implications of the tax exempt status associated with the royalty payments see Miranda Stewart, "Tax and Native Title," paper presented at the 28th National Convention, The Tax Institute, Perth (March 2013) <www.fdio.com.au/sites/fdio.com.au/files/Document_%20The%20Tax%20Institute%20Tax%20and%20Native%20Title%20paper.pdf>.
19. Andrew Burrell, "Pilbara indigenous community split over Fortescue mines claim" (*The Australian*, 11 August 2015) <www.theaustralian.com.au/news/inquirer/pilbara-indigenous-community-split-over-fortescue-mine-claim/news-story/33f4b6d0c17aff1dfdbf83eb61fcf336>.
20. Rio Tinto, "Compensation and benefits for land access guidance" (*Rio Tinto*, 2015) in Rio Tinto "Why agreements matter: How to guide" (*Rio Tinto*, March 2016) 73 <https://www.riotinto.com/documents/Rio_Tinto_Why_Agreements_Matter.pdf>.
21. Amos Aikman, "Existing land rights law fails traditional owners" (*The Australian*, 25 July 2018) 4 <https://www.theaustralian.com.au/subscribe/news/1/?sourceCode=TAWEB_WRE170_a_GGL&dest=https%3A%2F%2Fwww.theaustralian.com.au%2Fnation%2Fpolitics%2Flaws-failing-traditional-owners%2Fnews-story%2Fbb144590e9918143fa785a83d6095d91&memtype=anonymous&mode=premium&v21suffix=60-a>.
22. Rio Tinto (n 20) 73.
23. Ibid.
24. Fortescue Metals Group, "Fortescue enters into ground-breaking deal for first Aboriginal iron ore mine" (*Media Release*, 14 September 2015) <http://fmgl.com.au/media/2644/media-release-2015-14-september-aamc.pdf>.
25. Maureen Teha and Lee Godden, "Legal forms and their implications for long-term relationship and economic, cultural and social empowerment," in Marcia Langton and Judy Longbottom (eds), *Community Futures, Legal Architecture: Foundations for Indigenous Peoples in the Global Mining Boom* (Routledge 2012) 111, 127.

26. Rio Tinto, "Iron Ore's landmark Indigenous employment result" 15 January 2018, <https://connect.riotinto.com/content/news/article/5a5c4a9f76012095a89368bd>.
27. Andrew Burrell, "Rio Tinto snubbed by Pilbara's Aboriginal Elders" (*The Australian*, 6 August 2016) <https://www.theaustralian.com.au/subscribe/news/1/?sourceCode=TAWEB_WRE170_a_GGL&dest=https%3A%2F%2Fwww.theaustralian.com.au%2Fbusiness%2Fmining-energy%2Frio-tinto-snubbed-by-pilbaras-aboriginal-elders%2Fnews-story%2F32fb4168c6d295c63dce2ea95afcafef&memtype=anonymous&mode=premium&v21suffix=60-a>.
28. Minister for Aboriginal Affairs Legalwise Speech 17 June 2017, Western Australian Treasurer, Hon. Ben Wyatt MLA, "Native Title Priorities: Self-Determination and Collaboration" (copy of speech held by author).
29. Brad Thompson, "Mining leases in limbo as Christian Porter rejects native title quick fix" (*Financial Review*, 17 June 2017) <at www.afr.com/business/mining-leases-in-limbo-as-attorney-general-rejects-native-title-quick-fix-20180616-h11h51>.
30. The NTA provides for three types of ILUAs. (1) A body corporate agreement; (2) an area agreement; and (3) an alternative procedure agreement (NTA (n 5) ss 24BD, 24CD, 24DE).
31. Briana Shepherd, "Banjima people celebrate after Pilbara native title deal signed in Kings Park ceremony" (*ABC News, 4 November 2015*), <www.abc.net.au/news/2015-11-04/bhp-billiton-and-nanjima-people-sign-pilbara-native-title-deal/6913522>.
32. AAP, "Rio Tinto signs huge $2b native title deal" (*ABC News*, 5 June 2001) (ABC News, 5 June 2000), <www.abc.net.au/news/2011-06-03/rio-tinto-signs-huge-2b-native title-deal/2743734>.
33. John Southalan and Joe Fardin, "Free, prior and informed consent: how and from whom? An Australian analogue" (2009) 37(4) Journal of Energy & Natural Resource Law 365.
34. NTA (n 5) s 24CG(3).
35. *Kemppi v Adani Mining Pty Ltd (No 4)* [2018] FCA 1245 [64]–[65].
36. NTA (n 5) s 24EA.
37. *Fair Work Act 2009* (Cth), enterprise agreements, Part 2–4.
38. Transparency International Australia, *Corruption Risks: Mining Approval in Australia—Mining for Sustainable Development Programme*, October 2017, 42.
39. (1911) 27 TLR 451.
40. Ibid 452.
41. *Platara v Dempster*, Owen J in *Jetcity Pty Ltd v Yenald Nominees Pty Ltd*, unreported, BC 9901772, WA Supreme Court, 9 April 1999, "*All of the these cases clearly show that in Australia there is little difference between 'best endeavours' and 'reasonable endeavours.'*"
42. *Rhodia International v Huntsmand International*, [2007] 2 Lloyd's Rep 325, "… there may be a number of reasonable courses of action which could be taken in a given situation to achieve a particular aim. An obligation to use reasonable endeavours to achieve the aim probably only requires a party to take one reasonable course, not all of them, where as an obligation to use best endeavours probably requires a party to take all reasonable course he can."
43. *Electricity Generation Corporation v Woodside Energy Ltd* (2014) 251 CLR 640 [656]–[657].
44. Ibid.
45. For example, *Iron Ore (Robe River) Agreement Act 1964* (WA), s 3(2) of sch 8.
46. *Re Gaffney and Department of Jobs, Tourism, Science and Innovation* [2019] WAICmr 3 (15 February 2019).
47. See Jason MacLean, "Impact Benefit Agreements, Transparency, and Subsidiarity", in Ibironke T. Odumosu-Ayanu and Dwight Newman (eds.), *Indigenous-Industry Agreements, Natural Resources, and the Law* (Routledge 2021); Bram Noble, "The Relationship Between Indigenous-Industry Agreements and Environmental Assessment", in Odumosu-Ayanu and Newman, ibid.

48. Commonwealth Government Response to "Nineteenth Report of the Parliamentary Joint Committee on Native Title and the Aboriginal and Torres Strait Islander Land Fund: Second Interim Report for the Section 206(d) Inquiry: Indigenous Land Use Agreements, 3 November 2005 (copy of response held by the author).
49. Ciaran O'Faircheallaigh, "Implementing Agreement Between Indigenous Peoples and Resource Developers in Australia and Canada" Aboriginal Politics and Public Sector Management Research Paper No 13 (Griffith University 2013) 6.
50. J. Robertson, "Adani's compensation for traditional owners 'well below' industry standard, report finds" (*ABC Radio*, 1 December 2017) <abc.net.au/news/2017-12-01/adani-compensation-well-below-industry-standard-report-finds/9212058>.
51. Rio Tinto (n 20) 72.
52. K. Barndon, "Making up the numbers or making a mark", Australian Mining Monthly (5 July 2018).
53. Department of Jobs, Tourism, Science and Innovation, "Western Australian Iron Ore Profile" (*Government of Western Australia*, June 2019) <https://www.jtsi.wa.gov.au/docs/default-source/default-document-library/wa-iron-ore-profile-0619.pdf?sfvrsn=ca9d701c_4>.
54. Comments attributed to Josie Alec in Y Redrup, "Indigenous entrepreneurs targeted with Investible startup accelerator program" (*Australian Financial Review*, 7 January 2018) <afr.com/technology/indigenous-entrepreneurs-need-more-help-than-just-ticking-a-box-20180105-h0e6fv>.
55. The CATSI Act outlines five positive duties on corporation directors—duty of care and diligence; duty of good faith; duty not to improperly use position and information; duty to disclose material personal interest; and duty to not trade while insolvent—see CATSI Act, ss 265–271.
56. A related party benefit is when a corporation gives a financial benefit to a person or organization with a close relationship to the corporation—see CATSI Act, s 293.
57. While related party transaction is not directly defined in the ACNC Act, the term "related party" is defined in Australian Accounting Standards (AASB) 124 Related Party Disclosures.
58. Transparency International Australia (n 38) 44, 57.

15 Canadian Law and Realpolitik Regarding Indigenous-Industry Agreements

Thomas Isaac and Arend J.A. Hoekstra

I. Introduction

The practice of Indigenous-industry agreements in Canada has been dominated thus far by the use of Impact Benefit Agreements (IBAs).[1] IBAs are private contractual agreements negotiated between project proponents and Indigenous peoples.[2] Drafted correctly, IBAs can help mitigate risk for proponents and Indigenous peoples, including by providing mechanisms for consultation and evidence of mutually acceptable accommodation. As private contractual agreements, IBAs can be tailored for, and responsive to, market, legal, and political forces. In this paper, we consider increasingly common arguments that IBAs should be subject to government regulation, ultimately urging significant caution on any such regulation. We develop that argument in the subsequent sections by considering the nature, legal bases, and political bases for IBAs before going on to consider the ways in which imprudent regulation could interfere with, and cause uncertainty for, existing established practices. By way of context, though, we first set out how IBAs are responsive to interests on all sides.

IBAs are a product of both the increased recognition of Aboriginal and treaty rights and proponents' desires for greater regulatory certainty and risk management. Canadian governments are evolving their decision-making processes to better reflect the Crown's duty to consult and promote reconciliation with Canada's Indigenous peoples. Canadian courts are considering how the rights of Indigenous peoples should be reconciled with other Canadian interests—with "reconciliation" a dominant theme in the jurisprudence on the recognition and affirmation of Aboriginal and treaty rights in section 35 of Canada's *Constitution Act, 1982*.[3] In this evolving legal landscape, project proponents are faced with uncertain and shifting parameters for advancing projects which may impact the Aboriginal and treaty rights of Canada's Indigenous peoples.[4]

IBAs can be a useful tool for development proponents to manage risk in the context of such legal, regulatory, and societal uncertainty. By obtaining Indigenous support for a project through an agreement, proponents can mitigate the risk of delay or obstruction or legal challenge, potentially avoiding significant cost and risk.[5]

IBAs offer significant advantages to Indigenous peoples as well. IBAs, as private and negotiable agreements, can address specific project impacts, through compensation, mitigation, and avoidance measures. In many instances IBAs can help to address socio-economic risk factors within Indigenous communities, including in relation to skills development, employment, environment, health, and the potential biophysical effects of resource development.[6] Indigenous peoples can negotiate the provision of specific benefits through IBAs; some Indigenous peoples are deriving millions of dollars a year in revenue for their communities from natural resource development.[7] One source suggests that "First Nations took in $321 million of revenues from natural resources in 2015–2016."[8] The natural resource economy alone has the potential to provide tens of thousands of jobs for Indigenous peoples.[9] Making available employment opportunities, opportunities for training and skills development, and opportunities for Indigenous peoples to build their own companies and expertise, can all be negotiated and directed through an IBA.

Many Indigenous peoples assert that they have an inherent right to lands and resources within their traditional territories, including the explicit right to manage and participate in the development of resources.[10] IBAs can allow Indigenous peoples to have a meaningful say in how natural resources are developed, how project impacts can be minimized, and how project benefits can be obtained. IBAs represent a pragmatic model for mineral development—a model of bilateral cooperation between proponents and Indigenous peoples—a model that operates outside, but in contemplation of, regulatory regimes and the Crown.[11]

IBAs can also serve governments' interests. Canada's Constitution binds Indigenous peoples and governments together; it is the Crown's responsibility to fulfil the Crown's duty to consult.[12] With each regulatory decision which could adversely impact Aboriginal or treaty rights, the Crown is exposed to risk that its decision could be overturned, the proposed project could be prevented or delayed (as was seen in 2016 in *Northern Gateway* and again in 2018 in *Trans Mountain Expansion)*, and that the attractiveness of investing in Canadian projects may be adversely impacted. In order to give confidence to its decision making process, the Crown or Crown delegates (including regulators), frequently look to whether an IBA exists. The existence of an IBA can be evidence that the Crown's duty to consult has been satisfied, or that an approval by the government will not be challenged.

The Crown's interest in the completion of IBAs invites the question examined further in this paper: should the Crown regulate IBAs? At least some commentators argue that the Crown's absence in the negotiation and completion of IBAs is problematic since it is the Crown's "legal duty to promote reconciliation of aboriginal and non-aboriginal interests."[13] However, while IBAs are often used as evidence of the Crown's duty to consult having been fulfilled, IBAs are, with few exceptions, private contracts. IBAs are negotiated within a spirit of tension between proponents and Indigenous governments: proponents risk unfavourable regulatory decisions including unsatisfactory conditions and costly delays; Indigenous peoples risk having projects approved despite their objections, without their direct input, and without the potential socio-economic benefits which often flow from IBAs. As this paper develops in the next sections, any regulation with respect to IBAs may alter the tension that is required to bring both the Indigenous peoples and the proponents to the bargaining table and produce a fair and reasonable outcome. Disrupting this tension could discourage infrastructure and resource investments, thereby reducing the economic benefits available to Canadians generally, including Indigenous Canadians.

II. The Nature of IBAs in Canada

In Canada, IBAs have become common in natural resources and energy projects[14] and are also increasingly used in both public and private infrastructure projects. IBAs are commonly negotiated between Indigenous communities and project proponents. Indigenous communities may be represented by band councils, chiefs, representative organizations, or Indigenous development corporations. Some Indigenous communities in Canada have found that having one development corporation or institution represent several Indigenous communities or land owners in their negotiation with private sector resource companies can be effective, provided that good communication and community consultation mechanisms are established.[15]

IBAs provide mechanisms for establishing formal relationships between proponents and Indigenous peoples. The process of negotiating IBAs will typically include meetings between proponents and community leaders, and may include information efforts to inform Indigenous communities about the terms of the IBA before it is executed.

In their most basic form, the IBA seeks to address the adverse effects of a project on an Indigenous community through negotiated terms rather than rely on regulator-imposed terms. In many cases, the negotiated terms will not only reflect the potential impact, but will also share benefits in proportion to the value of the proposed project, ensuring that Indigenous peoples receive benefits from the development of resources or lands.[16]

Benefits provided through IBAs may include provisions for: royalties or lease payments; support for community-based business development; education, training, and employment opportunities; infrastructure and social development; and cultural retention programs.[17] IBAs will often include provisions on how the parties will work together going forward, including through environmental management schemes and dispute resolution and arbitration processes.

In exchange for sharing benefits created by the proposed project with the potentially impacted Indigenous peoples, the proponent will seek assurances that the Indigenous peoples will support the project. In some instances, this support may be unqualified, while other instances may allow for opposition only after reasonable efforts have failed to satisfy an objection.

The Ekati Diamond Mine in Canada's Northwest Territories concluded IBAs with the Tłı̨chǫ Government, Akaitcho Treaty 8, North Slave Métis Alliance, and the Hamlet of Kugluktuk/Kitikmeot Inuit Association. The IBAs establish commitments to funding, training, preferential hiring, business opportunities, and communications.[18] The Ekati mine offers apprenticeships to enhance the skills of their workforce and has a preferential hiring policy in place so that preference is given to northern residents and, in particular, northern Indigenous peoples. In 2016, the overall employment of northern Indigenous employees made up 36% of their employees, excluding contractors.[19] Additionally, preference is given to Indigenous businesses, and $144 million or 43% of the northern business spend, went to Indigenous businesses in 2016.[20]

III. Key Legal Bases for IBAs in Canada

Within Canada's Aboriginal law jurisprudence, the principle of "the honour of the Crown" requires that the Crown act honourably, in accordance with its historical and future relationship with Indigenous peoples.[21] The Crown's duty to consult derives from the honour of the Crown[22]—"The Crown, acting honourably, cannot cavalierly run roughshod over Indigenous interests ... the honour of the Crown may require it to consult with and reasonably accommodate Indigenous interests."[23]

The Crown's duty to consult is triggered when the Crown has knowledge, real or constructive, of the potential existence of an Indigenous or treaty right and contemplates conduct that might adversely affect that right.[24] The extent to which the Crown has a duty to consult is context specific and is directed by: the strength of an Indigenous people's claim to Indigenous or treaty rights; the seriousness of any potential impact of the proposed Crown action; and the history of dealings between the Crown and the Indigenous group, where relevant.[25]

The Supreme Court of Canada has emphasized that the duty to consult lies with the Crown and the Crown cannot delegate the ultimate responsibility associated with the duty.[26] However, the Crown may delegate procedural aspects of consultation to third parties, including proponents.[27] The Crown can also rely on certain regulatory bodies, such as the National Energy Board, to fulfill its duty to consult because where a "regulatory agency exists to exercise executive power as authorized by legislatures, any distinction between its actions and Crown actions quickly falls away."[28]

In assessing whether the duty to consult has been met, the court engages in a two-stage analysis. In the first stage of analysis, the court will consider whether the Crown appropriately identified the level of consultation required. The court will not give deference to the Crown's assessment at this stage and instead requires the Crown's assessment to be correct.[29] In the second stage of the analysis, the court will look at whether the consultation undertaken was reasonable. The consultation need not be perfect and mistakes will be tolerated so long as they do not strike at the heart of what is fair and reasonable in the circumstances.[30] Even if the court incorrectly assessed the level of consultation that is required in the first stage, the Crown may still have met the level of consultation that is required to satisfy the duty.[31] As a result, the Crown is incentivized to require a higher level of consultation than the assessed level as a precaution in case the assessment was wrong.

The existence of an IBA will often be considered by the Crown before it makes a decision which invites the Crown's duty to consult, such as a necessary project permit or authorization. However, while IBAs are frequently used to see whether the procedural aspect of the Crown's duty to consult has been satisfied, they are not by themselves "process" agreements. The commitments from Indigenous communities within IBAs are typically twofold: that the Indigenous community will not challenge or obstruct the project, and that the Indigenous community will make statements before regulators attesting to the satisfaction of the duty to consult. As a result, while IBAs provide a basis through which project support is granted by the Indigenous community, they do not ensure that consultation itself has occurred, only that the Indigenous community will attest that it has been satisfied, and will not challenge the project. For Crown decisions-makers, including regulators, the attestations of Indigenous communities can be relied upon to reduce the risk of an appeal regarding the fulfillment of the Crown's duty to consult, and may make a decision-maker more confident in approving a project.

In general terms, there is currently no constitutional or common law obligation on proponents or private parties to enter into IBAs. However, several modern treaties and several legislative frameworks do set out requirements for consultation and the negotiation of benefits, effectively requiring IBAs.

In terms of modern treaties, the Nunavut Land Claims Agreement signed in May 1993 is the largest land claim in the history of Canada, and led to the creation of a new federal territory in April 1999.[32] Under the Nunavut Land Claims Agreement, no major development project may commence on Inuit owned lands, with exceptions, until an IBA is finalized in accordance with Article 26 of the Nunavut Land Claims Agreement. There are also guiding principles provided including that the "benefits shall not place an excessive burden on the proponent and undermine the viability of the project."[33] Under the Nunavut Land Claims Agreement, there are also arbitration processes set out should the parties be unable to come to an agreement.[34]

The Inuvialuit Comprehensive Land Claim Agreement came into effect on July 25, 1984[35] and includes participation from the Government of Canada, the Government of the Northwest Territories and the Government of Yukon. Where a resource proponent has approval from the Government of Canada to access resources underneath Inuvialuit land, there is a requirement for the parties to enter into a participation agreement, or in other words, an IBA.[36] Where the parties are not able to agree on the terms of the IBA, the matter is referred to the Arbitration Board which may select the proposal, submitted by each party, it considers the more reasonable or may, after consultation with the parties, make a compromise ruling.[37] The fees paid under the IBA are of fair compensation to the Inuvialuit for use of lands, damage to lands, and any diminution of the value of their interests in their lands.[38]

The Gwich'in Comprehensive Land Claim Agreement (Gwich'in Agreement)[39] was signed on April 22, 1992 between the Government of Canada, the Government of the Northwest Territories, and the Gwich'in. The Sahtu Dene and Metis Comprehensive Land Claim Agreement (Sahtu Agreement)[40] was signed a little more than a year after the Gwich'in Agreement and is nearly identical to the Gwich'in Agreement. The land claims include explicit provisions that require the negotiation of agreements between affected Indigenous peoples and developers, thereby assuring that some of the benefits from development will accrue to Indigenous peoples whose traditional lands are affected by the project. Both agreements require consultation, in the manner provided in the agreement, before resource developers engage in exploration or production on certain lands.[41] The agreements also established the Surface Rights Board, which has jurisdiction over matters relating to surface entry and compensation for Indigenous owned lands.[42] Although the agreements do not require an IBA, the process under the Surface Rights Board essentially establishes a process whereby if no agreement is reached by private parties and the affected Indigenous group, then the Board will determine compensation for rent by assessing factors such as potential damage that may be caused to the land, the impact on wildlife, and the cultural significance of the land.[43]

The Tlicho Land Claims and Self-Government Agreement[44] (Tlicho Agreement) was signed on August 23, 2003 and is more expansive in both the land and resources transferred to the First Nation. It also provides for self-government whereby the Tlicho Government was granted law-making authority over Tlicho citizens and communities on Tlicho lands.[45] The Tlicho lands were granted in fee simple[46] which means that the Tlicho government controls all the mineral rights below their land and mining proponents require consent from the Tlicho government before exploring or extracting minerals on Tliicho lands. The Tlicho Agreement also contains consultation processes and provides that if there is a major mining project in the treaty region then proponents must enter into negotiations for an IBA.[47] IBA negotiations cannot "place an excessive burden on the proponent *and* undermine the viability of the project" [emphasis added].[48]

The Labrador Inuit Land Claims Agreement (LILCA) was signed in 2005 by the Labrador Inuit, represented by the Labrador Inuit Association, and the governments of Canada and Newfoundland and Labrador.[49] The LILCA includes self-government provisions that enable the creation of the Nunatsiavut Government.[50] Under this agreement, no major development may commence in the specified zone until an agreement has been concluded between the resource developer and the Nunatsiavut Government in accordance with the LILCA. The IBA negotiations "shall not place an excessive burden on the Developer *or* undermine the viability of the Major Development" [emphasis added] and the benefits should reflect the scale of the project.[51] If the parties cannot come to an agreement, the matter may be referred to the arbitration process outlined in LILCA.[52]

When a modern treaty, such as a comprehensive land claim agreement or settlement agreement, has been duly executed and ratified by all parties, the resulting agreement is brought into force under federal legislation and becomes constitutionally protected under section 35.[53] As a result, these modern treaties establish constitutionally protected IBA requirements in Canada.

In addition to modern treaties, certain legislation also requires IBAs to be negotiated. First, the Yukon *Oil and Gas Act*[54] requires a benefits agreement to be entered into if an oil and gas developer would like to carry on oil and gas activity in the Yukon, and anticipates that costs will be in excess of $1,000,000 in any 12-month period.[55] The legislation provides a process for developers to follow and if an agreement cannot be reached, there is a dispute resolution process available.[56] The Act also allows for the Yukon First Nation and the Minister to agree to waive the requirement.[57]

Second, the *Canada Petroleum Resources Act*[58] also requires a benefits plan, as opposed to an agreement, when active on certain federal lands and waters. The plans are intended to provide opportunities for all Canadians, not Indigenous peoples specifically, to participate in work and other activities. No work or activity on any frontier lands, as defined in the *Canada Petroleum Resources Act*, that are subject to any former exploration agreement, former lease, former permit, former special renewal permit, exploration licence, production licence, or significant discovery licence shall be commenced until the Minister has approved or waived the requirement of approval of the benefits plan.[59]

Third, the Government of Newfoundland and Labrador also mandated in its Aboriginal Consultation Policy that "[a]ny financial consideration in regard to accommodation of the infringement of Aboriginal rights will be the responsibility of the proponent."[60] This is contrary to the Supreme Court of Canada's statement in *Haida Nation* where the "legal responsibility for consultation and accommodation rests with the Crown."[61]

IV. Political and Practical Bases for IBAs

Privately negotiated IBAs between proponents and Indigenous peoples offer advantages, including through risk management, to the Crown, Indigenous peoples and proponents. Although the duty to consult and, where appropriate, accommodate, falls on government, it is the proponents who are best situated to communicate technical elements of a project and identify and provide accommodation within the scope of the project. Proponents are also best situated to determine what accommodation is reasonable within the context of a project and the capacity of a project to offer benefits. As a consequence, bilaterally negotiated IBAs offer a practical solution to accommodation as well as an effective political tool for satisfying governments' obligations to Indigenous peoples.

The Crown ultimately bears the burden of ensuring that the duty to consult has been discharged.[62] IBAs typically offer confirmation that Indigenous peoples are satisfied with the consultation undertaken, which the Crown may rely on when deciding to approve a project. Support provisions within IBAs, which reduce risk for proponents, also mitigate the risk that the affected Indigenous group will later pursue legal action against the Crown for failing to comply with the duty to consult.

There is a political risk that if government authorization is given for a development without a negotiated IBA, and against the will of the Indigenous peoples, the relationship between Crown and Indigenous peoples will be adversely impacted. Conflict between Indigenous peoples and governments can become public, shaping public perceptions, and can interfere with other important discussions. Securing Indigenous consent through an IBA may help to avoid direct conflict between Indigenous parties and governments.

There is a risk that the government will approve projects on lands later proven as Aboriginal title lands, which was the case in *Tsilhqot'in Nation.*[63] Projects on lands which are later found to be held by an Indigenous people through "Aboriginal title" could be subject to expropriation or significant oversight and taxation by the title-holders. Such a finding could undermine investor confidence and impose compensatory liabilities (legal or political) on governments for financial damages. IBAs can help to address the risk of a future finding of Aboriginal title in two ways. First, consent by an Indigenous people to a project may preclude an Indigenous people from later attempting to block or expropriate the project. Second, IBAs may provide mechanisms to address the future establishment of Aboriginal title over a project area, including provisions to restrict Indigenous taxation to levels consistent with those which are imposed by government over Crown lands.

IBAs offer a number of advantages to Indigenous peoples, including risk management regarding the development of a project, support for self-government, and the provision of benefits.

IBAs serve as a means for Indigenous peoples to ensure that a project is developed in a manner that the Indigenous group finds acceptable, and is an opportunity to extract legally binding contractual commitments from proponents.[64] The Crown's duty to consult includes considering project impacts on the rights of Indigenous peoples[65] and balancing "Aboriginal concerns reasonably with the potential impact of the decision on the asserted right or title and with other societal interests."[66] Where this process is done without an IBA, the Indigenous peoples may have limited ability to influence the accommodation provided. While an Indigenous people may have a preferred accommodation measure in mind, the Crown may not believe such accommodation is necessary, or may determine that another form of accommodation will satisfy the Crown's duty to consult and, where appropriate, accommodate. As a consequence, without an IBA, Indigenous peoples are exposed to risk that their preferred methods of project development may not be incorporated.

The negotiation of an IBA as well as processes set out therein, may provide an Indigenous people greater opportunities to influence a project, especially early on. For instance, an Indigenous party could request consultation before a project is designed and submitted to regulators, allowing them greater influence in how the project is designed. Similarly, an IBA can prescribe clear project accommodation processes, including through joint environmental committees, building standards, and reclamation standards.

IBAs can also help advance self-government. IBAs may provide funding to support capacity building for Indigenous governments. IBAs may also include committees and oversight bodies which complement capacity-building initiatives and provide opportunities for an Indigenous people to negotiate for, and advance their collective interests through a governing body. Additionally, IBAs can be used to provide evidence of public acceptance of an organization which claims to represent an Indigenous people, and can encourage internal acceptance among Indigenous peoples of an organization claiming to be the authorized community representative. This is often observed among non-*Indian Act* communities, including Métis communities.

Finally, IBAs offer a potentially significant source of benefits for Indigenous peoples, including economic, cultural, health, and skills development benefits, as described in greater detail above. Under the Crown's duty to consult, there is no obligation to compensate for adverse effects, only to "balance" interests.[67] As a consequence, an Indigenous people without an IBA could be left disadvantaged overall as a result of a project. With an IBA, an Indigenous people has the potential of offsetting any adverse effects on rights with socioeconomic benefits, and are likely to receive a net overall benefit from the project.

For proponents, IBAs are typically sought in order to manage regulatory risk and the risk of public opposition and obstruction. Without an IBA, proponents risk delays, unfavourable project conditions, or the denial of authorizations. This risk to proponents arises from the Crown's risk that a Crown decision could be challenged and overturned through claims that the Crown's duty to consult has not been fulfilled. If the Crown is assured that Indigenous groups have been adequately consulted, it will be more likely that the authorizations and licences that are required for development will be granted. Mitigation against the risk of delay can significantly improve project economics. According to a study conducted by the Harvard Kennedy School, a major, world-class mining project with capital expenditure of between US$3–5 billion would suffer costs of roughly US$20 million per week of delayed production in Net Present Value terms. For an initial mineral exploration project, daily delays are estimated to cost US$10,000.[68] IBAs can be mutually beneficial and by entering into agreed upon terms with Indigenous groups, proponents benefit by reducing the risk of delayed regulatory proceedings or judicial challenges.

Proponents also face a public perception risk as a result of Indigenous opposition. As seen recently with the Trans Mountain Expansion Project, regional public opposition (in the case of the Trans Mountain Expansion Project, from the Province of British Columbia, the City of Burnaby, and the City of Vancouver) can lead to development obstacles including legal challenges, attempts to impose additional constraints or prohibitions, and public acts of obstruction and civil disobedience. These efforts can raise costs, cause delays, increase physical project risks, and negatively impact public perceptions of a proponent. Entering into IBAs can help to evidence Indigenous support and portray a project as being a net benefit to Canadian society.

V. IBAs as Risk Management Tools

IBAs are negotiated and concluded within the currently existing positive "tension." Parties are encouraged to collaborate on the development and conclusion of IBAs in response to the uncertainty arising from the Crown's determination of whether it has fulfilled the Crown's duty to consult, and from the strong mutual interest in the benefits that can be provided. This incentive is partially offset by the confrontational structure in which IBAs are negotiated: many of the benefits shared through an IBA are tied to the finite value of a project, and both the Indigenous party and the proponent are incentivized to maximize their capture of the potential project value.

Leverage exists on both sides. Indigenous peoples know that without their consent or commitment not to publicly oppose a project, the Crown may suffer greater uncertainty and a proponent could face costly delays, including through legal action brought by an Indigenous people to challenge a Crown authorization. Proponents know that Indigenous groups are incentivized to negotiate and enter into IBAs because Indigenous peoples have a reciprocal obligation to the Crown to act in good faith[69] and act in a way that fosters dialogue by engaging in the process.[70] There is also no need for consent from Indigenous peoples[71] and no stand alone duty to accommodate.[72] That means that if an Indigenous people refuses to engage in IBA negotiations or fails to resolve an IBA, proponents can proceed with development after making efforts to fulfill the duty to consult in good faith, provided that the Crown acted honourably in its attempts to consult.

Regulating IBAs could adversely impact the current positive tension that exists between Indigenous peoples and proponents. As noted, for most projects there is a finite project value which can be distributed between Indigenous parties and proponents. With few exceptions, regulating IBAs can only increase leverage for Indigenous parties. Regulations cannot undermine or weaken the Crown's duty to consult, since this duty arises from the constitutional principle of the honour of the Crown. If an Indigenous party is unable to secure desirable IBA terms, they can always add pressure through the consultation process, as is presently possible.

Regulations which create greater leverage for Indigenous parties, including through requirements to conclude such agreements, risks disrupting the current shared interest in negotiating an effective IBA. While at present, an Indigenous party must balance an interest in maximizing benefits with the possibility that a proponent can proceed without an IBA, regulating IBAs reduces the need to balance interests, and may shift the focus to maximizing benefits. Not only does this shift the nature of negotiations from balanced to adversarial, it also shifts the allocation of finite project value. Where multiple Indigenous groups seek to maximize regulated IBA benefits, the available project benefits may not meet the expectations of the parties and may significantly delay a project or undermine its viability.

While IBAs are helpful tools for managing risk arising from the Crown's duty to consult, they do not fit squarely within the legal process of consultation. As a result, regulating IBAs within the context of consultation risks distorting the purpose of consultation and the realistic and sustainable ends of reconciliation.

The content which defines the Crown's duty to consult is based on a proposed project's potential impact on Aboriginal and treaty rights. In contrast, the content which defines the commitments available through an IBA is based on the nature and scope of a project, without direct regard to its impact. In many cases, an IBA may only be achievable where a project is capable of producing enough benefit to offset the potential perceived adverse effect of a project. From that "breakeven" point, the benefits derived through a project IBA are likely to correlate with the economic potential of a project, increasing as the project increases in value. This increase in benefits correlates to the value of the uncertainty to the proponent: a delay in a high-value project is more costly to a proponent in present-value funds than a similar delay for a marginally economic project.[73] This principle is reflected in the Tlicho Agreement, where one of the principles for the required negotiation of an IBA is that negotiations should not place an "excessive burden on proponents *and* undermine the viability of the project [emphasis added]."[74] As a consequence, the anticipated value of IBAs under the Tlicho Agreement should be expected to increase as the value of a project increases, up to the point that such benefits place an excessive burden on a proponent and undermine the viability of the project. Another modern treaty, the Acho Agreement in Principle,[75] similarly requires that negotiations should not put an "excessive burden on proponents *nor* undermine the viability of the project [emphasis added]."[76]

A negotiated IBA will necessarily shift the focus of consultation to the value of a project from the adverse impact to Aboriginal rights. This shift carries a number of challenges. Consultation requires the Crown to discharge its duty to consult and specifically to uphold the honour of the Crown. The honour of the Crown is highly nuanced, changing based on different circumstances. As a consequence, the honour of the Crown rests with the Crown and cannot be delegated.[77] The negotiation of an IBA between two private parties cannot fulfill the honour of the Crown and cannot be guided effectively by the honour of the Crown. A proponent is incapable of carrying or assessing the honour of the Crown. As a consequence, there is no way for a proponent to determine whether IBA benefits are sufficient to discharge the Crown's duty.

Without a basis in the honour of the Crown, there is no clear basis for what constitutes appropriate "benefits" within the context of an IBA. Legislated IBAs are likely to result in similar benefits for differing Indigenous groups, regardless of the degree of impact (except where the net adverse effect is so great as to increase the minimum acceptable benefit value for an individual party). This is because the source of the leverage will come from the regulatory requirement for an IBA, rather than the obligation of the Crown to act honourably when it impacts Aboriginal rights. Creating stand-alone IBA requirements is also likely to increase the desire for participation among minimally impacted Indigenous peoples seeking to apply the leverage available through the regulatory regime, with the potential of diluting the benefits available to the most adversely impacted parties.

Regulating IBAs also shifts the focus of the Crowns' decisions from reconciliation—the pursuit of reconciling "aboriginal societies with the larger Canadian society of which they are a part"[78]—to the provision of benefits through rent-seeking. While there is nothing wrong with seeking to share benefits generally, and particularly with disadvantaged communities, a focus on benefits does a disservice to reconciliation's role in creating a sustainable system capable of respecting the interests of different peoples while considering objectives such as the pursuit of economic and regional fairness among Indigenous and non-Indigenous peoples.[79] If not conducted carefully, a focus on benefits may distract from the Crown's heavy burden to advance reconciliation.

VI. Possible Outcomes from Government Intervention with IBAs

There are several dangers posed by government intervention into IBAs. First, government intervention into privately negotiated IBAs risks undermining key attributes of the Crown's duty to consult as set out by the Supreme Court of Canada. Second, on the specific issue of confidentiality of IBAs, there are sound reasons to keep IBAs confidential. Third, the indirect government intervention into IBAs through anti-corruption legislation illustrates again the need for caution in any rush to regulate.

Mandating IBAs risks providing Indigenous parties with a near-veto. *Haida Nation* states explicitly that consultation does not provide for a veto for Indigenous peoples.[80] A veto might be appropriate in certain circumstances, for example, modern treaties where Indigenous peoples own their lands in fee simple, to the exclusion of others including other Indigenous peoples. A veto may also be appropriate where an Indigenous peoples, such as for example the Tsilhqot'in, have established Aboriginal title to lands, though courts have repeatedly stated that Aboriginal title is not absolute, and can be infringed by the Crown provided that infringement is justified.[81]

However, in circumstances where Indigenous groups are not land owners or have not proven Aboriginal title, mandating IBAs risks creating an imbalance in bargaining power which allows Indigenous groups to capture significantly more of a project's economic value than would be available at present[82] even if compensation for the adverse impact on their Aboriginal and treaty rights are minimal compared to the captured value. Participants in a study conducted by Public Policy Forum suggest that "... First Nations are starting to demand benefits beyond benefits from a project and are looking to achieve much more significant shares of the project revenues so that they can truly maximize economic benefits from their territory."[83]

Significant leverage and bargaining power may result in a short-term increase in rent capture for Indigenous peoples as projects which are already partially funded seek to recover sunk costs. However, a new generation of investments in projects may be curtailed, as investors begin to realize that a significant portion of a project's value will need to be surrendered.

Indigenous groups may also be disadvantaged if regulatory oversight of IBAs includes constraints and requirements for Indigenous parties. Potentially paternalistic regulatory guidelines risk limiting an Indigenous peoples' ability for self-determination through the unrestrained negotiation of IBAs.

If governments decide to regulate IBAs, it is critical that they establish structured regimes for how benefits are allocated between Indigenous groups. When there are multiple affected Indigenous groups, the use of bilateral negotiation strategies may result in competition among affected communities.[84] In an unstructured regime, Indigenous groups must compete over finite resources. With more parties, it will be increasingly difficult for a proponent to manage expectations and satisfactorily allocate the finite available project value. Even if these negotiations can be resolved, risk of no resolution, or the significant dilution of proponent value, may discourage potential proponents from formulating a project proposal.

Proponents may believe that regulation will introduce more certainty in the project development process, including through standardized parameters for the negotiation process.[85] In particular, some have stressed that guidelines which clarify expectations could be beneficial for both sides of the negotiation table.[86] However, because of section 35, a government imposed regulatory regime would be binding on the proponent but not necessarily on Indigenous peoples. Indigenous peoples are not precluded from pursuing litigation to attack the regulatory regime set by government if they feel that the regime does not honourably address the development's potential adverse impacts on their rights. As a consequence, imposing content requirements for IBAs will effectively set a minimum standard that proponents have to meet without creating a corresponding limit on satisfactory (maximum) compensation. This minimum standard is also likely to be higher than the standard determined by the free market because, as stated earlier in this paper, the government is incentivized to go above and beyond minimum requirements to ensure that the Crown's duty to consult is satisfied.

Apart from these more general issues on regulation, IBA confidentiality is often raised as in issue, out of various concerns about the effects of confidentiality. These include arguments that IBAs may preclude Indigenous peoples from knowing what other Indigenous peoples have been able to negotiate and concerns that IBA confidentiality interferes with the public interest in other ways.[87]

From a practical standpoint, though, IBA confidentiality remains important. IBAs are typically comprehensive documents which contain sensitive financial information.[88] They often include sensitive information about profit and equity sharing, compensation, land-use payouts, and royalties which can be commercially sensitive for the parties.[89] Some Indigenous peoples have raised concerns that any funds received from IBAs will be considered as "Indian revenue moneys" within the meaning of the *Indian Act*[90] and potentially subject to federal regulation.[91] Section 69(1) of the *Indian Act* gives the Crown power to disallow the band to control, manage, and expend in whole or in part its revenue moneys. Some Indigenous peoples are also concerned that the federal government will expect Indigenous groups to use any funds generated through IBAs for basic community programs such as education or social assistance and will reduce the amount the government currently provides by the amount that the Indigenous group acquires by virtue of an IBA.[92]

One more specific context in which issues about IBA confidentiality may arise is the anti-corruption context. Legislation such as the *Corruption of Foreign Public Officials Act*[93] (Canada), *Bribery Act*[94] (UK), and *Foreign Corrupt Practices Act*[95] (US) restrict the bribing of government officials. Corruption can result in diverted wealth in the hands of certain private interests.[96] Compliance with anti-corruption legislation shows commitment to the rule of law and requires strong institutions to set the standard and ensure compliance.[97] There is an increased risk of misappropriation when working with organizations with government-like powers and which are subject to low transparency community approval processes. Indigenous groups have government-like powers; it is important that benefits provided through IBAs be transparent to community members. Institutions need to be in place to ensure that any benefits derived from development projects is fairly distributed amongst the impacted community. These institutions must be transparent while evidencing clear government policy and employing sound business and accounting practices.

The *Extractive Sector Transparency Measures Act*[98] (ESTMA) was enacted "to implement Canada's international commitments to participate in the fight against corruption through the imposition of measures applicable to the extractive sector"[99] and to support prohibitions on bribing domestic or foreign public officials found in the *Criminal Code*[100] and the *Corruption of Foreign Public Officials Act*.[101] ESTMA applies to Indigenous governments and requires every "entity" to disclose to the Minister all payments it has made to Indigenous governments if the total amount of payments within a category of payments made to the same payee in the financial year exceeds $100,000 or such other amount prescribed by regulation to the applicable category of payment.[102]

Many Indigenous communities are worried that the confidential information concerning their IBAs could become public as a result of ESTMA.[103] ESTMA does increase accountability and could be used to address the lack of transparency in current Indigenous governance in the natural resources sector, but it is unclear whether ESTMA was truly enacted to address corruption in the international sphere or to enhance transparency on a more domestic level. ESTMA also does not address the transparency concerns outlined above because it does not impose obligations on Indigenous governments to be transparent about how benefits are allocated amongst a community. Industry and Indigenous peoples alike have expressed concerns about ESTMA, noting that the mandatory reporting obligation might significantly undermine the trust and goodwill developed between industry and Indigenous entities over a particularly sensitive juncture.[104] While ESTMA was not framed directly as an intervention in IBA practice, it may have effects on it. All government regulation of IBAs must be considered with caution and prudence.

VII. Free, Prior, and Informed Consent

The United Nations Declaration on the Rights of Indigenous Peoples (UNDRIP) is being raised by many Indigenous peoples as an important indication of where Canada and its legal regime should head.[105] Section 35 of Canada's *Constitution Act, 1982* is unique at law internationally and provides for the recognition and affirmation of existing Aboriginal treaty rights in the Constitution of Canada and in a manner which, at times, can limit the power of the Crown. It is against this complex and unique legal backdrop that we must consider how UNDRIP would fit into Canada's legal regime, if at all. In particular, the concept of "free, prior, and informed consent" (FPIC) is a broad and inflexible concept, whereas section 35 of the Canadian Constitution requires balancing and taking into account the rights of others.

It is through a reasonable, transparent and considered balancing of competing interests that section 35's ultimate purpose is achieved: reconciliation.[106] FPIC suggests that Aboriginal and treaty rights should always be interpreted to prevail over rights of other affected individuals or groups. This standard of consent is inconsistent with relevant Canadian jurisprudence. In *Mikisew Cree*,[107] the Supreme Court of Canada stated that the "fundamental objective of the modern law of aboriginal and treaty rights is the reconciliation of aboriginal peoples and non-aboriginal peoples and their respective claims, interests and ambitions."[108] The concepts of balancing competing rights and reconciliation are central to understanding Canada's constitutional protection of Indigenous rights. UNDRIP is not necessarily the standard to achieve, particularly given Canada's unique and sophisticated legal regime relating to Aboriginal and treaty rights.

FPIC would also destroy the tension required to bring parties to the bargaining table for IBAs. If FPIC was the standard, there would be no incentive for Indigenous groups to negotiate so that benefits of development are shared. Instead, Indigenous groups would be rational to adopt the view that "development should occur only if the affected communities realize the maximum possible benefits from any specific project."[109] In this environment, proponents would have less incentive to advance projects on account of greater uncertainty and reduced potential profits. Similarly, incentives to undertake mineral exploration may be reduced if the potential value of any finding could be captured by Aboriginal and treaty right holders.

VII. Conclusions

This paper does not reject the regulation of IBAs, but it calls for a cautious and prudent approach moving forward. Any regulation of IBAs should occur only through a thoughtful and principled approach, considering the balance of leverage between the parties and the existing positive tension. With the rising prevalence of IBAs, the accustomed public reaction is to rally for regulation. This paper highlights the issues that should be considered if there is to be government regulation of IBAs and encourages governments to ensure that any intervention is principled and consistent with a long-term sustainable approach from a public policy perspective. Any involvement by governments should not disrupt the role of market forces, or remove incentives for the parties to negotiate for mutual benefit.

Although it is unclear what the purpose of IBAs *could* be if legislated, it is clear that IBAs presently serve a number of important functions. An IBA can be a business risk mitigation tool, a tool for socioeconomic change, and a method of accommodating potentially impacted Aboriginal and treaty rights. Some pressure exists for government regulation of IBAs, spurred by the many important advantages of IBAs, their prevalence in a seemingly tripartite environment, and their use by governments as evidence in assessing whether the Crown's duty to consult has been satisfied. However, government intervention which impacts the development of IBAs must be thoughtful, prudent, focussed on long term considerations, and recognize the significant risks of interfering with the positive tension that currently exists between Indigenous peoples and proponents when negotiating IBAs.

The legal landscape for Aboriginal law is rapidly changing, dynamic, and uncertain. Project development is inextricably tied to this legal landscape, and government, Indigenous peoples, and proponents alike are exposed to increased risks in this area. IBAs are an effective risk management tool widely used and any changes to this tool should be taken cautiously.

Notes

1. In some instances, IBAs may be referred to by other names including socio-economic benefits agreements, cooperation agreements, accommodation agreements, and participation agreements. For an argument that this form may shift in future, see also Ken Coates, "Towards Comprehensive Engagement: Indigenous-Industry Agreements in the Natural Resource Sector in Canada" in Ibironke T. Odumosu-Ayanu and Dwight Newman (eds) *Indigenous-Industry Agreements, Natural Resources, and the Law* (Routledge 2021).
2. *Indigenous peoples*, for the purpose of this paper, are those peoples possessing Aboriginal and treaty rights protected by, Canada's *The Constitution Act, 1982* (Canada), being Schedule B to the Canada Act 1982 (UK), 1982, c 11, s 35.
3. Ibid.
4. Indigenous opposition to project development led to judicial reviews of the consultation process offered in relation to the Northern Gateway and Trans Mountain Expansion pipelines, resulting in government authorizations being revoked. See *Gitxaala Nation v. Canada* [2016] FCA 187 [*Northern Gateway*]; *Tsleil-Waututh Nation v Canada (Attorney General)* [2018] FCA 153 [*Trans Mountain Expansion*].
5. On the role of IBAs in risk management, see also Dwight Newman and Levi Graham, "Indigenous-Industry Agreements, Legal Uncertainty, and Risk Allocations" in Ibironke T. Odumosu and Dwight Newman (eds) *Indigenous-Industry Agreements, Natural Resources, and the Law* (Routledge 2021)..
6. Courtney Fidler and Michael Hitch, "Impact and Benefit Agreements: A Contentious Issue for Environmental and Aboriginal Justice" [2007] 35 Environments Journal 49, 50 [Fidler].
7. Ravina Bains and Kayla Ishkanian, "Government Spending and Own-Source Revenue for Canada's Aboriginals: A Comparative Analysis" (*Fraser Institute*, 2016) <www.fraserinstitute.org/studies/government-spending-and-own-source-revenue-for-canadas-aboriginals> accessed 20 June 2019.
8. Germain Belzile, "The First Entrepreneurs: Natural Resource Development and First Nations" (*Montreal Economic Institute*, 2018) <www.iedm.org/85482-first-entrepreneurs-natural-resource-development-and-first-nations> accessed 20 June 2019.
9. Dwight Newman and Kaitlyn S Harvey, *Stepping Into the Sunshine Without Getting Burned: The Extractive Sector Transparency Measures Act (ESTMA) and Aboriginal Communities*, (Macdonald-Laurier Institute 2016) 5.

10. Gordon Shanks, *Sharing the Benefits of Resource Developments: A Study of First Nations-Industry Impact Benefits Agreements* (Public Policy Forum 2006) [Shanks].
11. Fidler (n 6) 51.
12. *Haida Nation v. British Columbia (Minister of Forests)* [2004] SCC 73 [*Haida Nation*].
13. Fidler (n 6) 52.
14. Emilie Cameron and Tyler Levitan, "Impact and Benefit Agreements and the Neoliberalization of Resource Governance and Indigenous-state Relations in Northern Canada" [2014] 93 Studies in Political Economy 25.
15. Irene Sosa and Karyn Keenan, "Impact Benefit Agreements Between Aboriginal Communities and Mining Companies: Their Use in Canada" [2001] Environmental Mining Council of British Columbia, the Canadian Environmental Law Association and Cooper Accion: Accion Solidaria para el Desarrollo 3 <www.cela.ca/sites/cela.ca/files/uploads/IBAeng.pdf> accessed 20 June 2019 [Sosa].
16. Ibid 2.
17. Newman and Harvey (n 9) 5.
18. Dominion Diamond Corporation, "Aboriginal Partnerships" (2016) <http://responsibility.ddcorp.ca/2015/aboriginal-partnership.php> accessed 23 June 2019.
19. Dominion Diamond, "2016 Ekati Diamond Mine, 2016 Socio-Economic Agreement Report" (*Mining North*, 2016) 9 <www.miningnorth.com/_rsc/site-content/library/diamondmining/ekati-2016-sea-report-final.pdf> accessed 24 June 2019.
20. Ibid 19.
21. *Taku River Tlingit First Nation v. British Columbia (Project Assessment Director)* [2004] SCC 74 [24].
22. Thomas Isaac, *Aboriginal Law*, 5th ed (Canada: Thomson Reuters Canada, 2016) 101. On the duty to consult generally, see also Dwight Newman *Revisiting the Duty to Consult Aboriginal Peoples* (Purich Publishing 2014).
23. *Haida Nation* (n 12) [27].
24. Ibid [25].
25. *Rio Tinto Alcan Inc. v. Carrier Sekani Tribal Council* [2010] SCC 43.
26. Ibid [53].
27. Ibid [53].
28. *Clyde River (Hamlet) v. Petroleum Geo-Services Inc* [2017] SCC 40, 411 DLR (4th) 571.
29. *Ahousaht First Nation v. Canada (Fisheries and Oceans)* [2008] FCA 212 [34], 297 DLR (4th) 722.
30. *Katlodeeche First Nation v. Canada (Attorney General)* [2013] FC 458 [183].
31. *Beckman v. Little Salmon / Carmacks First Nation* [2010] SCC 53 [*Little Salmon*].
32. Canada, *Agreement between the Inuit of the Nunavut Settlement Area and Her Majesty the Queen in Right of Canada* (Indigenous and Northern Affairs 1993) (Nunavut Land Claims Agreement) enacted by the Nunavut Land Claims Settlement Act 1993, c 29.; Isaac (n 22) 186.
33. Nunavut Land Claims Agreement, ibid art 26.3.3.
34. Ibid arts 26.5.1–26.6.5.
35. Department of Indian Affairs and Northern Development (Canada), *The Western Arctic Claim: The Inuvialuit Final Agreement* (Indian Affairs and Northern Development 1984) (*Inuvialuit Final Agreement*).
36. Ibid s 10.
37. Ibid ss 10(8)–(9).
38. Ibid s 10(1).
39. Department of Indian Affairs and Northern Development (Canada), *Comprehensive Land Claim Agreement Between Her Majesty the Queen in Right of Canada and the Gwich'in as Represented by the Gwich'in Tribal Council* (Indian Affairs and Northern Development 1992) [*Gwich'in Agreement*].

40. Department of Indian Affairs and Northern Development (Canada), *Sahtu Dene and Metis Comprehensive Land Claim Agreement* (Indian Affairs and Northern Development 1993) [*Sahtu Agreement*].
41. Ibid s 22.
42. *Gwich'in Agreement* (n 39) s 26.2.
43. Ibid s 26; *Sahtu Agreement* (n 40) s 27.
44. Department of Indigenous and Northern Affairs Canada, *Land Claims and Self-Government Agreement Among The Tlicho and The Government of the Northwest Territories and the Government of Canada* (Indigenous and Northern Affairs Canada 2003) [*Tlicho Agreement*].
45. Northwest Territories, "Concluding and Implementing Land Claim and Self-Government Agreements" (Executive and Indigenous Affairs), <www.eia.gov.nt.ca/en/priorities/concluding-and-implementing-land- claim-and-self-government-agreements/tlicho> accessed 23 June 2019.
46. *Tlicho Agreement* n (44).
47. Ibid ss 23.4.1.
48. Ibid ss 23.4.3.
49. Office of the Auditor General of Canada, *Report 3—Implementing the Labrador Inuit Land Claims Agreement* [3.5] <www.oag-bvg.gc.ca/internet/English/parl_oag_201602_03_e_41060.html>.
50. Ibid [3.5].
51. Department of Indigenous and Northern Affairs Canada, *Land Claims Agreement Between The Inuit of Labrador and Her Majesty the Queen in Right of Newfoundland and Labrador and Her Majesty the Queen in Right of Canada* (Indigenous and Northern Affairs Canada 2005) s 6.7.4 [LILCA].
52. Ibid ss 6.7.8–6.7.9.
53. Sandra Gogal, Richard Riegert, and Joann Jamieson, "Aboriginal Impact and Benefit Agreements: Practical Considerations" [2005] 43 Alta L Rev 129, 136.
54. *Oil and Gas Act*, RSY 2002, c 162.
55. Ibid s 68.
56. Ibid s 68(9).
57. Ibid s 68(4).
58. *Canada Petroleum Resources Act*, RSC 1985 (2nd Supp), c 36 [Canada Petroleum Resources Act].
59. Ibid s 21.
60. The Government of Newfoundland and Labrador, *Aboriginal Consultation Policy on Land and Resource Development Decisions* (Newfoundland and Labrador 2013) 4 [*Aboriginal Consultation Policy*].
61. *Haida Nation* (n 12) [53].
62. Ibid.
63. *Tsilhqot'in Nation v. British Columbia* [2014] SCC 44 [*Tsilhqot'in Nation*].
64. Shanks (n 10) 7.
65. *Chippewas of the Thames* (n 15) [47].
66. *Haida Nation* (n 12) [50].
67. Ibid [50]; See, for example, *Ktunaxa Nation v. British Columbia (Forests, Lands and Natural Resource Operations)* [2017] SCC 54, where the Court found that project could advance despite irreparable damage to "spirit bear"; see also *Chippewas of the Thames* (n 15) where the only accommodation offered was conditions on operations.
68. Rachel Davis and Daniel Franks, "Costs of Company-Community Conflict in the Extractive Sector" Corporate Social Responsibility Initiative Report No. 66 (Harvard Kennedy School 2014).
69. *Haida Nation* (n 12) [42].

70. *Canada (Attorney General) v. Long Plain First Nation* [2015] FCA 177, 388 DLR (4th) 209 [158].
71. *Behn v. Moulton Contracting Ltd* [2013] SCC 26 [29].
72. *Little Salmon* (n 31) [32].
73. The authors intend to further explore this relationship in a future publication.
74. *Tlicho Agreement* (n 44) s 23.4.
75. Government of Northwest Territories, *Acho Dene Koe First Nation Fort Liard Métis: Agreement in Principle* (Government of Northwest Territories 2014) s 6.7.4 [*Acho Agreement in Principle*].
76. Ibid s 10.5.0.
77. *Haida Nation* (n 12) [53].
78. *R v. Gladstone* [1996] 2 SCR 723 [73].
79. Ibid [75].
80. *Haida Nation* (n 12) [48].
81. *Delgamuukw* (n 23) [160]; *Tsilhqot'in Nation* (n 63) [77]–[88].
82. Shanks (n 10) 7.
83. Ibid 26.
84. Sosa (n 15) 26.
85. Shanks (n 10) 21.
86. Ibid 21.
87. See, for example, Sosa (n 15) 81; Newman & Harvey (n 9); Newman and Graham (n 5).
88. Fidler (n 6) 58.
89. Ibid 58.
90. *Indian Act* 1985, RSC 1985, c I–5.
91. Ibid s 69(1).
92. Shanks (n 10) 10.
93. *Corruption of Foreign Public Officials Act* 1998, SC 1998, c 34.
94. Bribery Act 2010 (UK) c 23.
95. Foreign Corrupt Practices Act of 1977, 15 USC § 78dd–1.
96. Newman (n 9) 4.
97. Milos Barutciski and Sabrina A. Bandali, "Corruption at the Intersection of Business and Government: The OECD Convention, Supply-Side Corruption and Canada's Anti-Corruption Efforts to Date" [2016] 53 Osgoode Hall LJ 231, 262–263.
98. Extractive Sector Transparency Measures Act 2014, c 39 (ESTMA).
99. Ibid s 104.
100. *Criminal Code*, RSC 1985, c C-46 ss 119–121.
101. *Corruption of Foreign Public Officials Act* 1998, c 34 ss 3–4.
102. Isaac (n 22) 14.
103. Newman and Harvey (n 9) 5.
104. Ibid 9.
105. Isaac (n 22) 59.A bill that would have attempted to enact UNDRIP into Canadian statutory form narrowly missed becoming law in June 2019, as Bill C-262 died on the Senate order paper at third reading. The issues raised in Bill C-262, though, will no doubt return.
106. Isaac (n 22) 5.
107. *Mikisew Cree First Nation v. Canada (Minister of Canadian Heritage)* [2005] SCC 69, [2005] 3 SCR 388.
108. Ibid [1].
109. Shanks (n 10) 7.

16 Towards Comprehensive Engagement: Indigenous-Industry Collaboration in the Resource Sector in Canada

Ken Coates

I. Introduction

Many analyses of Indigenous-industry agreements, including several chapters in this volume,[1] tend to see a set of fixed features to these agreements and to assume that they will continue in basically their present form. Those assumptions must yield, though, to an emerging reality that Indigenous relations are by no means static. The present moment is one of the most dynamic times in history on the place of Indigenous peoples in economic and commercial worlds. The trendlines underlying the present dynamism have emerged over recent decades, and they point towards a different reality than the present state of Indigenous-industry agreements. The trend is towards more comprehensive engagement and, indeed, engagement with Indigenous peoples throughout the life cycle of resource projects.

As I show in Part II, the reasons for these trends are not mainly in international developments. Rather, as I show in Part III, a pragmatic response not only to possible Indigenous legal claims, but also to various emerging realities of the benefits of doing business with Indigenous peoples, has sustained significant changes to date. In Part IV, I will suggest several likely further developments that will alter the shape of Indigenous-industry agreements as presently understood.

By way of background, it is worth noting that over the last 40 years the engagement of Indigenous peoples in the natural resource economy has changed dramatically. As recently as the 1970s, Indigenous communities had no precise legal rights over resource development and received few benefits from the development of mines, oil and gas properties, forestry projects, and hydroelectric dams on their traditional territories. By the early years of the 21st century, driven largely by favourable Supreme Court of Canada decisions in cases like *Haida Nation v British Columbia (Minister of Forests)*,[2] *Taku River Tlingit First Nation v. British Columbia (Project Assessment Director)*,[3] and dozens of others, Indigenous communities had more clearly defined roles and opportunities within the resource economy and a level of participation that would have seemed extremely unlikely three decades earlier. Because the law is a perennial work in progress and because recognition of Indigenous and treaty rights has been comparatively recent, it is not yet clear how Indigenous participation in the resource economy will evolve.[4]

Developments in the energy sector, including direct Indigenous investments, the exploration of equity options, and the proposal active at the time of writing that a group of First Nations purchase all or part of the Trans Mountain pipeline, suggest that Indigenous aspirations continue to expand. But there are complications. On the one hand, the Canadian federal government has had trouble shedding its paternalistic tendencies, moving forward without full consultation on the cancellation of the Enbridge pipeline project, implementing a ban on tanker traffic on the Northwest coast, and stopping oil and gas exploration in the Arctic. Conversely, internal jurisdictional conflicts among the Wet'suwet'en in 2019 stalled the construction of the Coastal Liquefied Natural Gas (LNG) pipeline through northern British Columbia, and highlighted complexities in the structures of Indigenous leadership and decision-making.

Indigenous engagement in the resource sector continues to evolve, from a small and largely inconsequential base in the 1970s, as Indigenous communities develop greater expertise, as companies and Indigenous governance test new models of participation, and as the human capital within the Indigenous population expands in line with growing levels of activity. The arrangements vary substantially across the country, based on the size and expected lifespan of the resource project, the nature of the company or companies involved, the preferences of Indigenous communities, the degree of engagement by anti-development environmentalists, and the market forces of price and demand. Multi-million-dollar community agreements, complex impact and benefit agreements (IBAs, the most common form of Indigenous-Industry agreements in Canada thus far), comprehensive employment and training programs, and preferential business opportunities have become commonplace. To say that the resource landscape has changed is to understate the situation dramatically.[5]

The transformation is far from over. The process of defining and clarifying Indigenous rights to active involvement continues through the courts, in regional, national and international politics, and through unrelenting Indigenous pressure. First Nations, Metis, and Inuit people have brought forward hundreds of cases before Canadian courts, testing and refining earlier agreements and continuing the never-to-be-completed process of defining Indigenous rights under Canadian law.[6] While there are Indigenous activists and sovereigntists who decry the reliance on the Canadian legal and political system, a growing number of First Nations have focussed more on capitalizing on the hard-won Indigenous rights than extending the boundaries of their legal authority. The result has been an historic expansion of Indigenous engagement in the resource sector with substantial financial returns to communities, business people, and individual workers.

II. Role of International Developments

International developments in the early 21st century altered the Canadian dynamics, albeit in uncertain ways. The United Nations Declaration on the

Rights of Indigenous Peoples (UNDRIP) and, in particular, the provisions calling for "free, prior and informed consent" on developments on Indigenous lands, have become an active part of the Canadian lexicon on Indigenous legal and political rights.[7] When the United Nations voted on UNDRIP, Canada, Australia, New Zealand, and the United States voted against the declaration. By 2010, all four of the states that had voted against had now endorsed the document, leaving it to individual countries and the institutions of international law to determine the authority and utility of the declaration. UNDRIP remains substantially untested, in large part because of its uncertain status within the Canadian political and legal systems. The former Conservative government of Prime Minister Stephen Harper endorsed the agreement in 2010, but viewed it as an "aspirational" rather than a practical document. Prime Minister Justin Trudeau reversed this approach, declaring his support for UNDRIP in the 2015 federal election campaign and restating his endorsement when his government introduced what were arguably the most pro-Indigenous policy commitments in Canadian history.[8]

The Trudeau government's initial enthusiasm proved overly optimistic. Within a year of being elected, they backed away from a verbal commitment to make UNDRIP part of Canadian law, only to reverse their reversal a few months later. The Liberals supported a 2018 private member's bill that called on the government to harmonize federal legislation and regulations with UNDRIP, although the bill made its way through the parliamentary steps only to die just before third reading in the Senate due to the end of the parliamentary session in 2019.

While UNDRIP did not immediately transform Indigenous participation in the resource economy, the Canadian endorsement of the United Nations declaration sharpened the debate and supported Indigenous demands for greater control over the use of their traditional territories. While there have been numerous commentaries by Indigenous leaders about the applicability of UNDRIP in the Canadian context, the discussion of "free, prior and informed consent" has been moderate and contextualized by the extensive Indigenous engagement in the natural resource economy in Canada.[9]

The constraints of UNDRIP as a foundation for Indigenous rights in Canada are generally well-understood—it is a non-binding text. There will, no doubt, be numerous legal tests of the applicability of UNDRIP in the coming decades. UNDRIP will likely have more impact on Indigenous aspirations than on the practical legal and political implications.[10]

Indigenous interest in the resource sector is driven by much more practical factors than the desire to see UNDRIP principles enacted in Canadian law. First Nations, Inuit, and Métis peoples experience substantial poverty, and the social, cultural and political displacements associated with being without the money needed to cover basic necessities. Indeed, from the expansion of the Indigenous rights movement in the 1960s, community leaders criticized the welfare dependency that accompanied the expansion of the social welfare state in the post-war era and argued that they deserved to share in the general prosperity of the country. The battle for Indigenous rights—and it is vital to recall that Indigenous peoples were not "given" rights under Canadian law but had to fight for decades to secure recognition of what the Supreme Court of Canada has repeatedly recognized as inherent or treaty rights. While numerous Indigenous leaders remain focussed on securing even greater recognition of their Aboriginal and treaty rights, many others are determined to convert recognized rights into practical and positive outcomes for their communities.[11]

III. Indigenous Legal Claims and Resulting Canadian Trendlines

Indigenous aspirations for a place in the Canadian economy do not mean that they seek to enter the Canadian mainstream. The battle for resource rights and control over traditional territories was designed to give communities and Indigenous people the choice to continue their traditional lifeways, in whole or in part, or to participate in the wage and commercial economy at a level, time, and intensity of their choice. Indigenous leaders sought, as well, to secure the financial resources needed to secure autonomy from government and to address housing, educational, and other challenges in their communities.

As a result of Indigenous legal actions and the resulting Supreme Court of Canada decisions, Indigenous people secured the power necessary to negotiate better financial arrangements in the resource sector. All current pipeline proposals, several of which are managed by Indigenous business people, make provision for Indigenous equity, thus already moving beyond the form of IBAs towards joint ownership. The legal decisions clarified, without providing a great deal of precision, the rights of Indigenous people to be consulted on developments on their traditional lands and to be accommodated for any socio-economic dislocations associated with resource activity. As is the norm with such judgements, there was limited specificity in several key areas, such as the appropriate level and nature of consultation, the standard for community accommodations, expectations of financial returns, and the best structure for formal agreements between Indigenous governments, companies, and governments. The fundamental requirements are simple. If the Indigenous peoples and the company are in agreement that conditions have been met, then a suitable arrangement is deemed to be in place. If Indigenous peoples feel an offer is too low, or the company feels Indigenous communities are being unfairly obstructionist, both have the option of resorting to the courts for an adjudication. Through the negotiation of agreements and a variety of court decisions where settlements could not be reached, the contours of acceptable settlements have been roughly defined.

That many, indeed most, Indigenous communities are engaged with resource development is not because they are enthusiastic about the exploitation of traditional territories. Indeed, the Indigenous response to a pipeline, mine, forestry operation, hydroelectric project or other such development is not much different than that of most non-Indigenous communities. If the citizens of Mississauga can rise up in protest about a natural gas plant and many people in the Lower Mainland of British Columbia vigorously oppose the construction of the Trans

Mountain pipeline, it is hardly surprising that some community members—and occasionally entire communities—oppose a mine, forestry operation or other development. Some people oppose the projects, largely for environmental reasons, but most accept development as an integral and necessary part of the modern industrial economy. So it is with Indigenous peoples, who recognize that there are few, if any, economic alternatives beyond the resource economy.

There are a growing number of examples of Indigenous communities changing their stance on resource development. The Cheslatta First Nations in Northern British Columbia participated extensively in the successful 1990s opposition to the Kemano Complete Project, which called for the construction of a water control dam in the middle of their homeland. More recently, the Cheslatta have been involved in discussions about a new dam, one they would build and own in part. The differences, in large measure, include the Cheslatta's opportunity for partial ownership, the associated employment and revenue flows, and the control that they would exercise over planning, construction, and operations.[12]

Indigenous engagement with the resource sector is defined by conflicting priorities: the positive desire for employment and business opportunities; and long-standing concerns about the social, economic, cultural, and environmental impacts of major projects on their traditional territories. There is sustained anxiety in Indigenous communities across Canada regarding the out-migration of residents to larger towns and cities. The movement of young people, seeking what some perceived to be a more exciting lifestyle, a formal advanced education, or better job opportunities, remains a serious worry on many reserves and remote centres.[13] Communities that aligned themselves with the Mackenzie Valley Pipeline, for example, highlighted the importance of sustainable well-paid job opportunities for young people.[14] The grinding poverty in many Indigenous communities, clearly not alleviated by several generations of dependence on government transfers and still largely disconnected from the mainstream Canadian economy, can be seen in serious deficiencies in health, education, and social outcomes, and the distressing aspects of Indigenous social pathology that is evident in many communities.[15] Engagement with the resource sector is increasingly seen as one route—perhaps the only route for many communities—out of economic despair and entrenched marginalization, but it possesses risks and uncertainties.

Following a period of trial and error, and only after extensive and often intense community debate, Indigenous groups found ways to reach acceptable agreements with resource companies. There are hundreds of Indigenous agreements with mining companies and forestry operators. Indigenous communities are collaborating on numerous renewable energy projects, ranging from solar parks to run of the river installations. Hundreds of communities have negotiated favourable agreements with pipeline and service companies, creating opportunities for members and revenue for local government.

While there is considerable opposition to some resource projects—such as the controversies over uranium mining in northern Saskatchewan,[16] the Ring of Fire projects in northern Ontario,[17] and the Kinder Morgan Trans Mountain pipeline expansion project[18]—Indigenous communities in Canada are much more open to resource development than media coverage suggests.[19] That First Nations are exploring the possibility of purchasing a share of the Trans Mountain pipeline is a sign of substantial Indigenous support for the industry or, more accurately, for the financial and employment benefits arising from resource development and equity investment.[20] First Nations were not unanimous in opposing the Energy East pipeline or the Northern Gateway.[21] Some of the northern British Columbia First Nations are upset with the Government of Canada for unilaterally imposing a tanker ban on the BC coast,[22] just as the Inuit of Nunavut are angry about the federal government's hastily imposed restrictions on Arctic oil and gas.[23] First Nations have been strongly engaged in LNG development in British Columbia; the Haisla stand to benefit substantially from the $40 billion investment in the LNG Canada plant under development in Kitimat, B.C.,[24] as does the Squamish First Nation from a planned LNG plant in their territory near Vancouver.[25]

Despite the general pattern of mutually beneficial engagement between Indigenous communities and resource companies, approaches are fragmented and occasionally confrontational. While constructive patterns and models of negotiation have emerged,[26] there is no rule book on consultation, compensation, and appropriate impact and benefit or collaboration agreements. Many factors—market demand for resources, wealth, size, and experience of the resource firm, community preparedness, local leadership, richness, and likely longevity of the development, and anticipated impact on the Indigenous people and territories, among others—influence the negotiation processes and shape outcomes. Due to the complexity, it would be unrealistic to expect there to be a uniform approach to consultations.

In short order, Indigenous communities in Canada developed comprehensive strategies and processes for the negotiation of agreements with resource companies. For their part, the resource companies moved to bring their negotiation and consultation processes in line with both the preferences of First Nations, Metis, and Inuit communities and the requirements of evolving Indigenous legal rights. The processes were far from ideal. Efforts to secure Indigenous support for Enbridge's Northern Gateway Pipeline foundered, in part, due to complications and misunderstandings around consultations and agreements.[27] Similarly, efforts to develop the rich mineral resources of the Ring of Fire district in northern Ontario failed to proceed after many expensive and, for both sides, extremely frustrating attempts at commercial reconciliation that involved recourse to the courts.[28] In many instances, protracted negotiations were required before communities and companies found common ground. In some instances, as with the Tahltan in Northwest British Columbia, the development process sparked intense debate and political conflict among the Indigenous population.[29]

Participants in the Indigenous-corporate interactions developed, over time, considerable personal and collective experience in negotiations and consultations. Several companies—Vale,[30] Cameco,[31] Gold Corp,[32] and others—established particularly effective systems. Some of the smaller firms, particularly the high risk, high return exploration firms that lead the resource sector into new development zones, adopted short-term approaches to their relations with Indigenous communities. While some of these arrangements worked out, others suffered from a lack of clarity or produced unrealistic expectations among Indigenous peoples.

Canada produced a substantial consultation and negotiation professional sector, with individuals and firms moving from one development field to the next, capitalizing on the rapid accumulating knowledge about effective commercial relationships between resource companies and Indigenous communities.[33] For their part, Indigenous communities hired experts from this emerging cadre of professionals while also consulting extensively with other Indigenous communities about their experiences with negotiations in general and with specific companies. While many of the financial terms of agreements remained confidential, there was an increasingly rich understanding of Indigenous and corporate expectations and the general negotiating parameters and needs on both sides of the tables.

New realities have taken over the natural resource sector in Canada. While Indigenous peoples have been gaining strength in negotiations—possessing an authority which can be used most effectively when there is a rich deposit combined with high global demand—companies generally have significant advantages. Resource companies, particularly larger companies like Rio Tinto,[34] Suncor,[35] BHP,[36] and others, have extensive legal and negotiation departments, access to capital, global expertise, and international professional networks. Indigenous communities, in contrast, typically have fewer resources, small administrative teams, and rarely have the local capacity to respond quickly to the companies' interventions.

Shared understandings have settled in across Canada. Some Indigenous communities remain strongly opposed to resource development; others look enthusiastically for opportunities to collaborate. The issue at the root of the national and international debate about FPIC and UNDRIP—whether or not UNDRIP calls for an Indigenous veto on resource development and whether UNDRIP has substantive legal standing in the country[37]—has become secondary within the industry. Veto or not, resource firms worry about the prospect of major and costly delays. They understand, within fairly clear commercial parameters, that Indigenous communities control much of the agenda. For their part, Indigenous governments and communities understand the practical limits of their authority; too much interference and too many delays can result in corporate withdrawal and the loss of employment and other economic opportunities.

Indigenous communities have increasingly come to realize, through difficult experiences, that forces well beyond their control, and the control of the resource firms, can scupper a well-planned collaboration. In areas where corporate profit margins are tight or unreliable—as happened recently with a carefully negotiated hydroelectric project in northern Saskatchewan[38]—the planned resource development can be cancelled, with few results to show for what are often years of consultations and negotiations. The evidence of the past decade shows that many—likely most—Indigenous communities are looking for responsible developments, undertaken with collaborative and trustworthy partners. There have been enough successful negotiations to demonstrate that the companies and their Indigenous partners have changed dramatically in both their approaches and negotiating successes.

For much of the period after the 2004 Supreme Court of Canada's decision on the duty to consult in *Haida*, attention focussed on the financial aspects of the negotiations and agreements. Resource companies and Indigenous partners made a great deal about the often-substantial community investment funds, itself a carryover from the early times of corporate social responsibility, that often-emphasized physical assets, like school or recreational buildings. Other high-profile commitments, including aggressive employment targets like those outlined in agreements with the Baffinland iron ore mine in Nunavut,[39] the Diavik diamond mine in the Northwest Territories (NWT),[40] Voisey Bay in Labrador,[41] Cameco's uranium operations in Saskatchewan,[42] and preferential contracting arrangements, demonstrated the growing complexity of collaboration agreements and corporate-Indigenous collaborations. Other elements, ranging from commitments to recognizing Indigenous knowledge,[43] local participation in environmental assessment and monitoring,[44] and commitments to Indigenous capacity building,[45] showed the expanding scope of the accords and the growing integration of local communities into company operations.

While problems persisted, the involvement of hundreds of Indigenous communities and resource companies created a matrix of corporate and local involvement that inevitably includes zones of conflict and disagreement. Over time, and following further negotiations, the difficulties were often resolved to the satisfaction of all parties, but often with a residue of discontent and even bitterness. Conditions had improved to the point where, in 2018, a survey of mining companies in Ontario—one of the most contested zones in the country—had resource companies identify relations with Indigenous governments as the fourth most significant challenge facing company operations, well behind federal and provincial government policies and general environmental regulations.[46]

Relations are occasionally less than ideal, with Indigenous communities, or groups within the community, opposing either an entire project or aspects of it. The example of Attawapiskat First Nation in Northern Ontario, with its complex and often confrontational relationship with the nearby De Beers Mine, shows that even sizeable annual payments to the community, and efforts to expand Indigenous employment are no assurance of ongoing local support.[47]

Overall, the experience of Indigenous communities has been much better than in the past, carefully constructed through extensive consultations and negotiations, and general significant returns to Indigenous peoples. However, the returns are not spectacular and have often fallen well short of expectations. Resource companies complain—more quietly than in the past—that Indigenous peoples want resource projects to compensate for all measure of social, infrastructure, cultural, and economic needs. Nonetheless, taken as a whole, the resource industry has been restructured substantially, creating much more space and more positive returns for Indigenous peoples.

The most successful arrangements—and there are a fair number from Voisey's Bay to Diavik, Suncor to Gold Corp in the mining sector alone—are those that are not constrained by the technical terms of the agreements. Partners in these accords view them as living agreements, subject to modification by mutual agreement and designed to accommodate the unanticipated. These arrangements have informal or formal dispute mechanisms, open discussions between company and community reputations, and a focus on both long-term collaboration and sustainable partnerships. There are occasional troubles even in these carefully negotiated and well-managed arrangements, particularly if there are significant environmental challenges or mishaps, major market-enforced modifications in employment or operations, or local political entanglements. Discussions with Indigenous and corporate partnerships typically emphasize the fundamental importance of key personnel on both sides. Responsive Indigenous administrators and experienced and culturally aware company employees contribute a great deal—beyond the formal terms of the agreements—to the success of the collaborative ventures. Where and when collaborative arrangements work, all parties focus on real partnerships and the establishment of foundations for long-term collaboration and mutually beneficial structures and processes. Indigenous companies are looking, in their dealings with the resource companies, for the positive and sustainable systems that they often had with the historical fur trade.[48]

IV. Twenty-First Century Strategies for Relations Between Resource Industry Proponents and Indigenous Communities

New strategies are emerging for 21st century accommodations between natural resource companies and Indigenous communities. Substantial differences remain across the sector. Indigenous peoples typically expect a greater return than resource companies are prepared to offer. In almost every Indigenous community, there are members who resist development on cultural and environmental grounds; they are not easily swayed. The vulnerability of companies to global market realities often works at cross-purposes with Indigenous peoples' desire for sustainable, long-term benefits. With the passage of time and growing experience, Indigenous communities have come to understand what likely works the best and resource companies recognize the many benefits of strong local and regional connections and positive relations with Indigenous organizations and governments. Several key elements have emerged in recent settlements and negotiations, as always framed by the legal options that Indigenous groups have if they feel that their rights have not been addressed appropriately. These emerging elements include:

1 **Comprehensive and pro-active approaches:** Legalistic and minimalist initiatives are no longer sufficient. Indigenous communities look for early pro-active engagement, with resource companies making connections as early in the process as appropriate. From the outset, the corporate

approach must be inclusive and wide-ranging, based on an understanding of Indigenous culture and local realities. Communities are looking for evidence of a long-term, flexible arrangement and not technical contracts and carefully drafted legal provisions.

2 **Indigenous clarity**: It is equally important that Indigenous communities be as clear as political circumstances permit regarding their preparedness for resource development. Participants realize that circumstances change. But to the greatest degree possible, Indigenous governments should provide a clear statement of their willingness (or lack thereof) to support collaborative resource development. Companies may still decide to proceed as "duty to consult and accommodate" requirements and FPIC do not, at this point, constitute a veto on projects. But clarity from the Indigenous side of the negotiations is instrumental in ensuring constructive discussions.
3 **Pre-discovery evaluation of cultural and ecological sites**: Perhaps the greatest challenge facing resource development relates to the Indigenous insistence, which is entirely appropriate, that the proposed project be ecologically safe and not infringe on vital cultural sites. Under present arrangements, the appropriate site evaluations typically occur after early stage exploration has occurred and promising deposits have been identified. It is possible to head off subsequent tensions and difficulties by having pre-exploration assessments done of traditional territories. This work is properly a responsibility of governments—federal, Indigenous, provincial, and/or territorial—and would represent a major contribution to Indigenous confidence in the development process. Pre-exploration assessments would also provide corporations with a clear upfront understanding of limits on development activity.
4 **Laying the foundations for Indigenous engagement**: By the time resource companies arrive in an area, it is likely too late for Indigenous communities to capitalize fully on the employment and commercial opportunities from developments. Working closely with Indigenous groups, federal and territorial governments should focus on regional training and employment programs (including a substantial emphasis on the skills needed in the future for more heavily technology-driven jobs) and on the improvement of regional business capacity. This approach is, in its broad contours, being followed in Northern Quebec and Nunavut. Waiting until projects are identified and are in the approval process is several years too late for Indigenous peoples to prepare fully for the available opportunities.
5 **Financial return from the exploration phase**: At present, returns to Indigenous communities typically commence after preliminary exploration and the identification of potentially viable projects. This means that Indigenous peoples do not extract financial or other benefits from their traditional territories at the point where the entire land area has potential but as yet unrealized commercial value. It is vital, as Indigenous peoples continue to insist, that communities get some return from early stage development, in the form of jobs, business contracts, and financial returns from either governments or companies.

6 **Indigenous responsibility for environmental oversight and monitoring**: When Indigenous communities debate possible resource projects, much of the conversation focusses on questions of environmental oversight and protection. A long history of mining projects with unfortunate environmental consequences—some of them catastrophically so—has heightened concern at the community level. Companies have increasingly understood the value of direct Indigenous involvement in environmental monitoring, including through the hiring of Indigenous-owned assessment firms. On major projects, including pipelines, firms are recognizing the value of Indigenous participation in environmental oversight.

7 **Opportunities for equity investment**: Twenty years ago, the primary focus on Indigenous-corporate engagement was on job creation and employment; for more than a decade, communities have insisted on greater access to business development opportunities. Since 2010, there has been a growing emphasis on Indigenous access to equity investment. For some Indigenous communities, the request came in the form of an allocation of shares in the development company; in a growing number of cases, the Indigenous governments or their development corporations seek the opportunity to make equity investments on a standard business-case basis. In either case, Indigenous communities have recognized that partial ownership provides better access to project information, a possible role (such as a seat on the Board of Directors) in management, and greater financial returns for the community.[49]

8 **Comprehensive business engagement**: The growth of Indigenous business engagement in the natural resource sector has been extensive in recent years. This aspect of industry participation has become a primary focus for many Indigenous communities, who seek both the opportunity to employ more residents and to secure a greater financial return from participation in the project. Resource companies understand the value of these commercial collaborations and have been willing to expand joint venture operations and preferentially contracting arrangements. As Indigenous businesses gain expertise, which they have done over the past 20 years, this element of the collaboration gains in value to all parties.[50]

9 **Long-term monitoring and remediation**: Resource development is focussed on Indigenous communities as short-term operations (with important exceptions like hydro-electric stations, the oil sands, and Cameco's uranium operations in northern Saskatchewan). But the environmental consequences could be much longer, as situations like the Cypress-Anvil mine at Faro, Yukon,[51] and the gold mines at Yellowknife, NWT,[52] have demonstrated. It is vital that collaboration processes, involving both governments and corporations, include both long-term monitoring of environmental conditions and pro-active remediation efforts to address lingering ecological issues. Ensuring that funding is set aside for downstream responses has become a requirement of government permitting processes; it is important that these commitments and associated funding, be connected to Indigenous governments and communities. Environmental monitoring and

remediation can be seen as part of the broad package of initiatives designed to support Indigenous socio-economic development while protecting ecological integrity.

These trends mark developments beyond the limited contents of IBAs and towards a more comprehensive, full-cycle participation. These arrangements, plus the expanding involvement of Indigenous representatives in governance, oversight, and environmental assessment processes, will likely increase Indigenous support for development.

V. Conclusions

The primary surprise in Indigenous resource development is not the presence of conflict, as debate about appropriate and accepted use of resources is a key element in the entire sector. It is not that there are numerous court cases involving Indigenous-corporate disputes about specific projects and the financial and organizational arrangements emerging out of consultations and negotiations. It is not that many Indigenous people and communities have significant concerns about the protection of the environment and traditional territories in the face of substantial development pressures. Rather, the major surprise is the comparative peace in the resource sector. Where there are conflicts—Trans Mountain Pipeline and the Site C dam, both in British Columbia—it is typical that there will be Indigenous peoples on both sides of the debate.[53] Satisfaction is far from uniform on both sides of the Indigenous-corporate divide, as is to be expected in a situation where all participants are seeking to maximize their returns from resource projects.

If relations continue along the current trajectory, selective conflicts will continue but the general pattern of accommodation and collaboration will continue and likely improve. Indigenous engagement with resource companies remains a work in progress. As time passes and as Indigenous expertise expands, the exercise of Indigenous legal rights and powers will increasingly be seen as a sign of failure, not achievement. Companies that collaborate will do better and attract investment. As recent experiences in Yukon suggest, even the smaller junior firms that typically locate and develop new resource properties have integrated more comprehensive engagement with Indigenous peoples. It is instructive that the Canadian Mining Association, the lead lobby group for the mining sector in Canada, stood apart from much of the resource sector in support the Government of Canada's Bill C-69, which introduced new assessment procedures.[54] Companies that seek to impose the legal rights of development will not proceed easily or successfully. Additionally, Indigenous communities that respond too assertively (unless they are determined to shut down resource activity) to development projects can find themselves isolated from the resource economy. Balancing corporate and Indigenous interest has become the hallmark of the sector, to a much greater degree than is seen anywhere else in the Canadian economy.

There is a core message for governments in the experience of the last two decades. To a surprising degree, authority and decision-making have shifted away from government, save for the increasingly complex work of environmental regulations and permitting. Governments no long factor prominently in the negotiation and collaboration processes relating to resource projects. They are expected to provide basic infrastructure—roads, rail links, power, etc.—to ensure that projects proceed at an appropriate pace, and to defend legal rights and processes. Major commitments to new roads in Yukon, the federal government's intervention on the Trans Mountain Pipeline, and discussions about infrastructure across the sub-Arctic and Arctic are all examples of appropriate government involvement.

Indigenous involvement in the resource sector is not a panacea or a simple solution for the challenges facing Indigenous peoples and communities. Major projects will not and cannot produce full Indigenous employment or bring prosperity, in the short and medium term, to the many rural and remote communities that need real opportunity. Many Indigenous governments have enhanced their revenue streams, including from government resource revenue sharing, and have the opportunity to assert their autonomy from the Government of Canada and address some urgent community needs. Resource development is an important piece of a complex puzzle, but it is only one piece. Over the last 30 years, Indigenous peoples managed to convert major court victories into practical and applied power within the Canadian natural resource economy, with the benefits accruing to Indigenous participants growing substantially over time. As a means of addressing the socio-economic and other challenges facing Indigenous communities, the resource sector is only a partial solution. As a symbol of what it possible when Indigenous peoples secure recognition of their rights and then learn to apply them effectively, Indigenous involvement in the natural resource economy stands as an important illustration of what is possible in Canada.

Notes

1. See Thomas Isaac and Arend J.A. Hoekstra, "Canadian Law and Realpolitik Regarding Indigenous-Industry Agreements" in Ibironke T. Odumosu-Ayanu and Dwight Newman (eds), Indigenous-Industry Agreements, Natural Resources and the Law (Routledge 2021); Dwight Newman and Levi Graham, "Indigenous-Industry Agreements, Legal Uncertainty, and Risk Allocations" in Odumosu and Newman (eds) ibid; Ciaran O'Faircheallaigh, "Negotiated Agreements, Indigenous FPIC, and the Mine Life Cycle" in Odumosu-Ayanu and Newman (eds) ibid. This is not a critique of those chapters but a possible nuancing of the assumptions on which they are built.
2. 2004 SCC 73.
3. 2004 SCC 74.
4. Ken Coates and Brian Lee Crowley, *New Beginnings: How Canada's Natural Resource Wealth Could Re-Shape Relations with Aboriginal People* (Macdonald-Laurier Institute 2013).
5. On impact and benefit agreements, see K.J. Caine & N. Krogman, "Powerful or Just Plain Power-full? A Power Analysis of Impact and Benefit Agreements in Canada's North" (2010) 23(1) Organization & Environment 76; E. Cameron & T. Levitan, "Impact and Benefit Agreements and the Neoliberalization of Resource

Governance and Indigenous-state Relations in Northern Canada" (2014) 93(1) Studies in Political Economy 25; G.P. St-Laurent & P. Le Billon, "Staking Claims and Shaking Hands: Impact and Benefit Agreements as a Technology of Government in the Mining Sector" (2015) 2(3) Extractive Industries and Society 590; Ciaran O'Faircheallaigh, "Community Development Agreements in the Mining Industry: An Emerging Global Phenomenon" (2012) 44(2) Community Development 44(2) 222.

6. Bill Gallagher, *Resource Rulers: Fortune and Folly on Canada's Road to Resources* (Bill Gallagher 2012); Dwight G Newman, *The Duty to Consult: New Relationships with Aboriginal Peoples* (UBC Press 2009).
7. This is not uniform. Some Indigenous peoples, including in northern British Columbia, emphasize the importance of UNDRIP. Other Indigenous peoples, particularly those with modern treaties, are less concerned about the United Nations' agreement.
8. Ken Coates and Blaine Favel, *Understanding UNDRIP: Choosing Action on Priorities over Sweeping Claims about the United Nations Declaration on the Rights of Indigenous Peoples* (Macdonald-Laurier Institute 2016) [Coates and Favel].
9. Ibid. In Yukon, for example, a researcher found little evidence that First Nations people focussed on UNDRIP.
10. Duane Champagne, "UNDRIP (United Nations Declaration on the Rights of Indigenous Peoples): Human, Civil, and Indigenous Rights" (2013) 28(1) Wicazo Sa Review 9; Ken Coates, "From Aspiration to Inspiration: UNDRIP Finding Deep Traction in Indigenous Communities" (*Ken Coates*, 18 September 2013) <http://kencoates.ca/from-aspiration-to-inspiration-undrip-finding-deep-traction-in-indigenous-communities/>; Elivira Pulitano (ed), *Indigenous Rights in the Age of the UN Declaration* (CUP 2012).
11. Greg Poelzer and Ken Coates, *From Treaty Peoples to Treaty Nation: A Road Map for All Canadians* (UBC Press 2015).
12. The Cheslatta are working with other First Nations on a collective effort through the First Nations Major Projects Coalition (FNMPC). For more information on the FNMPC, see <http://www.fnmpc.ca/>.
13. Chris Andersen and Claude Denis, "Urban Natives and the Nation: Before and After the Royal Commission on Aboriginal Peoples" (2003) 40(4) Canadian Review of Sociology/Revue canadienne de sociologie 373.
14. Paul Sabin, "Voices from the Hydrocarbon Frontier: Canada's Mackenzie Valley Pipeline Inquiry (1974–1977)" (1995) 19(1) Environmental History Review 17; C.M. Chambers, *For our children's children: An educator's interpretation of Dene testimony to the Mackenzie Valley Pipeline Inquiry* (1991); Walter Strong, "Mackenzie Valley pipeline project officially one for the history books" (*CBC News*, 28 December 2017) <https://www.cbc.ca/news/canada/north/mackenzie-valley-gas-project-no-more-1.4465997>.
15. Lynn F. Lavallee and Jennifer M. Poole, "Beyond recovery: Colonization, health and healing for Indigenous people in Canada" (2010) 8(2) International Journal of Mental Health and Addiction 271.
16. Bethany Haalboom, "Confronting risk: A Case Study of Aboriginal Peoples' Participation in Environmental Governance of Uranium Mining, Saskatchewan" (2014) 58(3) The Canadian Geographer/Le Géographe canadien 276.
17. Heather Hall and Ken Coates, *Missed Opportunities, Glimmers of Hope: Aboriginal Communities and Mineral Development in Northern Ontario* (Macdonald-Laurier Institute 2017).
18. Russ Diabo, "Pipelines, Climate and 'Indigenous Consent'" (2016) 27(3) Indigenous Policy Journal; the work of the Union of B.C. Indian Chiefs can be found at <https://www.ubcic.bc.ca/>.

19. Interestingly, Indigenous involvement with resource development has led to growing tensions with environmental organizations, which have capitalized on Indigenous protests to develop public support for their opposition to projects. See Gary Mason, "Environmentalists' Next Opponent? First Nations" (*The Globe* and Mail, 17 January 2019).
20. The Indian Resource Council is leading this effort.
21. Brian Lee Crowley and Ken Coates, *The Way Out: New Thinking about Aboriginal Engagement and Energy Infrastructure to the West Coast* (Macdonald-Laurier Institute 2013).
22. See for example Justin Giovannetti, "First Nations Lobbying for Lift on Tanker Ban off B.C.'s Coast" (*The Globe and Mail*, 7 December, 2018) <https://www.theglobeandmail.com/canada/british-columbia/article-first-nations-lobbying-for-lift-on-tanker-ban-off-bcs-coast/>.
23. See for example John Van Dusen, "Nunabut, N.W.T. Premiers Slam Artic Drilling Moratorium" (*CBC News*, 22 December 2016) <https://www.cbc.ca/news/canada/north/nunavut-premier-slams-arctic-drilling-moratorium-1.3908037>.
24. For a commentary on Haisla involvement, see Chief Councillor Crystal Smith, "An Open Letter on why Haisla Nation Stands Behind LNG" (*Haisla Nation*) <https://haisla.ca/an-open-letter-on-why-haisla-nation-stands-behind-lng/>.
25. On the deal, promising more than $200 million in benefits to the Squamish First Nation, see The Canadian Press, "Squamish Nation Inks Deal with Woodfibre LNG" (*Global News*, 30 November 2018) <https://globalnews.ca/news/4717709/squamish-nation-inks-deal-with-woodfibre-lng/>.
26. See Ginger Gibson and Ciaran O'Faircheallaigh, "IBA Toolkit" (Walter and Duncan Gordon Foundation 25 June 2015) <http://gordonfoundation.ca/resource/iba-community-toolkit/>.
27. See Coates and Crowley (n 21).
28. Hall and Coates (n 17)
29. Monte Paulsen, "A Gentle Revolution" (*The Walrus*, December 2005) <https://thewalrus.ca/2006-01-politics/>.
30. "Voisey's Bay" (*Vale*) <http://www.vale.com/canada/EN/aboutvale/communities/voiseysbay/Pages/default.aspx>.
31. "Indigenous Peoples Relations" (*Cameco*) <https://www.cameco.com/sustainable_development/2016/supportive-communities/indigenous-peoples-relations/>.
32. Newmont Goldcorp <http://csr.goldcorp.com/2010/5_indigenous.php>.
33. For a critical review of this sector, see Frances Widdowson and Albert Howard, *Disrobing the Aboriginal Industry: The Deception behind Indigenous Cultural Preservation* (McGill-Queen's Press-MQUP 2008).
34. "Indigenous Peoples" (*Rio Tinto*) <https://www.riotinto.com/canada/indigenous-peoples-17540.aspx>.
35. "Aboriginal Relations" (*Suncor*) <https://www.suncor.com/sustainability/community-consultation/aboriginal-relations>.
36. "Indigenous Peoples" (*BHP*, 2019) <https://www.bhp.com/our-approach/operating-with-integrity/indigenous-peoples>.
37. Coates and Favel (n 8).
38. "SaskPower Puts Brakes on $630M Hydro Project in Northern Sask." (*CBC News*, 25 September 2017) <https://www.cbc.ca/news/canada/saskatchewan/saskpower-puts-brakes-on-630m-hydro-project-in-northern-sask-1.4306393>.
39. "Inuit Impact and Benefit Agreement" (*Baffinland Iron Mines Corporation*) <http://www.baffinland.com/inuit-impact-and-benefit-agreement/?lang=en>.
40. Alfredo Barrios, "Statement of Commitment for Indigenous Peoples" (*Rio Tinto*) <https://www.riotinto.com/canada/statement-of-commitment-for-indigenous-peoples-17582.aspx>.

41. Evan Careen, "Almost $24 million in funding announced for indigenous people in Labrador" (*The Telegram*, 29 June 2018) <https://www.thetelegram.com/news/regional/almost-24-million-in-funding-announced-for-indigenous-people-in-labrador-222682/>.
42. See <https://www.northernontariobusiness.com/industry-news/mining/new-awakening-in-indigenous-engagement-371721/>.
43. Newmont Goldcorp (n 32).
44. John Acharibasam and Bram Noble, "Assessing the Impact of Strategic Environmental Assessment" (2014) 32(3) Impact Assessment and Project Appraisal 177.
45. A recent confidential survey of a provincial mining sector revealed that half of the companies invested directly in capacity building at the community level.
46. Information provided by the Ontario Mining Association, July 2018.
47. Joseph Quesnel, "Attawapiskat could have more prosperity, but not by getting local diamond mines to shut down" (*Financial Post*, 17 March 2017) <https://business.financialpost.com/opinion/attawapiskats-refusal-to-support-a-diamond-mine-misses-an-opportunity-for-better-prosperity>.
48. Arthur J. Ray, *Indians in the Fur Trade: Their Role as Trappers, Hunters, and Middlemen in the Lands Southwest of Hudson Bay, 1660–1870: With a New Introduction.* (University of Toronto Press 1998).
49. An examination of the importance of equity investment to Indigenous peoples is being written by Ken Coates and Joseph Quesnel and will be produced by the Macdonald-Laurier Institute.
50. Indigenous business development is being monitored and assessed by the Canadian Council of Aboriginal Business. Their work can be accessed at <https://www.ccab.com/>.
51. Anne Dance, "Northern Reclamation in Canada: Contemporary Policy and Practice for New and Legacy Mines" (2015) 41 Northern Review 41; Arn Keeling and John Sandlos, "Environmental Justice Goes Underground? Historical Notes from Canada's Northern Mining Frontier" (2009) 2(3) Environmental Justice 117; John Sandlos and Arn Keeling, "Aboriginal Communities, Traditional Knowledge, and the Environmental Legacies of Extractive Development in Canada" (2016) 3(2) The Extractive Industries and Society 278; Liza Piper, *The Industrial Transformation of Subarctic Canada* (UBC Press 2010).
52. Chris Paci and Noeline Villebrun, "Mining Denendeh: A Dene Nation Perspective on Community Health Impacts of Mining," (2005) 3(1) Pimatisiwin: A Journal of Aboriginal & Indigenous Community Health 71; Heather E. Jamieson, "The Legacy of Arsenic Contamination from Mining and Processing Refractory Gold Ore at Giant Mine, Yellowknife, Northwest Territories, Canada" (2014) 79(1) Reviews in Mineralogy and Geochemistry 533.
53. Wendy Holm (ed), *Damming the Peace: The Hidden Costs of the Site C Dam* (James Lorimer & Company 2018).
54. Pierre Gratton, "Bill C-69: A Step Forward for Canada's Mining Sector" (*Globe and Mail*, 16 September 2018) <https://www.theglobeandmail.com/business/commentary/article-bill-c-69-a-step-forward-for-canadas-mining-sector/>.

Index